THE TRUTH ABOUT
ROMANTICISM

How have our conceptions of truth been shaped by romantic literature? This question lies at the heart of this examination of the concept of truth both in romantic writing and in modern criticism. The romantic idea of truth has long been depicted as aesthetic, imaginative, and ideal. Tim Milnes challenges this picture, demonstrating a pragmatic strain in the writing of Keats, Shelley, and Coleridge in particular, which bears a close resemblance to the theories of modern pragmatist thinkers such as Donald Davidson and Jürgen Habermas. Romantic pragmatism, Milnes argues, was in turn influenced by recent developments within linguistic empiricism. This book will be of interest to readers of romantic literature, but also to philosophers, literary theorists, and intellectual historians.

TIM MILNES is Senior Lecturer in English Literature at the University of Edinburgh.

CAMBRIDGE STUDIES IN ROMANTICISM

This series aims to foster the best new work in one of the most challenging fields within English literary studies. From the early 1780s to the early 1830s a formidable array of talented men and women took to literary composition, not just in poetry, which some of them famously transformed, but in many modes of writing. The expansion of publishing created new opportunities for writers, and the political stakes of what they wrote were raised again by what Wordsworth called those 'great national events' that were 'almost daily taking place': the French Revolution, the Napoleonic and American wars, urbanisation, industrialisation, religious revival, an expanded empire abroad and the reform movement at home. This was an enormous ambition, even when it pretended otherwise. The relations between science, philosophy, religion, and literature were reworked in texts such as *Frankenstein* and *Biographia Literaria*; gender relations in *A Vindication of the Rights of Woman* and *Don Juan*; journalism by Cobbett and Hazlitt; poetic form, content, and style by the Lake School and the Cockney School. Outside Shakespeare studies, probably no body of writing has produced such a wealth of comment or done so much to shape the responses of modern criticism. This indeed is the period that saw the emergence of those notions of 'literature' and of literary history, especially national literary history, on which modern scholarship in English has been founded.

The categories produced by Romanticism have also been challenged by recent historicist arguments. The task of the series is to engage both with a challenging corpus of Romantic writings and with the changing field of criticism they have helped to shape. As with other literary series published by Cambridge, this one will represent the work of both younger and more established scholars, on either side of the Atlantic and elsewhere.

For a complete list of titles published see end of book.

Edinburgh University Library

Books may be recalled for return earlier than due date;
if so you will be contacted by e-mail or letter.

Due Date	Due Date	Due Date

THE TRUTH ABOUT ROMANTICISM

Pragmatism and Idealism in Keats, Shelley, Coleridge

TIM MILNES

University of Edinburgh

CAMBRIDGE
UNIVERSITY PRESS

CAMBRIDGE UNIVERSITY PRESS
Cambridge, New York, Melbourne, Madrid, Cape Town, Singapore,
São Paulo, Delhi, Dubai, Tokyo

Cambridge University Press
The Edinburgh Building, Cambridge CB2 8RU, UK

Published in the United States of America by Cambridge University Press, New York

www.cambridge.org
Information on this title: www.cambridge.org/9780521198073

First published 2010

Printed in the United Kingdom at the University Press, Cambridge

A catalogue record for this publication is available from the British Library

Library of Congress Cataloging-in-Publication Data
Milnes, Tim.
The truth about Romanticism : pragmatism and idealism in
Keats, Shelley, Coleridge / Tim Milnes.
p. cm. – (Cambridge studies in Romanticism ; 83)
Includes bibliographical references and index.
ISBN 978-0-521-19807-3
1. English poetry–19th century–History and criticism. 2. Romanticism–Great Britain.
3. Pragmatism in literature. 4. Idealism in literature. 5. Keats, John, 1795–1821–Criticism
and interpretation. 6. Shelley, Percy Bysshe, 1792–1822–Criticism and interpretation.
7. Coleridge, Samuel Taylor, 1772–1834–Criticism and interpretation. I. Title. II. Series.
PR590.M54 2010
821'.709145–dc22

2010004396

ISBN 978-0-521-19807-3 Hardback

To Michelle, with all my love

Contents

Acknowledgements

The bulk of this book was written during a sabbatical year generously granted by the University of Edinburgh and funded partly by the Arts and Humanities Research Council. Its earliest, incondite ideas were licked into shape at conferences in Aberystwyth, Nottingham, and Bristol, and by colleagues in the Department of English Literature at Edinburgh. Later revisions were greatly assisted by the patient and thorough commentary of the two anonymous readers for Cambridge University Press, and by the helpful oversight of James Chandler. Particular thanks are due to Liz Barry, Alex Benchimol, Liz Brown, Damian Walford Davies, Lesel Dawson, A. C. Grayling, Paul Hamilton, Sara Lodge, Susan Manning, Uttara Natarajan, Tom Paulin, Randall Stevenson, Jules Siedenburg, Samira Sheikh, Kerry Sinanan, Richard Marggraf Turley, Jane Wright, and Duncan Wu. Among my considerable non-academic obligations are those I owe to my parents, Les and Audrey Milnes. My largest single debt, however, is to the support and encouragement of my wife, Michelle Milnes, to whom I dedicate this book with love and gratitude.

The pragmatics of romantic idealism

O friend! Truth! Truth! but yet Charity! Charity!

Coleridge's plea comes in the midst of an 1804 notebook entry that characteristically combines self-mortification with self-justification. The poet confesses to 'Drunkenness' and 'sensuality', but begs his future reader to consider, in mitigation, that he 'never loved Evil for its own sake'.[1] 'Charity', he suggests, is the prerequisite for interpreting the 'Truth' of his life's work. The passage presents Coleridge at his most strategically disarming, yet it would be wrong to dismiss his appeal as wishful thinking or crafty manipulation. The request for trust, the assumption of generosity on the part of his reader, is no mere sleight of hand. By refusing to subordinate friendship and charity to an abstract idea of truth, Coleridge trades on a network of romantic ideas concerning the nature of the relationships between truth, charity, and friendship. This network, which forms the central interest of this study, can be characterised broadly as an interest in the interdependence of truth and intersubjectivity. More concisely, and contentiously, it can be described as a kind of pragmatism.

In choosing the last descriptor, I am not claiming that the writers discussed here are essentially pragmatists: as I argue below, the growth of naturalism in the nineteenth-century forms a formidable barrier between the romantics and pragmatists such as William James and John Dewey. When, for example, Coleridge defines the 'Ideal' as the 'union of the Universal and the Individual', he subjects the possibility of redescription to a transcendental ideal in a way that is quite alien to pragmatism.[2] This romantic tendency to idealise or hypostasise 'Truth' is well documented. However, modern criticism (largely thanks to its preoccupation with Hegel and German idealism), has fixated upon and internalised the romantic idealisation of truth to the exclusion of historical and alethic alternatives. Chief among the latter is a British discourse of communicative rationality that insists upon the inseparability of truth and dialogue, as well as the embeddedness of all thought in social values, the normative weave of life. I argue that it is this discourse, captured by Coleridge's dictum that in the 'affectionate seeking after the truth' we must presuppose that 'Truth is the correlative of Being', which can be characterised as 'pragmatic' or 'holistic'.[3]

Stated plainly then, the argument of this book is that much modern criticism and commentary on romantic literature is written in the shadow of a bad romantic idea: the idealised or hypostasised notion of truth. Against this tendency, I highlight and defend a valuable but now marginalised romantic idea, a 'holistic' conception of truth and communication. In doing so, I adopt an openly normative approach that I see not only as unavoidable, but also as one way of putting the most helpful romantic ideas to work in historical interpretation. At its best, romantic writing shows how thought depends fundamentally upon dialogue and communication, and how dialogue in turn presupposes a shared concept of truth and a commensurable background of values. This tells us something important about the futility of subjecting the normativity of our beliefs to the radical suspicion fostered by what Thomas Pfau dubs the 'conspiratorial hermeneutics' of modern commentary.[4] It also highlights a point made recently by Nikolas Kompridis: namely, that the refusal to hypostasise the 'normative' (as in, for example, 'the romantic ideology') is the prerequisite for a future-orientated criticism of historical texts.[5] In other words, once we treat the normative dimension to our theories and beliefs from a pragmatic point of view, the romantics can be seen, in Richard Rorty's phrase, to 'enlarge the realm of possibility'. Viewed as good 'private' philosophers rather than poor 'public' ones, they enable us to imagine the experience of better possible futures.[6]

Reading Coleridge, Shelley, and Keats in this way also alerts us to the fact that finding a common ground between persons, cultures, and historical eras is the precondition, not the product, of interpretation. In other words, if we are to interpret the romantics at all, we are compelled to treat them as inhabiting a conceptual- and value-space that is at least commensurable (that is, comparable) with our own. Consequently, the method of the present study is 'romantic', not because of its 'immanence to' or 'transcendence of' a romantic paradigm, but because it rejects such terms as outworn and metaphysical. It sees no coherent alternative to interpretation based on the presuppositions of fallible truth-claims couched in an openly evaluative vocabulary.[7] Like the romantic discourse it describes then, the outlook of this book is reformist rather than revolutionary: it does not offer a *theory* of 'reading', 'truth', or 'romanticism'. Instead, it endeavours, in a piecemeal way, to counter, amend, and extend other readings of Keats, Shelley, and Coleridge, and, in doing so, to recover a romantic concept of communicative action generally forgotten or discredited by modern criticism.[8]

This is not to say that the discourse of communicative rationality identified here has gone unnoticed. Kathleen Wheeler, Paul Hamilton, Angela Esterhammer, Richard Eldridge, Russell Goodman, and Jerome Christensen, among others, have all written books that stress the pragmatic, future-directed accent of romantic literature.[9] What remains to be explored, however, is *why* so much romantic writing appears to veer between a thoroughly pragmatic attitude towards truth, interpretation and self-description, and a propensity to hypostasise key concepts as transcendent ideals. I believe that such ambivalence is best explained against the background of two competing strains of British empiricism: representationalism, and a linguistic 'turn' in late eighteenth-century thought.

The first of these can be traced to the seminal 'idea' idea in Descartes and Locke, which centred the regulation of beliefs in the mind and made *contemplation* the defining characteristic of knowledge. As Rorty argues, Locke's move to identify belief-justification with the causal explanation of mental representations secured the priority of 'knowledge of' to 'knowledge that', and thus the primacy of 'knowledge as a relation between persons and objects rather than persons and propositions'.[10] This shift has profound consequences, not least of which is the reorientation of philosophy away from divinity and morality and towards epistemology, and the forging of a new discourse of idealism, dealing in 'faculties' of the 'imagination' and 'understanding', and the 'association' of 'ideas' and 'impressions'. From this point, as James Engell demonstrates, it is possible to narrate the surpassing of empiricism by romanticism as the inflation of an idealised mental sphere already present in the older tradition, that is, as the evolution of a naturalistic British representationalism into a supernaturalised Germanic idealism.[11]

It would be wrong to suppose, however, that representationalism passed uncriticised even within the schools of eighteenth-century empiricism. Thomas Reid's attack on the Lockean 'idea' idea is effectively an attack on epistemology itself as a way of thinking about the regulation of belief. By abandoning an epistemological apparatus of ideas and their causes for a linguistic model of natural and artificial 'signs', Reid lays the groundwork for a linguistics of knowledge.[12] Subsequently, as W. V. Quine notes, John Horne Tooke's etymological deconstruction of the 'idea', and Jeremy Bentham's 'shift of semantic focus from terms to sentences' indicate a new willingness to think of knowledge in terms of communication and interpretation rather than representation and confrontation.[13] I argue further that when considered alongside the admissions by empiricists such as Hume and Dugald Stewart regarding the unsustainability of the representational model these developments indicate a powerful crosscurrent in late eighteenth-century thought. Towards the end of the century, the language of British empiricism (particularly within dissenting and radical circles) is increasingly antidualist and anti-representationalist. Consequently, it is less concerned with the problem of representing truth, and more with the problem of how truth operates within a community concerned with mutual understanding. This concern is illustrated in the 'Introduction on Taste', which opens the second edition of Edmund Burke's *Philosophical Enquiry into the Origin of our Ideas of the Sublime and Beautiful*:

On a superficial view, we may seem to differ very widely from each other in our reasonings, and no less in our pleasures: but notwithstanding this difference, which I think to be rather apparent than real, it is probable that the standard both of reason and Taste is the same in all human creatures. For if there were not some principles of judgement as well as of sentiment common to all mankind, no hold could possibly be taken either on their reason or their passions, sufficient to maintain the ordinary correspondence of life.[14]

Burke's treatment of 'the standard of reason and Taste' as a problem for the pragmatics of communication rather than for epistemology or metaphysics suggests that truth is neither a 'thing' to be possessed, nor a 'context' about which one may or may not have a theory, but that which is 'sufficient to maintain the ordinary correspondence of life'.

This appeal to the pragmatic preconditions for dialogue represents a tradition that has been overshadowed by associationism and romantic theories of the imagination, overwhelmed by the introduction to Britain of German idealism, and generally overlooked by modern commentary and criticism. And yet, Coleridge, Shelley, and Keats each inherits, absorbs, and modifies the linguistic and pragmatic turn of late eighteenth-century empiricism. In this new understanding of the intimate relationship between communication and the concept of truth, rational norms are aligned with the pragmatic boundaries determined by free discourse within the public sphere. Rejecting both subject-centred reason *and* hypostasised negations of reason, it attempts to give an account of the conditions of living a coherent life from *within* a coherent lifeworld, from within an inhabited framework of goods and values. In so doing, it assumes that there is no 'truth' outside dialogue, but also that *because of this*, there can be no dialogue without a shared concept of truth.

HOLISM VERSUS HYPOSTASIS: 'SOCRATIC' EMPIRICISM

The difference between the two varieties of empiricism I distinguish reflects a debate in late eighteenth-century Britain over whether truth is an object that the mind strives to represent (sometimes referred to as the 'correspondence' theory of truth) or a human creation. The second idea is commonly seen as a distinguishing feature of romantic writing. Here, however, a further distinction needs to be drawn: between the idea of truth as the creation of the *mind*, and as the creation of *communication*. The first trades upon the idea of a centred subject, the second invokes the notion of intersubjectivity.

The romantics are conscious of this difference, not only through their schooling in a native philosophical tradition, but also thanks to their awareness of a similar ambiguity within Platonism. This ambiguity has been studied in a revealing essay by Donald Davidson. In 'Plato's Philosopher', Davidson writes of how he was once puzzled by the ancient philosopher's return to the Socratic dialogue in the *Philebus*, a method that Plato's later works had suggested 'might be supplemented or replaced by techniques with loftier aims'.[15] Davidson came to realise, however, that far from signalling a failure this absence of a clear and settled method illustrates Plato's idea of what Davidson elsewhere calls the 'holism of the mental'.[16] According this picture, as old beliefs are destroyed and new ones forged in the crucible of the Socratic dialogue, what emerges is an awareness of the *interdependence* of subjectivity, intersubjectivity, and truth. For Socrates, Davidson argues, either all of these elements come into play at once, or none of them does.

Part of my argument is that tensions between representational/idealist and dialogic/pragmatic forms of late eighteenth-century empiricism, together with an analogous ambiguity in Platonism, alert the romantics to the 'holism of the mental'.[17] Kathleen Wheeler has made a similar point in her study of the relations between romanticism, pragmatism, and deconstruction, identifying in the work of Shelley and Coleridge a 'dynamic synthesis of Platonic/Socratic philosophy with empiricism'.[18] While I agree with this formulation, and extend it to Keats, I see the romantic attitude as more cautiously experimental than triumphantly synthetic. This is partly because I disagree with Wheeler on the relevance of German idealism when dealing with the philosophical discourse of British romanticism.

For Wheeler, romantic pragmatism/deconstruction is an umbrella category that unites Coleridge, Shelley, the German romantic ironists, and other antirationalist thinkers such as Hegel, Nietzsche, and Heidegger. The problem with this view is that it implies that the Kantian, *transcendental* ground at stake in the work of all the German writers mentioned above is also (at least analogously) a focal concern of British romanticism, when, Coleridge aside, the concept of such a ground does not enter the mainstream of British intellectual life until the 1830s.[19] Consequently, I maintain that the 'Socratic empiricism' of Coleridge, Shelley, and Keats is most usefully considered not in the context of transcendental idealism, but within a native tradition of empiricism torn between an idealism that preserves the dualism of subject and object (albeit often at the price of the object) and a new discourse of communicative rationality that stresses the role of language in shaping belief. It is this latter view of language that Angela Esterhammer describes as 'inherently pragmatic and dialogic'. The same discourse, as Russell Goodman and Richard Poirier argue, ultimately exerts a strong influence over American pragmatism.[20]

In overestimating the ability of German analogues to unpick the alethic ambiguities of British romanticism, Wheeler is following a well-trodden path. For at least half a century, Anglo-American criticism and commentary has generally considered the romantics as most philosophically interesting when read alongside their German contemporaries. It is difficult to overstate the consequences of this assumption, and two are of particular concern here. The first, already mentioned, is the eclipse of the linguistic empiricism of the late eighteenth century as a formative influence on romantic writing (tellingly, Wheeler does not consider the work of Reid, Tooke, or Bentham to be significant in her pragmatic/deconstructive reading of romanticism).

The second is an unwholesome preoccupation in much modern romantic criticism with reflexivity and the dynamics of 'immanence' and 'transcendence'. This preoccupation begins with Hegel's concept of immanent critique. As Jürgen Habermas argues, Hegel is the first thinker to diagnose the malady of modernity, an 'epoch that lives for the future', as the need '*to create its normativity out of itself*'. This need, he adds, 'explains the sensitiveness of its self-understanding', as the post-Kantian subject struggles with the responsibilities of self-redescription.[21] Hegel's immanent or dialectical critique is designed to overcome the Kantian gulf between spontaneity and reflection by reconstituting the subject as inherently relational. However, as Habermas argues, it is important to distinguish between the young Hegel, who based his metacritique of 'the authoritarian embodiments of a subject-centered reason', upon 'the unifying power of an intersubjectivity that appears under the titles of "love" and "life" ',[22] and the post-Jena Hegel, for whom the philosophical absolute is 'a further presumption under which alone philosophy can resume its business'.[23] Under the sign of the absolute, the later Hegel extends mistrust of subject-centred reason into a suspicion of epistemology itself. This effectively *radicalises*, at the same time that it ostensibly abolishes, the critique of knowledge, since the totalising or dialectical critique perpetuates, by inversion, the Enlightenment quest for a foundational discipline of thought: 'Hence what starts out as immanent critique covertly turns into abstract negation'.[24]

For Habermas, the outcome of this move is the denial 'to the self-understanding of modernity the possibility of a critique of modernity'.[25] Divested of its assurance of an absolute, metacritique as negativity abandons genuine understanding in favour of a hypostasised discourse of otherness, of 'truth/power', 'absent causation', and so on. Habermas demonstrates that this hypostasisation is inverted idealism, albeit one cramped by its inability to configure its own conclusions as epistemic gains. In this respect, modern thought, and particularly certain forms of postmodern theory and historiography, remains trapped within the shadow of German idealism. Modern romantic criticism is unusually sensitive to this confinement, in that the aporia in its own subject positioning is bound up in complex ways with its subject matter. Consequently, the dialectical methods invoked by postmodern historicism are beset by paradoxes of 'immanence' and 'transcendence', what Marjorie Levinson calls the dilemmas of 'empathy and contemplation'.[26] My argument here is that such impasses are avoidable, the unhappy descendants of the romantic idealisation of truth and Hegel's ambiguous radicalisation of the critique of knowledge.

WITHOUT THE 'OUTSIDE': DIALOGUE AND METACRITIQUE

Nonetheless, postmodern historicism's immersion in the language of 'immanence' and 'transcendence' reveals a great deal about how it remains spellbound by romantic idealism. Captivated by the image of a hypostasised otherness but lacking a basis for critique, it risks overlooking genuine romantic insights. Instead, it has become increasingly preoccupied with methodology, fixated on the metaphysical question of what is 'inside' and 'outside' romanticism. That we continue to struggle with the question of intellectual transcendence in the course of reading a literature that explores such transcendence suggests to many not just that our self-conscious reading of romantic literature is caught in a hermeneutical circle, but that the hermeneutical circle *is* romanticism. If, as some have suggested, romanticism comes to signify not a doctrine but the very condition in which criticism operates, it becomes difficult to outmanoeuvre precisely because of the way in which it styles its own critique as self-overcoming.[27] Michael Scrivener captures such concerns in a string of questions in a recent review article: 'are we still reading Romanticism by means of its own constructions, or have we so far removed ourselves from the assumptions of Romantic texts that we are finally outside of Romanticism? Do we want to be outside of Romanticism? Is it possible to get outside of Romanticism? Are we finally free of Romantic ideology?'[28]

I argue that such metacritical questions are misconceived because the radicalised doubt that informs them is incoherent. Fear of repeated or 'reinscribed' romantic transcendence is merely an offshoot of a wider postmodern suspicion of truth. In seeking a context for thought itself, historicism's metacritique becomes what Fredric Jameson calls 'metacommentary': the attempt, by situating itself *outside* interpretation – in the 'strangeness, the unnaturalness, of the hermeneutic situation' – to explain 'not the nature of interpretation, but the need for it in the first place'.[29] Many critics position metacommentary in Foucault's zone of the 'unthought', where the dialectic between present and past is played out against the more fundamental otherness of a configuration of power and truth, itself the fundamental condition or 'historical *a priori*' of the western *episteme*.[30] Others, in turn, insist on subjecting *every* position to the labour of historical dialectic. As James Chandler has demonstrated, contextualising the very idea of intelligibility means that investigation must extend to historicism's *own* rubric of history and dialectic.[31]

If Habermas is correct, however, then the language of 'inside' and 'outside' is simply a remnant of the Hegelian radicalisation of epistemology. This has the merit of explaining why, as recent commentators have noticed, postmodern historicism is so uneasy in its own skin.[32] Untethered from critique, dialectic institutes a quasi-knowledge or anti-knowledge that vacillates between the detection and confession of cognitive contamination. The result is a criticism that, while searching for symptoms of givenness or failure of dialectic, always redeems itself through self-reflexive awareness – awareness that smacking immediately of transcendence only falls under further suspicion. This yields a paradox: on one hand, constantly reviewing one's own thought for symptoms of transcendence and ideological contamination itself draws the suspicion of unacknowledged positivism (that is, of the assumption that ideology is an illusion that can be treated or weeded out); on the other hand, the very confession of one's ideological investment, one's cultural situatedness, can attract the very same suspicion (that is, of a disarming candour that promotes critical immunity). Between suspicion and confession, the voice of critique is lost.[33] Instead, as Paul Hamilton observes, by folding suspicion into suspicion, postmodern historicism invariably produces the kind of repetition it sets out to avoid: a critical chiasmus.[34]

The imperative here, then, is not to enable a critique of idealism that is somehow resistant to the remainders of idealism, but to avoid constructing a self-immunising metacommentary that repeats (by inversion) the hypostasising manoeuvre that makes idealism problematic in the first place. This means giving up the idea that 'difference', 'negativity', 'totality' or other signs of radical otherness are trump cards in the language game of interpretation. I argue instead that we should accept Rorty's argument that rationality is 'a matter of conversation between persons, rather than a matter of interaction with a nonhuman reality'.[35] Rethinking objectivity as intersubjectivity means taking seriously the idea that when it comes to truth 'there is only the dialogue'.[36] One casualty of this arrangement is the goal of immanent critique: if thought has no radical exteriority, it makes no sense to think of interpretation as either 'immanent' or 'transcendent'. A second consequence is the rehabilitation of the concept of truth, albeit hypostasised in the weakest possible way as the indefinable absolute of discourse (if, as Davidson claims, truth has no explanatory use, we can, in Rorty's words, 'safely get along with less philosophising about truth than we had thought we needed').[37]

Some critics deplore this move, claiming that pragmatism's insistence on translatability and communicability is precisely what renders it inadequate as an aesthetic theory. Charles Altieri, for example, argues that pragmatism is ill-equipped to explain the relationships we have with certain objects, such as works of art, which do not have practical designs upon us. In particular, he claims, it lacks a 'powerful language for dealing with the otherness of objects from the past, or of objects which set themselves goals alien to pragmatist principles'.[38] Altieri contrasts the pragmatist's limited lexicon of otherness with that of Hegel, whose 'concern for what cannot be treated as "truth" per se, except dialectically, … provides us a stance from which we might be able to characterize why artists labor to get something right as a highly worked singular project'. Compared to Hegel's approach, he maintains, Rorty and Davidson's assertions regarding the futility of metatheories of truth effectively silences fundamental dialogues (between cultures, as well as between individuals and art objects) before they can begin, producing 'an Occam's razor that risks becoming an instrument of cultural castration'.[39] The basic flaw in Rorty's approach to poetry, Altieri complains, is the former's assumption that the value and meaning of aesthetic performance can readily be cashed out into hypothetical statement.

Altieri's critique, however, offers a limited picture of the ways in which pragmatic approaches to problems of truth and interpretation might engage with artistic and literary works. In fact, the concern of thinkers like Rorty, Putnam, and Davidson with translatability is not heretically paraphrastic. Their approaches neither insist upon propositional articulacy nor disregard the performative or non-sentenceable features of aesthetic objects. Instead, they merely demonstrate that the commensurability of such features with the interpretive practices of the reader or spectator is itself a precondition of interpretation and critique. In contrast, Altieri's method implies that truth can be treated from the 'outside' as well as the 'inside'. In doing so, it subjects the ways upon which literary and artistic works communicate to a hypostasised otherness that renders interpretation simultaneously aporetic and dialectically negotiable. If what is gained in this picture is a critical language that gestures towards vague ideas of singularity and the 'self-reflexive structurings of imaginative energies', what is lost is the idea of constructive critique and the notion of art as, fundamentally, a form of communication.[40]

Another unwelcome consequence of Altieri's insistence on the untranslatable and therefore incommunicable power of aesthetic objects has more immediate relevance to the present inquiry. Like other attempts to account for the power of the aesthetic through notions of radical otherness, Altieri's critique harbours a resistance to *involvement* with different cultures and historical eras. And yet, it is this very sense of involvement that Poirier identifies in Emerson's claim that historical thinking always involves an acknowledgement of shared reality. 'Far from suggesting that we work our way into the past so as to recognize its otherness', Poirier notes, Emerson argues that history 'forces upon us a recognition of likeness, a participation in past productions, however monstrous these may be'.[41] Such recognition stems from Emerson's holism, his understanding that agents, actions, and words work altogether or not at all, and that 'each discovers ... an inconvenient dependency on the others, and a disconcerting necessity, therefore, to move on to the next transition, toward a similar but again only temporary fusion'.[42]

As I note below, Emerson's holism forms a bridge between pragmatism and what Habermas identifies as the 'counterdiscourse' of romanticism. This counterdiscourse, the offspring of the radical, linguistic empiricism of Reid, Tooke, and Bentham, understands 'truth' as an indispensable presupposition, an absolute limit-concept of the pragmatics of communication. Drawing upon what Habermas describes as 'the paradigm of mutual understanding between subjects capable of speech and action', it stresses the intersubjective basis of reason.[43] Indeed, it pursues neither transcendence nor immanence because it implies that such terms have no purchase on life stronger than the concepts and values that give life its coherence. Accordingly, instead of asking, 'what are the (impossible) conditions of my knowledge of life?' it asks, 'what does it mean to live a good life?'[44] Old habits of thinking, however, die hard. Caught between an established tradition of representational (ideal) empiricism and a more recent, dialogic concept of self, British romantic writers vacillate between the hypostasised language of self, mind, imagination, and truth, and weak idealisations of community: what Rorty calls 'solidarity', and I term holism.[45]

TRUTH AND INTERSUBJECTIVITY

In reading the romantics pragmatically and the pragmatists romantically, this book strives to instigate not a reconciliation or synthesis of perspectives, but a useful dialogue between them. In doing so, it builds upon the work of Rorty, Habermas, and Charles Taylor, all of whom stress the role played by the literature and culture of the romantic period in shaping the outlook of modern pragmatism. Rorty, in particular, has sought to isolate the romantic celebration of creation from what he perceives to be its nostalgia for absolute grounds, arguing that we should exchange the 'romance and idealistic hopes' of the pursuit of objective truth for 'a rhetoric that romanticizes the pursuit of intersubjective, unforced agreement among larger and larger groups of interlocutors'.[46] However, by acknowledging that the rhetoric of romanticism is vital to the pursuit of solidarity, Rorty, unlike Habermas, underplays the 'pursuit of intersubjective, unforced agreement' within romanticism itself. As in daily life, the conversation between romanticism and pragmatism is a two-way street.

Accordingly, the first two chapters of the present study attempt to initiate this dialogue from different directions. In Chapter 1, I explore in greater detail the ideas of pragmatist thinkers with a view to alleviating some of what Rorty calls the 'critical cramps' of modern commentary. Crucial to this project is overcoming the hypostasised discourse of postmodernism. Thinking seriously about the self as constituted by intersubjectivity demands that we abandon the notion of an 'outside' of thought, an *un*thought. As Davidson maintains, accepting that our awareness floats upon a sea of presuppositions means that it is impossible to question the totality of our beliefs at any particular time. The very act of holding a belief presupposes a limit concept of truth, in so far as it is impossible to communicate without such a concept. The dependence of truth upon dialogue, in turn, completes Davidson's picture of the holism of the mental. This, like the 'Best Account' of human life described by Taylor, rejects the unhelpful vision of total redescription in favour of an account of thought's preconditions based in the narrative of an unfolding life as the embodiment of value.

Pragmatists are apt to trace their holism back to Hume. Rorty, Quine, Putnam, Davidson, and Taylor all agree that the Scottish philosopher loads empiricism with an ambivalent legacy. The breakdown of correspondence between mind and world in Hume's work leaves subsequent thinkers with a dilemma: whether to grasp the horn of idealism, or look elsewhere (to language and communication, primarily) for an explanation of how belief, truth, and meaning connect. The first of these recourses has become so widely identified with romanticism that today the term 'romantic idealism' sounds like a tautology. Following Habermas, however, I find in romantic writing an emergent, broader idea of the holistic creativity and coherence of thought, one that not only attests to the interdependence of truth and interpretation within life, but explains how we are compelled to treat romantic writers themselves as agents and innovators rather than prisoners of language and ideology.

Correspondingly, Chapter 2 explores the background of romantic pragmatics, whereby a late eighteenth-century 'counterdiscourse' of reason gradually relinquishes philosophy's goal of a neutral subject position in favour of a regulative ideal of coherence. This realignment takes place on two separate fronts: Scottish commonsensism and linguistic materialism. In Scotland, Thomas Reid and Dugald Stewart respond to Hume's scepticism by retreating from the epistemology of representation and stressing (respectively) the roles of interpretation and transcendental argument in regulating the web of belief. Meanwhile, materialist theorists of language, in particular John Horne Tooke and Jeremy Bentham, undermine correspondence theories of truth and meaning by arguing that epistemic norms – what Bentham calls the 'logical fictions' of discourse – are formed within linguistic protocols that are themselves the necessary conditions of maintaining (to quote Burke again) 'the ordinary correspondence of life'.

The ideas of Tooke and Bentham are particularly important in encouraging the emergence of a culture in which the concepts of 'truth' and 'communication' are treated as mutually supporting vectors.

John Keats's familiarity with this discourse, through his connections with the culture of dissent, is well documented. In Chapter 3, I claim that his 'Cockney School' contact with the politics of linguistic reform produces a tension in his writing between what I identify as two different forms of 'correspondence': epistemological and epistolary. Where the first produces idealism, the second is closely linked to the radical empiricism of dissenting culture. Against New Historicist interpretations, I argue that Keats's poetry and prose display a sense of thought not as pulled apart by negativity, but as bound together by a concept of deixis. This concept suggests that the relation between truth and communication is fundamentally one of interdependence. For Keats, the 'beauty' of the concept of truth consists in its status as the nonideal absolute in knowledge that makes dialogue – even imaginary dialogue with an urn – possible.

In a similar way, Shelley's writing reveals that the principal philosophical struggle in his work is not primarily between empiricism and transcendentalism (or materialism and idealism), but between two competing conceptions of how truth relates to language and communication. Shelley is still widely read as a Platonic idealist who dabbled in radical materialism. In Chapter 4, however, I show how Shelley's readings in philosophy and contemporary language theory spur his engagement with a Socratic, elenctic method of inquiry. This allows him to argue that, in so far as truth depends upon interpretation, and interpretation always *presupposes* a limit concept of truth, the development of human intelligence is an 'education of error'. In this respect, other aspects of Shelley's thought – his refusal to separate facts from values; his claim that thought is a relation rather than a thing, and that love (a going-out of our nature into otherness) has a *constitutive* role to play in human knowledge – all reveal his engagement with a holistic conception of reason that echoes the radical empiricism of Tooke, Godwin, and Bentham.

Much of Coleridge's reputation today rests upon his status as the only 'major' British romantic writer to engage wholeheartedly (though some would say, misguidedly) with German idealism. In Chapter 5 of this study, however, I argue that the conversion narrative that propels Coleridge from a radical eighteenth-century materialism into a quietist nineteenth-century idealism (obligingly pressing many of the key buttons of modern commentary as it goes) elides three vital aspects of his thought.

The first of these is 'etymologic,' the theory of language and logic that Coleridge adapted from Tooke; the second is his interest in the holistic potential of Kant's transcendental argument; the third is what might be dubbed the ethics of the interpersonal in his later theosophy. Taken together, I argue, these half-submerged elements of Coleridge's thought form a network of concerns that constitute romantic holism. This forms a counterdiscourse to idealism and its alter ego, hyperscepticism, or what Coleridge calls 'hypopœsis'.

CHAPTER I

Romanticising pragmatism: dialogue and critical method

Rorty's call for 'a rhetoric that *romanticizes* the pursuit of intersubjective, unforced agreement' (my emphasis) reflects his view that pragmatism extends some of the key ideas of romanticism. This in turn raises the question: which ideas? Kathleen Wheeler characterises the antirationalistic strain of thought linking romanticism, pragmatism, and deconstruction as a thoroughgoing rejection of dualism in all its guises.[1] Rorty himself is more cautious, picking his way between the possibilities of redescription implicit in what he identifies as 'the romantic notion of man as self-creative', and the equally romantic but (for him) less laudable aspiration that the vocabulary for that redescription be final, grounded in the noncontingent foundations of a 'transcendental constitution'.[2] Consequently, Rorty argues, although Coleridge, Shelley, and Wordsworth may have taught William James and John Dewey that truth is a human creation, the pragmatists had to find out for themselves that creation is not the act of an individual (or universal) consciousness, but is embedded within social interaction and communication. Habermas's argument, in turn, cuts between Wheeler's inclusiveness and Rorty's caution. His articulation of a romantic counterdiscourse of communicative rationality unsettles the assumption that romantic writers have no way of expressing the idea of self-creation without hypostasising it as an ideal. In subsequent chapters, I trace a distinctly British and empirical form of this counterdiscourse through the work of Keats, Shelley, and Coleridge.

In this chapter I build on Wheeler's work on James and Dewey by assessing the potential contributions of six recent pragmatist thinkers to romantic criticism and commentary: Rorty, W. V. Quine, Hilary Putnam, Davidson, Charles Taylor, and Habermas. I begin with Rorty's suggestion that outworn paradigms and problems should simply be set aside, rather than answered (an idea, which, as I argue below, is particularly attractive in the case of postmodern historicism), as well as his belief that it is generally more useful to emphasise commonalities between writers than differences. I then turn to pragmatist attacks on two Humean dualisms: W. V. Quine's assault on Hume's fork of logical and factual truth and Hilary Putnam's dismantling of Hume's 'fact/value' dichotomy. Pragmatists treat the normative from a holistic point of view, eschewing the radical suspicion of many postmodern thinkers. This in turn enables Charles Taylor to rehabilitate transcendental argument, pioneered by Dugald Stewart and Immanuel Kant, as a non-logical way of understanding the material and normative conditions of thought. Taylor's notion of transcendental argument as 'embodied' narrative is itself, I suggest, thoroughly romantic.

Another useful pragmatic precept concerns the redundancy of metacommentary. Quine's linking of truth-values to systems of meaning has been seen by many as opening the gates to Foucauldian notions of incommensurable discourses: of 'systems' of truth in fluid relationships with channels of social power. However, as Davidson points out, to say that there is no escaping one's conceptual scheme is simply to say that there is no meaning that can be attached to the very idea of a conceptual scheme, or to concomitant notions of 'immanence' and 'transcendence'.[3] As I argued in the Introduction, this means dropping the 'problem' of whether we are 'inside' or 'outside' romanticism, and of what kind of metacommentary we must evolve to negotiate the 'incommensurability' of past discourses to our own. If it follows from the explanatory redundancy of the concept of truth that we need no epistemology or 'theory' of truth, then it further follows that we need no anti-epistemology or theory of 'untruth'. Davidson's own, holistic account of the interdependence of truth, interpretation, and belief obviates the paradoxes of postmodern metacommentary, and is broadly in line with Habermas's own pluralistic conception of reason as communicative action.

One important consequence of the demise of metacommentary is the abandonment of disciplinary thinking and its association with what Rorty calls the 'pretense that philosophy and literary criticism are "disciplines" with "methods" and "research techniques" and "results"'.[4] Indeed, as Winfried Fluck observes, there is, strictly speaking, 'no pragmatist method' of interpretation.[5] Pragmatic interpretation is tactical in its manoeuvres rather than strategic: as such, it forsakes the notion of 'interdisciplinarity'. As Rorty contends using theory or philosophy in literary interpretation 'isn't exactly bringing philosophy and literature together. It's just saying, "Here's this particular philosophical view that might relieve your critical cramps."'[6] Consequently, he insists, only the 'low cunning' of pragmatism offers an escape from the constraints of disciplinarity, adding that '[i]n so far as pragmatism privileges the imagination over argumentation, it's on the side of the Romantics'.[7] This statement has more truth in it than Rorty acknowledges. While romantic criticism is certainly well-advised to abandon hypostasisation for holism, I maintain that by treating interpretation as a conversation in which boundaries are determined pragmatically rather than metaphysically, we are ultimately exchanging one romantic policy for another (better) one.

HISTORICISM AND CRITICAL CHIASMUS

Among the metacritical 'cramps' to have afflicted romantic criticism and commentary in the past few decades, the problem of repetition is one of the more intractable. Postmodern historicism in particular faces the conundrum of how to validate critical gains when confronted by a romantic milieu in which ideas of historical relativity, aesthetic reflexivity, and interpretive indeterminacy are already parts of the discourse. In this context, any claim to have transcended past thought-structures can seem merely to reveal its dependence upon romantic paradigms, just as any declaration of critical 'immanence' might appear to betray a desire for critical supervenience. This question of whether criticism of romantic literature is fated to repeat the rhetoric or ideology of romantic literature has prompted historicists such as Marjorie Levinson to develop a method that recognises the 'complex repetitive temporality' upon which all criticism depends.[8] Alternatively, Jerome Christensen has attempted to take advantage of the chiasmus in postmodern criticism, affirming the '*commission* of anachronism' as the means by which the critic 'romantically exploits lack of accountability as the emergence of unrecognised possibility'.[9] In this way, romantic commentators frequently divide in their approach to the problem of repetition along Marxist and Nietzschean lines, either translating repetition into historical negativity or celebrating its affirmation of the 'untimely' or anachronistic in all thought. What Neo-Marxists and Neo-Nietzscheans agree upon, however, is that the tension between 'immanence' and 'transcendence' is a *problem* that criticism must negotiate.

Those who respond to the problem of repetition by rallying to Jameson's cry 'Always historicize!' generally do so under the banner of dialectic.[10] Jerome McGann's work establishes the fundamental task facing romantic historicists by demanding that any interpretation guided by subject-based categories of agency or intentionality give way to an account whereby historical reflexivity is identified as constitutive of poetry as such. 'Poems,' he inveighs, 'at once locate a dialectical encounter between the past and the present, and they represent, through processes of reflection, a particular instance of dialectical exchange which is taken in the present as given from and through the past.' McGann insists that taking seriously the dialectic of meaning means appreciating how 'reflection of the art work is itself a doubled event, involving as it does the act of reflection on the part of the reader or critic as well as the fact of reflection which is preserved in the received work'.[11] For McGann, Marx and Engels's stipulation that people make their own history, but in historical conditions not of their own making, serves as a model whereby the reader's hermeneutical freedom is itself conditioned by the historical determinations of the text being read. This approach takes to heart Sartre's stipulation that any theory of knowledge must allow that 'the experimenter is a part of the experimental system'. In such a way, the action of interpretation, '*in the course of its accomplishment*, provides its own clarification'.[12]

Consequently, interpretation as dialectic conceives itself as patrolling an asymptotic relation between immanence and transcendence. And yet, while postmodern historicism insists on difference as a means of avoiding the repetition of romantic categories, its wariness of turning difference into a form of transcendence (itself the repetition of a romantic trope) propels it back into repetition. Marjorie Levinson's account of the temporality of reading as a process of repetition with change is one attempt to deal with this tension. By rejecting the model of interpretation as ventriloquism for a model of interpretation as translation constituted by a 'complex repetitive temporality', Levinson attempts to steer a course between the Scylla of difference and the Charybdis of Hegelian synthesis.[13] To ask, 'might we not be part of a developing, leap-frogging logic?' she claims, is not just 'to wonder who we are that we produce the Romantics in just this way. It is also to inquire who *they* are, to have produced *us* in just this way'.[14] For Levinson, the indifference or detachment that Liu diagnoses as the postmodern malady of New Historicism, itself the product of dialectic, will only be overcome by dialectic.[15] As she reminds us, 'the dialecticity we restore to the work through our criticism – its agency in the past – is also its agency in the present'.[16]

It is unsurprising, then, to find that a postmodern criticism intent on dissolving the metaphysics of romanticism into its dialectical material conditions should in turn have given rise to a *new* romantic poetry, one which, by a curious doubling, resists such indifference. It is, indeed, the romantic introduction of an otherness within truth (and with it the concept of an 'outside' to truth) that initiates the modern project to negotiate the relationship between the 'liberating' and 'oppressive' legacies of Enlightenment discourse. Thus, what Levinson calls the 'nonstrategic indifference'[17] of romanticism, its 'infinitely recuperative' assimilation of 'history, politics, or other people', is itself the negation of the incommensurable otherness it preserves in the figure of the sublime.[18] Through the liberating agency of modern criticism, the romantic dialectic ensures that wherever cancelled otherness reappears. From the perspective of postmodern historicism, then, the paradox of immanence and negativity is something that criticism must endure. Levinson maintains that having 'found out the barbarism in those high-romantic texts, we must submit to their civilizing hints or else worsen our own barbarism'. Dialectic will never allow itself to settle into indifference, she maintains, because the ceaseless vigilance that it enjoins regarding the reflexivity of criticism's self-positioning involves the same 'paradoxical commitment to immanence and negativity' that shapes our ever-mobile relationship with romanticism.[19]

As I argued in the Introduction, however, far from being inescapable, this 'paradoxical commitment' is merely the product of a dichotomy between immanence and transcendence that is in turn based upon the questionable assumption that thought has an incommensurable but conditioning outside, a radical 'otherness'. At stake here is what Bernard Williams identifies as a tension between 'truth' and 'truthfulness'. According to Williams, the 'intense commitment to truthfulness – or, at any rate, a pervasive suspiciousness, a readiness against being fooled', that inflects postmodern discourse is allied to 'an equally pervasive suspicion about truth itself'. Thus, paradoxically, the 'desire for truthfulness drives a process of criticism which weakens the assurance that there is any secure or unqualifiedly stateable truth'.[20] In modern thinkers such as Foucault, this quest for 'truthfulness' without 'truth' involves establishing a perspective outside thought itself. Consequently, criticism is beset by an indeterminate 'doubling' of perspectives, whereby the groundlessness of the unthought or antireason that interrogates reason from the 'outside' itself becomes, functionally, a foundation of critique.

This doubling reflects an ambivalence in postmodern historicism between two competing instincts, both of which are exhibited and analysed by James Chandler's *England in 1819*: the desire that a dialectical reading should 'sustain a certain reflexivity throughout',[21] and the desire to understand the 'preconditions that make our own (my own) historicism practicable'.[22] The first is the imperative of dialectic; the second, however, denotes an inquiry shaped by the analysis of preconditions and presuppositions, known to Stewart, Coleridge, and Kant as transcendental argument. Although this seems a minor ambiguity, it leaves open the possibility that one of the preconditions of our historical understanding is that we do *not* view it as determined by negativity, absent causation, or complex repetitive temporality. Indeed, I would contend this very conclusion is pressed upon us as much by Levinson's conception of dialectical criticism as involving a 'paradoxical' commitment to immanence and negativity, as by Chandler's exhaustive historicising of the distinction between referential and 'worklike' functions of texts. Like Levinson's work, *England in 1819* attempts to satisfy Liu's stipulation that 'no understanding of the text as action is possible without a theory; and no theory of the New Historicism is possible without a fully historical sense of the method'.[23] A key part of Chandler's enterprise involves reading the historicism of the 1980s as a complex repetition of the Sartre and Lévi-Strauss history debate in the 1960s, and that in turn as repeating the debates over historical consciousness in 1819. Ostensibly then, Chandler's is a historical dialectical critique of dialectical historicism.

Chandler's work pushes the methodological hygiene of postmodern historicism to its limit. As with any putatively 'immanent' methodology, the problem for historicism lies in articulating its own critical position without slipping into the kind of knowingness that might be classed as 'transcendence'. By insistently 'doubling' its perspectives, however, *England in 1819* suggests not that negativity exhaustively determines, but that it simultaneously provokes and defers the very moment of recuperative awareness or epistemological transcendence that it sets out to avoid. So long as thought is seen as merely a phase of negativity, the problem of how negativity can *make sense of itself* will recur. In this way, historicism's preoccupation with radical otherness, combined with its commitment to *think* that otherness as part of its own project, ensures that the dichotomy of inside/outside is preserved by being sent into dialectical freeplay. Rather than dispensing entirely with the dichotomy between immanence and transcendence, this strategy finesses the division to the point where the inquiring subject and the subject of inquiry are indeterminate fields. Thus, by historicising the very distinction between 'marking and making history', Chandler holds immanence and transcendence in a suspension whereby historical knowledge is linked to a transformed present and future. However, to render a dichotomy indeterminate is one thing, to collapse it another.

By contrast, abandoning the idea that thought has an 'outside' means discarding the idea that it makes any sense to talk of 'negativity' or 'contingency' as powers that trump thought's understanding of its own conditions of possibility. Simply put, it means giving up the futile attempt to situate *thought itself,* and recognising that all argument ultimately takes the form of transcendental argument, or argument from basic presuppositions. In its adherence to metacommentary, however, post-modern historicism fails to consider the possibility that the removal of the 'immanent/transcendent' boundary might lead to an enhanced, rather than a relentlessly mediated practice of rational inquiry.

ROMANTIC PRAGMATISM: RORTY AND HABERMAS

The differences between pragmatism and historicism should not be overstated. As Frank Lentricchia observes, the two theories find common ground in their abandonment of epistemology and their denial of 'the classical claim of philosophy for representational adequacy,' their insistence on the fundamental 'instrumentality of ideas', and their elevation of rhetoric and dialogue over notions of neutrality and factuality.[24] Furthermore, as Rorty argues, there are good pragmatic reasons for not being too schismatic. Acknowledging the commonalities between theories answers to the pragmatist pursuit of intersubjective agreement or solidarity, the intuition that rather than being unbridgeable 'distinctions between cultures, theories, or discourses ... represent no more than differences of opinion – the sorts of differences that can get resolved by hashing things out'.[25]

Solidarity notwithstanding, there is one core issue on which pragmatists and historicists diverge: the nature of truth. For Lentricchia, truth is determined by social and historical totality; for Rorty, it is subject only to the pragmatics of communication. Accordingly, Lentricchia complains that 'pragmatism drains from its epistemology all but a minimal residue of history and society'.[26] Rorty's notion of a communicative space in which differences 'get resolved by hashing things out', he argues, remains blind to the power structures that define that space. Thus, while exchanging 'confrontation' for 'conversation' may appear appealing as an ideal, in reality '[y]ou cannot jump into this conversation and do what you please'.[27] Lentricchia quickly fastens upon a term that captures what worries him most about Rorty's thought: romanticism. By concentrating above all upon the need of the individual to communicate, to be edified, Rorty revives a language of 'liberal, personal needs ... celebrated from Addison to Wordsworth'.[28] However, the utopia of 'a fully socialized Romanticism,' based on agreement and solidarity rather than 'objective' truth, takes no cognisance of the economics of modern subjectivity, of how the personal freedom envisaged by Addison and Wordsworth is commodified by capitalism and virtualised by postmodern technologies. 'The missing term in Rorty's analysis', Lentricchia concludes, 'is "society" '.[29]

Historicism, however, has long since given up on the idea of a Marxist science of society. Lentricchia himself sees Marxism as 'a kind of rhetoric ... an invitation to practice'.[30] From a pragmatist perspective, the problem is one of how historicism accesses the totality (or negative causality) supposedly 'outside' everyday communication when there *is only* the 'practice' of dialogue and interpretation. By postulating a hypostasised totality from which one may interrogate the intersubjectivity upon which communication and knowledge rest, historicism offers only a perspective outside perspective, a view from nowhere. And yet, as Rorty observes, '[t]o say that we should drop the idea of truth as out there waiting to be discovered is not to say that we have discovered that, out there, there is no truth'.[31] Indeed, Rorty argues (following Davidson) that the claim that we cannot step outside our conceptual scheme is equivalent to the claim that there is *no such thing as* a 'scheme' or 'regime' of truth: there is just truth. This is not to make a foundation of truth, merely to affirm that truth is one of the things required for intelligent interaction with others and with the world. Beyond this, no theory can penetrate: 'when we hypostatize the adjective "true" into "Truth" and ask about our relation to it,' Rorty maintains, 'we have absolutely nothing to say'. Of course, '[w]e can, if we like, use this hypostatization in the same way that admirers of Plato have used other hypostatizations – Beauty, Goodness, and Rightness. ... But the point of telling such stories is unclear'.[32]

While Rorty's treatment of truth may appear more brisk and less 'cramped' than that of historicists, Lentricchia's second point remains unanswered: just how 'romantic' is intersubjectivity? A key argument of this study is that the 'holistic' approach to truth favoured by pragmatists such as Rorty, Davidson, and Habermas revives a romantic discourse of communicative rationality that modern theory and historicism (still swayed by the post-Hegelian radicalisation of Enlightenment scepticism) has either forgotten or discounted. As I indicated at the beginning of this chapter, Rorty's own relation to the romantics is ambivalent. On one hand, he attaches great importance to 'the romantic notion of man as self-creative'[33] and to the way in which, as he sees it, romanticism 'inaugurated an era in which we gradually came to appreciate the historical role of linguistic innovation'. Above all, he argues, romanticism glimpses the possibilities of redescription 'in the vague, misleading, but pregnant and inspiring thought that truth is made rather than found'.[34] Furthermore, in fashioning her cultural role 'as auxiliary to the poet rather than to the physicist',[35] Rorty's ironist reveals her 'indebtedness to Romanticism'.[36] Like Shelley and Coleridge, she strives for metaphorical renewal, seeing language as an evolutionary process in which 'new forms of life [are] constantly killing off old forms'.[37] By rejecting commonsense realism and reorienting thought towards innovation, however, the romantic pragmatist 'can only hope to trace the outlines of what Shelley calls "the gigantic shadows which futurity casts upon the present" '.[38] Consequently, Rorty is untroubled by accusations that pragmatism merely repeats the romantic elision of social and historical reality. Pragmatists and romantics 'make more vivid and concrete our sense of what human life might be like in a democratic utopia ... They do little to justify the choice of such a utopia or to hasten its arrival. But they do show how the creation of new discourses can enlarge the realm of possibility.' For this reason, they should be read as 'good *private* philosophers' rather than merely as 'bad *public* philosophers'.[39]

Rorty is, nonetheless, guarded about other aspects of romanticism. While he is keen to revive within cultural commentary and theory a romantic emphasis on spontaneity, creativity, and metaphor, he is wary of the romantic tendency to hypostasise its ideals in the form of a transcendental constitution. Kant and Hegel in particular are guilty, in Rorty's view, of confusing the important idea that nothing has a nature or an essence with the unhelpful notion that space and time are ideal. Thus, what is 'misleading' in the otherwise 'inspiring' romantic idea that truth is made rather than found is the suggestion that truth is the creation of consciousness or an absolute mind. 'What is true about [the first] claim', Rorty counters, 'is that *languages* are made rather than found, and that truth is a property of linguistic entities, of sentences'.[40] In dismantling representationalism, then, the pragmatist must complete a job that the romantics left half-finished. By maintaining that the human self is created by a contingent, constantly changing vocabulary, the pragmatist avoids the romantic mistake of viewing metaphorical expressions as 'mysterious tokens or symbols of some higher reality'.[41] She thereby obviates the romantic compulsion 'to justify ... metaphors by philosophical argument'.[42]

Rorty, then, presents his own ambivalence about romanticism as a simultaneous embracement of romantic irony and rejection of romantic hypostasisation. This reading of romantic discourse contrasts with that of Habermas. Habermas is critical of what he sees as Rorty's counterintuitive 'epistemization of the idea of truth', whereby 'the truth of a proposition is

conceived as coherence with other propositions or as justified assertibi-
lity'.[43] By arguing that there is nothing to truth apart from justification,
Rorty attempts to eliminate from dialogue the *presupposition of
context-independent truth*. However, Habermas claims, Rorty fails to
distinguish between the reflexivity of philosophical discourse, which
suspends the preconditions of everyday thought, and the dialogue of
the 'lifeworld', for which a concept of objective truth is a necessary
precondition. Without such a presupposition, Habermas maintains, the
pragmatics of communication break down. 'This supposition of an
objective world that is independent of our descriptions,' he argues, 'fulfils
a functional requirement of our processes of cooperation and communication. Without this supposition, everyday practices, which rest on the . . .
Platonic distinction between believing and knowing unreservedly, would
come apart at the seams'.[44] For Habermas, any pragmatic account of truth
must accommodate 'the entwining of the two different pragmatic roles
played by the Janus-faced concept of truth in action-contexts and in
rational discourses respectively'.[45]

What the Rorty/Habermas debate brings into focus is the extent to
which the romantic tension between holism and hypostasis persists in
modern pragmatism. Rorty sees himself as arguing on behalf of reform
rather than revolution, for the beauty of intersubjectivity rather than the
sublimity of incommensurable phrase-regimes.[46] Consequently, he is
perplexed by Habermas's reluctance to embrace a playful romantic irony:
'Romanticism,' he notes, 'seems to make Habermas nervous. He does not
discuss Schiller's exhaltation of "play," nor is he inclined to follow Shelley
(as Dewey did) in thinking of poets as unacknowledged legislators'.[47] In
Habermas's picture of truth as 'Janus-faced', alternating between system
and lifeworld, Rorty detects the vestiges of an essentially religious worldview, a yearning for an encounter with a nonhuman reality. 'As I see it,' he
counters, 'philosophers who think that we have a duty to truth, or that we
should value truth, or that we should have faith in truth, are engaging in
needless, and philosophically mischievous, hypostatization'.[48] Rorty contrasts such 'hypostatization' with a pragmatism that combines romantic
ideas about the redescriptive possibilities of language with a Darwinian
account of how language evolves blindly. It is this *naturalised* romanticism
that he claims to find in the work of John Dewey:

For Dewey, it is the Romantic strain, rather than the rationalist strain, that
should be preserved from Hegel and Marx, and combined with a Darwinian
naturalism. Such naturalism is fairly difficult to combine with traditional

religions, but fairly easy to combine with the Romanticism that is the least common denominator of Wordsworth and Byron, of Emerson and Nietzsche.[49]

Habermas, on the other hand, is puzzled by what he sees as Rorty's *lack* of pragmatism. The latter's heroic, romantic defiance of commonsense realism refuses to acknowledge 'the *pragmatic dimension*' played by normativity in 'a particular deployment of the [truth] predicate'. Minimalist or deflationary theories of truth are fine for reflective thinking, Habermas acknowledges, but 'in everyday life we cannot survive with hypotheses alone, that is, in a persistently fallibilist way'.[50] Rorty's extreme aversion to the strong notion of context-independent truth is still more surprising, he observes, when one realises that in the notion of 'solidarity', or extending the circle of dialogue and agreement even he smuggles a 'weak idealization into play'.[51] Despite Rorty's protests, hypostasisation is clearly not without its uses.

This brings us back to Rorty's call for solidarity or intersubjectivity to be 'romanticized'. On the face of it, this call sits uneasily with his simultaneous attempt to 'naturalise' romanticism. Rorty, however, insists that his is a '*non-reductive* naturalism'.[52] To be a naturalist in this sense is not to privilege scientific or materialist accounts of causality; on the contrary, it is to allow a plurality of explanations of the web of relations that constitute truth and subjectivity.[53] In this way, as Rorty puts it, '*holism takes the curse off naturalism*'.[54] For Habermas, however, the implications of 'romanticising' intersubjective agreement are quite different. From this perspective, holism means incorporating, at least within the lifeworld, a minimised idealism by allowing the notion of objective truth to be a basic presupposition of dialogue. As I discuss below, this raises further problems about the very possibility of distinguishing systematic from lifeworld thought (or as Hilary Putnam puts it, 'norms' from 'values'). Nonetheless, Habermas's account of the conditions of communicative rationality enables him to identify a different form of 'pragmatised' romanticism from that of Rorty, one in which holism 'takes the curse off', not naturalism, but the *ideal* of truth. I will return to this point, which has significant implications for the critique of romanticism, in Chapter 3. At this stage, however, it is important to clarify what is meant by 'holism'.

MEANING HOLISM: QUINE

As a term that has bearings on the nature of definition, 'holism' is, unsurprisingly, not an easy idea to pin down. One can begin, however, by distinguishing between *epistemological* holism and *semantic* holism.

The first is crisply described by Rorty as 'the view that people change their beliefs in such a way as to achieve coherence with their other beliefs, to bring their beliefs and desires into some sort of equilibrium – and that that is about all there is to be said about the quest for knowledge'.[55] The holistic picture of knowledge is, above all, antifoundational. On Rorty's view, the vessel that floats our awareness of the world is not built in dry dock or upon the *terra firma* of a neutral objectivity, but at sea, with whatever materials come to hand. Semantic holism shares this perspective in its account of how language hooks onto the world, of how meaning relates to truth. For W. V. Quine, the collapse of the positivist conception of analyticity (the idea that certain statements are true by virtue of the *meaning* of the terms used) entails giving up any foundationalist notion that language maps onto the world in a logical way.[56] Quine's central argument is that the notions of 'analytical truth' and 'synonymous meaning' presuppose, rather than (as positivists like Carnap and Ayer would have it) explain each other. The whole edifice of logical positivism was built upon a hopelessly circular argument. 'Let us face it,' Quine urges, 'our socialized stimulus synonymy and stimulus analyticity are still not behavioristic reconstructions of intuitive semantics, but only a behavioristic ersatz'.[57]

This finding leads Quine to draw two important conclusions. The first is that the notion of a quantifiable thing or relation called 'meaning', according to which the intensions and extensions of individual terms can be determined by the truth-conditions for whole sentences, should be dropped in favour of a holistic picture in which the only criteria for deciding such things are associated with language-practices as a whole. Language, he decides, is a social art, based 'entirely on intersubjectively available cues as to what to say and when'.[58] Indeed, since reference is indeterminate, Quine argues, it is better to talk of 'interpretation' than 'meaning'. Moreover, since the death of analyticity also means the demise of the synthetic, we must finally ditch the view that the world is somehow *given* to the senses: objects are theoretical through and through. 'Entification,' as he puts it, 'begins at arm's length'.[59] This in turn entails dropping the idea of truth as correspondence for one of truth as immanent to a conceptual scheme, a language. Truth becomes 'disquotation'. The referent of 'a rabbit', in short, can only be a rabbit. From this discovery Quine draws a second conclusion: ontological relativity. For Quine, an empiricism *without* dogmas casts knowledge as a Kuhnian field of force in which no data is 'hard' or unrevisable, and in which any 'conflict with experience at the periphery occasions readjustments in the interior of the field'.[60] Consequently, since '[a]ny statement can be held true come what may, if we make drastic enough adjustments elsewhere in the system . . . by the same token, no statement is immune to revision'.[61] There are no rules for this, just as there are no rules for interpretation. Meaning holism entails truth relativism.

In so far, then, as it affirms the anatomical connections between referential systems and other forms of human life, Quine's meaning holism falls into the broader category of what Jerry Fodor and Ernest Lepore describe as '*anthropological* holism'. Fodor and Lepore add that among the adherents of this theory can be numbered '*almost* everybody in AI and cognitive psychology; and . . . absolutely everybody who writes literary criticism in French'.[62] The inclusion of the last category is telling, in that it conforms to a long-standing tendency among many commentators to depict Quine's arguments as coterminous with currents in 'continental' postmodernism. In the case of Fodor and Lepore, the reasons for this relate to the three major consequences that they see as arising from Quinean holism. The first of these is the evaporation of the intentional (since 'meaning holism is incompatible with a robust notion of content identity, and hence with a robust notion of intentional law').[63] This problem leads to the second consequence, namely the end to any putatively 'scientific' theory of rationality. Quine himself seems quite comfortable with such an outcome. Indeed, he confirms that his argument that no statement has its own fund of empirical data means the end of positivist-epistemological attempts to reduce sentences to observational and logico-mathematical terms. Accordingly, 'rational reconstruction' in philosophy should give way to 'naturalised' epistemology, or practical psychology.[64]

However, it is the third of the ramifications that Fodor and Lepore identify that has particular salience in the present context. Fodor and Lepore claim that the truth-relativism that stems from Quine's account of the indeterminability of translation results in a situation where different conceptual schemes have different truth-values *because* they are different systems of meaning. If Quine is right, and entification always occurs 'at arm's length', meaningful cross-cultural and cross-historical comparisons are impossible. If all objects are theoretical from the start, having formed within the conceptual matrix of a given linguistic culture, we are committed to talking not about different theories of the same things, but about different *things*. For example, rather than viewing ancient Greek astronomers as having a different theory about the nature of the stars from us, we are committed to denying that the things they referred to were *stars* at all. On this scheme, Fodor and Lepore claim, 'it may well turn out that scientific theories are empirically incommensurable unless their ontological commitments are more or less identical'.[65] Again, Quine does little to discourage this view, insisting that ontological relativity goes all the way down. However, like Hume, he tempers his account with a naturalist appeal to the human instinct for epistemic conservatism. This conservatism, or 'a favoring of the inherited or invented conceptual scheme of one's own previous work', provides a less mobile centre around which more radical changes to meaning and belief systems can occur without causing conceptual chaos.[66] The supposed necessity of mathematical truths, for example, merely 'resides in our unstated policy of shielding mathematics by exercising our freedom to reject other beliefs instead'. Quine is all for conservatism, so long as we realise that, like epistemic virtues such as generality, simplicity, and refutability, truth is simply part of the language-game of science. 'It is well,' as he concludes, 'not to rock the boat more than need be'.[67]

FACTS AND VALUES: PUTNAM

Fodor and Lepore's arguments reveal why semantic holism is often seen to support the theory of incommensurable discourses. The latter theory, which dates back to Spinoza, takes its modern form in Kuhn's vision of scientific paradigm shifts as inaugurating radically different worlds, and becomes the cornerstone of Foucault's and Lyotard's accounts of how developments in knowledge are triggered by contingent changes in discourse.[68] Accordingly, while for the early Foucault the emergence of man as an empirico-transcendental doublet in late eighteenth-century discourse is the product of an inexplicable 'breach . . . distributed across the entire visible surface of knowledge',[69] for Lyotard the abyss separating empirical and transcendental language-games marks the point at which heterogeneous 'phrase regimes . . . cannot be translated from one into the other'.[70] Working through the implications of incommensurability for interpretive practice has become one of the defining activities of postmodern literary criticism and historicism.

As Putnam and Davidson demonstrate, however, semantic holism need not yield incommensurability. Putnam's work attempts instead to link Quine's semantic holism with a wider, epistemological holism. Quine himself was prepared to adopt Humean, commonsense measures for what was good in the way of belief in the light of the theory-ladenness of experience. Putnam, however, argues that once we consign the dichotomy of 'fact' and 'value' to the same bin as that other

Humean totem, the analytic/synthetic boundary, there remains no reason to separate the 'theoretical' from the evaluative.[71] For Putnam, meaning holism entails belief holism, but what makes our beliefs cohere itself depends upon a network of *evaluative* decisions. Accordingly, he proposes recasting what Quine identifies as the indeterminacy of translation as 'the *interest relativity* of interpretation'.[72] Putnam further agrees with Quine that there are no experiential inputs to knowledge that are not already shaped by concepts, by discourse. However, he insists, this need not mean the death of realism. We need not equate truth merely with what is rationally acceptable or permissible within a given cultural discourse or local knowledge if we conceive of truth as 'an *idealization* of rational acceptability' – itself, of course, a sound epistemic value.[73] We can, in short, be both 'internalists' and 'realists' about truth.

While Putnam's internal realism involves accepting an objectivist view of truth, this objectivism strips away many of the problematic features of traditional realism. Indeed, it seeks to bypass the relativist/realist debate by rejecting the dichotomy of perspectives whereby historical and cultural contingency is pitted against the notion of a transcendent, ahistoricial organon of reason. What is required, as Putnam argues, is an account of truth and interpretation enabled by the understanding that 'the mind and the world jointly make up the mind and the world'.[74] Putnam's point is that accepting the Nietzschean claim that factual statements always presuppose value-judgements does not necessarily lead to a radically relativised notion of truth. Indeed, the identification of truth with historical or cultural conventions merely repeats the same old dichotomy of fact and value on a procedural level (as in: is it *true* that truth is a convention?) Only an *a priori* scepticism would infer from the collapse of this dichotomy that the concept of truth must be understood through, say, notions of 'difference' or 'power'.

By contrast, Putnam adopts a pragmatic tack, arguing that, since our frameworks of rationality and coherence are ineluctably historical and cultural, no historical or cultural understanding of rationality and coherence (whether 'dialectical' or 'archeological') can adopt a perspective that itself transcends those frameworks. There is no special exemption clause in our basic notions of coherence or truth: they are ineliminable conditions of discourse itself. Whether an idealisation of rational acceptability, as Putnam maintains, or the irreducible presupposition of meaning as argued by Davidson and the later Habermas, truth is not something that can be examined, as it were, from the outside.

Consequently, the close connection between truth, coherence, and value does not mean that judgements of value are radically relative. By emphasising the plurality in such judgements, we may allow that they can be objectively indeterminate or context-sensitive with the proviso that they can also be *right*. To say truth is 'relative' to our framework of understanding, on the other hand, is merely to say that the concept of truth that we have is the one that we have. As Putnam observes, 'if all is relative, then the relative is relative too'.[75]

Putnam's account of truth has important ramifications for reading literature of the romantic period. His work indicates that the perspectival paradoxes encountered by postmodern historicism are alleviated when we recognise the futility of attempting to describe our interlacing framework of truth and value from the 'outside', as an 'ideology' or a 'regime of truth'. The attempt to avoid transcendence through metacommentary rests upon the misconception that there is a metaphysically interesting distinction to be made between 'immanence' and 'transcendence'. For Putnam, however, there are good reasons for treating reason as both immanent *and* transcendent. This means, for instance, that we are bound to treat romantic writers as interlocutors: 'We are committed by our fundamental conceptions to treating not just our present time-slices, but also our past selves, our ancestors, and members of other cultures past and present, as *persons*; and that means ... attributing to them shared references and shared concepts, however different the *conceptions* that we also attribute'.[76] Like Rorty and Habermas, Putnam maintains that the prospect of a radically external perspective on questions of truth and value is merely the ghostly remainder of a value-free rationality. Indeed, the persistence of relativism in the work of writers such as Paul de Man and Paul Feyerabend reveals the grip that the Kantian–Hegelian fantasy of absolute knowledge continues to exert over modern thought. 'Talk of "otherness," "exotopy," and "incommensurability," ' he notes, 'would not be as widespread as it is if the ideas of perfect knowledge, of falling short of perfect knowledge, and of the falsity of everything short of perfect knowledge did not speak to us'.[77] The best alternative to such talk is to treat historical knowledge, evaluation, and interpretation holistically. This avoids hypostasising the background historical presuppositions of thought as something radically 'external' to thought itself, thereby obviating the unhelpful notion of historically or culturally incommensurable 'systems' of thought. As Rorty observes, one of the most compelling accounts of such 'holistic' thinking is set out in Donald Davidson's defence of 'radical interpretation'.

TRUTH AND INTERPRETATION: DAVIDSON

Though he broadly accepts Quine's semantic holism, Davidson, like Putnam, draws different conclusions. Epistemic conservatism aside, for Quine ontological relativity means rejecting the fantasy of a *theory* of meaning that might render the relations between different discourses commensurable. There is, he maintains, no theory-neutral way of determining meaning – or rather, what is 'assertible' in a particular context. Against this, Davidson argues that anyone in the position of a radical interpreter – that is, in the position of having to interpret a previously unknown language 'from scratch' – is entitled to treat any evidence that that language is, in principle, untranslatable as evidence that they are not dealing with a language at all. Similarly, any system of belief that appears to be a candidate for complete incommensurability with that of the interpreter is, to that extent, a candidate for some status other than that of 'system of belief'. Indeed, as Davidson points out, an interpreter would never be in a position to recognise such a candidate, since recognition itself presupposes commensurability.

This in turn calls into question the very notions of 'systems of belief', 'conceptual schemes' and, indeed, of 'discourses' – concepts essential to much modern literary criticism and theory. From Davidson's perspective, Kuhn's account of different worlds of knowledge inaugurated by paradigm shifts simply amounts to saying that the truth-value of a sentence is relative to the language in which it is articulated. To take the further step of claiming that this truth is incommensurable with other truths in other discourses is to make the unwarranted assumption that it makes sense to conceive of a single space within which each scheme has a position and a perspective that is *not itself* a space of reasons. It is this assumption that underlies Foucault's idea of the *episteme* as a field 'in which knowledge, envisaged apart from all criteria having reference to its rational value or to its objective forms, grounds its positivity'.[78] For Davidson, however, it is meaningless to talk of reason outside a space of reasons. There is no sensible way of talking about incommensurably relative truths. The concept of truth may be indeterminate, but truth itself is not plural. In this way, Quine's ontological relativity becomes Davidson's 'anomalous monism'.[79]

Consequently, Davidson replaces Putnam's account of reason as both immanent and transcendent with a mental holism that resists any 'basic division' within thought itself. This, he claims, leaves us 'free to give up the search for the "right" theory of truth'.[80] For Davidson, truth is not the sort of thing about which it is worth having a theory, because it is not a *thing* at all. Indeed, he concludes, 'if we cannot intelligibly say that schemes are different, neither can we intelligibly say that they are one'.[81] Once the notion of truth-relative-to-a-scheme (or paradigm or *episteme*) is exposed as the last dogma of empiricism, the idea that meaning is determined by a particular *regime* of truth can be reduced to the idea that meaning is determined by truth. In this way, it can be seen that removing the final traces of the 'given' or theory-neutral in human knowledge leads not to conceptual relativism but rather to a new objectivism about truth. As Davidson puts it, by giving up the 'given', 'we do not give up the world, but reestablish unmediated touch with the familiar objects whose antics make our sentences and opinions true or false'.[82]

Thus, while Davidson's objectivism is antifoundationalist, it is also anticonventionalist. While it rejects the picture of truth as ideal, it also resists the attempt to explain truth in terms of 'conventions' or 'discourses'. Davidson argues that we need to understand in full the implications of Quine's claim, following Tarski, that truth is 'disquotation', or (to put it in pragmatic terms) affirmation.[83] For Davidson it follows from this that truth can only be understood through its triangular relationship of interdependence with intentionality and intersubjectivity. When one of these elements is removed, the others fall, but when taken together they are mutually sustaining. Thus, to have an intention or to hold a belief presupposes a shared concept of truth, which would be impossible without communication between persons, which in turn requires that they hold beliefs (and so on). In this way, Davidson seeks to extend Quine's holism, arguing that intelligent, socially engaged life sustains truth, but that without truth, human intelligence would be impossible. Truth, then, is not some transcendent ideal. Since truth determines meaning holistically, through the beliefs of interpreters, there is 'no going outside this standard to check whether we have things right'.[84]

This in turn explains Davidson's insistence that 'radical interpretation' is always possible. One of the misconceptions that feeds theories of culturally or historically incommensurable conceptual schemes, Davidson argues, is the assumption that language is the *medium* of thought. From a holistic perspective, by contrast, 'language' is determined by the communicative *acts* in which people engage in the attempt to understand each other. Truth determines 'meaning' via belief, through what participants in communication hold to be true. As Davidson demonstrates, a minimum condition for understanding any statement is understanding what it would be for that statement to be true: without the possibility of error, communication would be impossible. Quine showed that there can be no rules or conventions for this. Yet for precisely this reason, Davidson insists that an interpreter can never sustain the kind of suspicion enjoined by various brands of postmodernism. Instead, she is bound to proceed on the assumption that her beliefs and those of the person she interprets share common ground.

This 'principle of charity' forms the cornerstone of Davidson's defence of radical interpretation against the claim of incommensurability.[85] The holistic interdependence of thought, truth, and communication means that finding a common ground, a shared way of life, is not subsequent to interpretation, but a condition of it. By equating language with interpreting the beliefs of others, Davidson erases 'the boundary between knowing a language and knowing our way around the world generally'.[86] We have no choice in interpretation but to begin *in medias res*, when we are already at sea, which means assuming, first, that those we interpret share a substantial number of our basic beliefs, and second, that to say this is just to say that most of their basic beliefs must be *true*. By the same token, we can only *mean* what we are able to imagine others as being able to interpret. Crucially then, recognising that meaning is determined by truth 'necessarily requires us to see others as much like ourselves in point of overall coherence and correctness – that we see them as more or less rational creatures mentally inhabiting a world much like our own'.[87]

Davidson's arguments have significant consequences for critical theory. First, they offer an account of the indeterminacy of 'meaning' without losing a foothold in truth or undermining human agency. In describing language in terms of a pragmatics of communication that has the possibility of error as its cornerstone, Davidson is clear that any interpretation must at some point engage with human intentions. This, of course, is not to identify meaning with psychological origins: Davidson concurs with Putnam on the principle that ' "meanings ain't in the head" '.[88] The meaning of a text 'is the product of the interplay between the intentions of the writer to be understood in a certain way and the interpretation put on the writer's words by the reader'.[89] By accounting for how both are transformed by the act of interpretation, Davidson is able to account for how our 'passing' theories of interpretation successfully accommodate unusual or convention-defying linguistic events. For Davidson, language always harbours a tension between such passing but transformative theories and the stability of our presuppositions, our 'prior' theories. In this respect, challenging works of literature are analogous to malapropisms: writers like Joyce and Shakespeare take us to the limits of what is acceptable in language, to 'the foundations and origins of communication'. Linking evolution and revolution in language with the cycle of 'destruction and return to the point of origin', they compel us 'to share in the annihilation of old meanings and the creation ... of a new language'.[90] As Reed Way Dasenbrock indicates, Davidson's anticonventionalism places 'innovation and creativity at the very heart of language use'.[91] Yet, like malapropisms, literary innovations commandeer and rely upon 'a common conceptual space'.[92] Only within the context of a great number of shared beliefs and presuppositions – which is to say, only with a shared concept of *truth* – can the Dionysian business of language take place. Davidson's account explains how, indeterminacy notwithstanding, we *do* understand what Joyce means, just as we understand what Mrs Malaprop means. Moreover, it does so while retaining a notion of writer and reader as *agents* in the activity of interpretation.

The recovery of agency in interpretation in turn produces a second major consequence of Davidson's arguments: the close connection between method and learning. Davidson bases his holism upon the 'good Socratic intuition' that 'it is only in the context of frank discussion, communication, and mutual exchange that trustworthy truths emerge'.[93] The Socratic elenchus, he maintains, is a method that, rather than *establishing* truth, proceeds on the basis that there is good reason to believe that the *assumption* that dialogue leads to truth is true, that when 'our beliefs are consistent they will in most matters be true'. Davidson's method, then, is based on a truth-enabling network of mutually dependent presuppositions. It is dialectic, but dialectic based in a pragmatics of dialogue rather than an *a priori* notion of negativity. Moreover, by rejecting the conventionalist dictum that all interpretation is ultimately self-validating, Davidson shows how we adjust our theories to fit our experience, even as our experience is shaped by our theories. Theories of interpretation have a mutually sustaining rather than a self-confirming relationship with truth. While the principle of charity prevents us from dispensing with the majority of our beliefs and values at any given moment, it also guarantees that some of them will be sacrificed as our assumptions are challenged and overturned. Dialogue invariably effects some kind of change or transformation in all parties. In our encounters with texts, no less than with people, our interpretive assumptions are constantly revised. Davidson's account of interpretation intimates how we can conceive of this revisionary process as a process of *learning*.

Davidson's original claim is that 'intra-attitudinal' holism, the interdependence of beliefs in interpretation, is forced upon us by the way in which belief connects meaning and truth. Like Putnam, however, he sees no reason to privilege cognitive over connative attitudes. On the contrary, intentions are always 'caught up in the web of evaluative attitudes and practical knowledge'.[94] Since meaning is as entangled with desire as it is with belief, holism applies inter- as well as intra-attitudinally. Indeed, Davidson finds for 'a thoroughgoing holism, not only with respect to meanings and beliefs, but also with respect to the relations between the cognitive and the evaluative attitudes'.[95] Once again, he insists on separating the question of determinacy from that of objectivity. In the end, we should accept that some questions of value and interpretation are simply vague: it is consistent with objectivity, as Davidson insists, that in some cases 'there should be no clear answers about what is right'.[96]

What this means for our own practices as readers and interpreters is that we are mistaken if we think that our positioning with respect to the text is something that can be determined by a choice of 'method'. At its most fundamental level, the search for a methodology is pointless, since, if Davidson is right, the *basis* of intercultural and historical comparisons could never be something that might be accepted by one person or society, but not by another. 'The only way we have of knowing what someone else's values are,' he maintains, 'is one that (as in the case of belief) builds on a common framework'.[97] This 'basis', such as it is, is a presupposition we make by engaging in interpretation in the first place. We do not 'choose' our values any more than we 'look' for truth. In literary criticism, as in life, 'we do not have to establish, argue for, or opt for, a basis for such judgements. We already have it'.[98]

TRANSCENDENTAL ARGUMENT AS NARRATIVE: TAYLOR

So far, I have suggested that the work of Rorty, Habermas, Quine, Putnam, and Davidson might 'pragmatise' romantic criticism by providing a view of interpretation that trades upon a holistic conception of truth connected to intersubjectivity. Significantly, however, most of these thinkers already emphasise the links between their own work and models of communicative rationality developed in the late eighteenth and early nineteenth centuries. Quine, for example, stresses that his theory of ontological relativity is 'a consequence of taking seriously the insight that I traced from Bentham – namely, the semantic primacy of sentences'.[99] Similarly, Putnam traces the problems of modern thought to the aftermath of Hume's division of everyday and reflective consciousness, while Rorty has compared

Davidson's work on language, ostensibly rooted in Platonic conceptions of dialogue, to romantic paradigms (moreover, as I argue below, Davidson's Socratic-elenctic method of inquiry is prefigured in Keats, Shelley, and Coleridge). Other philosophers such as Habermas and Charles Taylor, moreover, follow Rorty in making a more direct connection between their 'romanticised' pragmatism and the pragmatics of romanticism.

Taylor's findings are the product of his broader attempt to redefine rationality in terms of a 'substantive' conception of the good rather than a 'procedural' methodology. He traces the procedural conception of ethics shared by Kantians and utilitarians to two ideas, promulgated by Locke and still influential today: the punctual self and the instrumentality of language. The first, he argues, misconceives the subject as a neutral cognitive zone and postulates 'the self that Hume set out to find and, predictably, failed to find'. The idea of the punctual self can be laid to rest, Taylor maintains, and its postmodern shadow exorcised, only when we realise that humans 'exist only in a certain space of questions, through certain constitutive concerns'.[100] The second notion, closely associated with the representational theory of knowledge, is what Davidson dismissively refers to as the view that language 'is just the sometimes awkward tool we use to express our thoughts'.[101] Against this, Taylor advocates what he sees as a 'Romantic theory': an 'expressivist understanding of language and art', which 'stresses the constitutive nature of language'.[102]

Taylor argues that selfhood involves possessing a concept or intuition of the good (and that both the 'self' and the 'good' are created as much as discovered through communication). Adopting this perspective, however, entails acknowledging the entanglement of thought with the everyday qualitative distinctions that constitute the framework within which human beings live. There is, in other words, no stepping outside *life*, either through positivist analysis or through the postmodern reflex that simply repeats 'the epistemological démarche in the negative mode'.[103] Attempts to transcend this framework come up against what Taylor calls the best account or 'BA principle', according to which no external description can ever supersede the network of values within which our own descriptions are constituted. After all, as he asks, what 'ought to trump the language in which I actually live my life?':

What is preposterous is the suggestion that we ought to disregard altogether the terms that can figure in the non-explanatory contexts of living for the purposes of our explanatory theory. ... What we need to *explain* is people living their lives; the terms in which they cannot avoid living them cannot be removed from the explanandum. ... We cannot just leap outside of these terms altogether ...[104]

According to Taylor, to give an account of the conditions of knowledge without the radical dichotomy of 'within/without' is to engage in 'an exploration of the limits of the conceivable in human life, an account of its "transcendental conditions"'.[105] Taylor's claims are supported by Putnam and Davidson, who see the appeal to basic presuppositions as paradigmatic of holistic rationality. Moreover, Taylor argues, the aura of foundationalism that hangs over transcendental argument disappears with the demise of the fact/value antinomy. Putnam, for example, is prepared to describe his own method as transcendental, but insists that 'arguing about the nature of rationality . . . is an activity that presupposes a notion of rational justification wider than the positivist notion, indeed wider than institutionalized criterial rationality'.[106] Transcendental arguments can only be set to work, he contends, within an understanding of rationality as eudaemonia, or the complete development of human values.

In many ways, Taylor's account goes further than Putnam. Transcendental argument, he proposes, possesses four salient features: it marks the threshold of coherent human activity; it enhances knowledge by transition rather than deduction; it is apodictic yet defeasible; it has its roots in biographical narrative. Crucially, it determines the point at which 'a total lack of coherence in our perception would be a breakdown in awareness'.[107] Here, however, Taylor notes a peculiar feature of transcendental argument: it proceeds by the *enhancement* of knowledge rather than by deduction. Once the baseline of our conceptions is seen to be holistic rather than logical, transcendental argument sheds its attachment to foundations. When arguing from the presuppositions of our thought and beliefs, he claims, we find that 'the first stage is different in nothing from the later stages, except in being easier to grasp'. It is this epistemic gain through the enhancement of awareness rather than empirical aggregation or logical inference that Taylor identifies as the move from 'sketchier to richer descriptions' inherent in all constructive dialogue.[108]

Engaging in transcendental argument is not a matter of giving basic reasons, then, but of 'reasoning in transitions. It aims to establish, not that some position is correct absolutely, but rather that some position is superior to another'.[109] Hence the apparent paradox that the conclusions of transcendental arguments are *at the same time* apodictic and always open to debate: '[t]he deeper we go, that is, and the richer the description, the more a cavil can be raised'.[110] It is, however, the fourth feature of transcendental argument – its autobiographical dimension – that is most significant to the present discussion. By acknowledging that understanding peoples, cultures, and texts depends upon our values and commitments, Taylor argues, we come to see how closely interwoven such understanding is with a conception of one's own life as an unfolding *narrative*. Echoing Keats's claim that 'axioms in philosophy are not axioms until they are proved upon our pulses', Taylor maintains that the sense one makes of the world and the sense one makes of one's own life cannot be prised apart.[111] In this way, accepting an argument or taking a position is, as he puts it, always 'connected in a complex way with our being *moved* by it'.[112]

Once the spectre of *transcendence* is dispelled, then, transcendental argument emerges as the means by which we endeavour to understand the *conditions* of thinking and living in the absence of abstract foundations. For Taylor, our statements, interpretations, and judgements only become intelligible against a presupposed background of what Putnam identifies as eudaemonia and Taylor calls the 'moral ontology' that articulates intuitions of the good life.[113] While these values will inevitably vary (as Putnam argues, plurality is itself part of the desideratum), commensurability between values (as Davidson has shown) remains a precondition of holding values at all.[114] In this way, Taylor's account introduces the possibility of viewing the romantic, 'expressivist' narrative of self as an 'embodied' rather than abstract transcendental argument that attempts, as Richard Eldridge puts it, 'to achieve fluency in the exercise of human powers to shape a life as an embodiment of value'.[115] At its most holistic, then, romantic writing embodies 'transcendental' argument, not according to the Kantian model of establishing the *a priori* conditions of experience, but in a way that approaches what Taylor describes as an appeal to our ' "agent's knowledge" ', a knowledge of the background conditions without which 'our activity would fall apart into incoherence'.[116]

ROMANTIC COUNTERDISCOURSE: HABERMAS

Taylor's rehabilitation of transcendental argument through the nonfoundational language of 'embodied' reason bears comparison with Habermas's attempt to recover a counterdiscourse of decentred rationality in Enlightenment and romantic culture. Habermas notes that the romantic revolt against instrumental reason is commonly depicted as a straightforward, albeit unstable, hypostasisation of the aesthetic: the antithesis of reflective thought. The problem with this assumption, he counters, is that it overlooks the relationship between the newly forged concept of the aesthetic and the Enlightenment-romantic discourse of communicative reason. Here, rather then fleeing from 'truth' to 'life', romanticism prospects a mediating role between life and thought, or, in Habermas's terms, between a pre-given 'lifeworld' (one that is 'constitutive', 'already interpreted', 'intersubjectively shared', and determined by the pragmatic considerations of speech acts that collectively underpin communicative rationality) and a presupposed and regulative 'system' (a world determined by considerations of truth and falsity, in which thought itself is made the object of reflection).[117] This mediation Habermas identifies as the basis of a form of self-critique, whereby, rather than the 'dirempted totality . . . felt primarily in the avenging power of destroyed reciprocities' (the legacy of Hegel's radicalisation of epistemology), we find 'the aesthetic, body-centred experiences of a decentred subjectivity that function as the placeholders for the other of reason'.[118] In this way, he locates a model of reason based on communication rather than subjectivity or consciousness. Furthermore, by treating communication as a matter of pragmatics rather than semantics (and the meaning of an utterance as inextricably bound up with its truth), he is able to admit values as *constitutive of*, rather than separate from, the rationality of the lifeworld. Thus, with Taylor and Putnam, he contends that 'the truth of statements is based on anticipating the realization of the good life'.[119]

And yet, Habermas's theory of communicative rationality is not without its problems. In particular, Rorty and Putnam have queried the division of 'system' and lifeworld' thought. Habermas believes that by its very nature communication between individuals 'conceptually forces participants to suppose that a rationally motivated agreement could in principle be achieved . . . if only the argumentation could be conducted openly enough and continued long enough'.[120] As Putnam indicates, this is very close to his own 'internal realist' claim that 'truth is an *idealization* of rational acceptability'.[121] However, rather than inferring from this simply that communication, rational thought and truth are interdependent, Habermas deduces the separation of the everyday lifeworld and a presupposed limiting horizon of objective truth that alone 'can be understood as the correlate of the totality of true propositions'.[122] This world of systematic reflection, he maintains, becomes the normative guarantee for all thought. In maintaining this, however, Habermas introduces the notion of a normative plane in human knowledge that passes beyond questions of value. According to Putnam, Habermas's system/lifeworld division is essentially a norm/value division: unlike norms, 'values can be made plausible only in the context of a particular form of life'.[123]

The trouble with this, Putnam claims, is that 'the objectivity Habermas posits for norms *presupposes* the objectivity of at least some values'.[124]

Habermas, he claims, is still haunted by the thought that without some Archimedean point, reason remains vulnerable to sceptical attack. And yet the dichotomy between evaluative and normative stances weakens his general case that cultural and historical relativism is otiose. As a consequence, new life is breathed into the old conflict between immanence and transcendence, only now the paradox lurks between the planes of the 'constitutive' and the 'regulative', the 'intramundane' and the 'extramundane'. Still more troubling, potentially, is the way in which Habermas's value/norm dichotomy results in the isolation of literature from philosophy and science. '[I]llocutionarily *disempowered*' by their limited validity claims, literary works are denied the very ability to '*criticize* one another' that he allows to philosophical texts.[125]

Putnam's objection to Habermas's separation of norms and values echoes Rorty's refusal to see truth as 'Janus-faced'. From a Habermasian perspective, however, such arguments fail to grasp the fact that the presupposition of unconditional truth is *pragmatically* indispensable to the speech-act situation. As I show below, this tension between communication and idealisation is something that pragmatism and romanticism share. Nonetheless, Habermas's work, like that of Rorty and Taylor, broadly supports one of the main argumentative strands of this book: the 'counterdiscourse' of romanticism (that which refuses to shadow-box with a subject-centred reason) is holistic. Moreover, by offering an account of truth as a key presupposition in the pragmatics of communication, Davidson and other pragmatists demonstrate how transcendental argument best articulates how we orientate ourselves in respect to the historical texts *we* study. Dispensing with concepts of 'immanence' and 'transcendence' alleviates the critical 'cramp' of metacommentary and obviates the obstinate question of whether it is possible or desirable to get 'outside' romanticism. In this way, by reading the romantics 'holistically', we not only come to see how romantic writing frequently shapes its argument by affirming a shared concept of truth as a precondition of living a life; we also come to see how the same presuppositions determine our ability to interpret them.

CHAPTER 2

Pragmatising romanticism: radical empiricism from Reid to Rorty

In Chapter 1, I argued that the metacritical 'cramps' of modern romantic commentary are allayed by incorporating the 'romanticised' pragmatisms of Rorty, Habermas, and Taylor, and registered some helpful ideas concerning the relationship between truth and interpretation provided by Quine, Putnam, and Davidson. Pursuing this line of inquiry has meant delaying until now any further exploration of the connections between pragmatism and romanticism. In particular, it has meant deferring any assessment of the extent to which pragmatic or holistic attitudes to questions of truth and meaning already figure within romantic literature. While, at first glance, the latter might appear to be an unpromising enterprise, the very suspicions held by critics and historians regarding the hidden agendas of modern pragmatism would suggest otherwise. If, as Lentricchia and others have claimed, there is an underlying complicity between 'romantic' and 'pragmatic' worldviews, then it is not unreasonable to suppose that a strain of pragmatic thinking is already active within romantic culture. Given this, what is required at this stage is an explanation of why the attempt to 'pragmatise' the romantics should appear counterintuitive.

Accordingly, in this chapter I argue that such an account involves making a clear distinction between two empirical traditions within (and against) which British romantic writers work. The first of these is a doctrine of representational or epistemological empiricism that dates back to Locke and reaches its nadir in Hume's *Treatise of Human Nature* (1739–41). Central to this system is the idea that truth is determined by the degree of *correspondence* between a mental entity and a non-mental reality. The second is a movement of the late eighteenth century: initiated by Thomas Reid's attack on the mentalistic bias of the philosophy of 'ideas', it stresses the constitutive role of language in shaping belief. Instead of confrontation with a non-human reality, its leading metaphor is that of free *communication* between individuals. Within this second, 'linguistic' variety of empiricism, truth becomes the indefinable, untheorisable limit-concept for weak idealisations of human community and intersubjectivity (what Rorty calls 'solidarity'), but loses its status as a hypostasised, non-human ideal.

One of the main obstacles to distinguishing these two forms of empiricism, and to understanding the pressures exerted by them upon the British romantic imagination, arises when they are misleadingly related to (or worse, subsumed by) categories derived from contemporary German idealism. Deploying Kantian or Hegelian paradigms in such contexts can be problematic in two ways. First, as I argued in Chapter 1, the 'exteriority' that preoccupies much modern commentary is the legacy of a peculiarly German (Hegelian) restructuring of critique, one that would have made little sense to British romantic writers. Moreover, the way in which this legacy perpetuates an idealised 'Truth' through the agency of a hypostasised 'otherness', highlights a second hazard in 'Germanising' the romantics. Here, the philosophical tenor of romantic writing is distorted by the supposition that its aspirations can be readily translated into the categories of German idealism.

Even pragmatist readers of the British romantics are not immune to this assumption. Kathleen Wheeler and Richard Rorty argue that romantic philosophy models itself on 'friendly conversation', or, as Wheeler describes it, 'a dynamic synthesis of Platonic/Socratic philosophy with empiricism'.[1] Both commentators, however, base their accounts of romantic irony upon a German, transcendental model that culminates in Hegel's demonstration that 'Reason's other, its opposite, is part of itself', and that, as a consequence, 'Words are saturated with a residue of meaninglessness'.[2] By doing so, they overlook a peculiarly British conception of the role of truth within 'friendly conversation', one that seeks to reconceptualise reason as a process of charitable dialogue rather than as parasitic upon a hypostasised otherness. Thus, while Wheeler in particular stresses the *revolutionary* character of romantic 'antirationalism', I detect a strategy of *reform* that operates outside the polarising framework of German idealism, one which, as Angela Esterhammer argues, conceives of the products of reason 'not as given, but as *intersubjectively experienced* through a series of discursive interactions'. Indeed, as Olivia Smith notes, even politically revolutionary texts such as Thomas Paine's *Rights of Man* (1791) tend to be epistemologically reformist, replacing the conventional wisdom that 'refinement and lack of concreteness' are the hallmarks of rational discourse with a style that is open, conversational, dialogic.[3] In this chapter, I examine the way in which this new, counterdiscourse of communicative rationality emerges, as a moribund form of representational empiricism gives way to a linguistic and anthropological turn in late eighteenth-century British thought.

To understand how this occurs, we must first consider the condition of British epistemology in the wake of Hume's impressionistic empiricism. As I have argued elsewhere, for writers of the romantic generation the implications of Hume's work extend further than is generally acknowledged.[4] In particular, English romanticism, like modern philosophy, is stalked by the shadows of two Humean dichotomies: the division between facts and values, and a strict distinction between synthetic and analytic truths. Hume introduces these dichotomies with little fanfare. The division of fact and value occurs in a throwaway remark made in the third volume of the *Treatise* regarding the relation between 'is' and 'ought' propositions. Hume queries the easy transition in works of moral philosophy between statements that use 'is' and those that use 'ought'. Since 'this *ought*, or *ought not*, expresses some new relation or affirmation,' he observes, with customary irony, ''tis necessary that it shou'd be observ'd and explain'd'.[5] Similarly, the distinction between analytic truths dependent upon '*Relations of Ideas*', and contingent truths based on '*Matters of Fact*' is introduced in the *Enquiries Concerning Human Understanding* with little further explanation.[6] It has been left to subsequent philosophers to puzzle over these far-reaching dichotomies.

Hume's scepticism regarding both the epistemological status of 'ought' statements and the possibility of building knowledge upon the 'relations of ideas' stems from his unflinching empirical method. It is this approach that leads him to argue in the *Treatise* that the 'idea' idea measures up very poorly on empirical standards. A moment's reflection, he argues, is sufficient to demonstrate the objects with which we are most immediately and intimately acquainted are not ideas, but impressions. And yet, the testimony of the impressions proves to be an inadequate foundation for scientific knowledge, the meaning of abstract concepts such as causation, and (Hume is mortified to discover) knowledge of self. Other determinants, such as habit, custom, and the power of human sentiments, must be invoked in order to explain the possibility of belief. At this point, however, representational epistemology gives way to naturalistic behaviourism as the privileged language of explanation.[7] By setting the bar for the experiential authenticity of speculative thought at such a high level, Hume's impressionistic empiricism engineers its own collapse.

Hume's own response to this predicament is to forgo the study for the street, precipitating a gulf between reflective and quotidian consciousness. In Hume, these separate spheres are bound together by the practiced confidence of the Enlightenment belletrist, whose philosophical failures are recuperated by a cultivated style of suasive indifference.[8] Accordingly, every philosophical paradox becomes an opportunity to assert the genial authority of the Enlightened citizen of the world. In the longer term, however, Hume burdens British empiricism with an acute apprehension of the chasm between thought and 'life'. This problem, as Hilary Putnam observes, is not just a problem for philosophers, but is by its very nature existential. Since 'the question of fact and value is a forced choice question for reflective people', the empirical underdetermination of lifeworld normativity and rationality raises disturbing questions about the relationship between thinking and living a human life.[9] As a result, Hume ensures that a deep suspicion of thought becomes part of romanticism's troubled intellectual inheritance.

Hume rides the metaphors of representational empiricism into the ground, demonstrating that the notion of 'correspondence' explains neither the truth of the concepts with which we think, nor the words we use to express those concepts. It is tempting to see the romantic reaction to this collapse as both heroically idealist and hopelessly lopsided, vaunting the pyhrric victory of the mind over an objective world to which it cannot possibly correspond. And yet, while familiar, this picture is incomplete. As the romantics were aware, the late eighteenth century witnessed the emergence of responses to the 'Humean' condition that rejected outright the vocabulary of correspondence. By demonstrating that the meaning of words cannot be cashed out in terms of corresponding impressions, and that the truth of ideas cannot be determined by their correspondence to the data of the senses, Hume shows that the relationship between belief, language, and the world is poorly comprehended by metaphors of representation. For some writers, this in turn raises the possibility of establishing a closer relationship between truth and *meaning*. One manifestation of this linguistic turn in empiricism, as I discuss below, is Jeremy Bentham's use of Hume's distinction between impressions and ideas to argue that 'soft' linguistic fictions, rather than 'hard' empirical data, determine reason. Accordingly, as empiricism shifts from a model of truth-as-representation to one of truth-as-coherence, truth ceases to be the (attainable or unattainable) object of desire, and becomes instead what ultimately makes sense within a community of belief.

It is a measure of the effectiveness of Hume's attack on representational empiricism that the appetite for epistemological debate in Britain over succeeding decades is severely blunted. The materialistic theories of Hartley, Priestley, and Godwin, for example, deal with the sceptical implications of Hume's work largely by not dealing with them, while other thinkers move to replace the 'first philosophy' of Descartes and Locke with naturalistic, commonsensical, or linguistic accounts of human knowledge. The latter tendency signals the eclipse of epistemology by socialised explanations of truth and meaning (explanations whose roots lie deep in the 'public sphere' discourse developed in the first half of the century). In this complex development, four innovations in particular demand attention here: Thomas Reid's move to replace a philosophy based on correspondence and representation with one based on language and interpretation; Dugald Stewart's discovery of the transcendental presuppositions that underlie empirical reflection; John Horne Tooke's claim that the basic components of reason are words, not ideas (introducing the idea that communication is *constitutive* of truth); and Jeremy Bentham's discovery that the basic presuppositions of knowledge (Stewart's transcendental principles) are fictions, supported not by facts or laws, but by the pragmatic necessities of communication.

Reid's realignment of perception and appeal to 'natural' language is a direct response to Hume's dismantling of doctrinal certainty for belief. In the 1764 *Inquiry into the Human Mind, on the Principles of Common Sense*, he agrees with Hume that 'our belief of the continuance of nature's laws is not derived from reason'.[10] What this means for Reid, however, is that the link between nature and intelligence is not representational but interpretive. Consequently, in Reid's work the raw data of sensation become the *signs* upon which experience is built. Reid divides these signs into those, such as conventions constructed by humans, in which the connection between the sign and the thing signified is entirely arbitrary, and those, such as the sensation of hardness, in which the connection is 'established by nature'[11] through 'the original constitution of our minds', or common sense.[12] In this way, Reid supplants Hume's representational model of experience with one that is fundamentally hermeneutic: 'All our knowledge of nature, beyond our original perceptions,' he maintains, 'is got by experience, and consists in the interpretation of natural signs'.[13]

Among the many ramifications of this strategy, one of the more significant is the way in which Reid describes this 'original constitution' of the mind in terms of dispositions and innate anticipations. Indeed, he claims that the very *predisposition* to interpret other people and the world through 'natural' signs is the basis of our linguistics of experience. Reid is struck by the fact, as he sees it, that the 'signs in the natural language of the human countenance and behaviour, as well as the signs in our original perceptions, have the same signification in all climates and in all nations'.[14] This commonality leads him to postulate:

an early anticipation, neither derived from experience, nor from reason, nor from any compact or promise, that our fellow-creatures will use the same signs in language, when they have the same sentiments.

This is, in reality, a kind of prescience of human actions; and it seems to me to be an original principle of the human constitution, without which we should be incapable of language, and consequently incapable of instruction.[15]

Without 'prescience,' in other words, or the *expectation* that interpretation is at least possible, language and knowledge are impossible. Reid encapsulates his argument in '*the principle of veracity*' and '*the principle of credulity*', which stipulate that knowledge is only possible because of our disposition (more often than not) to be truthful, and because of the presupposition that what others tell us will be (more often than not) truthful.[16] In Reid's hermeneutics of experience, then, sincerity and charity in interpretation become the (mutually sustaining) pragmatic preconditions of understanding.

Reid's idea of the 'prescience' of human intelligence is echoed by Dugald Stewart, who in the *Elements of the Philosophy of the Human Mind* (1792–1827) identifies such nonempirical truths as 'part of the original *stamina* of human reason, which are equally essential to all the pursuits of science, and to all the active concerns of life'.[17] Nonetheless, Stewart criticises Reid for failing to distinguish the primary elements of human thought from 'those prejudices to which the whole human race are irresistibly led, in the first instance, by the very constitution of their nature'.[18] He insists that the former 'are of an order so radically different from what are commonly called *truths*, in the popular acceptation of that word, that it might perhaps be useful for logicians to distinguish them by some appropriate appellation, such, for example, as that of *metaphysical* or *transcendental* truths'.[19] Consequently, while both Reid and Stewart move to liberate empiricism from a correspondence model of truth by rethinking the *presuppositions* that underlie both empirical judgements and ordinary communication, neither is prepared to abandon the assumption that knowledge must have foundations. For Reid, common sense remains 'an original principle of the human constitution', while for Stewart, the framework for understanding the '*stamina*' of human reason is defined by purely '*metaphysical*' truths of consciousness.

This brings us to John Horne Tooke and Jeremy Bentham, whose attempts to dispense with these very foundations form a major part of the backdrop to the holistic counterdiscourse of romanticism identified in this study. Tooke has a particular significance in the present context because of his direct influence on Keats, Shelley, and Coleridge. Following the collapse of his trial for treason in 1794, Tooke became a key figure in Jacobin circles and something of a father figure to young radicals (the guest lists for his literary dinners included Paine, Godwin, Coleridge, and Leigh Hunt).[20] His philosophical importance, however, stems from the way in which he develops the materialism of David Hartley into the arena of language and meaning. Furthermore, by extending the attacks of the Scottish commonsense school upon the philosophy of 'ideas', Tooke energises the debate over the relationship between the language of reform and the reform of language. In particular, by drawing together the concepts of truth and communication, he helps to found the notion of what might be called a *civic* conception of truth, according to which, as Olivia Smith puts it, 'truth, freedom, and good government are interdependent'.[21]

The immediate aim of Tooke's dialogue on philology, *Epea Pteroenta, or the Diversions of Purley* (1786–1805), is destructive, attacking the 'nonsense' of '*Metaphysic*' in modern thought (of which, he claims, the 'rights of man' philosophy is particularly guilty).[22] As 'H' reflects, in one of the opening passages:

Yet, I suppose, a man of plain common sense may obtain [truth], if he will dig for it; but I cannot think that what is commonly called Learning, is the mine in which it will be found. Truth, in my opinion, has been improperly imagined at the bottom of a well: it lies much nearer to the surface: though buried indeed at present under mountains of learned rubbish . . . .[23]

At the same time, *Diversions* seeks to overcome the malaise that had afflicted empiricism since Hume. By reconfiguring the relationship between thought and language, Tooke attempts to answer the question: how are we to treat the concepts of truth, self, and meaning, when representation (epistemological and political) is in crisis, and, above all, once we have lost our faith in the correspondence of mind and world? From the beginning, he insists that '*truth*' and the '*good*' are 'inseparably connected'[24] with the nature of language, the function of which is not to denote ideas or '*things*'[25] but 'to *communicate* our thoughts'.[26] Ideas are words: indeed, beyond having 'Sensations or Feelings', all the operations of the mind 'are merely the operations of Language'.[27] W. V. Quine hails this shift in the debate 'from ideas to words' as one of 'Five Milestones' since the Enlightenment 'where empiricism has taken a turn for the better', arguing that 'Tooke appreciated that the *idea* idea itself measures up poorly to empiricist standards'. None the less, he dismisses as 'needless and hopeless' Tooke's 'heroic' further attempt to explain the problem of how grammatical particles were definable in sensory terms, by arguing that language (originally consisting of nouns and verbs but torn between the imperatives of signification and the need for abbreviation) descends into generality and abbreviation. Instead of arguing that meaning resides in the etymological origins of single words, Quine maintains, Tooke need only have recognised, as Bentham did later, that words 'are *syncategorematic*. They are definable not in isolation but in context'.[28]

Quine's criticisms notwithstanding, Tooke's arguments have powerful implications for the development of romantic holism. First, by arguing that the basic units of thought are words, not ideas, Tooke subordinates reason to communication, deflating the idea of truth into that which is coherent or acceptable within a natural language. Indeed, Tooke suggests, truth should be seen primarily not as the goal of communication, but as its fundamental *presupposition*:

TRUE ... means simply and merely – That which is TROWED. ... TRUTH supposes mankind: *for whom* and *by whom* alone the word is formed, and *to whom* only it is applicable. If no man, no TRUTH. There is therefore no such thing as eternal, immutable, everlasting TRUTH; unless mankind, *such as they are at present*, be also eternal, immutable, and everlasting. Two persons may contradict each other, and yet both speak TRUTH: for the TRUTH of one person may be opposite to the TRUTH of another.[29]

As Olivia Smith notes, Tooke's etymological transvaluation of 'think' from 'thing' 'seems slightly less bizarre when one knows that "thing" is now derived from the Old-English term meaning "discussion" '.[30] Thus, in the conditional, 'If no man, no TRUTH', Tooke formulates the watchword of an emerging counterdiscourse of reason based in the pragmatics of communication. This in turn promotes the redescription of subjectivity as selfhood becomes relational, that is, conceivable only within the space of reasons and values that Bentham would later call the necessary 'fictions' of discourse. In this respect, Tooke's work cuts against the grain of a culture increasingly inclined to intensify rather than disperse the field of subjectivity. As a consequence, while the language of selfhood constructs meaning (as Paul de Man argues) as a self-positing 'intent' of consciousness, in Tooke semantic relations are materialised into the pragmatics of everyday communication. In effect, Tooke responds to the challenge of Hume's philosophy by dissolving the boundary between questions of truth and questions of meaning, thereby creating a space in which reason can be defined holistically rather than in the language of foundations.

A key agent in the extension of Tooke's ideas about truth, language, and thought in the early nineteenth century is Jeremy Bentham. Bentham's direct influence upon the romantics (with the notable exception of Shelley)[31] is minimal. His works on logic and language, written between 1810 and 1815, remained unpublished until 1843. Moreover, Bentham has little time for epistemology – like Hegel, he does not see the avoidance of error as the overriding imperative of coherent thought. Unlike Hegel, however, for Bentham this is less to do with the fact that philosophy has to build *beyond* epistemology, and more to do with the subordination of philosophy itself to the concerns of eudaemonia, or the good life. Indeed, Bentham would never have concerned himself directly with the relation between language and truth if had it not been for a problem he encountered while writing *An Introduction to the Principles of Morals and Legislation* (1789). In the course of tackling this problem, however, Bentham came to articulate the public-sphere rationality of late Enlightenment culture in ways that not only cut across his more noted contributions to political philosophy, ethics, and jurisprudence, but which are also consonant with the discourse of romantic holism.

While working on the vital chapter 'Of Motives' in the *Introduction*, Bentham realised that the word 'motive' has two distinct meanings; one literal and legitimate, the other figurative and fictitious. On one hand, it may be 'any of those really existing incidents from whence the act in question is supposed to take its rise'; on the other, the term may mean 'a certain fictitious entity, a passion, an affectation of the mind, an ideal being'. Returning to this difference over two decades later in his essays on logic and language, Bentham designates the latter sense as a 'logical fiction'.[32] Logical fictions (for example, motives) differ from poetical fictions (for example, centaurs) in that they are indispensable to thought. Indeed, as he probes further into this question in the *Introduction*, Bentham finds that logical fictions link to a web of figures that stretch much deeper into human thought and language than he had anticipated. This in turn reinforces the idea that the language of reform and the reform of language are inseparable: 'Confining himself to the language most in use, a man can scarce avoid running, in appearance, into perpetual contradictions. ... To obviate this inconvenience, completely, he has but this one unpleasant remedy; to lay aside the old phraseology and invent a new one'.[33] How is this renewal of language to be achieved? For Bentham, it is not at all clear that abstract and empirically dubious language, the 'nonsense' of metaphysics of which Tooke had complained, can be resolved within a 'neutral' database suitable for utilitarian calculus. One cannot explicate individual terms by tracing them back to simple ideas or primitive perceptions, as Hume had initially hoped, since simple ideas are the most fictional of all our mental entities. Since sensation is *itself* determined in a pain/pleasure manifold, sense-impressions are always already evaluated within a utilitarian economy of well-being: as such, they cannot be construed as stable referents or units of meaning. In this way, Bentham's utilitarianism leads him away from the correspondence theories of truth and reference, as he comes to realise, albeit belatedly, that there is no Archimedean point in discourse. This forces him to confront the idea that language itself *creates* ideas. By accepting that figuration goes all the way down to the referent, Bentham suggests that meaning is not psychological and causal, as Hume and other empiricists supposed, but holistic and relational. He is thus able to allow that it is perfectly possible for a word to be used correctly and successfully by a number of people who associate with it quite different ideas/sensations, or even no ideas/sensations at all. The meaning of a term is determined not by causation, but by context.

A number of important consequences follow from this argument. First, Bentham claims, the basic units of meaning are not single terms, but whole statements, speech acts, or propositions; second, the reform of language cannot look to foundations of any kind for its bearings. Thus, in order to create a 'new phraseology', Bentham develops a method of contextual definition, or explication by paraphrase, which he calls 'paraphrasis'. Among his many accounts of this method, one of the clearest is in his 'Essay on Logic' (1813–15): 'By the word paraphrasis may be designated that sort of exposition which may be afforded by transmuting into a proposition, having for its subject some real entity, a proposition which has not for its subject any other than a fictitious entity'.[34] Ultimately, by rejecting Hume's argument that in order to know the meaning of a term we need to find some object in experience to which it refers or corresponds, Bentham argues that what counts as a 'real entity' is ultimately a matter of coherence. 'Meaning' depends upon context, not upon correspondence between word and object: upon sentences, not things. Like Reid, then, Bentham sees truth as dependent upon interpretation, and interpretation in turn as dependent upon the assumptions and predispositions of individuals. Like Tooke, however (and unlike Reid), he argues that truth is man-made, a 'necessary fiction' of discourse.

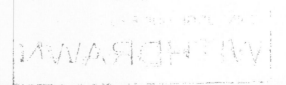

Indeed, since, as Bentham puts it, '[t]he discourse that ... is *not* figurative is the discourse in which ... no other fictions, – no other figures are employed than are *absolutely necessary*', there are few regions of mental life that are untouched by figuration.[35] 'Literal' meaning and 'factual' truth emerge only through communication, through an interpretive community. In this scheme, as Olivia Smith observes, 'legitimate government and correct reasoning either co-exist or do not exist at all'.[36] In this way, Tooke and Bentham undermine the Humean boundaries between truth and meaning, fact and value, and prepare the ground for a form of empiricism with no index of neutrality. This in turn creates room for the emergence of a discourse in which truth and *coherence* are closely intertwined, and fact and *value* intricately entangled.

As Esterhammer argues, by determining that literal meaning and factual truth emerge only through communication, Bentham 'developed the most important theory of his time about the way language shapes reality'. And yet, Bentham was not alone in coming to the realisation that meaning resides in statements rather than words. Around the time that he was developing his theory of paraphrasis or contextual definition, Dugald Stewart was assembling along similar lines an argument against Tooke's particularist view of language. In his essay 'On the Tendency of Some Late Philological Speculations' (1810), Stewart takes issue with the idea that single words acquire meaning by corresponding to single ideas or sensations:

In reading, for example, the enunciation of a proposition, we are apt to fancy that for *every word* contained in it there is an *idea* presented to the understanding ... So different is all this from the fact, that our words, when examined separately, are often as completely insignificant as the letters of which they are composed; deriving their meaning solely from the connexion, or relation, in which they stand to others.[37]

In Stewart's scheme, however, this does not imply that language determines thought. It is merely an illustration of the fact that 'the function of language is not so much to *convey* knowledge ... from one mind to another, as to bring two minds into *the same train of thinking*, and to confine them, as nearly as possible, to the same track'.[38] For Stewart, it remains the case that knowledge is constituted entirely upon consciousness as its *foundation*: while the *nature* of the mind may be material, he allows, 'all our knowledge of it is to be obtained by the exercise of the powers of Consciousness and Reflexion'.[39] Hence his criticism of Tooke's linguistic deflation of 'true', which if accepted, he claims,

'would completely undermine the foundations both of logic and of ethics'.[40]

None the less, Stewart's thought, like Bentham's, indicates how models of language and belief were shifting during this period, turning away from the representationalism of the eighteenth century, and towards accounts based on relationality and the natural preconditions of human behaviour. Thus, Stewart, his insistence on the philosophical primacy of consciousness notwithstanding, abandons the notion of correspondence in meaning and truth in favour of a paradigm that simultaneously stipulates the dependence of meaning upon a linguistic framework, and the reliance of knowledge upon natural conditions that form the transcendental 'stamina' of human reason. Characterising this new direction in British thought, however, remains a challenging endeavour. It necessitates, for example, revising our image of Tooke as an etymological pedant; of Bentham as a thinker whose utilitarianism committed him to a straightforwardly literal and factual view of the world; and of Stewart himself as a thinker stranded between empiricism and idealism.

And yet, in facing this challenge, encouragement can be drawn from recent work in adjacent fields. Simon Swift's work on the 'new' Kant, in particular, complements the present study's attempt to recover a decentred discourse of rationality in late Enlightenment and romantic culture. Drawing on the work of Kant scholars, Swift traces a theory of 'expressive rationality' in German thought that seeks to explain meaning in terms of the linguistic *act* rather than as a form of representation, thereby avoiding the elision of social and ethical questions.[41] For Swift, Kantian reason is not simply based upon noumenal law, but incorporates 'standards derived from a community of rational beings in order to keep the individual's philosophical speculations on a self-regulated path, and to prevent the slide of thinking into enthusiasm and fanaticism'.[42] Understood properly, Swift argues, Kant's naturalised, 'transcendental anthropology' can become 'a model for a renewed understanding of the philosophical importance of Romantic discourse'.[43] In this discourse, the maligned romantic symbol offers not the false promise of aesthetic plenitude, but 'a type of anthropological "orientation", or a pragmatic human capacity to find our way in a world whose final determination escapes us'.[44] How the romantics endeavour to communicate this 'pragmatic human capacity' in poetry and prose (and how they do so largely without the intervention of German philosophical models) forms the subject of the remaining chapters of this book.

ABSOLUTES WITHOUT IDEALISM

At the beginning of this chapter, I reviewed my twin claims that pragmatic accounts of truth and interpretation help to explain the nature of the metacritical assumptions that form the background to our reading of the British romantics, and that, conversely, reading the romantics pragmatically sheds light on modern pragmatism's 'romanticisation' of its own sense of validity, by revealing how deeply entrenched romantic writing is within the holistic 'counterdiscourse' of the late Enlightenment. In addition, I claimed that defending these arguments entails not only an examination of the 'romantic' debts of modern pragmatism, but also an explanation of why corresponding attempts to 'pragmatise' the romantics should seem counterintuitive.

So far, in pursuing the second goal, the current chapter has identified a longstanding bias in late twentieth-century criticism towards viewing the philosophy of British romanticism, methodologically and historically, through the lens of German idealism. This tendency, I have argued, not only obscures the extent to which the problems and paradoxes of (post)modern commentary themselves stem from the German idealist radicalisation of Enlightenment critique, it also underplays the significance of moves made by British writers to break away from bankrupt 'correspondence' theories of truth and meaning through forms of what Swift calls 'transcendental anthropology'. These movements broadly reject subject-centred views of reason in favour of a decentred, holistic discourse that foregrounds the pragmatics of mutual understanding, and in particular the interdependence of belief, communication, and presupposition.

Reading the romantics through the pragmatists and the pragmatists through the romantics inevitably involves courting a certain degree of hermeneutical circularity, but from a pragmatist perspective there is no reason why such circularity should be viewed as vicious (indeed, from a pragmatist perspective, no such circle is truly 'vicious'). Moreover, it bears repeating that in 'pragmatising' the romantics, in claiming that they adopt a far more pragmatic position on questions of truth and meaning than has generally been recognised, I am not arguing that Keats, Shelley, or Coleridge *are pragmatists*, at least, not in the sense that the term is widely applied today. As I have shown, in terms of contemporary thought, the poetry, prose, and aesthetics of these writers can be read as an attempt to navigate between two competing empirical traditions: a moribund representationalism, first instigated by Locke and long since dismantled by Hume, and a more recent, linguistic, anthropological, and holistic turn signalled by the work of writers such as Reid, Tooke, and Bentham. Even here, however, one should proceed with caution. It barely needs stating, for example, that the views of Bentham on most matters do not map those of Coleridge. I will argue in Chapter 5, however, that, despite appearances, the two thinkers end up defending surprisingly similar arguments about the nature of the relationship between truth and communication.

Indeed, the most interesting difference between the romantic writers discussed below and their eighteenth-century empiricist forebears is not idealism (the attempt to outmanoeuvre the correspondence view of truth by inflating empiricism's field of consciousness), but absolutism. In struggling to express the unconditional presuppositions of discourse, the romantics evince a far stronger concern than the philosophical radicals with what is at stake in the notion of truth as the limit-concept or 'absolute' of communication. Thus, whereas a writer such as Tooke takes the view, like Rorty, that 'truth' is a concept whose discursive privileges should be revoked, Keats, Shelley, and Coleridge adopt a position closer to Habermas and Davidson, maintaining that the possibility of communication within the public sphere depends upon a notion of truth that is absolute and therefore indefinable, but (crucially) not *ideal*. For the romantics, it is the absoluteness, not the ideality of truth, which fascinates.

Among the more significant corollaries of this swing from a hypostasised to a communicative concept of truth is the diminution of the ideal of truth as the *goal* of inquiry. As Lorraine Daston and Peter Galison detail, Kant's redrawing of subjectivity undermines the Enlightenment model of scientific inquiry as engaged in the genial identification and depiction of a typology based upon idealised and 'universal' images of '"what truly is"'.[45] According to Daston and Galison, the ontological assumption of 'truth-to-nature' that underpins eighteenth-century scientific endeavour cannot withstand the influence and implications of Kant's idea of an actively legislating, transcendental subjectivity. After Kant, they argue, the practised self of the Enlightenment savant that refines the sensations of crude experience into knowledge appears more like a burdensome shadow of consciousness, trapped by its own preconceptions of what constitutes truth. This leads scientists to underplay the metaphysical paradigm of scientific inquiry as the pursuit of truth in favour of the epistemological goal of acquiring knowledge. Stimulated by the development of photography, the concept of *objectivity* emerges as a new, strictly mechanical and non-interventionist 'code of epistemic virtue'.[46] Galison, in particular, sees romanticism's involvement in the emergence of this 'virtue' as critical, forming the crucible wherein the objective, scientific self 'grounded in a will to willessness' is fashioned as the antipode of 'an artistic self that circulated around a will to wilfulness'.[47] Indeed, seen from this perspective, '[o]bjectivity is Romantic'.[48]

Daston and Galison accurately depict how the notion of ideal truth as the goal of thought unravels in the early decades of the nineteenth century. Their adherence to a familiar, metaphysical/epistemological image of the romantic self, however, means that they overlook the ways in which many romantic writers respond to the challenge of an overde-termining subjectivity not by embracing idealism, but by redescribing truth itself along social and *intersubjective* lines. Crucial to this redescription is a rethinking of the relationship between reason and the quotidian. Foucault's work in this area highlights the important fact that the problems described by Daston and Galison are not confined to the systematic fields of science. Writers of the early nineteenth century inhabit a milieu in which the paradox of immanence and transcendence has permeated the discourse of the lifeworld. No longer is it possible to pass off the 'strange empirico-transcendental doublet' of modern subjectivity as a purely intellectual conundrum, as Hume once tried to do.[49] This in turn changes the relationship between 'thought' and 'life', a relationship that Lockean empiricism, whose ideals of contemplation and correspond-ence ultimately precipitate the epistemological crisis, is ill-equipped to address. As confidence in what Taylor calls the 'procedural' methods of representational empiricism (shared by Locke, Hume, Reid, and Bentham) ebbs, however, interest in more 'expressive' forms of understanding grows. These developments enshrine Taylor's principle that the terms in which people live their lives should not be left out of *explanations* of their lives.[50] The normative framework of life becomes, pragmatically (not epistemo-logically) the transcendental condition for communication, and thus for understanding. One consequence of this is that the relationship between life and thought is increasingly explored in the process of *writing one's life*. In this way, the narrative of romantic autobiography comes to bear the burden of simultaneously thinking *of* and *within* a lifeworld.

This conception of thought as *embodied* by life need not, however, be articulated autobiographically. As I argue below, the case of Shelley's changing views on thought and language forms a striking example of the romantic reconceptualisation of 'life' and its further implications for the relationship between thought, communication, and truth. Initially, in his 1819 essay, 'On Life', Shelley's revocation of materialism takes the form of a Berkelian idealism whereby the duality of idea and object is annulled. 'I confess,' Shelley writes, 'that I am one of those who am unable to refuse my assent to the conclusions of those philosophers who assert that nothing exists but as it is perceived'.[51] At this stage at least, Shelley is also inclined to view as incontrovertible the empirical doctrine that perception *precedes* the letter: sticking firmly to the Lockean tradition, he affirms that words and signs are the markers of ideas and that language is the instrument of thought. However, this in turn raises the possibility – given that the difference between the various modifications of the 'one mind' of which we are parts is 'merely nominal' – that language plays a *constitutive* rather than merely instrumental role in the mind's construction of difference.[52]

This ambiguity has provoked a debate between what might be called 'centrifugal' and 'centripetal' readings of Shelley. On one side, commentators such as Jerrold Hogle read Shelley as attempting to reconcile two views of language. The first, held by Tooke, Godwin, Coleridge, and Bentham, sees language as constitutive of thought; the second, advocated by Locke, Berkeley, Rousseau, and Monboddo, describes language as an instrument created by the mind for the purpose of communicating ideas. The guiding principle of Shelley's centrifugal and 'transferential' universe, according to Hogle, is that everything is mediated: in this way, all dualities, even opposed philosophical positions, depend upon a more fundamental relationship of codependence. On this reading, endorsing Berkeley's *esse est percipi* doctrine is just Shelley's way of affirming that any thought is already interpreted, determined by a transferential matrix of signification.[53] William Ulmer, on the other hand, contends that Shelleyan transference is a logocentric scheme in which the lost correspondence between mind and world is displaced into the pursuit of an unattainable ideal of presence. For Ulmer, the centripetal assumption – shared, he claims, by both sides of the eighteenth-century language debate – that language is underpinned by truth as 'presence' means that Shelley's Platonic erotics of negativity is always more of a sentimental and nostalgic response to the referential inadequacy of language than a challenge to referentiality as such. Worse still, in its 'assumptions about truth and language, Shelley's poetry internalizes the hierarchical structures and institutional violence endemic to Western culture'.[54]

A further possibility, however, is overlooked by both interpretations. Appreciating this involves taking careful note of Shelley's suggestion that 'Life' is both opaque *and* 'that which includes all'.[55] Life, he memorably claims, 'is at once the centre and circumference; the point to which all things are referred, and the line in which all things are contained'.[56] Since there is, in other words, no *outside* or radical exteriority to life, the relation between immanence and transcendence is folded *into life itself.* Seen from this perspective, Ulmer's charge that Shelley's dialectic confirms itself by denying the parasitic dependence of meaning upon a more fundamental otherness or absence begs the question of whether it even makes sense to conceive of such 'otherness' as a kind of space *outside* life. While Shelley agrees that we will always find instability and indeterminacy in life, he suggests that life also ensures that we assume that at least some things are true. Consequently, there is no tension for Shelley between the *centrifugal* claim that 'almost all familiar objects are signs, standing not for themselves but for others, in their capacity of suggesting one thought, which shall lead to a train of thoughts', and the apparently *centripetal* consequence that our 'whole life is thus an education of error'.[57]

Shelley then, does not simply assume the existence of truth (including the truth of other persons and the world), as Ulmer claims; he argues that such things cannot *but* be assumed if we are to live a coherent life. As Satya Mohanty has argued, the possibility of error is the *corollary*, not the antithesis, of the idea that all questions set out from value assumptions that are 'historically and socially embedded'.[58] Similarly, for Shelley, objectivity is not neutrality: life itself presupposes truth, and truth presupposes the possibility of error. Viewed in these terms, Hogle's claim that the relational character of knowledge necessitates a notion of 'radical transference' is misconceived, as is Ulmer's claim that the presence of truth in Shelley's work betrays a metaphysical homesickness. Indeed, for Shelley, any theory can be *sacrificed* to thought: '[t]he relations of *things*, remain unchanged, by whatever system', he affirms, adding that by 'the word *things* is to be understood any object of thought, that is, any thought upon which any other thought is employed'.[59] For Shelley, there is only one conceivable plane to thought and that plane is thought itself.

In his mature poetry, Shelley rejects the notion of a fundamental dichotomy between immanence and transcendence. Thus, 'The Triumph of Life' suggests that the narrator's thirst for a knowledge that trumps life itself is destined to end in the defeat prefigured by Rousseau's disfigurement, and by the pageant of:

> "Chained hoary anarch, demagogue and sage
> Whose name the fresh world thinks already old –
> "For in the battle Life and they did wage
> She remained conqueror –
> ('The Triumph of Life', ll. 237–40)

As Paul Hamilton observes, what Shelley's poem problematises is the very attempt to move 'outside' thought, expressed by the narrator's insistent question, ' "Then, what is Life?" ' The hypostasising assumption behind this question, he claims, is 'the error which allows life to be felt as an intolerable imposition from without'.[60] For Shelley, since life, like truth, has neither 'outside' nor 'inside', both ideas remain indefinably absolute (and absolutely indefinable), conceivable only as the preconditions of thought and communication.

HOLISM AND THE 'AMERICAN ROMANTIC PHILOSOPHICAL TRADITION'

My description of the romantics' wavering resistance to hypostasisation, the refusal to see life, in Hamilton's words, as 'an intolerable imposition from without', shares some features with Stanley Cavell's account of romanticism as a response to philosophy's (particularly Kantian episte-mology's) failure to cope with the 'tragedy' of scepticism. Like Cavell, I locate in romantic writing an impatience not with empiricism as such, but with a certain *kind* of philosophical thinking (what I variously term epistemology, representationalism, or the correspondence view of truth, and Cavell calls the quest for certainty) that precipitates, simultaneously, a suspicion of philosophy and a craving for limitation. Moreover, Cavell's work engages in a longstanding debate over the historical and philosoph-ical links between romanticism and modern pragmatism. Since both issues have a considerable bearing upon the question of the 'pragmatism' of romanticism, they will form the principal points of focus for the remainder of this chapter.

For Cavell, philosophy shares with modernity the burden of being defined both by its own self-questioning and its own inescapability. He agrees with Wittgenstein that epistemological problems arise mainly when philosophy abandons the quotidian, and that they terminate 'when we have gone through a process of bringing ourselves back into our natural forms of life'.[61] There is, in this key respect, no difference in kind between philosophical thinking and everyday discourse. And yet, rationalising according to a criterion we cannot identify means that we don't always mean what we say, or say what we mean. Bereft of foundations, the task of the philosopher is to cope with the partiality of her perspective, and to express her worldview as best she can. This does not imply the death of rationality, merely the recognition that as in aesthetic disagreements, a 'familiar lack of conclusiveness' in dialogue, 'rather than showing up irrationality, shows the kind of rationality it has, and needs'.[62]

In breaking from foundationalism, Cavell further inherits from Wittgenstein (as well as from Dewey and Austin) the conviction that what is needed in the knowledge of other minds in particular is 'a special concept of knowledge ... which is not a function of certainty'.[63] Certainty is the tragic lure of modern (post-Cartesian) thought, in so far as the idea that 'we can save our lives by knowing them' collapses into scepticism the moment that epistemology sets out on its quest.[64] For Cavell, knowledge cannot be abstracted from its interpersonal basis, from the act of *acknowledgement*. This has a number of consequences, foremost among which is the introduction of moral responsibility in knowing: for while the failure of certainty is figured as an 'absence ... a blank', failure of acknowledgement remains 'the presence of something, a confusion, an indifference, a callousness'.[65] For this reason, scepticism is depicted by Cavell not as a paradox or as a cruel maladaptation of reason, but as a thoroughly human *tragedy*, one through which we must pass in order to appreciate that the 'presentness' of the world to us 'cannot be a function of knowing', but must instead 'be *accepted*; as the presentness of other minds is not to be known, but acknowledged'.[66]

At this point, Cavell's work on scepticism takes a distinctly romantic turn. Attuned, in his reading of literary texts, for the kind of engagement with otherness forsaken by philosophy, Cavell is struck by the parallels between his own thinking on scepticism and philosophy and that of the romantics. In particular, he finds in romantic writing an understanding that if 'skepticism is the playing out of a tragedy', then 'our ordinary lives partake of tragedy in partaking of skepticism'.[67] Writing in the wake of Hume's alienation of ordinary thinking and philosophical reflection, the romantics know this 'everyday' tragedy by a number of names: for Coleridge and Wordsworth it appears as despondency or dejection; for Emerson, it is melancholy; for Thoreau, quiet desperation. Cavell argues that although they do not quite overcome scepticism the romantics hover on the brink of passing beyond epistemological tragedy into a new understanding of the relationship between everyday rationality and philosophical reason.

However, romantic despondency is likely to be misunderstood if it is seen merely as a response to the threat of scepticism. For Cavell, romanticism is a reaction both to scepticism and 'to a disappointment with philosophy's answer to this threat'.[68] Unhappy with Hume's attack on reason, the romantics are also unwilling to accept the bargain struck by Kant for the recovery of knowledge: a division between the phenomenal and the noumenal (knowing and unknowing) modes of being. As a result, romantic writing is haunted by a 'perception of human doubleness' and the spectre of a life, like that of the Ancient Mariner, lived 'between worlds'.[69] Cavell finds Coleridge's poem, with its symbolic landscape of liminality (of 'lines' and 'Life-in-Death' (l.193)) particularly suggestive in this regard: a depiction of scepticism as the killing of knowledge through a refusal of acknowledgement or 'attunement'. In slaying the albatross, the Mariner exempts himself from the community of nature, enacting a fantasy of cognitive autonomy that strips language of its communality. The Mariner is thus condemned to *live* his scepticism, isolated in a world in which the uncommunicating 'stony eyes' (436) of the dead crew mirror his own 'breaking of attunement' with others, the product of a sceptical 'craving for exemption from human nature'.[70] It is only when, in a final act of acknowledgement, he blesses God's creatures, that the Mariner's penance begins.

Coleridge's poetic nightmare exemplifies the romantic refusal of scepticism and of the philosophical yearning for certainty that gives rise to it. For Cavell, the romantics are the first to identify scepticism as a product *of*, rather than a subject *for* philosophy. Scepticism, they find, is first and foremost a refusal to recognise that the transcendental conditions of knowledge – acknowledgement and attunement – are interpersonal in nature. None the less, the idea of limitation, of boundaries and foundations, remains a lure. Accordingly, Cavell portrays romantic writing as inaugurating 'the (modern) struggle of philosophy and poetry for and against one another, for and against their own continued existence'.[71] While the current study broadly echoes this picture, its main vectors of pragmatic absolutism and epistemological idealism cut across Cavell's categories of 'poetry' and 'philosophy' (thus, idealism – offering a completion of dialogue through the agency of constitutive forms – may be expressed through a variety of modes and genres). In addition, it foregrounds the specific contribution of an eighteenth-century tradition of Socratic or 'radical' empiricism as crucial to the development of a romantic counterdiscourse of rationality based upon a concern with the holistic relationships of interdependence between truth, communication, and subjectivity. Finally, it highlights the lines of pragmatism and romanticism that link writers such as Keats, Coleridge, and Shelley, with later thinkers such as Emerson, James, Dewey, Putnam, Davidson, Taylor, Habermas, and Rorty.

This brings us to the 'romantic pragmatic' tradition. For Cavell, the responses of Emerson and Thoreau to scepticism are comparable to those of Wordsworth and Coleridge because 'the transcendentalism established in their pages is what became of romanticism in America'.[72] Russell Goodman uses this observation as a starting-point in his attempt to trace the course of an 'American Romantic philosophical tradition'.[73] Accordingly, he details the direct influence of Coleridge upon Emerson, of Wordsworth upon James, and of Keats, Shelley, and Coleridge upon Dewey (including the latter's late admission that Coleridge's *Aids to Reflection* ' "represents pretty much my religious views still" ').[74] More broadly, Goodman argues that American philosophy extends romantic ideas and themes in five key areas. As he puts it, the 'ideas and projects of the European Romantics – "the feeling intellect," the "marriage of self and world," the human mind as a shaper of experience, the criticism and expansion of empiricism, and the naturalization and humanization of the divine – developed in a philosophically distinctive way on American soil'.[75] I will briefly examine each of these areas in turn.

Goodman's work reveals the deep strain of romantic thought that persists within American pragmatism to this day. In the notion of 'the feeling intellect', for example, he isolates a shared concern with the affective dimension of knowledge. According to Goodman, Emerson, James, and Dewey inherit from the romantics 'a voluntarist picture of knowledge' whereby to know something invariably involves assuming a 'special attitude or stance'.[76] In particular, James's emphasis on the constitutive role of mood in knowledge and Dewey's attempt to combine emotion and science within a praxis of imagination represent, he argues, variant forms of 'Romantic empiricism'.[77] Another way of thinking about this connection is in terms of the treatment of values. What Goodman identifies in 'the feeling intellect' can be redescribed as a refusal to draw a firm boundary within the make-up of experience between 'hard' facts and 'soft' values.

The idea that romantic writing tests the boundary between fact and value is well attested. Laurence Lockridge notes the widespread resistance in writing of this period to the bifurcation of the descriptive and the evaluative. 'The ethics of Romanticism', he finds, consists in 'a will to value in the face of a prevailing reduction of value'.[78] So pronounced is this resistance in a writer like Charles Lamb, for example, that it surfaces at the level of the thematic. Elia's imperfect sympathies with Scots, who 'appear to have such a love of truth (as if, like virtue, it were valuable for itself) that all truth becomes equally valuable', counters emphatic Caledonian naturalism with a bravura performance of the noncommittal, which in turn testifies to Lamb's sense that human flourishing is based on a plurality of virtues that do not reduce to the cognitive.[79] Indeed, so impressed was Dewey by Lamb's coded attack on the means–end logic of utilitarianism in 'A Dissertation Upon Roast Pig', that he draws upon this essay in his 'Theory of Valuation'. The 'Dissertation,' Dewey argues, points up 'the absurdity of any "end" which is set up apart from the means by which it is to be attained and apart from its own further function as a means'.[80] In Lamb's yarn, the pyromaniac pursuits of the Chinese swine-herd's son Bo-bo indirectly lead the residents of the village (including the Judge who tries him) into arson as they attempt to reproduce his fortuitous discovery of pork crackling: 'Thus this custom of firing houses continued, till in process of time, says my manuscript, a sage arose, like our Locke, who made a discovery, that the flesh of swine, or indeed of any other animal, might be cooked (*burnt*, as they call it) without the necessity of consuming a whole house to dress it'.[81] For Dewey, Lamb's playful essay discloses how the '*value* of enjoyment of the object *as* an attained end is a value of something which in being an end, an outcome, stands in relation to the means of which it is the consequence'.[82] This continuum of 'means' and 'ends' loses its paradoxical air when we jettison the idea that ends are determined by theoretical considerations that are themselves *outside* the field of value, and accept that 'improved valuation must grow out of existing valuations'.[83] All that prevents us from realising this continuum, according to Dewey, is the empirical dogma that Lamb rightly refuses: that there is a separation 'between the "world of facts" and the "realm of values"'.[84]

This refusal can be seen, in turn, as the corollary of another leading idea shared by romanticism and pragmatism: what Cavell and Goodman describe as the 'marriage' of self and world, a nonreductive, symbiotic partership between mind and nature. At the heart of this idea is the constitutive role of volition: the agency of our *willing* selves in knowing the world around us. Hence Coleridge's philosophical elevation of Will, and his longstanding dissatisfaction with the cold, purely conceptual apparatus of the Kantian critique. Cavell and Goodman argue that behind the nightmare figure of 'Life-in-Death' in the 'The Rime of the Ancient Mariner' and the 'grief without a pang, void, dark, and drear' (l.21) of 'Dejection: An Ode', is Coleridge's belief that before the question of *knowing* arises other minds must first be *acknowledged* and the natural world *accepted*. The same idea influences not only Emerson's conception of the '"intimate separation" between ourselves and the world', but also James's search for a 'middle ground' between real and ideal.[85]

The third and fourth points that Goodman claims mark intersections between romanticism and pragmatism are closely related. The theory that the mind shapes its own experience has long been recognised as a theme common to the work of Coleridge, Shelley, Dewey, James, and Rorty.[86] Accordingly, the romantic rejection of the 'correspondence' theory of knowledge prepares the ground for pragmatists to collapse the dualisms of experience and nature, subject and object, knowledge and action, and (in the case of Dewey) to eulogise art as the 'highest because most complete incorporation of natural forces and operations in experience'.[87] Less remarked, though central to the argument of this book, is romanticism's hand in reforming empiricism. Goodman, for instance, observes that James and Dewey 'follow Emerson in focusing on the shaping power of the human mind' and 'in criticizing the paltry notion of experience with which empiricism traditionally operates'.[88] And yet, as I endeavour to show below, the possibility of a richer, less rigid empiricism – one in which the 'paltry' notion of representation or correspondence is jettisoned, and the boundaries between experience and language dissolved – is already prospected by Keats, Shelley, and Coleridge.

While not always in agreement, attempts by Cavell and Goodman to construct the narrative of an American philosophical tradition based upon the persistence of romanticism in pragmatism are further buttressed by commentators such as Wheeler, Eldridge, and Rorty.[89] Thus, Goodman's contention that the romantic 'naturalization and humanization of the divine' is the *sine qua non* of Dewey's developments in *Art as Experience*, of 'a vitalized and deepened experience, an extraordinary ordinary'.[90] This is elsewhere echoed by Wheeler, who maintains that an emphasis on action 'forms the most consistent character of Coleridge's Jamesian, dynamic philosophy: not idealism, not transcendentalism, so much as an evolving, natural supernaturalism'.[91] Goodman, indeed, sees Putnam's support for the idea that 'the mind and the world jointly make up the mind and the world' as a more recent return to the American tradition of philosophy represented by Emerson, James, and Dewey, and thus as a further 'perpetuation in philosophy of the original Romantic enterprise'.[92]

Here, however, a degree of caution is advisable. The idea of the natural supernatural, in particular, is a fluid dynamic in which the 'natural' and the 'supernatural' is never in equipoise. In dealing with the 'evolving' relationship between the ordinary and the extraordinary, there is always the temptation to ask: which is more fundamental? The romantic and the pragmatist typically deliver different answers to this question (or rather, they present different attempts to finesse it). In the case of the former, the very ambiguity of 'natural supernaturalism' reflects the precariousness of the relationship between romantic pragmatism and romantic idealism. This precariousness is notably less pronounced in James and Dewey. Certainly, James's characterisation of truth as 'a mere aspiration or *Grenzbegriff*, marking the infinitely remote ideal of our thinking life' echoes many a romantic pronouncement on the subject.[93] What matters, however, is the significance attached to this 'infinitely remote ideal'. As the adjective 'mere' suggests, James, like Dewey, tends to be reductively eliminative when it comes to truth, effectively identifying it with what works. In this respect, the missing link between romanticism and pragmatism is Darwin, and the possibility of a purely behaviouristic explanation of human belief. There is in James and Dewey a subordination of philosophy to biology, such as in Dewey's 'empirical naturalism' and his Darwinian notion of organic, 'adaptive adjustment'. It is hard to imagine Coleridge, Shelley, or Keats applauding James's dictum that '[t]he true is the name of whatever proves itself to be good in the way of belief', much less Dewey's claim that '[t]he adverb 'truly' is more fundamental than either the adjective, true, or the noun, truth'.[94]

It is, then, easy to overstate the affinities between the pragmatists and their romantic forebears.[95] Indeed, James and Dewey take pains to distance themselves from some of the romantics' more extravagant expressions of epistemological longing. When James dismisses Schopenhauer's 'ontological wonder-sickness' he expresses a distaste, shared with Nietzsche, for what he sees as romantic idealism's nostalgia for objective truth.[96] Similarly, Dewey's impatience with romantic sentimentality is implied in his claim that it is 'difficult to estimate the harm that has resulted because the liberal and progressive movement of the eighteenth and earlier nineteenth centuries had no method of intellectual articulation commensurate with its practical aspirations'.[97] Trapped within the binary of scepticism and idealistic absolutism, Dewey argues, romanticism's lack of practical sense even handicaps its artistic productions: glorifying flux and evolution for its own sake, romantic art is 'not art' in so far as it employs the 'sense of unachieved possibilities...as a compensatory equivalent for endeavour in achievement'.[98]

If not the shared manifesto depicted by Goodman and Wheeler, natural supernaturalism none the less remains the obstinate *question* to which romantic writers and pragmatist philosophers repeatedly return. Indeed, the problem continues to bedevil pragmatist thought. Thus, Dewey's naturalist disdain for romanticism's 'compensatory' ideals of 'unachieved possibilities' is echoed by Rorty's suspicion of Habermas's conception of truth as 'Janus-faced', that is, as simultaneously involving the unconditional claims of systematic thought and the intersubjectivity of the lifeworld.[99] This brings us back to the question that divided Rorty and Habermas in Chapter 1, which now re-emerges as one of the central dilemmas of romantic natural supernaturalism: must truth, as Rorty maintains, be deflated into an naturalistic account of the shifting sands of coherence that underlie everyday language games, or is it possible, as Habermas argues, to preserve a notion of the *absoluteness* of truth within a pragmatic account of the speech-act situation without falling prey to the perils of hypostasisation? Like Dewey, Rorty is convinced that truth can be explained nonreductively within a naturalistic language '[o]nce one drops the traditional opposition between context and thing contextualized'. Without such an opposition, 'there is no way to divide things up into those which are what they are independent of context and those which are context-dependent'. Holism, he maintains, '*takes the curse off naturalism*'.[100]

The writers discussed below have no clear answer to this problem, but their ambivalence between idealism and pragmatism appears far from naïve when viewed alongside Davidson's or Habermas's finely-balanced adjudication between truth's unconditionality and the role that it plays within communicative practice. In many ways, indeed, the alethic manoeuvres of the romantics appear more 'pragmatic' when read alongside modern thinkers like Putnam and Taylor than they do when compared to the Darwinian naturalism of James and Dewey. Admittedly, if, as one recent commentator maintains, pragmatism is 'fundamentally a theory about truth', in which ' "truth" is practice-oriented, situational, provisional, experimental and processual in the sense that it is constantly emerging anew in never-ending processes of adaptation to experience and readjustment to intersubjective encounters', then the lines that connect the romantics to the 'American philosophical tradition', as described by Cavell, Goodman, and Wheeler, will always be evident.[101] The radical achievement of Keats, Shelley, and Coleridge, however, lies in their disclosure of the deep connections between intersubjectivity and truth, and thus of how, to adapt Rorty's phrase, holism takes the curse off absolutism.

CHAPTER 3

This living Keats: truth, deixis, and correspondence

Keats remains, for many readers, the epistolary poet par excellence. Few today would countenance Paul de Man's claim that the importance of Keats's letters is easily 'exaggerated'; indeed, it is more common to find critics insisting on their centrality to interpreting his poems.[1] In particular, the letter Keats writes from Hampstead in late December 1817 to his brothers George and Tom, contains what must be one of the most critically overdetermined passages of prose in English literature: the rumination on 'Negative Capability, that is when man is capable of being in uncertainties, Mysteries, doubts, without any irritable reaching after fact & reason'.[2] Like Keats's later denigration of the literal as antithetical to the 'life of allegory', this abdication from 'fact and reason' can be depicted as contesting a second, important sense of 'correspondence': that of agreement or accord. By questioning the literal foundation of meaning and the factual status of belief, Keats undermines an empirical topos whereby correspondence is held to be the key relation underpinning meaning and truth – respectively, between the referring sign and its referent, and between the idea and its object. Through the 'correspondence' of letters, then, Keats subverts the 'correspondence' of epistemological harmony.

This anti-epistemic turn in Keats's writing has been interpreted in a number of ways: as evidence of a nascent Neo-Platonism imbibed from Benjamin Bailey's bookshelves; as the revival of eighteenth-century theories of sympathetic imagination modelled on Shakespeare; and as evidence of a developing engagement with Hazlitt's theories of art, knowledge and power.[3] At the same time, Keats's 'negative' conception of poetic identity and 'allegorical' view of life has resonated with modern commentators, some of whom have linked it to a shift in early nineteenth-century thought from a broadly Kantian to a Hegelian model of determination. In this transition, the Enlightenment idea that meaning and truth are underpinned by 'correspondence' is rejected in favour of a picture of thought and communication as governed by a 'negative' form of relationality. Indeed, for some, even talk of literary 'influence' imports assumptions of agency and intentionality that are merely the interpretive residue of a subject-based metaphysics of presence, a hangover from the old Kantian order. Such commentators are inclined to view Keats's letter as exemplifying the negativity that simultaneously sustains and undermines both the Enlightenment *cogito* and a long tradition of exegetical positivism. Accordingly, an influential strain of commentary has detected in Keats's work not just the familiar negation of instrumental rationalism (the overcoming of calculating intellect) but the negation of the negation, a dialectical resistance to repeating the objectivity (in the form of a transcendent or ideal aesthetic) first erased from the mechanistic. According to this perspective, Keats the dreamer, the transcendental escapologist, is *at the same time* Keats the radical, the dialectical acrobat. His life and work perform (whether he knows it or not) the negativity that Hegel, Marx, Adorno and others expose at the heart of the romantic will to 'value', 'beauty', and 'truth'.[4]

In this chapter, however, I argue that there is a form of rationality in Keats's writing that has escaped both formalist approaches and the suspicions of postmodern and New Historicist approaches. This rationality is intimately bound up with his life in letters. Keats's thought, indeed, is split between two different ways of conceptualising truth, subjectivity, and meaning in the wake of the collapse of the Enlightenment masterparadigm of a grounding correspondence between self and world, responses I have characterised as 'hypostatic' and 'holistic'. On one hand, viewed from the 'outside', Keats's dream of truth bankrupts the epistemic. Like Hume's final demand for authenticity, Keats's insistence on a knowledge that might be worthy of imagination proves more than any model of 'truth as correspondence' can sustain. Overextended, idealism loads contemplative knowledge with a significance that it cannot sustain. As a result, and having equated the failures of instrumental reason with those of coherent thought as such, Keats is half-inclined to follow his mentor Hazlitt and renounce the cognitive completely.

This is a well-known Keats, the Keats who suspects that all thought tends to abstraction and commodification, the 'false coinage' of Wordsworthian speculation.[5] The same Keats assumes that knowledge refines rather than enriches, producing women who are 'everything in nothing',[6] and who himself, accordingly, affirms 'nothing' but the heart's affections, and rescues poetry, 'being in itself a nothing',[7] from the trade of reason through a consecrating kind of sensation. As reason lurches into

scepticism, and thence into alienation and indifference, the consolation of
the aesthetic is increasingly imbued with the power of alterity. Thus, the
well-known tropes of Keatsian negativity – nothingness, half knowledge,
indolence, death, sensual immediacy – all assume the numinous aura of
the 'other' of thought; a hypostasised, incommensurable, yet determining
non-thought.

Coexisting with this, however, is a second strain in Keats's writing,
one that allows him to assemble ontologies of '[t]hings real … Things
semireal … and Nothings', and postulate an ideal of coherence according
to which 'evey [*sic*] point of thought is the centre of an intellectual
world'.[8] We need look no further than the addressee of these remarks to
identify the catalyst for such speculative turns: it is Bailey who, in the
autumn of 1817, introduces Keats to the possibilities and resources of
philosophical discourse. Keats's stay in Bailey's Oxford rooms has been
linked with the acceleration of his interests in history, moral philosophy,
Platonism, and – perhaps most importantly – Hazlitt's own regenerate
brand of empiricism. Yet it is also likely to have intensified Keats's
awareness of a tradition of dissenting and reformist thought for which
he had already been primed, as Nicholas Roe has shown, by the principles
and practices of his 'Cockney schoolroom' education.[9]

This education was itself shaped by the philosophical debates taking
place within the culture of rational dissent, particularly those concerning
the relation between the language of reform and the reform of language.
On one level, these were arguments about the direction of empiricism. As
confidence in the Cartesian/Lockean correspondence model of truth and
knowledge broke down, tensions emerged that would ultimately polarise
empiricism into idealistic/psychological and linguistic/anthropological
strains. On one hand, writers such as Hume, Abraham Tucker, Alexander
Gerard, Archibald Alison, and later, Hazlitt, adopted an 'idealistic' stance,
stressing the constitutive role of the imagination. On the other, prompted
in part by the physiological reductionism of Hartley and by attacks by
Reid and the Scottish commonsense school upon the philosophy of
'ideas', materialists like Priestley, Tooke, and Bentham came to see
such idealism itself as empirically dubious, arguing that knowledge was
determined by language.[10]

Between them, these camps struggle to answer the pressing question of
how to treat the concepts of truth, self, and meaning, once confidence in
the *correspondence* of mind and world is lost. Idealists such as Hazlitt use
the compensatory inflatus of imagination or the 'formative' mind to
overcome the embarrassing failure of empiricism to provide doctrinal

security for belief. And yet, the anti-epistemic, noncognitive tendency in this tradition, evident in Hume's ironic indifference as much as Hazlitt's exaltation of mental power, signals their reluctance to countenance any alternative to truth as correspondence. This position contrasts strikingly with that of materialists like Tooke and Bentham, who, by deflating the concept of truth into what was coherent or acceptable within a language, suggested that truth was the *presupposition* of communication rather than its goal. Accordingly, while the field of subjectivity expands in Tucker and Hazlitt to the point where it overpowers its object, selfhood becomes entirely relational for the materialists, conceivable only within a space of reasons and values: what Bentham would call a necessary 'fiction'. Similarly, while 'meaning' becomes an increasingly problematic concept for idealism, a hazy and distant intent of consciousness, it is dismantled, etymologically by Tooke, and paraphastically by Bentham, into the practical, social business of interpretation and communication.

An understanding of both traditions is vital for appreciating the true character of Keats's alethic ambivalence. Critically, it is the second movement that presents the possibility of disconnecting rational thought as such from the purely instrumental and representational rationalism that Keats gently mocks in his 'Godwin-methodist' friend Charles Dilke, who 'will never come at a truth as long as he lives; because he is always trying at it'.[11] Ironically, it is partly through reading Godwin's *Political Justice* that Keats encounters the holistic and pragmatic idea of truth and interpretation being developed by reformists and radicals. From this outlook, truth is relational and embedded in communication, determined by the interdependent relations obtaining between the self, other people, and a presupposed world. Thus, Keats's depiction of the webs of belief spun by human beings as constituting a centreless community of coherence, a 'fellowship' or 'grand democracy of Forest Trees',[12] answers to an essentially social conception of truth. Indeed, it is this conception that underlies the general ability of much romantic writing to see itself, as Richard Eldridge puts it, as in touch with truth and yet 'always already underway in culture'.[13]

Keats's uneasiness about reasoning, however, has been allowed to obscure the extent to which a 'philosophical' discourse of radical empiricism makes its presence felt in his poetry and prose, and in particular how it affects his handling of questions of truth, subjectivity, and meaning. As I argue below, the enigma of 'truth' and 'beauty' in the 'Ode on a Grecian Urn' unravels when truth is disconnected from correspondence and recast as the *presupposition* (rather than the goal) of discourse. Indeed, as 'Lamia'

suggests, if objective truth is itself based upon social contact, rather than
metaphysical givenness, the fate of the self must be linked to *communication*, not the destructive gaze of a spectating consciousness. In turn, once
language is seen as bound up with the deictic gesture that underwrites the
pragmatics of communication, 'meaning' appears less as a *thing* endlessly
deferred, than as the *activity* of interpretation itself. Conceived as
elenchus, a dialogue through which all participants are transformed in
the course of submitting their intentions to the 'fellowship' of communication, the understanding of others is expressed most tellingly in Keats's
writing – and above all in 'The Fall of Hyperion' – by the figure of the
warm contact of the human hand. Even Keats's conviction that all axioms
of philosophy must be tested upon the 'pulses', is based more upon a trust
in the resources of communicative reason than upon a conception of
immediacy as givenness.[14]

The extent of Keats's ambivalence, then, can only be realised when his
negativity, his unwillingness to own 'one Idea of the truth of any of my
speculations', is weighed against the constitutive role of dialogue in his
formal and informal writings.[15] At this point, the true significance of
'correspondence' in Keats's writing becomes clear. Understanding the
subtle relation in Keats's writings between the epistolary and the epistemological means appreciating the fundamental importance in his work
of the connection between everyday communication (with all its indeter-
minacies) and a presupposed concept of truth. In turn, this relation belies
the idea that the story of the breakdown of the empirical topos in Keats's
writing is that of the inexorable triumph of negativity over subjectivity.
Epistemological correspondence, the foundation of the factual and the
literal, is most seriously challenged in Keats not by negation, but by what
might be called the correspondence of the letter – in other words, by
communication. Within Keats's holistic counterdiscourse of reason, it is
in this *epistolary* sense alone that truth amounts to 'correspondence'.

NEGATIVITY AND NEGATIVE CAPABILITY

Amidst all the differences in method, argument, and emphasis in recent
historicist commentary (and passing over, for the moment, those increasingly vocal parties who dissent from the Neo-Nietzschean–Hegelian
orthodoxy in modern criticism altogether) negativity remains the master-
trope of modern romantic criticism and commentary.[16] Having entered its
postmodern phase transformed by the concept of incommensurability,
dialectical method drives an endless spiral of suspicion, cancellation, and

regrounding by considering questions of truth, meaning, and knowledge primarily under the sign of otherness. In this way, any reading becomes both a study of, and subject to, the (in)determination of thought by the 'unthought', and of truth by a powerful 'untruth'.[17] In romantic criticism, and in Keats studies in particular, historicism has imposed a considerable levy of reflexivity upon the reader, and particularly upon the interpreter of Keats's concept of negative capability. According to this model, a thoroughly dialectical reading must at some point register how the knowing modern overdetermination of this concept is *itself* shaped by a thoroughly Keatsian model of 'half knowledge' or aesthetic (mis)understanding.[18]

From the perspective of postmodern historicism, then, Keats's rejection of the verificationist values of the Enlightenment raises the possibility that the aesthetic is the uncanny and vengeful double of truth as well as its consummation; that 'beauty' shadows the 'truth' it completes with the unassimilable 'untruth' of a determining otherness. Viewed this way, the echoes of Hazlitt's account of Shakespearean genius that resound in Keats's idea of negative capability acquire new significance.[19] Enabled by a 'half knowledge' that cannot be laid out as facts or reasons, the beauty that Shakespeare catches from the Penetralium of mystery 'obliterates all consideration', including the truth it perfects. According to this picture of Keats, the Shakespearean self is instructive precisely because of the way in which it presents itself as incapable of self-determination: the punctual ego is always secretly bound to chameleonic nonidentity, to heterogeneity. In Keats, when subjectivity (having been untethered from its correspondence with objective reality) falls to pieces, it is not saved by aesthetic grace. Instead, it exposes the dependence of truth and meaning upon the hidden life-support machine of negativity and incommensurable difference: of signatures, bodies, and the exchanges of material culture. Accordingly, Keats's life becomes a performance of its own negativity. By throwing back the curtain on the conditions of intentionality, the ideal 'allegorical life' rematerialises as its own 'life of allegory'.[20] Such, it is argued, is the significance of Keats's 'disquisition with Dilke':

I had not a dispute but a disquisition with Dilke ... & at once it struck me, what quality went to form a Man of Achievement especially in Literature & which Shakespeare possessed so enormously – I mean *Negative Capability*, that is when man is capable of being in uncertainties, Mysteries, doubts, without any irritable reaching after fact & reason – Coleridge, for instance, would let go by a fine isolated verisimilitude caught from the Penetralium of mystery, from being incapable of remaining content with half knowledge. This pursued through

Volumes would perhaps take us no further than this, that with a great poet the sense of Beauty overcomes every other consideration, or rather obliterates all consideration.[21]

And yet, there is, lurking about Keats's concept of 'half knowledge', something that conforms neither to the scepticism of a moribund empiricism nor to the dialectics of negativity. To see this, we must register how ambiguity affects the above passage on two levels. The first and most obvious equivocation lies between the enabling absence of 'half knowledge' and the recuperative presence offered by 'the sense of Beauty'. The rhythms and rhetoric of Keats's prose embody the difference between these notions: where the idea of 'half knowledge' appears, almost as an afterthought, at the end of a ruminative passage marked by equivocation, hesitation, and parenthesis, the consideration of 'beauty' brings the discussion to an abrupt halt. Keats manages the transition between these notions with the brisk stroke of his pen, opting for a shortcut 'through Volumes' that itself attests to the noncognitive character of his argument. But this argument bypass, an overcoming of reason en route to revealing how the sense of beauty itself 'overcomes every other consideration', exposes the very ambiguity that makes the move from half knowledge to the aesthetic so problematic: the equivocation between the idea of 'overcoming' as *obviation* and the idea of 'overcoming' as *obliteration*. This second, more fundamental ambiguity complicates the apparently confident Keatsian transition from indeterminacy to aesthetic plenitude. Indeed, it cuts across both these positions, raising further questions in its wake: do we interpret 'half knowledge' as *incomplete* knowledge or a *kind* of knowledge that negates the rational? Similarly, does the sense of beauty overcome the 'considerations' of thought by replacing them with other (better) considerations, or obliterate them in an act of sensory violence?

What is at stake in both these questions is the real force and direction of the counterepistemic trajectory of negative capability. This in turn can be formulated as the question: if subjectivity collapses, does rationality fall with it? On this question, there is a surprising convergence between traditional readings of negative capability as a species of scepticism, and postmodern–historicist detections of relativity: both, in fact, answer in the affirmative, albeit for different reasons. Stuart Sperry, for example, is alive to the ambiguities in Keats's thought when he notes how the ostensibly nondoctrinal, heuristic status of the notion of negative capability is severely tested by the fact that (in writing as in life) Keats finds it difficult to realise his ideal of the poet as an individual whose chameleonic lack of identity permits no fixed beliefs. Sperry locates one source of this difficulty in the way in which eighteenth-century empiricism had loaded the concepts of 'thought' and 'sensation' with complex and often contradictory significations. The example of Hazlitt's hero, Abraham Tucker, for example, might have reassured Keats that thought was simply the 'coalescence' of sensation, and as such entirely in harmony with the ideals of art. On the other hand, the apparently impenetrable pronouncements of Hazlitt's bugbear, Jeremy Bentham, would have alerted him to the possibility that reflective thought was constitutionally inclined to slide into alienating abstraction. This dilemma alone would have been tricky enough for Keats to navigate. 'The problem,' as Sperry observes, 'was that most of the time it was difficult to avoid seeing thought from both points of view – as process and effect'.[22]

However, while Sperry's identification of Keats's ambivalence is astute, he assumes that in confronting the dilemma of thought and sensation Keats was completely circumscribed by the metaphysics of subjectivity. Thus, when he claims that Keats's use of the term 'verisimilitude' rather than 'truth' suggests 'a form of verification that proceeds not through the rules of logic but by means of that imaginative convergence', Sperry infers that Keats is attempting 'to justify poetry as a kind of thinking we might consider unconscious or preconscious – a form of apprehension proceeding by relationships and laws distinct from those of the reason'.[23] The discourse of subjective idealism, he implies, is the only language-game of rationality in town. Transcendence by imaginative synthesis, after Tucker's model of association, becomes a bolthole for thought in its escape from the desiccating effects of abstract rationality. However, by identifying rational thought with the combined cells of binding logic and truth-as-correspondence, Sperry misses two possibilities: first, that *subjectivity* rather than rationality is the source of the problem for Keats; second, that the goal of 'unconscious' verification only makes subjectivity *more* coercive, more oppressive. He assumes that even if reason harbours further resources Keats was unaware of them. In other words (to come back to my original point), Sperry passes over the possibility that 'the sense of Beauty' might *obviate* rather than *obliterate* the perplexing 'considerations' of thought. He shares with more recent commentary the assumption that the aesthetic impulse in Keats is an antirational reflex that remains caught up in the contradictions of subjectivity.

Contrary to both perspectives, however, Keats's writing at times insists that the resources of reason outstrip those of subjectivity, and that while the disintegration of truth-as-correspondence entails the fragmentation of consciousness, the same is not necessarily true of rationality.

Consequently, readings of Keats's aesthetic as either the 'transcendence' or the 'negation' of the rational both tend to overplay the consequences of the collapse of one particular, consciousness-based model of rationality. That Keats is at least aware of the potential of an *alternative* paradigm is reflected in the fundamental ambivalence in his work between a subject-centred and a holistic conception of thought. Again, there are two Keatses at work here: one whose indifference, like that of Hume, is the by-product of his struggle with a consoling but ultimately oppressive subjectivity; and another who is prepared to countenance notions of reason and truth not grounded in the correspondence between the world and consciousness (notions, indeed, that are not 'grounded' at all). It is the first, 'indifferent' Keats who posits 'halfseeing'[24] and 'half knowledge' as a *kind* of apprehension distinct from the everyday. This is what Sperry reads as 'preconscious' aesthetic awareness, and what New Historicism tends to bracket as the purely 'negative' knowledge of thought's incommensurable otherness. According to this view, 'beauty' becomes the remedy for rational thought itself (for Sperry, the negation of the rational; for historicism, the negation of the negation).

For 'holistic' Keats, however, negative capability is a challenge to monolithic subjectivity, but not to reason itself. The halfseeing that underlies it is an awareness of the limitations of knowledge rather than the transcendent sense of the aesthetic or the negativity of dialectical knowledge. Encouraged by the example of Bailey, this Keats finds that he 'can have no enjoyment in the world but continual drinking of Knowledge', announcing his intention 'to follow Solomon's directions of 'get Wisdom – get understanding'[25] and to ask Hazlitt 'the best metaphysical road I can take'.[26] While sceptical about what can be known, 'holistic' Keats is not defeatist about the possibility of knowledge or the resources of reason. His argument is with a particular philosophy, which, by installing a self-identical consciousness at the centre of its considerations, constructs an alienating dogma of subjectivity. What is objectionable about this philosophy is not that it entertains a concept of objective truth, but that it conceives objectivity in terms of correspondence between a subject and the world, the inevitable failure of which provokes the false currency of thought characteristic of the 'egotistical sublime'.[27] Against Wordsworth's noumenal compensation for a defeated consciousness, Keats offers the holistic vision of ' "The Vale of Soul-Making" ', whereby the 'three grand materials' of intelligence, heart, and world 'act one upon the other' in shaping a human life. Critically, none of these is foundational; but collectively, through triangulation, each becomes the condition of possibility for the others. As Keats concludes, with a performative spiral of reasoning:

> I began by seeing how man was formed by circumstances – and what are circumstances? – but touchstones of his heart – ? and what are touch stones? – but proovings of his hearrt? … – and what was his soul before it came into the world and had These provings and alterations and perfectionings? – An intelligence – without Identity – and how is this Identity to be made? Through the medium of the Heart? And how is the heart to become this Medium but in a world of Circumstances? –[28]

For Keats, if objectivity is always embodied – emerging only through the interdependence of intelligent awareness, the contingencies of circumstance and the cultivation of value (the 'provings' of the heart) – then the fate of reason itself is not bound to a notion of truth as correspondence. At this point, Keats's notion of beauty re-emerges with new significance. For if objectivity is always the presupposition of *living* a rounded, intelligent life, not a thing to be captured or the goal of an abstract subjectivity, beauty might just turn out to be precisely what Keats claims it is: the surrogate for a concept of truth so basic it cannot be known.

None of this is to deny the presence of Keats the idealist. In the end, idealist Keats and holistic Keats are as irreconcilable as the Hume of the study and the Hume of the street. None the less, by underplaying the voice of *communicative* reason in Keats's writing we risk underestimating the involvement of his notion of truth in our own interpretations. This is not to deny the political or rhetorical dimensions of Keats's aesthetics of 'embarrassment'. Yet a less 'mediated' interpretation of that embarrassment might shed some light on our own discomfiture – that is, upon the embarrassment of overdetermination in modern criticism. What is meant by this is the kind of awkwardness to which Chandler admits, for example, when he confesses his failure to persuade his students of the pivotal significance of the pun on the word 'graves' in Shelley's sonnet 'England in 1819' (I shall return to this particular pun later). For Chandler, this embarrassment is profitable precisely because it becomes 'a way to test the limits of the poem's performative self-consciousness about historical representation – of its apparent commitment to the notion of changing history *by* interpreting it … – by pushing (as Blake might say) beyond "enough" in the analysis to "Too much" '.[29] Our overdetermination, as well as Shelley's, is licensed by the historical dialectic of exegesis, whereby we change the meaning of a text, and are in turn changed, by the act of reading.

However, if critics come to see overdetermination as a necessary part of dialogue and communication rather than hypostasised dialectic – that is, as entirely consistent with a notion of objectivity now uncoupled from any putatively 'neutral' spectatorial position – they might find a reason not to blush when their interpretations of Keats's embarrassment become 'Too much'. Similarly, the knowing overdetermination of 'negative capability' need not be characterised by negativity. This, then, is a second reason why rediscovering the 'holistic' Keats is worthwhile and valuable: in short, by demonstrating the indispensability of the concept truth to all communication, his work contains a lesson for all interpretive practices. Following this lesson, criticism might come to a view of the relation between negative capability and beauty that obviates both the displacements of transcendentalism and the neuroses of negativity. This will remain difficult, however, so long as we remain in thrall to foundationalist conceptions of truth and their parasitic negations.

THE PHILOSOPHICAL DIVERSITY OF DISSENT

These considerations make all the more urgent the task of re-examining the way in which much modern criticism continues to assume as its starting point of investigation an inverted version of Enlightenment foundationalism, in the form of a hypostasised (cultural, historical, semantic) otherness. As I argued in Chapter 1, Habermas shows how postmodern historicism, by extending suspicion to the heart of thought itself, perpetuates the Hegelian radicalisation of epistemological doubt. It comes as no surprise then, that such criticism has come to focus on the negationist implications of what Keats refers to as 'half knowledge'.[30] Such implications appear less than inevitable, however, if we resist the conclusion that the breakdown of the correspondence theory of truth central to most empiricist epistemologies inevitably signals the end of objective 'truth'. Indeed, they appear still less unavoidable when one considers Keats's awareness of the alternative ways in which truth was being reconceptualised by the culture of dissent.

Habermas's commentary is again helpful here, in that it describes a space within which a notion of rational discourse continued to function despite the ebbing of the age of reason. Above all, Habermas shows how it remained possible for writing of this period, by replacing the paradigm of observation with 'linguistically mediated interaction', to avoid the paradox that '[n]o mediation is possible between the extramundane stance of the transcendental I and the intramundane stance of the empirical I'.[31]

In this way, romantic writers retained the wherewithal to dissent from the rationalism that Hume unravelled, thereby avoiding the hypostasisation of the subjective 'aesthetic gateway' as the other of reason, and reinvesting thought with a 'critical capacity for assessing value'.[32] Indeed, following Putnam, it is possible to go further than this, registering the ways in which romanticism pursues the revaluation of thought within value to the point where the division between 'within' and 'without', 'immanent' and 'transcendent', loses all focus. For 'holistic' Keats, writing as a form of transcendence or as a form of negation only makes sense against a background in which it is seen as a process entangled with value and everyday existence, an activity that articulates the conditions of living a good life. In this respect, the transvaluation of values always leads back to truth, not least because a limit-concept of truth is the very condition of talking about value, indeed of communicating at all.

However, Keats's underlying sense of truth as communicative action is not heaven-sent. Nor is it constant and unshaken. Its deepest roots lie in the break-up of a consensus in the political left in the late eighteenth century. At its peak in the early 1780s during the coalition government of the Rockingham Whigs, this included figures like Bentham, Burke, and Priestley.[33] Thanks to the radical educational programme developed at Enfield School by its founder John Ryland (a friend of Priestley) and continued by John Clarke, the father of Charles Cowden Clarke, Keats's early reading was grounded in this culture, with its commitment to disinterested inquiry, communication, and the energetic exercise of reason. But as Keats was poring over the school's copy of *The History of America*, William Robertson's account of man's advancement and of 'how the faculties of his understanding unfold' and 'progress through the different stages of society' was already sounding hollow in light of the upheavals of the 1790s and the first decade of the new century.[34] By the time he left Enfield in 1811, the politics of dissent had long since fractured along a variety of fault lines. One of the most fundamental of these fissures was the question of how events (including mental occurrences) relate to truth. This in turn meant completely rethinking the nature of reason. If, as Roe claims, the 'culture of progressive knowledge fostered by Ryland and the Clarkes transformed Keats with the intensity of a religious conversion and ... subsequently encouraged his developing sense of calling as a poet', Keats now found that the ideals of progressive knowledge, poetry and progressive politics seemed to pull in different directions.[35]

One way in which these pressures play out in Keats's intellectual life is in his increasingly mixed feelings about philosophy or speculative

thought, an ambivalence reflected in his attitudes to two people who
figure prominently in his life between the autumn of 1817 and the spring
of 1818: Benjamin Bailey and Charles Wentworth Dilke. Bailey and Dilke
quickly become stand-ins respectively for Hazlitt and Godwin, the two
brightest stars in Keats's intellectual firmament. It is Bailey, the Oxford
scholar, who introduces Keats to philosophical dialogue, renews his
interest in the dissenting concept of disinterestedness,[36] and becomes, at
least for a time, a personified ideal of rational speculation, the 'human
friend Philosopher'.[37] Bailey also encourages Keats to read Hazlitt,
through whom Keats accesses the idea of a sympathetic, projective
imagination asymptotically in pursuit of 'Truth' – an ideal entity, which,
in both writers, gradually exceeds its compensatory function, becoming a
power that supercedes the epistemic.[38] Thus, just as Hazlitt is increasingly
inclined to polarise art and knowledge, poetry and prose, Keats eventually
forsakes the Apollonian wisdom or historical 'knowledge enormous' of
the 'Hyperion' poems for the world of 'Lamia,' in which truth, once
grasped, vanishes forever (though, as I argue below, this vanishing has
further implications). Dilke meanwhile, affectionately becomes the
'Godwin perfectibil[it]y Man', whipping boy of a debunked and hopelessly unfashionable 1790s ultra-rationalism that continues to beat a
straight line towards truth.[39] Indeed, as Roe claims, it is likely that Keats
has Godwin in mind when he expresses his doubts to Bailey that any
'Philosopher ever arrived at his goal without putting aside numerous
objections'.[40]

Between them, these two figures of philosophy map out much of the
intellectual landscape that shapes Keats's subsequent career. Godwin lurks
behind the 'disquisition' with Dilke that crystallises Keats's rejection of
the 'dogmatic single-mindedness' that he finds so at odds with Shakespearean, negative capability.[41] Conversely, it is the chivalric performances
of Bailey, which raise and dash the expectations of the 'literal'-minded
Reynolds sisters,[42] that elicit a defence, courtesy of Keats's newfound
idealism, of the 'continual allegory' by which every man shapes his
existence, and of which Shakespeare's life is the most complete example.[43]
None the less, Keats would have been aware that the positions they
represented left a great expanse of reason uncharted. Despite their differences, Godwin and Hazlitt both assume that truth is a matter of
correspondence. Godwin, for the most part, clings to Paine's positivist
mantra that 'such is the irresistible nature of truth, that all it asks, and all
it wants, is the liberty of appearing';[44] while Hazlitt takes the infinite
recession of truth from perception as indicative of the formative power of

the imagination. Either way, the only *concept* of truth assumed to be at issue is one of concurrence between mind and world. Yet the possibilities that went into the diverse mix of dissenting discourse raised further options, one of which is implicit in the claim that Keats encountered near the beginning of Godwin's *Inquiry*, where he remarks that 'if there be such a thing as truth, it must infallibly be struck out by the collision of mind with mind'.[45] What Godwin taps into here, apparently without realising it, is a contemporary and competing view of truth as the inter-subjective coherence of belief, the social glue that makes communication possible. It is at this point that we need to register a divergence within the currents of philosophical radicalism: between the discourses of truth-idealism and truth-holism.

In one respect at least, it is curious that the gateway to idealism for Keats should be Hazlitt, for at first sight the implications of Hazlitt's thought appear to be the reverse of the idealistic. Indeed, on the face of it, Hazlitt's sustained assaults on ethical egoism and the dichotomy of abstract and particular attacks empiricism at its most vulnerable point: the relationship between form and content. To the ethical egoist's ques-tion, 'how is disinterested action conceivable?' Hazlitt's answer may be paraphrased as: under the same conditions that action, identity and ideas are conceivable. For Hazlitt, each of these cruxes depends upon the problem of determination, or, more specifically, of how practical reason, personhood, and concepts in general acquire *content*. In each case, he finds that content is critically underdetermined by objects encountered in the 'outside' world: there is, in other words, a failure of correspondence between mind and reality. Givenness gets us nowhere; sensation, taken *simpliciter*, is dead, unintelligible.

The only answer, Hazlitt infers, is that the mind's shortfall in content is underwritten by the formative power of the mind itself. Accordingly, all ideas, rather than subdividing into particular and abstract (as Locke would have it), or merely constituting a residue of linguistic abbreviations or 'subauditions' (as John Horne Tooke would have it) are, to a greater or lesser extent, abstract.[46] Without 'the cementing power of the mind', Hazlitt argues in his 1812 lecture on Tooke, 'all our ideas would be necessarily decomposed and crumbled down into their original elements and flexional parts'.[47] Similarly, just as action (whether of the selfish or benevolent kind) is inconceivable without personhood, so identity is impossible without the power by which the mind coalesces the bundle of perception into a coherent self: without it, 'I am not the same thing, but many different things'.[48]

Accordingly, in his *Letter to William Gifford, Esq.*, which Keats read, Hazlitt defends the composing power of mind on the grounds that without it, the 'present moment stands on the brink of nothing'. He maintains that the objective world, the idea of a future self and the notion of other selves are all 'fashioned out of nothing' by imagination.[49] By inflating the constitutive role of the mental, however, Hazlitt deepens rather than annuls the binary model of knowledge. This in turn ensures not only that both writers continue to be stalked by the shadow of Hume, but that Keats, so long as he follows Hazlitt's lead, enters into a language of entification that is ripe for the kind of negativity brought to bear by postmodern and historicist commentary. For his own part, Hazlitt, like Hume, remains ambivalent about the cognitive status of imagination. He shifts uneasily between his claim (in 'Coriolanus') 'that the imagination, generally speaking, delights in power, in strong excitement, as well as in truth, in good, in right, whereas pure reason and the moral sense approve only of the true and good',[50] and his insistence (in the *Letter to Gifford*) that 'an abstract principle is alone a match for the prejudices of absolute power', and that the 'love of truth is the best foundation for the love of liberty'.[51] Hazlitt feels able to have it both ways here because, as he sees it, the formative power that makes the world intelligible, that endows language with meaning and gives content to our beliefs, is the same power 'that breathes into all other forms the breath of life, and endows our sympathies with vital warmth, and diffuses the soul of morality through all the relations and sentiments of our social being'.[52] None the less, his brand of idealism remains rooted in a correspondence view of truth, albeit one in which, without the normative force of 'reasoning imagination',[53] the 'thing itself is a non-entity'.[54]

Elsewhere, however, the debate over abstraction throws up the possibility that the correspondence model is *itself* a hindrance to understanding the relationship between truth and meaning. The point, some argue, is not to establish how the relation between idea and object is calibrated, but to understand the links between truth and language, or communication. A suspicion of all dualities pervades this counterdiscourse. While empiricism supported a view of language as the reflection of truth and value, thinkers within the culture of dissent begin to see meaning and truth as entangled. Paine's question, 'When men are sore with the sense of oppressions . . . is the calmness of philosophy, or the palsy of insensibility, to be looked for?' draws much of its rhetorical strength from his assumption that the possibility of reason rests upon free communication and debate.[55] Indeed, Paine's celebrated 'familiar' style reflects his assumption that a shared understanding between writer and reader is the condition of interpretation as dialogue or conversation. Thus, his claim that 'Reason, like time, will make its own way, and prejudice will fall in a combat with interest' can be read as a statement of the pragmatic constraints in all human interaction rather than a dogmatic assertion of the teleological destiny of reason.[56] As Olivia Smith observes of the language of *Rights of Man*:

> By frequent use of rhetorical questions and frequent reference to an understand-ing shared between himself and the readers, Paine brings his readers into the book. 'I' and 'we' become two identities which share a relation and various activities. ... Paine discusses his book as if it were a dialogue ... there is a sense that the writer and the readers are engaging in a conversation at its best – free-ranging, intellectual, and vivid.[57]

The same assumption reminds us in turn that for Godwin the ever-present possibility of error was not always governed by some immutable law, but was just as likely to rest upon the pragmatic consideration that '[w]e cannot make one false step, without involving ourselves in a series of mistakes and ill consequences that must be expected to grow out of it'.[58]

None the less, rescuing a public model of reason from the ruins of subjectivity where it had been abandoned by Hume would involve a rejection of the correspondence model more comprehensive than Godwin or Paine envisaged. As Olivia Smith notes, it meant challenging the 'belief that the self and language existed in a simple and direct relation',[59] an assumption that had encouraged eighteenth-century language theorists to draw parallels between, on one hand, the distinction between the 'particular' and the 'general' in thought, and, on the other, the distinction between the 'vulgar' and the 'refined' in language. Correspondence theory in contemporary philosophies of language thus served an established order whereby only '[t]hose who spoke the refined language were allegedly rational, moral, civilized, and capable of abstract thinking'.[60] Hazlitt's bargain with disinterested imagination seeks to undermine this hierarchy under the auspices of a powerful intellect, but in doing so effectively concedes the existence of a reality for which the mind has no corresponding representation, ensuring that the imagination remains as much a compen-satory as a formative power of thought. As a result, truth's role in discourse becomes ontologically obscure, moving from the everyday material world into an ever-receding horizon. As Hazlitt notes, rather uneasily: 'Truth is not one thing, but has many aspects and many shades of difference'.[61]

Coexisting with this romantic chiaroscuro, however, was a drive to deflate and demystify the concept of truth altogether, led by Tooke's insight that 'Truth ... has been improperly imagined at the bottom of a well: it lies much nearer to the surface'.[62] Tooke, as Tom Paulin points out, is in Hazlitt's book simply 'a materialist who resembles Bentham in his literalness and lack of imagination'.[63] Yet, as I argued earlier, Tooke's deconstruction of ideas into words, together with Bentham's conversion of the basic units of meaning from words into propositions or sentences, help to reconceptualise truth along naturalistic lines, depicting it as a precondition of language rather than an entity 'beyond' reason. Thus, while Tooke and Hazlitt share a common purpose in discrediting 'theories of language which asserted an extreme dichotomy between experiential and abstract modes of thought', their methods contrast starkly: while Hazlitt stresses the priority of mind, Tooke argues that truth and meaning only emerge within a linguistic system, an interpretive community.

These debates were very much alive during Keats's lifetime: he would have encountered them at school, in the pages of the *Examiner*, in the writings of Paine, Hazlitt, and Godwin, and at the literary dinners of Hunt (a self-declared convert to Tooke).[64] If this is true, however, our understanding of the set of assumptions with which he was working must be revised. Read alongside the predominantly idealist voices of Hazlitt, Coleridge, and contemporary German philosophy, for example, Keats's writing might appear to self-deconstruct in the way that Rajan describes when she demonstrates how an author-centred hermeneutics of productivity, developed to forestall the displacement of ideas by language, unwinds through the negativity of reading.[65] On the other hand, appreciating the extent to which idealism competes with a radical empiricism that requires no fixed centre (ideal or otherwise) for meaning – but which sees the everyday processes of interpretation and communication as the conditions of, rather than the 'supplements' of truth – brings out a different side of Keats. Competing with an idealist Keats who remains attached to Hazlitt's view of truth as the unattainable goal of imagination, there is a holistic Keats who sees that truth is impossible without communication and that what Bentham calls the 'fiction' of truth is the first presupposition of dialogue. In turn, this tension between truth as ideal and truth as dialogue casts new light on the problem of Keats's style and how it relates to his conception of language.

STYLE: KITSCH AND DEIXIS

Keats's doubts about his background and education, his own entitlement to the poetic vocation, and above all his ability to *communicate* with an audience are rarely far from the surface in his writing. 'Sleep and Poetry',

famously, has more than a few passages contorted by the wrestling match
between over-assertiveness and hand-wringing self-doubt:

> Will not some say that I presumptiously
> Have spoken? that from hastening disgrace
> 'Twere better far to hide my foolish face?
> That whining boyhood should with reverence bow
> Ere the dread thunderbolt should reach? How!
> [. . .]
> Ah! rather let me like a madman run
> Over some precipice; let the hot sun
> Melt my Dedalian wings, and drive me down
> Convuls'd and headlong! Stay! an inward frown
> Of conscience bids me be more calm awhile.
>
> ('Sleep and Poetry', ll.270–4; 301–5)

Since Christopher Ricks identified the 'slips and leaps of the mind' that
innoculate Keats's early verse with a self-conscious, enabling embarrassment, the infelicities and instabilities of Keats's style have been read as
markers bearing a broader cultural significance.[66] This quality has
attracted a long line of descriptors, from the 'unmisgiving' style portrayed
by Hunt and John Bayley, to Levinson's idea of a style so transparently
literary it becomes 'in effect, *anti*-Literature: a parody',[67] to Hamilton's
notion of Keatsian 'kitsch' as the self-wounding 'allegory of art'.[68] What
these approaches generally share is the intuition that there is a close
connection between Keats's style and the type of sensibility expressed by
his ideal of poetic nonidentity, or negative capability. In addition, they
tend to view this connection in terms of a perceived tension between the
mediating agencies of language and the imperatives of a sovereign subjectivity. Andrew Bennett, for instance, writes of such slips as textual instabilities
'by which "thought" – the ideational or "thetic" – is apparently subsumed
within the suffocating sensuousness of "language" '.[69] Indeed, for Bennett,
solecism 'constitutes the necessary faulture of poetry, the inescapable friction
of the "personal" with the "social" ', of which the figure of reading is the
master-trope. Keats's work, he claims, highlights – and struggles to come to
terms with – the impossibility of reading, which, he maintains (following de
Man), 'can only ever be other to itself, constituting *itself* as a kind of
remainder or supplement of writing, while Romantic writing calls for an
impossible coincidence of reading with the event of inscription'.[70]

As we have seen with Rajan, however, once one drops the assumptions
that reading is beset by 'incommensurable' temporalities, that interpretation necessitates a metaphysical coincidence of subject and object, and

that language 'mediates' human intentions right from the start (thereby dooming such coincidence to failure), there is no reason why reading or interpretation should be 'impossible'. Indeed, by replacing a subject-based conception of thought with one based on communication, the dissenting counterdiscourse of Tooke and others obviates the problems of mediating between the 'personal' and the 'social'. The threats posed to the concepts of truth, meaning, and self by the 'mediation' and 'indeterminacy' of language fail to bite, once one rejects the idea that these concepts are *things* that can only be got at 'through' language, and instead recognise in them the basic presuppositions of communication and thought, 'without which, unreal as they are', as Bentham puts it, '*discourse* could not, scarcely even could *thought*, be carried on'.[71] When there is nothing to mediate, indeterminacy and contradiction are untroubling to a communicative reason whose foundations extend no further than the fact that human beings manage, more often than not, to understand each other. Accordingly, Bentham's theory of fictions depicts language itself as no more than the prevailing success of communication through the interpretation of intentions. Thus, just as objective indeterminacy is accepted as part of everyday communication, the fact that doubt and contradiction are essential parts of literary interpretation does not undermine the fact that the only thing that makes reading possible is the possibility of error.

Another way of putting this is that language is fundamentally deictic. All communication *indicates*, by presupposing a shared 'limit-concept' (as Putnam calls it) of truth.[72] We do not interpret *through* the 'medium' of language; nor is language some tool, itself neutral, to be used in the excavation of 'meaning'. It is its deictic nature, rather than its conventionality, that is language's condition of possibility. Accordingly, Robert Brinkley and Michael Deneen have revived Peirce's concept of 'the indexical as deictic gesture' in support of their claim that reference always involves an existential relation that obtains 'irrespective of the interpretant'. By showing how '[n]ot every sign depends on interpretation because not every meaning is conventional', they argue, this indexical quality in language obviates the de Manian 'demystification' of romantic conceptions of meaning.[73] Yet careful reading of Paine, Tooke, Godwin, and Bentham shows that, despite their differences, such writers are *already* offering an account of the relation between truth and meaning according to which the deictic nature of communication consists in the *presupposition* of a shared community of belief, rather than in the existence of the object itself. In this respect, they open up a position that is happy to allow (*pace* Brinkley and Deneen) the dependency of meaning upon interpretation in so far as they deny (*pace* de Man) that the immanence of truth to a discourse implies the 'conventionality' of that discourse. As Davidson argues, there is in the end no intelligible way of distinguishing between the notion of 'truth-immanent-to-a-discourse' and truth itself.

For Davidson, language is action, not a medium: no more and no less than communication, the understanding of others. 'Meaning' depends upon a series of trade-offs between intentions rather than the location of a single intention or the following of a rule. Indeed, far from being determined by conventions, language depends upon the breaking of conventions, of our 'prior' and 'passing' theories of interpretation. We can claim, then, that 'meaning' (such as it is) is always mobile or indeterminate, once we accept that meaning is interpretation and that interpretation itself amounts to the understanding of (verbal, physical, typographical) gestures under the possibility of error. Significantly, Davidson observes that the deictic nature of communication is conspicuous in written personal correspondence, where confidence in a shared understanding of intentions is strongest. However, just as Peirce sees the indexical as a precondition of reference, Davidson sees the deictic as fundamental to all communication. 'Writing,' he points out, 'has its ways ... of establishing ties between writer's intentions, reader, and the world.' Thus, while a personal letter can 'take advantage of a world of established mutual connections', this merely indicates how 'almost all connected writing that involves more than a few sentences depends on deictic references to its own text'.[74]

This casts the epistolary dimension to Keats's writing in an interesting light. Keats's letters are not unusual in taking advantage of established or implied mutual connections between writer, world, and reader. However, Keats is no ordinary letter writer. As Bennett notes, the epistolary mode offered Keats the chance to explore the rhetorical variations of writing 'to', 'at', and 'for' a reader. For Bennett, these experiments betray the 'impossibility of *knowing* the humour of one's epistolary (let alone poetic) addressee: instead, one must figure the reader, construct a role for audience'. All writing, by extension, becomes 'a form of postscript, a writing that comes after, determining its context in its reading, a reading which is always already "figured" '.[75] However, we are now in a position to drop the assumption that Keats is bound to a conception of '*knowing*' that implies a metaphysical correspondence, a coincidence of mind and world or mind and mind. Consequently, we can see how, by innovating within a community of shared, albeit mobile beliefs, and by shifting between the voices of friend, brother, lover, and poet, Keats is able to explore the articulation of the *implicit* that lies behind communication.

More significantly, by modulating between everyday prose and metre, conversation and versification, Keats deictically embeds poetry in what Taylor calls 'a form of life, a "world" of involvements' that can only be understood transcendentally, through the articulation of what is implied in our everyday engagements with the world and with others.[76] Keats's epistolary transitions between prose and verse root poetry firmly in the correspondence of the letter, and thus in the deictic gesture that is the *sine qua non* of communication. Working in a context in which faith in the correspondence between mind and world has largely collapsed, Keats's poetry engages with what Habermas calls communicative reason, the unity of which 'only remains perceptible in the plurality of its voices',[77] and the validity of which, within 'the structures of possible mutual understanding in language constitute something that cannot be gotten around'.[78]

This in turn raises the question of how such a dynamic enters Keats's style, particularly the early, mannered verse that so offended the sensibilities of contemporary audiences (and which still retains the capacity to make modern readers feel queasy). What is the relation between the deictic and Keatsian 'kitsch'? Take, for example, the following passages from *Endymion*, in which Venus arrives among her Cupids to wake the sleeping Adonis:

> But all were soon alive:
> For as delicious wine doth, sparkling, dive
> In nectar'd clouds and curls through water fair,
> So from the arbour roof down swell'd an air
> Odorous and enlivening; making all
> To laugh, and play, and sing, and loudly call
> For their sweet queen:
> [...]
> Soon were the white doves plain, with necks stretch'd out,
> And silken traces tighten'd in descent;
> And soon, returning from love's banishment,
> Queen Venus leaning downward open arm'd:
> Her shadow fell upon his breast, and charm'd
> A tumult from his heart, and a new life
> Into his eyes.   (*Endymion* 11, ll.510–16; 523–9)

Writing Book 11 of *Endymion* at Hampstead in the summer of 1817, Keats was struggling to escape the stylistic influence of Hunt. Yet passages such as this, as Bate notes, 'share a common softness and moistness' with Hunt's verse: 'we think, as we go through the endless episodes of *Endymion*, of pastries crudely baked but abundantly topped with whipped cream'.[79]

It was the overabundant, cloying sweetness of 'Junkets' that nauseated the palates of John Gibson Lockhart in *Blackwood's* and John Wilson Crocker in the *Quarterly*, just as the onanistic inefficacy of 'Jack Ketch' revolted Byron. For modern critics such as Levinson, the offence lurking behind these complaints lies in the double negative whereby Keats's Poetry effects the 'demystification of a prestigious mode of literary production'.[80] As Hamilton argues, albeit in a slightly different vein, by calling in the numinous credit of romantic poetry, Keatsian kitsch sets up a run on art, exposing the bankrupt economy of aesthetic value when hypostasised outside the actual activity of human communication.

However, if we accept that Keats is able to draw from reserves of communicative reason that extend beyond the mere negation of idealism, our view of the cumulative effect of Keatsian 'badness' or 'kitsch' should change. A comparison with Cobbett is illustrative. Kevin Gilmartin demonstrates how, far from being 'a "naïve" dream that left key problems "unthought-out"', the dissenting conception of communicative reason was alive to how 'truly "animating" or transformative effects are the result of communicative acts under specific social and institutional conditions'.[81] Thus, the 'interventionist formal realism'[82] behind Cobbett's inclusion of straw samples in his letter to the Society of Arts is indicative of how 'Cobbett engaged his readers and his world through . . . indexical or deictic gestures' that challenged notions of 'what constituted a fact in political discourse'.[83] At first sight, Keats's idiom appears the very reverse of Cobbett's. And yet, the cultures within which each writer worked were remarkably similar. Indeed, the initial impression – the 'offence' – created by Keats's poetry is a key component in the inverted way in which his writing highlights the deictic gestures (rather than the 'correspondences' or 'conventions') that keep human communication going. If Cobbett jolts us into this realisation, Keats draws us into it almost without our noticing.

The manner in which Keats achieves this is similar to that of other 'Protean' or self-effacing writers such as Shakespeare and Joyce. Davidson notes how these writers self-consciously test and defy the linguistic conventions of their readers. By raising 'the price of admission' to language, he finds, they foreground the cycle of creation and destruction behind any interpretive engagement.[84] By effacing their own presence in the text, Shakespeare and Joyce distance their readers from 'meaning' (construed either as a convention or as an intent of consciousness). In doing so, they force their readers to confront the fact that the only thing sustaining interpretation is the *assumption* that they and the writer are working within sets of beliefs that, for the most part, overlap: that they are, as it were, speaking the same language. Davidson's point is that by doing so, 'Protean' writers reveal that 'speaking the same language' does not mean having similar intentions, or sharing a rule book or a set of conventions for expressing those intentions. Rather, it can only ever amount to the presupposition that both parties (speaker and hearer, writer and reader) are (mostly) comprehensible to each other. Davidson likens this process to understanding malapropisms, which is possible even though linguistic conventions have been violated, and despite the fact that the speaker/ writer may even be unclear about their *own* intentions. Interpretation occurs in the mix of communicated intentions: we understand Mrs Malaprop in the same way that we understand challenging passages from Shakespeare and Joyce: that is, fundamentally, because we *assume* that they are comprehensible. That Mrs Malaprop 'gets away with it' indicates that the only thing sustaining 'meaning' is the principle of charity in interpretation.[85]

Overcoming the suspicion, now deeply ingrained in modern criticism, that where 'subjectivity' and 'language' inhabit the same arena interminable conflict must ensue, and registering the full significance of Keats's grounding in a philosophical discourse of communicative reason, we are placed in view of a rather different relationship between Keatsian style and negative capability. Keats's style is not bound into any negative dialectic, nor is it bound to self-deconstruct. Like Shakespeare, 'Camelion' Keats estranges his reader not from meaning as presence, but from language as mediation. Unlike Shakespeare, he achieves this in his early poetry through a style that is self-consciously conventional rather than challenging. If Shakespeare raises the price of admission to language, Keats lowers it. The outcome, however, is the same: Keats's language is so rich and inviting that it becomes a site of resistance: it repels. The alienation that many readers of *Endymion* feel is the product of a style that challenges by enticing: like Lamia, it wants to be loved far too much for comfort. Language this conventional, one feels, cannot be taken at face value: it is too seductive to be true. It is, as Hamilton puts it, 'kitsch'.

As Gilmartin observes (and as Cobbett and Keats knew only too well), '[d]oing things with words goes beyond the figures on a page'.[86] It is towards this realisation that Keats's luxurious language leads the reader, not by overt use of the indexical, but by pushing what is conventionally acceptable to the limit, to the point where, without some form of ostension, some indication of a shared space of values, the reader is left grasping at straws. As he effectively embellishes himself out of existence, Keats tightens the focus of both writer and reader on the *presupposition* that they are indeed playing the same game and that they hold (mostly) the same beliefs, many of which they are prepared to sacrifice in the cause of better understanding – that is, of better *communication*. In this way, by alienating his reader from the 'medium', Keats teases his reader not so much out of thought, as out of language.

THE BEAUTY OF TRUTH: ELENCHUS
AND 'ODE ON A GRECIAN URN'

It is one thing to say that Keats is able to rely upon the assumption that language has a deictic relationship with truth; it is quite another to say that he carries this belief around with him like a doctrine: while the first is true, the second, clearly, is not. Keats does not have a 'theory' of truth in this sense, and any attempt to find one will be frustrated. None the less, his sense that a shared concept of truth is the presupposition of discourse is one that he shares with an identifiable philosophical strain within dissenting culture. When this tacit understanding meets Hazlitt's epistemological idealism, however, two figures struggle for dominance: on one hand, a sceptical, idealist, and ultimately negationist Keats, and on the other, a communicative, dialogic, and holistic Keats.

To unpick these entanglements, it is necessary above all to recognise how in Keats negativity is fed by idealism. Once truth is hypostasised as a thing, a possession of the mind; 'whatever imagination seizes' or 'Adam's dream', as he writes to Bailey in 1817, the impossibility of verification on the empirical model of correspondence ensures that aesthetic compensation quickly turns into negativity.[87] Like Hazlitt, Keats found the notion of a synthesis of truth and beauty, cognisable by a 'reasoning imagination', impossible to sustain.[88] Thus, two years later, he includes the sonnet 'Why did I laugh tonight?' in his journal letter to George and Georgiana Keats only after a prefaced apology reassures them that it was written 'with no thirst of anything but knowledge'.[89] This particular entry in the letter, dated Friday 19 March 1819, is significant in a number of respects, but two stand out in the present context. The first is the way in which it testifies to how, once the dream of imaginative truth breaks down, beauty returns to haunt thought with an unthinkable intensity. Keats's apology includes the excuse of 'a sort of temper indolent and supremely careless' acquired from having overslept, but this is clearly not the only influence under which he is writing.[90] Specifically, Hazlitt's notion of disinterestedness forms the background to Keats's attempt to 'reason'[91] on the prevalence of what Wordsworth calls the 'ellectric fire' of benevolence in human nature that like Keats's late morning 'langour' counteracts the 'animal' interests of poetry, ambition, and love.[92]

Keats's bulwark of 'disinterested' reason, however, is itself the cause of the very problem that it is enlisted to contain. It is idealism's very hypostasisation of 'truth' as an impossible goal, one which must be grasped sensuously as well as intellectually, that provokes both Hazlitt's suspicion that poetry is regressive (that it will more often than not sacrifice truth to power), as well as Keats's sense of poetry's inferiority to philosophy – '[f]or the same reason', as he puts it, 'that an eagle is not so fine a thing as a truth'.[93] In both writers, rational thought and aesthetic plenitude, initially seen as mutually sustaining, swiftly become antagonists. While in Hazlitt the epistemic imperative gives way to the psychology of power, in Keats the 'knowledge enormous' of 'Hyperion' (a poem that was foundering even as he wrote this letter) comes to be threatened by tropes of thoroughly noncognitive intensity that connote contingency and death. The closing couplet of the poem 'Why did I laugh tonight?' reveals how the inflatus of poetry and beauty merely provokes the horror of thought's negations, namely contingency (the 'Circumstances ... like Clouds continually gathering and bursting')[94] and death: 'Verse, fame and Beauty are intense indeed / But Death intenser – Death is Life's high Mead'.[95]

The story of how, under Hazlitt's influence, Keats vacillated between knowledge and poetry, truth and beauty, is a familiar one. The brief intermission (probably only a few weeks) required for Keats to reverse the closing lines of 'Why did I laugh tonight?' into the final motto of 'Ode on a Grecian Urn', is surprising only if one forgets how idealism in both Keats and Hazlitt is constructed in such a way as perpetually to vacillate between aesthetic consolation and aesthetic alienation. I have already argued that Keats was aware of a holistic alternative to Hazlitt's idealism currently emerging through the debates within dissenting culture. This alternative, however, which stressed the intimate connection between truth and communication, was in itself far from new. Indeed, Keats's citation of Socrates as (with Jesus) one of only two people he can think of who 'have hearts comp[l]etely disinterested' brings us to the second noteworthy feature of the 19 March letter: what it suggests about the extent to which holism was already bound up with Keats's understanding of Plato.[96]

The question of Keats's Platonism is often linked to that of whether – and if so, how – the closing lines of 'Ode on a Grecian Urn' articulate the 'leaf-fring'd legend' that 'haunts' about the 'shape' of the urn. Against those who dismiss Keats's acquaintance with Platonic philosophy as too slight to be of any importance, Douka E. Kabitoglou has sided with earlier scholars such as Gittings by suggesting that the poet's pivotal stay with Bailey at Oxford not only led him to read Wordsworth's 'Ode: Intimations of Immortality from Early Childhood' alongside Plato's *Timaeus*, but also prompted Keats to make the distinction between the 'old' philosophy of Platonism valorised in 'On Seeing a Lock of Milton's Hair' and the 'cold' philosophy of empiricism disparaged in 'Lamia'.[97] This claim has some plausibility, if for no other reason than that it tallies with Keats's famously ambivalent attitude towards philosophy, caught between his admiration for Bailey–Hazlitt idealism and his cheerful scorn for Dilke–Godwin perfectibilism. The 19 March letter entry appears to confirm that he connected Hazlitt's defence of disinterestedness to an ancient, Socratic tradition of thought. And yet, this tradition had a more obvious modern analogue in contemporary linguistic empiricism.

The tension in Plato's dialogues between doctrine and method, or more specifically between idealism and elenchus, is well attested. Kathleen Wheeler uses this friction as the basis for her argument that, in so far as it defines 'Knowledge and right opinion … as dynamic, as relational, as the connections between things – not as univocal, discursive statements couched in some notionally neutral (literal) language', romantic discourse is rooted in a tradition of 'Socratic anti-rationalism'.[98] Thus, Coleridge and Shelley's 'challenge to traditional philosophy takes the form of a dynamic synthesis of Platonic/Socratic philosophy with empiricism … expressing itself through the ancient conceptualisation of the reconciliation of opposites'.[99] As Davidson points out, however, elenchus in Socrates is carefully balanced by an understanding of the deictic element inherent in all communication. Plato's ultimately fruitless search for a method that might bring to the consistency and coherence of belief fostered by elenchus a measure of objectivity through correspondence, Davidson argues, finally led him to the realisation that objectivity itself depends upon the *assumption* that most of our beliefs cannot be false. 'Thus,' he observes, 'someone who practises the elenchus can, as Socrates repeatedly did, claim that he does not know what is true; it is enough that he has a method that leads to truth'.[100] Only in this way – that is, by understanding how the elenctic and the deictic are related in argument and everyday communication – can one see what was really at stake in the Socratic empiricism that Wheeler identifies in Coleridge and Shelley. It is likely that what Davidson calls the 'good Socratic intuition' that 'it is only in the context of frank discussion, communication, and mutual exchange that trustworthy truths emerge' struck as much of a chord with Keats, primed by the dissenting value of free debate, as any metaphysical doctrine.[101]

What, then, does this tell us about the 'Ode on a Grecian Urn'? First, it suggests that there is more going on in the famous closing lines than an idealist sleight of hand whereby the deathly intensity of beauty in the final couplet of 'Why did I laugh tonight?' reappears, inverted, as transcendent harmony:

> When old age shall this generation waste,
>   Thou shalt remain, in midst of other woe
> Than ours, a friend to man, to whom thou say'st,
>   'Beauty is truth, truth beauty,' – that is all
> Ye know on earth, and all ye need to know.
>   ('Ode on a Grecian Urn', ll.56–60)

The poem's idealism should be assessed according to how it deals with the problem of determination, a problem signalled not merely by the narrator's dogged engagement with the underdetermined, 'silent form' of the urn, but also, as Kabitoglou indicates, by the way in which the chiasmus 'Beauty is truth, truth beauty' indicates the disruption of conventional subject/predicate relations.[102] In the 19 March letter entry, poetry, ambition, and love are determined through a tranquillised disinterest that attests to the power of mind, seeming 'rather like three figures on a greek vase,' Keats writes, 'whom no one but myself could distinguish in their disguisement'.[103] In the 'Ode' however, the underdetermination of form is *not* answered by an act whereby the formative imagination manages somehow to wrest meaning from the incommensurable 'shape' of the vase. The rhetoric of projection, indeed, is notably absent from the poem.

What remains, then, is elenchus. For even as Hazlitt argued that the mind overdetermines its object, other influences (including what Wheeler calls 'Socratic' empiricism) indicated that *language* determines – and for Keats, like Bentham, 'language' meant *dialogue*. For these writers, the lesson of Socrates is that meaning is determined by discourse: that is, by the pragmatics of mutual understanding in which the possibility of error is ever-present. From this perspective, the determination of the content of the urn's 'leaf-fring'd legend' is attributable not to Platonic forms, the formative mind, or the incommensurable agencies of grammar or history. Instead, it is sustained by the poet-narrator's persistent questioning, by his assumption that the intelligibility of his own questions (the possibility that they might be true or false) is itself the condition of interpretation. With no objectivity other than what it gains through communication, truth is something that the 'Ode' moves *from* as much as *towards*. It has no inside or outside. If this means that truth itself is indeterminate, that it can never be defined, Keats remains unperturbed: all that we know of truth on earth, and all we need to know, is that it enables us to communicate, even when our questions struggle to bridge cultural, historical, and linguistic otherness. As Davidson notes, Socratic dialogue demonstrates that just because truth is an indefinable concept 'does not mean we can say nothing revealing about it: we can, by relating it to other concepts like belief, desire, cause and action' – or, Keats would add, beauty.[104]

LAMIA'S SYMPOSIUM

As he moved between the Isle of Wight, Winchester, and London through the summer and autumn of 1819, Keats's sense of the delicate interdependence between dialogue, truth and life helped to shape two of his most philosophically self-conscious poems: 'Lamia' and 'The Fall of Hyperion'. In different ways, both poems turn on problems of communication. In 'Lamia' the breakdown of communication between Apollonius, Lamia, and Lycius symbolically brings about the death of the lovers, while 'The Fall of Hyperion', like its predecessor, 'Hyperion: A Fragment', founders on the question of how the incommensurable language of the Gods can possibly be translated into a form fit for human understanding. Yet, while on one level the discovery of truth appears inimical to imaginative communion in 'Lamia', and resistant to language in 'The Fall of Hyperion', on another level both poems move to reconfigure truth and objectivity as *dependent* upon communication and contact between persons in a shared world.

Dialogue, indeed, plays a central role in 'Lamia', whose philosophical concerns are announced by the pre-Socratic backcloth of Corinth, by the fact that we first encounter Lycius 'lost, where reason fades, / In the calm'd twilight of Platonic shades' (1.ll.235–6), and in the way the final denouement travesties the dialogue form. Whether or not Keats read much Plato in Oxford, the peripatetic setting of the poem is particularly suggestive when read against the enforced silences of the final scene. An uninvited presence at the wedding feast, the reproving 'eye severe' (11.l.157) of the anti-Socratic Apollonius suppresses dialogue and gags debate. As in the *Symposium*, the party ends in chaos, but where the love-idealism debate of the *Symposium* breaks up in a riot of gatecrashers, in a curious and unsettling twist the banquet of 'Lamia' breaks *down* through a failure of argument, a refusal of communication. What is most striking about this closing passage is the way in which the triangulation required for mutual understanding quickly disintegrates once the demands of understanding others are subjugated to intellectual penetration. Gradually, the space of communication contracts and recedes into the unresponsive 'eye' of a beholding subject, an unresponsive spectator. This process is initiated by Apollonius, as we discover when Lycius turns:

> to beseech a glance
> From his old teacher's wrinkled countenance,
> And pledge him. The bald-headed philosopher
> Had fix'd his eye, without a twinkle or a stir
> Full on the alarm'd beauty of the bride   ('Lamia', 11.ll.243–7)

Lycius' desperate attempts at communication are frustrated by Apollonius' concentrated, Dilke-like *pursuit* of truth, a pursuit that annihilates speech:

> Poor Lamia answered not.
> He gaz'd into her eyes, and not a jot
> Own'd they the lovelorn piteous appeal:
> More, more he gaz'd: his human senses reel:
> Some hungry spell that loveliness absorbs;
> There was no recognition in those orbs   ('Lamia', 11.ll.255–60)

This breakdown in communication, as Levinson notes, is the result not so much of Lamia's duplicity as the penetrating, truth-seeking gaze of Apollonius. For Levinson, Apollonius' association with the school of Pythagoras in turn suggests 'an association of philosophy – indeed, *truth* – with mathematics', and thus the murderously contemplative discourse that commodifies quality as quantity.[105] If Apollonius represents the abstracting urge of empiricism distilled into its economic reality, the gaze through which Lamia's personhood is objectified out of existence, Lamia in turn becomes the capitalist-empirical ideal of signification: the perfect correspondence postulated by empirical rationalism in the form of 'an identity of thought and extension, form and content, Truth and Beauty'.[106] She is, in Levinson's view, money, the 'absolute' value refined into nothing by the economic logic of the very philosophical discourse that created her:

> 'Fool! Fool!' repeated he, while his eyes still
> Relented not, nor mov'd ...
> Then Lamia breath'd death breath; the sophist's eye,
> Like a sharp spear, went through her utterly,
> Keen, cruel, perceant, stinging: she, as well
> As her weak hand could any meaning tell,

Motion'd him to be silent; vainly so,
He look'd and look'd again a level – No!   ('Lamia', 11.ll.295–304)

Paul Endo takes this argument a stage further by claiming that Apollonius unwittingly exposes the 'romance' of truth at the heart of any discourse. By seeking correspondence where there are only conventions, Apollonius sees *through* Lamia's conventionality but *discovers* nothing. Lamia vanishes and Lycius dies because Apollonius strips away the romance of imagined social relations without which no subject can exist, what Endo calls 'the shared prejudices, conventions, recognitions, and misrecognitions ... that decide what can and cannot be accepted'. What Apollonius stumbles across, then, is the possibility that the 'authority of reason over romance may thus involve nothing more than the weight that makes its organizing protocols so much more difficult to ignore'.[107] Indeed, 'reason may be more deluded than romance insofar as it does not recognize, as Lamia does, that there exists an unassimilable other from which it must remain hidden'.[108] Apollonius inadvertently betrays that delusion, and thus the 'open secret' upon which truth depends, the 'fantastic belief that is not really a belief, that is never submitted (or never *allowed* to be submitted) to the testing conventionally believed to verify belief'.[109]

Such conventionalist readings of 'Lamia', however, tend to assume that the principal target in Keats's critique of Apollonius' 'cold philosophy' (11.l.230) is objectivity itself. Consequently, if 'Lamia' is an allegory, it would appear to be, as Bennett puts it, an allegory of the destructiveness 'of philosophy, reason, criticism, or allegorical reading' as well as 'the necessity, the inevitability, and the impossibility of allegorical reading'.[110] And yet, while Apollonius' 'cold philosophy' smacks as much of Newton as Pythagoras in its ability to 'Conquer all mysteries by rule and line' (11.l.235) and 'Unweave a rainbow' (11.l.237), he is repeatedly referred to as a 'sophist' (11.ll.172; 291; 299), whose ' "juggling eyes" ' (11.l.277), ' "impious proud-heart sophistries, / Unlawful magic, and enticing lies" ' are, for Lycius, as much to blame for Lamia's evaporation as any act of abstract analysis. The pre-Socratic Apollonius, then, embodies more than just Pythagorean number-fetishism; he is simultaneously associated with the 'juggling' rhetoric of relativism and the tendency of philosophy to think 'outside' the web of ordinary human relationships and communication. By combining Pythagorean analysis and Sophism in the figure of Apollonius, the poem suggests that alienating abstraction and worship of rhetoric are two of a kind. Both lose sight of truth: one, like Godwin, by aiming straight at it; the other, like Hazlitt, by insisting on the conventionality of human norms (imaginative projections).

Apollonius' gaze kills the lovers, then, not by objectifying Lamia as such, but by refusing the very communicative activity that *sustains* objectivity. Closing down conversation and silencing debate, it destroys the 'recognition' (11.l.260) of the intentions of others necessary for mutual understanding. Lamia's vanishing and Lycius' subsequent death on the 'sharp spear' of the 'sophist's eye' (11.ll.299–300) suggest that Keats's philosophical allegory is one in which both the dream of correspondence (the empiricist's fantasy) and negativity (the sophist's diagnosis) are seen as destructive to life. Thus, the denouement of 'Lamia' becomes the terrifying image of a world without dialogue. A travesty of the Socratic elenchus, it discredits idealism and relativism alike. If the 'open secret' of 'Lamia' is that truth cannot exist without communication, without 'organizing protocols' and interpretive practices, it is equally clear that there is no going 'outside' these practices to establish that we have things right or, indeed, to discover that what we consider to be 'right' is a relative matter. To accept this, however, is just to make the very admission that Apollonius and much modern commentary on Keats resist: that truth has *no* outside, no measure, no 'unassimilable other'. The 'fantastic belief that is not really a belief' at the heart of 'Lamia' is that the *sine qua non* of intelligent life is the *presupposition* of truth in communication. This presupposition is an act of charity in interpretation: once refused, truth falls apart, and with it the possibility of intelligent life. Significantly, death in 'Lamia' is peremptory and empty. Gone is the rich, sickly-sweet death of aesthetic negation; the dissolution here has the sudden emptiness and absence that marks the inconceivable:

> 'A Serpent!' echoed he; no sooner said,
> Than with a frightful scream she vanish'd:
> And Lycius' arms were empty of delight,
> As were his limbs of life, from that same night.   ('Lamia', 11.ll.305–8)

Like 'Ode on a Grecian Urn', 'Lamia' suggests that Keats was beginning to question the truth-hypostasising tendency of Hazlitt's idealism. At the same time, he was increasingly drawn to an idea of truth as the precondition of communicative action. To the end, his writing suspends itself between these two lines of dissenting thought. Against the Socratic empiricism that envisages truth as the indeterminate postulate of dialogue, there is the lure of Adam's dream, the promise of a perfect correspondence of conception and reality in the life of allegory, a harmony of word and object, figure and truth. Keats is aware that fantasies such as these feed on failures. If the correspondence model of truth worked, such fantasies would not exist. And yet, like Hazlitt, idealist Keats grasps for such remedies in case language moves to fill the divide between consciousness and world. For Socratic, holistic Keats, however, empiricism's greatest bogeys – relativism, and the spectre of knowledge determined by language – are themselves the by-products of its own ideal of correspondence.

HYPERION'S GRAVE

Key to understanding how Keats struggled to overcome the uneasy tension between these two views of language are the 'Hyperion' poems, and in particular the transition in Keats's thinking that occurred between the abandonment of 'Hyperion' in the spring of 1819 and the commencement of *The Fall of Hyperion* a few months later. The first 'Hyperion' fails for a number of reasons, but among these is the problem of translation: the logical snag of how to narrate the origins of a discourse that determines the poem's own telling. As Apollo pleads with Mnemosyne for the understanding through which he will create a new poetic language ('Point me out the way / To any one particular beauteous star, / And I will flit into it with my lyre' (III.ll.99–101)), the analogy with Keats's own problems in accounting for the 'mute' sources of his own language is clear. By attempting to tell the story of its own Apollonian inception, Keats's poetic narrative is faced with the same conundrum of an absent origin:

> 'Goddess benign, point forth some unknown thing:
> 'Are there not other regions than this isle?
> [. . .]
> 'Mute thou remainest – mute! yet I can read
> 'A wondrous lesson in thy silent face:
> 'Knowledge enormous makes a God of me.'
> ('Hyperion,' III.ll.95–6; 111–13)

Keats's description of Apollo's awakening recalls William Robertson's account of how the uneven progress of historical knowledge allows the attentive historian, having charted 'the progress of darkness' in a culture, to turn to the 'more pleasant exercise' of observing 'the first dawnings of returning light'.[111] However, as Keats knows, the image of historical data flowing freely into Apollo's brain highlights the indeterminacy of the relationship between (mental) 'form' and (historical) 'content'. It is this indeterminacy that undermines Robertson's assumption of the possibility of 'scrupulous accuracy' in 'evidence' and 'proof' in historical inquiry:[112]

'Majesties, sovran voices, agonies,
'Creations and destroyings, all at once
'Pour into the wide hollows of my brain
'And deify me . . .'   ('Hyperion', III.ll.115–18)

For all his confidence about the 'grand march of intellect', Keats had learned from Hazlitt that the interpretive mind exerts a formative influence on the past.[113] Yet Hazlitt's idealism demands a sublimation of historical truth ill-suited to Keats's epic mode and potentially compromising to his ostensibly neutral, third-person narrative. Apollo's mystification at his own enlightenment all too effectively figures the narrator's own lack of insight into the source of his own 'meaning'. This, according to Christopher Bode, is the logical faulture within the historical narrative of 'Hyperion'. Caught in 'a paradox of his own temporality', Keats has no choice but to abandon the poem.[114] For Bode, the crucial transition in Keats's thought that enables the poet to resurrect the project in *The Fall of Hyperion* is signalled by the reformulation of the 1817 poetics of 'negative capability' as the 1819 poetics of the 'vale of soul-making'. Only through the latter is Keats able to conceive of knowledge itself as historically relative, licensing the historically situated narrator of *The Fall* to incorporate temporality into the voice of the poem. Where 'Hyperion' is an unintended failure, Bode argues, *The Fall* is a 'necessary failure',[115] which self-consciously 'insists on being a translation', enacting 'the "necessarily false" transitional stage of communication'. Acknowledging the incommensurability of languages, *The Fall of Hyperion* demonstrates that in interpretation, 'periphrasis and catachresis are as close as one can get' to the understanding of otherness.[116]

Keats was certainly sufficiently concerned about the problem of language to open *The Fall* with a rather awkward apologia in which the poet is figured as visionary and intermediary rolled into one. The logic of this passage, which does little to support Moneta's later claim that 'The poet and the dreamer are distinct, / Diverse, sheer opposite, antipodes' (1.ll.199–200), suggests that all that distinguishes the dream of the poet from that of the 'Fanatic' and the 'savage' is that the first is written down:

For Poesy alone can tell her dreams,
With the fine spell of words alone can save
Imagination from the sable charm
And dumb enchantment. Who alive can say
'Thou art no poet; may'st not tell thy dreams'?
Since every man whose soul is not a clod
Hath visions, and would speak, if he had lov'd
And been well nurtured in his mother tongue.
                    (*The Fall of Hyperion*, 1.ll.8–15)

While the tensions in this fragment – between dream as innocence and escapism; between poetry as the guardian of imagination and the agent of social change – have exercised many commentators, it is conceivable that they were introduced as an opening dilemma that the poem was ulti-mately intended to resolve.[117] Yet though Keats had other concerns pressing upon him in the autumn of 1819, his inability to complete the Hyperion poem at the second attempt suggests his ongoing struggles with the conceptual framework of the poem. In this respect, Bode's diagnosis has a ring of truth to it: *The Fall*, no less than its predecessor, finds it difficult to reconcile the narrator's role as visionary and as translator. On one hand, the charm of Moneta's words instil within the poet:

> A power within me of enormous ken,
> To see as a God sees, and take the depth
> Of things as nimbly as the outward eye
> Can size and shape pervade.
> (*The Fall of Hyperion*, 1.ll.303–6)

Even as the narrator takes on the 'enormous' knowledge of Apollo, however, the mediating force of language intervenes. Indeed, the contra-diction at the heart of the poem is such that the more the speaker's insight gathers power the less the events in heaven seem commensurable with the human; similarly, the more the poet insists on the immediacy of his vision, the less the language of the Titans appears comprehensible. As Moneta cautions at the beginning of the second Canto:

> 'Mortal, that thou may'st understand aright,
> 'I humanize my sayings to thine ear,
> 'Making comparisons of earthly things;
> 'Or thou might'st better listen to the wind,
> 'Whose language is to thee a barren noise,
> 'Though it blows legend-laden through the trees.'
> (*The Fall of Hyperion*, 2.1–6)

Like the narrator, the reader is never far from the predicament of Apollo, surprised at the possibility of comprehending the mute testimony of an incommensurable discourse, yet understanding it none the less. At this point, one might be tempted to side with critics such as Bode and Bennett and find in the compositional history of the 'Hyperion' poems an allegory of the impos-sible necessity of interpretation. Certainly, the more one studies the 'Hyperion' poems, the more they seem to brood over the very (im)possibility of their own existence. The enigma they reveal is not so much that we do not 'understand', but that we do not understand *how* we understand. However, to view the *The Fall of Hyperion* as a 'necessary failure' begs the question of just what Keats saw to be at stake in interpretation. It assumes that his only way of framing our failure to know *how* we know is the self-deconstructing dream of truth, the image of a vision that repeatedly throws itself onto the thorns of language.

My argument in this chapter, however, has been that in Keats the negativity that might transform idealism into metaphysical irony is frequently obviated by a counterdiscourse of reason that refuses to hypostasise 'meaning' and 'truth'. Thus, what Bode sees as 'periphrasis' in Keats's poetry, I see as 'paraphrasis', in Bentham's sense: a non-foundational conception of translation that overcomes the paradox of the incommensurable. On this view, 'meaning' is seen as mobile; it is not a matter of correspondence, but of interpretation. Once it is allowed that 'meaning' consists in what a person can imagine others might imagine her to intend, language, whether written or spoken, becomes less of a mediating presence in communication and more like one among a number of deictic gestures by which we understand the world and other people. At the same time, objective truth is not compromised by the fact that interpreter and interpretant are altered in the act of communication: it *depends* upon it, just as that same act depends upon a shared concept of truth. Keats's background in radical, 'Socratic' empiricism enables him to conceive of elenchus as a process that transforms people *because* it presupposes truth. It is this presupposition, I would argue, that lies behind the paradoxes of the suggestive but mute Mnemosyne and the barren but 'legend-laden' wind mentioned by Moneta, both of which recall the pregnant silence of the urn, the incommensurable barrier of culture and history that Keats's poet overcomes with dialogic interpretation.

This is not to say that any of these poems should be read as hymns to holism. As the fractured remains of the 'Hyperion' poems attest, Keats's own tangled intellectual allegiances confound such pigeonholing. But this caution also applies to deconstructive and historicist readings of Keats that are so confident in their negativity that they are apt to overlook a more pragmatic Keats, the Keats who assures George and Georgiana that, having written 'Why did I laugh tonight?', 'Sane I went to bed and sane I arose'.[118] The afterthought is vital, for it is in the sanity of correspondence with friends, relatives, and lovers – in the democratic 'fellowship' of intelligence – that Keats's dream of truth is kept alive. For Keats, no less than for Shelley and Coleridge, philosophy and truth depend upon community. By ignoring this, one misses the significance of other deceptively casual phrases, such as those with which Keats closes the opening passage of *The Fall of Hyperion*: 'Whether this dream now purposed to rehearse / Be poet's or fanatic's will be known / When this warm scribe my hand is in the grave' (*The Fall of Hyperion*,' 1.ll.16–18).

The importance that Keats attaches to this 'induction' of *The Fall* is reflected in the fact that he included lines 1 to 11 in his letter of 22 September to Richard Woodhouse.[119] In the same letter, he complains of 'Isabella' that 'It is too smokeable ... There is too much inexperience of live, and simplicity of knowledge in it .... There are very few would look to the reality. I intend to use more finesse with the Public. It is possible to write fine things which cannot be laugh'd at in any way'.[120] The new, self-consciously indirect narrative of *The Fall*, together with its recondite 'induction' is a product of this determination. In the closing lines of the induction, however, Keats's 'finesse' consists in the performance of a deictic gesture of a particular kind, one that encourages the reader to 'look to the reality' behind what appears to be an expression of indifference, a resigned shrug of the poetic shoulders. In this way, what is, on the face of it, a disclaimer, a typical Keatsian deferral of authority to posterity, simultaneously relocates the authority of written testimony from the realm of the ideal to the sphere of communication.

This transfer of authority is achieved through the manner in which these lines deftly interleave three key aspects of Keats's thought: his view of writing as 'correspondence'; his idea of a fellowship of discourse in which interpretation is transformative; and his sense of the interdependence of the deictic and the elenctic in communication. To see this, we first need to be aware that the transfer of warmth through the contact of a human hand is for Keats a sign both of fellowship *and* of the change that we undergo through dialogue. The significance of this association of warmth, contact, and communication is evident from his earliest poetry. In the 1816 poem 'To Charles Cowden Clarke', for example, social contact, even everyday correspondence, becomes vital to the coherent flourishing of thought. Keats describes a process whereby the contemplation of nature and the writing of 'rhymes and measures' (l.98) leads him, 'as my hand was warm' (l.103), to write a letter to Clarke that itself *becomes* the poem, concluding with a handshake: 'Again I shake your hand, – friend Charles, good night' (l.132). Such complex relations between nature, language, and intersubjectivity underpin the close connection between poetry and correspondence. For Keats (in this vein, at least), all writing is 'correspondence', in so far as it depends for its truth upon human contact, and above all upon the transfer of 'warmth' that signifies not so much the 'presence' of meaning, as the *transformation* that we undergo in any act of communication.

It is no coincidence, then, that it is in correspondence that Keats's wordplay – the kind of punning that gives the final line of the 'induction' its significance – was allowed free rein. Punning is an important currency in the Keats circle – indeed, in Cockney culture in general – and, as James Chandler indicates in his close reading of Shelley's 'England in 1819', the possibilities of words such as 'grave' – suggesting not just death but burial, concealment, writing, and the forbidden image – are seldom over-looked.[121] What is striking about Keats's use of the term here, however, is not merely that it forges a strong connection between writing and the transformative/connective power of interpretation, but that in doing so it divests even the trope of death of its aura of incommensurable otherness. No longer, it seems, is it merely 'rich to die': the 'grave' itself ceases to be a barrier to mutual understanding once truth is seen as the product of a dialogue that takes place between peoples and cultures, past and present. The same idea is at work in the poem that Keats wrote on the reverse of his manuscript of 'The Cap and Bells':

> This living hand, now warm and capable
> Of earnest grasping, would, if it were cold
> And in the icy silence of the tomb,
> So haunt thy days and chill thy dreaming nights
> That thou would wish thine own heart dry of blood,
> So in my veins red life might stream again,
> And thou be conscience-calm'd. See, here it is –
> I hold it towards you.[122]

Just as in the 'induction' to *The Fall*, the power of this poem lies in the deictic gestures of '*This* living hand' and '*this* warm scribe my hand,' but it is above all the ostension 'See, here it is – ' that ensures that the readers 'look to the reality'. Immediacy here is not the merely 'given': it depends upon interpretation, upon dialogue, elenchus. Similarly, what *The Fall of Hyperion* indicates is something that is true for 'holistic' Keats generally, namely, that the value of our dreams and imaginings does not rest in an ideal inflatus that alternately privileges and negates poetic insight. Instead, it depends upon a notion of a truth that is presupposed by all communi-cative activity. Thus in poetry, just as in correspondence – indeed, in writing generally – the only test of authenticity is whether (pun intended) 'this warm scribe my hand is in the grave'.

CONCLUSION

I have argued that the celebrated anti-epistemic turn in Keats is multi-faceted in ways that commentary has tended to overlook. This oversight is largely down to the propensity in modern criticism to identify a traditional concept of 'truth' with a particular model of 'correspondence', and through that with specific ideals of subjectivity and neutrality. This is all the more remarkable when one considers that Keats was quite familiar with alternative models, foremost among which was the conception of truth as the presupposition of discourse, which, pioneered by Tooke and later Bentham, had already found its way into the language of philosophers such as Paine and Godwin. Consequently, negative capability translates into negativity less obligingly when Keats's self-effacing, hyper-conventional style is seen to highlight rather than deconstruct the deictic dimension of language. At the same time, Keats's indifference, his willingness never to be in the right, appears less carelessly noncognitive when it is read against a cultural climate in which the fusion of Socratic method with an otherwise moribund empiricism provided an opportunity to see objectivity itself as immanent to the elenctic method through which dialogue – and through dialogue, thought – was sustained. In short, 'indifferent' Keats morphs into 'holistic' Keats wherever he finds it possible to substitute the 'correspondence' of mind and world for the 'correspondence' between two or more people communicating in a shared world.

Throughout this chapter, I have suggested that a helpful way of thinking about Keats's dilemma is in terms of the relationship between form and content. Thus, while Hazlitt's postulation of the 'formative mind' as a means of overcoming the problem of underdetermination in traditional empiricist models of meaning and knowledge leaves 'indifferent' Keats vacillating between intensity and knowledge, 'holistic' Keats puts the dichotomies of form/content, mind/world, and reason/sensation on hold, opting instead for a view of meaning and knowledge as socially determined. 'Truth holism', of course, no more implies 'truth relativism' to Keats than it does to Tooke, Godwin, or Bentham. The relationship implied by the elenctic method of these 'Socratic' empirics is interdependent and holistic, not foundational: consequently, the idea that truth presupposes society is seen as entirely compatible with the proposition that discourse presupposes objective truth. As the 'Ode on a Grecian Urn' intimates, the 'beauty' of truth consists in its exquisite fineness: truth is sustained, only in as much as it is presupposed by communication and dialectic. Stepping beyond the sphere of dialogue into an inconceivable 'outside' or otherness is, as Hilary Putnam puts it, tantamount to mental suicide: it is such an extremity that Keats depicts in the denouement of 'Lamia'.[123]

'Lamia''s last act allegorises the dependence of 'life' upon the symbiotic relationship between truth and communication. As Apollonius discovers, interpretation is sustained by charity, by the presupposition between parties that the give-and-take in any dialogue is carried out against the possibility of error. Once this *assumption* is dropped, communication is impossible, and so, in the absence of any possibility of triangulation between individuals and a shared world, is truth. Consequently, the *deictic* function becomes crucial to Keats's writing. Implicit in his early style and integral to his letters, the 'truth' of Keats's epistolary mode is the indicative gesture of the warm, communicating hand.

It might be argued that such a reading of 'This living hand' falls into the trap of allegorising the 'body' or materiality of Keats's life and work, when, as Denise Gigante argues, what this poem really betrays is 'an existentialist nausea . . . the endgame of aesthetic taste' symptomatic of the failure 'to allegorize, or sublimate, the material substance of self'.[124] However, allegory is only a 'trap' when interpretation and truth are cast as antipodes. Against the long-standing tendency in romantic criticism to see interpretation as that which besets thought with a contingency intolerable to its ideal of consciousness, Keats's writing indicates that there is more to the 'life of allegory' than the story of a bankrupt subjectivity in hopeless dialectical flight from the incommensurable determinants of the body, or language, or history. His poetry testifies to how the interdependence of truth and interpretation, 'allegory' and 'life', is sustained in dialogue, in the 'fellowship' of belief found in correspondence, not in the over-inflation or the negation of an individual ego. This concept of truth, one that Keats inherits from the culture of dissent, looks to community and communication rather than determinacy or neutrality for its coordinates, for its sense of the real. Allowing our critical endeavours to be guided by similar notions today means acknowledging that when we write about Keats, we cannot grasp his 'meaning' without ourselves undergoing a change. But it also forces us to recognise that when we do, we write about *this* Keats, *here*.

CHAPTER 4

An unremitting interchange: Shelley, elenchus, and the education of error

Writing 'On Life' in Florence in late 1819, Shelley disavows the dogmatic materialism of his youth and, encouraged by the diverse lessons of Hume, Drummond, and Tooke, together with over a year's intensive reading of Plato, outlines an approach to experience and reality altogether less grounded and logocentric:

Whatever may be his [man's] true and final destination, there is a spirit within him at enmity with nothingness and dissolution. This is the character of all life and being. Each is at once the centre and the circumference; the point to which all things are referred, and the line in which all things are contained. ... Philosophy, impatient as it may be to build, has much work yet remaining .... It reduces the mind to that freedom in which it would have acted, but for the misuse of words and signs, the instruments of its own creation. ... Our whole life is thus an education of error.[1]

On one hand, this passage appears strikingly performative. Shelley's own writing, the self-consciously rhetorical use (rather than 'misuse') of words and signs, might itself be seen as an 'education of error'. Remarkably tenacious in this centrifugal action, however, is the centripetal function of philosophy, which has 'much work yet remaining' in monitoring the relationship between the 'centre' and 'circumference' of human life. Such persistence is thrown into even sharper relief by the fact that a little over a year later Shelley would famously supplant philosophy in his *Defence of Poetry* with the eternal creative cycle of figuration, which was 'at once the centre and circumference of knowledge'.[2] In 1819, it was philosophy's task to regulate the mind by superintending language; by 1821, however, it was poetry's responsibility to moderate knowledge. The 'point to which all things are referred, and the line in which all things are contained' are, in Shelley's schemes, apt to change, and even to be exchanged.

At the root of this problem is the figure of Hume. Shelley felt more keenly than Godwin the sceptical implications of the impasse in Hume's epistemology. Uneasily, he writes from Edinburgh to Hogg in November 1813

that 'I have examined Hume's reasonings with respect to the non-existence
of external things, and, I confess, they appear to me to follow from the
doctrines of Locke. What am I to think of a philosophy which
conducts to such a conclusion? – *Sed hæc hactenus*.[3] The baffled note
to Shelley's initial assessment of Hume is echoed a century and a half
later by Quine, who reflects on how little empiricism has progressed
over the intervening period with regard to the search for truth. On this
score, 'I do not see that we are farther along today than where Hume
left us', he admits: '[t]he Humean predicament is the human
predicament'.[4]

Indeed, Shelley's hesitancy between philosophy and poetry, the cognitive and the linguistic, is symptomatic of a wider, persistent struggle
within empiricism itself. Like Keats, Shelley finds that the intellectual
milieu of Socratic empiricism associated with the culture of dissent to
which he adheres harbours an ambiguity. On one hand, empiricism
presents various commonsense, sceptical, or (in the case of Hume himself)
stylistic attempts to finesse the collapse of the correspondence model of
truth; on the other, it eschews the epistemological imperative altogether,
transforming itself into the materialistic and therapeutic aids to coherence
offered by Tooke and Bentham. The Socratic tradition is similarly
double-edged. Running together with an ancient tradition of transcendental truth-mysticism that stresses the immediacy of intuition as a
remedy for the failures of calculating reason is a more recent, Enlightenment interest in the elenctic resources of truth suggested by Socratic
dialogue.

Thus, like Keats, Shelley's hesitation is a direct consequence of the fact
that he is writing in a milieu in which two recognisably modern forms of
empirical thought, the linguistic and the representational, are beginning
to take shape. In Godwin's writings, for example, these currents, while
identifiable, remain barely distinguished. Accordingly, the side of
Shelley's mind that is most impressed by Godwin's adaptation of Hume's
analysis of causation is also the side that is attracted by the sceptical ideal
of the mind's heroic and tragic exertions in the face of the unknowable.
This tendency lurks behind the preface to *Alastor*, where 'the pure and
tender-hearted' are doomed to 'perish through the intensity and passion
of their search after their communities, when the vacancy of their spirit
suddenly makes itself felt'.[5] At the same time, the part of Shelley that is
swayed by Godwin's utilitarian tendency to translate metaphysical problems into questions of solidarity and social coherence is more inclined to
stress the necessity of 'community spirit' for the operations of self,

including perception, since '[t]he intellectual faculties, the imagination, the functions of sense, have their respective requisitions on the sympathy of corresponding powers in other human beings'.[6] Whichever tack Shelley takes has important implications: is the 'generous error' of human thought an epistemological tragedy, or merely the *charitable* leap of belief that makes communication, and thus concepts such as truth and selfhood, possible?

As I argue below, Shelley never comes down firmly on either side of this debate. On one hand, encouraged by his 'Socratic' Godwinism to draw 'truth' and 'life' closer together, he suggests that truth is itself a property of communication, of social relation. At the same time, his attempts to *imagine* reason and *rationalise* imagination are frustrated by the persistence in his work of the Lockean view of language as the instrument of thought. In 'On Life', for instance, he maintains that 'Thoughts and feelings arise, with or without our will, and we employ words to express them'.[7] The Lockean word/idea dyad ensures that the notions of *reference* and *correspondence* remain locked into Shelley's thinking about meaning, the relation between truth and language. This in turn means that while he enthusiastically adopts Godwin's line on error as a condition of life, his conviction that this error occurs through language as the *medium* of thought, through what he calls the 'misuse of words and signs', stymies his broader endeavour to bring out the holistic, coherentist implications of his mentor's work. It is the same tension, in turn, that causes him, even in *A Defence of Poetry*, to hesitate in rejecting outright the key assumptions underpinning epistemology: the dualistic boundaries between imagination and reason, synthesis and analysis, language and idea, concept and content.

It is, then, hardly surprising that the new turn in Shelley's thought around 1819 remains unsteady, negotiating between two impulses or tendencies. On one hand, there is an inclination to configure the real as always already interpreted or overdetermined, the referential 'centre', forever subject to a centrifugal 'circumference'. On the other hand, there remains a centripetal desire signalled by the notion of a 'spirit' in humanity 'at enmity with nothingness and dissolution'. This is Shelley's version of the ideal inflatus that compensates the subject for the loss of correspondence between form and content, mind and world. In short, Shelley's writing manoeuvres between a model of truth based on relation and coherence, 'love' and dialogue, and a paradigm governed by correspondence, according to which language is merely the medium, the instrument of thought.

This impasse cannot be adequately described by the categories of epistemology and ontology. Shelley's dilemma does not lie between empiricism and transcendentalism, nor between materialism and idealism, but between two competing conceptions of truth and of how truth relates to human language and communication. Indeed, the image of Shelley as 'sceptical idealist' (what Hugh Roberts dismisses as 'one of the hoarier clichés of Shelley criticism') was for some time one of the principal obstacles to understanding this dynamic, in so far as it tended to reduce Shelley's thought to a dialectic of (Platonic) idealism and (Humean) scepticism.[8] As more recent commentary attests, and as I have argued in the case of Keats, the problem with this model is that it fails to interrogate the circle of support whereby scepticism, idealism, and indifference feed and reinforce each other. Attention in the early 1980s to Shelley's 'conflicted' philosophy of language went some way to disrupting the closed shop of metaphysics and epistemology.[9] However, it was not until deconstruction and new forms of cultural materialism and historicism got to work on the Shelleyan corpus that it became clearer that the dilemma of Shelley's writing is not between two forms of epistemology, but between the assumptions of epistemology and its alternatives.[10]

The story of Shelley's thought, then, is best described not as a flight from rationalism to poetic imagination or of materialism to idealism, but as an ongoing struggle between two kinds of rationalism, between two competing conceptions of what it is that sustains belief. Fundamentally, Shelley's attempts to overcome the 'calculating' reason that he deplores in the *Defence* are stymied by his adherence to an 'instrumental' view of language that kept him chained to the correspondence model of truth, the rationalism of Locke and Hume. Yet, as I demonstrate below, his refusal to divide matters of fact from questions of value; his insistence that thought is a relation and not a thing; his belief that love (a going-out of our nature into objects and other persons) has a constitutive role in knowledge, and that individual and social intelligence are interdependent (like the cloud of mind and the society into which it discharges its 'lightning') – all these elements indicate his commitment to a reform of reason broadly consonant with the radical empiricism of Tooke, Godwin, and Bentham.[11] With Shelley, no less than with our own discourse of modernity, weighing the difference between the 'reform' and the outright rejection of reason must finally be determined as a question about the nature of truth and the real character of what Shelley calls our 'education of error'.

SCEPTICISM AND THE NEW EMPIRICISM

Understanding what is at stake in the 'education of error' involves reappraising the intellectual and cultural landscape in 1819 against which Shelley struggles to transform his materialism into the new 'intellectual' philosophy. The linguistic materialism of Tooke and Bentham forms an important part of this landscape, and Shelley's engagement with this affects – and often discomfits – his absorption of transcendentalism, whether ancient and familiar (as in Plato) or newfangled and German (as in Coleridge and A. W. Schlegel). In order to see how this occurs, we need to tackle the perennial problem of Shelley's relation to Hume and scepticism.

The initial attractions of scepticism for Shelley are linked to its potential as a bulwark against the tyranny of the kind of *a priori*, dogmatical 'Truth' he associates with systematic or organised religion. In the *Philosophical View of Reform*, he praises Berkeley and Hume for having 'clearly established the certainty of our ignorance with respect to those obscure questions which under the name of religious truths have been the watchwords of contention and the symbols of unjust power ever since they were distorted by the narrow passions of the immediate followers of Jesus'.[12] Shelley is aware of the classical sceptical tradition, but what draws him to Hume's form of scepticism is the way in which its analysis of the concept of causation offered a two-pronged attack upon Christian doctrine. Hume's restriction of meaningful inductive inferences regarding cause and effect to those regarding 'particular instances, which have fallen under our observation', seem to Shelley to pull the rug from under the First Mover paradigm of God as a creator *ex nihilo* of the universe.[13] Accordingly, the note 7.13 to *Queen Mab* repeats his objection in *The Necessity Of Atheism* to the notion of a 'creative Deity' on the grounds that '[t]he only idea which we can form of causation is derivable from the constant conjunction of objects, and the consequent inference of one from the other', so that, in consequence, 'the generative power is incomprehensible'.[14]

Just as significant, however, are the epistemological inferences that Shelley draws from Hume's argument. In this, he is encouraged by William Drummond's *Academical Questions* (1805), which he reads between 1815 and 1817. It is significant that Shelley is at the same time studying Locke's *Essay Concerning Human Understanding*, since one of Drummond's principal targets is Locke's use of the notion of 'power' to explain both the perception of '*secondary*' qualities in objects – that is, those, such as colour, sound, smell, taste, which are not '*real Qualities*' inhering in objects like bulk or number – and the nature of human liberty. For Locke, secondary qualities were 'nothing but Powers, relating to several other Bodies, and resulting from the different Modifications of the Original Qualities ... to produce several *Ideas* in us by our Senses'.[15] At the same time, Locke distinguishes between '*Passive*' and '*Active*' power, attributing the first to the mind's ability to receive such ideas, and the second to its ability to direct its attention towards them. We need only introspect and 'we find in our selves a *Power* to begin or forbear, continue or end several actions of our minds', he claims, a power 'we call the *Will*'.[16]

Drummond's *Academical Questions* sets out from Hume's attack in the *Treatise of Human Nature* on Locke's identification of causation with power. Rejecting Reid's account of perception as the combination of passive sensation in the perceiver and an extramental and independent power in the object,[17] Drummond counters that such distinctions regarding passivity and activity 'can only be made, with respect to the order and associations of our own ideas'. For 'what are these qualities of external objects, unless they be sensations in our own minds?'[18] As for the 'doctrine of passive mental power', Drummond claims that this 'is one of the most singular among the fallacies, which deceived the excellent judgement of Locke'.[19] Consequently, '[t]here is no power, by which men can create, or destroy their feelings. Sensation alone overcomes sensation. Belief cannot be forced, nor can conviction be coerced'.[20] Such claims are eagerly seized upon by Shelley. Earlier, in *The Necessity of Atheism*, his anti-Christian conviction that 'belief is not an act of volition' had been grounded on a theory of mind as purely passive in sensation.[21] However, by extending Hume's epistemology of sensation into an interrogation of the active/passive dichotomy itself, Drummond's work offers a more promising line of attack. In particular, his assertion that the mind is incapable of creating the material of its own perception chimes with a motto that Shelley had encountered while thumbing Charles Lloyd's copy of Berkeley in the Lake District in 1812. He recalls the volume seven years later in a letter to Leigh Hunt:

I remember observing some pencil notes in it, apparently written by Lloyd, which I thought particularly acute. One especially struck me as being the assertion of a doctrine of which even then I had long been persuaded, and on which I had founded much of my persuasions regarding the imagined cause of the Universe. 'Mind cannot create; it can only perceive'.[22]

It is this conviction that in 1814 becomes the mainstay of the *Refutation of Deism*'s claim 'that mind is the effect, not the cause of motion, that power is the attribute, not the origin of Being'.[23] Drummond alerts Shelley to the way in which Hume's arguments pose a challenge to the very coherence of notions such as cause, effect, attribute, and origin. Thus, by 1819 and the 'intellectual philosophy' of 'On Life', the principle that 'Mind ... cannot create, it can only perceive' is explicitly linked to Drummond's argument that 'cause is only a word expressing a certain state of the human mind with regard to the manner in which two thoughts are apprehended to be related to each other'.[24] Drummond's scepticism is accordingly enlisted with Berkeley, Hume, and Hartley in the fight against the tyranny of a religious 'Truth' erected upon notions of volitional power (both metaphysical and psychological) and abstract reason.

The trouble with this campaign, however, is that Humean scepticism can be an unpredictable weapon. Once deployed, it has no more respect for the truths of Paine and Godwin than the eternal truths of religion. For Godwin, 'Nothing can be more certain than the omnipotence of truth',[25] a sentiment echoed by his eager new convert in 1811 when he writes to Elizabeth Hitchener that 'when I contemplate these gigantic piles of superstition ... I set them down as so many retardations of the period when truth becomes omnipotent'.[26] Between this claim and his warning in the *Defence* against sceptics who would 'deface, as some of the French writers have defaced, the eternal truths charactered upon the imaginations of men', Shelley retained an unwavering confidence in the objectivity of truth.[27] Significantly, this caution appears in a passage in the *Defence* in which Shelley is trying to put his earlier materialism into perspective (and utilitarianism in its place) by suggesting a role for the 'mechanist' in public affairs that is essential but none the less subordinate to that of the poet. In doing so, he foregrounds two theories that competed at that time to explain the connections between human action, language, and truth, explanations that John Stuart Mill was to formulate as the 'Benthamite' and the 'Coleridgian'.[28] While Shelley's *Defence* has usually been read as marking a decisive move towards the latter, closer scrutiny reveals a more complex picture.

What this examination shows is that Shelley's later work continues to hesitate between two concepts of truth: one based on ideal correspondence, the other on the pragmatics of communication. As it turns out, in this respect (as in so many others), Shelley continues to echo Godwin. In the *Inquiry Concerning Political Justice*, Godwin emphasises his empiricist credentials, acknowledging in a note that the arguments for his epistemology 'are for the most part an abstract, the direct one from Locke on the Human Understanding, those which relate to experience from Hartley's Observations on Man'.[29] It comes as no surprise, then, to find him arguing that ideas 'are regularly generated in the mind by a series of impressions, and digested and arranged by association and reflection'.[30] While denying the existence of any active power in the mind, however, Godwin draws back from full-blown materialism, arguing that thought is 'the medium of operation' in reasoning, rather than 'a mere superfluity' depicted by Hartley.[31] Shelley is aware that by stressing the phenomenal nature of perception, Godwin is, in reality, closer to Hume than to Hartley. This awareness would have been intensified by Godwin's Humean distinction between ideas and impressions.[32]

It is this very distinction, however, that lies at the root of Hume's scepticism. Hume insists in the *Treatise* that '*all our simple ideas in their first appearance are deriv'd from simple impressions, which are correspondent to them, and which they exactly represent*'.[33] One of the consequences of this for Hume is that in order to talk meaningfully about the world we do not require an 'object' world to correspond to our perceptions; instead, all talk of 'objects' should be reduced to talk of impressions. The ideal language of philosophy would thus be a phenomenal language of sense-impressions rather than the naïve discourse of objects in the 'external' world. The data of sensation, rather than the data of understanding, is the index of the real. While many (including, it appears, Godwin) accept Hume's settlement between epistemology and ontology without absorbing its full implications, others (including Shelley) see that it effectively severs the link between the perceiving subject and the 'external' world. The story of how Hume's impressionism develops into the all-conquering subjectivity of romantic literature has been told many times. What is less frequently reported, however, is the impact it has upon Bentham's theory of language, and thereby upon a strain of empirical thought that shifts the burden of reason from the punctual subject to linguistic coherence.

In an appendix to *Deontology: or Morality Made Easy*, Bentham refers to Hume's 'most important distinction between impressions and ideas', adding: 'I do not know what people did before this distinction. It was a great discovery'.[34] Most important for Bentham's purposes are the ramifications of the distinction for the question of reference. In effect, he takes Hume's proposal a stage further, arguing that once reference is reduced to the relationship between words and sense impressions (rather than between words and the world), the game is up for any correspondence theory of meaning. In the absence of a secure referential hook for words in the objective world, meaning in Bentham's hands becomes the property of statements, of sentences and propositions. At this point it is important to register that this linguistic holism is not, as some have suggested, a form of linguistic organicism.[35] On the contrary, there is no ideal relationship between form and content, part and whole, in Bentham's philosophy of language. Rather, as commentators such as Quine have noted, Bentham makes a decisive move towards a linguistic pragmatism by replacing Hume's semantic anchor in the data of experience with a notion of meaning as determined by linguistic context, a context that is potentially open-ended.

As Bentham admits, this development was not part of his original plan. Writing the chapter 'Of Motives' in his 1789, *An Introduction to the Principles of Morals and Legislation*, he found himself, as he recalls in his Preface, 'unexpectedly entangled in an unsuspected corner of the meta-physical maze'[36] brought on by the discovery that the term 'motive' has two distinct meanings; one literal and legitimate, the other figurative and fictitious. He finally emerged from this maze in the 1810s with a series of essays on logic and language: 'A Fragment on Ontology', the 'Essay on Logic', the 'Essay on Language', and 'Fragments on Universal Grammar'. These works argue that far from being reducible logical fictions are the presuppositions of discourse, distinguishable from poetical fictions not in *kind* but in *degree*.[37] As I showed earlier, Bentham's initial desire to ground language in a factual foundation ultimately led him to the realisation that facts themselves were, strictly speaking, fictitious entities, and that the concept of truth, while objective, was the ultimate fiction or *presupposition* of discourse, as well as its goal. Thus, as Frances Ferguson notes, when it comes to concepts such as personal identity, Bentham 'replaces the self-consciousness and self-expressiveness that we have so often associated with the Romantic period with a description of individuality that is not so much expressed as produced'.[38]

Shelley reports to Hogg in March 1814 that he had read Dumont's translation and arrangement of Bentham's notoriously disorganised manuscripts, a course of study that would have taken him through many of the materials that Bentham himself collated in his *Introduction*.[39] That these works made a favourable impression upon Shelley is supported by the fact that, in his 1819 letter to *The Examiner*, Bentham's name appears in the roll-call of deists invoked in the defence of Carlisle (together with those of Paine, Hume, Drummond, and Godwin).[40] Accordingly, when he advertises *A Philosophical View of Reform* to Hunt the following year, he presents it as 'a kind of standard book for the philosophical reformers politically considered, like Jeremy Bentham's something, but different & perhaps more systematic'.[41] This connection has led James Chandler to argue that under Bentham's influence Shelley extends his own scepticism about representative forms (in particular, that of an individual will as representative of a general will) into a full-blown 'new historicist conception of a human environment', a conception which involves the postulation of 'a "superstructure of maxims and forms" that can be traced to material historical origins and actually changed, even "overthrown"'.[42] Indeed, in the idea of 'a casuistry of the *general* will',[43] Chandler detects the emergence (in writers such as Shelley, Bentham, and Walter Scott) of 'a form of historical dialectic not reducible to Hegelianism'.[44]

It is equally possible, however, that Shelley's and Bentham's conception of the relation of representative forms (taken in the widest possible sense to include the epistemological as well as the political) does not correspond to a Hegelian model of dialectic because it is not dialectical at all. The assumption that political, epistemological, or semantic questions are fundamentally determined by the relationship between 'form' and 'content' establishes a line of inquiry almost guaranteed to culminate in the transcendental inflatus of imagination or the recuperative energies of dialectic. Much modern commentary continues to take the 'end' of such formalism as the starting point of its own dialectical critique, but in doing so it often overlooks other antiformalist alternatives embedded in romantic discourse.

One such alternative, articulated by Bentham, contains an idea to which Shelley is receptive. It is the idea that the objectivity of truth extends no further than the constitutive intersubjectivity of informed, reasonable, and freely communicating individuals. Reading the *Traités de legislation*, for example, Shelley would have encountered Bentham's analysis of the widespread desire for unanimity in debate: 'Unanimity pleases us. This harmony of sentiment is the only pledge we can have, apart from our own reason, of the truth of our opinions, and of the utility of the actions founded upon those opinions'.[45] The *pleasure* of unanimity is key for Bentham, since epistemic principle is itself rooted in social value. There is nothing 'given' or heaven-sent about this account, a quality it is unlikely that Shelley missed, and which forms the vital background for Bentham's deceptively reductive-sounding claim that '[t]he language of truth is uniform and simple. The same ideas are always expressed by the same terms. Everything is referred to pleasures or to pains'.[46]

Shelley's reading of Bentham is crucial then, not just in terms of his response to utilitarianism (which was qualifiedly positive) but with respect to his reception of Bentham's philosophy of language, which, like Tooke's, opens up entirely new ways of thinking about the relation between truth and meaning. This brings us back to Godwin, whose empiricism also engages with the pragmatic discourse of intersubjectivity that Shelley would have found in Bentham, and whose claims about the 'simplicity' of truth are also apt to be misconstrued as the dogmatic assertions of epistemological givenness commonly associated with representational empiricism. As in the case of Bentham, Godwin's claim that 'Truth is in reality single and uniform'[47] must be read alongside his suggestion that truth circulates within a society and cannot be disconnected from value, an argument that underpins his case regarding 'the tendency of truth in conducing to the perfection of our virtue'.[48] Thus, Godwin's correlation of the 'omnipotence of truth' with 'the connexion between the judgement and the outward behaviour' is grounded on the assumption not that truth exists in some Platonic hinterland, but that its unknowable, even indeterminate nature goes hand-in-hand with its status as social and objective. For *this* reason, 'if there be such a thing as truth, it must infallibly be struck out by the collision of mind with mind'.[49] Truth, in other words, is interwoven with the very fabric of human communication through the *possibility of error*. Consequently, just because we are capable of *knowing* truth does not mean that we are able to account for *how* we know.

If this were all Godwin had to say on the matter, then his message to Shelley would have been clear enough. However, Godwin's notion of 'error' vacillates between a Tookean/Benthamite conception based on the preconditions of communication, and a Lockean idea of failed correspondence, that is, between what I have characterised as 'pragmatic-communicative' and 'tragic-epistemological' conceptions of truth. Confirming this ambiguity is Godwin's decision to side with Locke, Rousseau, and Monboddo against Tooke and Bentham in the debate over the nature of language. 'Its beginning', he surmises, 'was probably from those involuntary cries, which infants for example are found to utter', which, 'being observed to be constantly associated with certain preliminary impressions . . . may afterwards be repeated from reflection'.[50] This association of 'primitive' society with infantile consciousness was a common theme in eighteenth-century thought, and Shelley was to reiterate the idea in the *Defence*. Significantly, however, this model generally promotes a picture of human intelligence that elevates the psychological over the linguistic. The litmus test for this question is whether abstraction is seen (as it is by Tooke and Bentham) as a by-product of language, or (as it is by Monboddo and Godwin) as 'one of the sublimest operations of the mind'.[51] Ensuring that communication remains the mere vehicle for, rather than the engine of thought, Godwin's conception of truth as regulated by social error is severely tested by the metaphysics of correspondence entailed by his acceptance of Locke's argument that *conceptualisation* is prior to communication.

Shelley inherits this ambiguity. Like Godwin, Shelley never manages completely to extricate himself from the form/content, word/idea binaries implicit in the Locke–Rousseau theory of language. At the same time, however, he is able to connect Godwin's nascent truth holism with a line of argument in Bentham that questioned all talk of meaning couched in terms of 'forms' and 'contents'. Though less clearly articulated than in Bentham, Godwin's conception of facts is of epistemic norms that are as much constituted *by*, as they are constitutive *of* discourse. Accordingly, rather than (as Chandler would have it) the development of a historical dialectic that moved beyond Hegelian logic, Shelley would have found in Bentham's idea of fictions an understanding of conceptual forms as dissolvable. It is against this background that Shelley's subsequent retreat from Godwinian rationalism should be considered, culminating in the *Defence*'s warning against the cultivation of knowledge at the cost of creative process and the promotion of science, to which 'man, having enslaved the elements, remains himself a slave'.[52]

Disenchanted with the philosophy of matter by 1819, Shelley's thought moves in two directions at once. He was beginning to realise that, by cleaving fact and value upon objective and subjective lines, Hume's philosophy imperilled truth as such (not just Truth as *a priori* dogma). In this light, the thesis that 'the mind cannot create', that it is powerless to swim against the necessitating current of sensation, no longer appears liberating. On one hand, Shelley's response to this is to push scepticism into the service of idealism, displacing into a noumenal ideal the truth underlying social change. This tactical move, once again, develops a line of thought already present in Godwin, who had also endeavoured to reconcile necessitarianism with scepticism: 'The discovery of truth is a pursuit of such vast extent, that it is scarcely possible to prescribe bounds to it. Those great lines, which seem at present to mark the limits of human understanding, will, like the mists that rise from a lake, retire farther and farther the more closely we approach them.'[53] The same 'sceptical idealism' informs Demogorgon's claim that Asia's questions could be answered only:

> – If the Abysm
> Could vomit forth its secrets: – but a voice
> Is wanting, the deep truth is imageless;
> For what would it avail to bid thee gaze
> On the revolving world? What to bid speak
> Fate, Time, Occasion, Chance and Change? – To these
> All things are subject but eternal Love.
> (*Prometheus Unbound* II.iv.ll.114–20)

The ease with which this move from materialism to idealism is achieved, however, betrays the fact that it does not, in itself, necessitate a changed view of the nature of *truth*. Indeed, Shelley's lingering attachment to the idea of correspondence as the fundamental principle of truth and meaning makes him more amenable to the idealism of Coleridge, A. W. Schlegel, and Hazlitt.[54] These theorists taught him that healing the divide between fact and value, objective and subjective, is a function of a *creative* mind – and, furthermore, that poetry is the realm in which such reconciliations are effected. At the same time, however, other aspects of Godwin's work (in particular his suggestions regarding the basis of truth in error) coalesce with arguments Shelley had encountered in Tooke and Bentham regarding the determination of semantic and epistemic 'forms'. This second, radical strain of empiricism enabled Shelley, like Keats, to make a connection between the theory of truth as communication and Socratic notions of elenchus and deixis. While Keats tropes this connection as beauty, however, for Shelley the 'imageless' status of truth is only comprehensible in terms of love.

DIALOGUE AND INDETERMINACY

Scepticism in Shelley's writing is a creature that turns upon its creator. Deployed initially to combat the 'Truth' of religion – namely, prejudice and superstition – it comes to threaten the very foundations upon which Shelley hopes to ground revolutionary principle. Accordingly, after 1819, Shelley begins to see that the effects of scepticism are lethal for *any* conception of objective truth, not just dogmatism. However, despite his endeavours to overcome alienation in knowledge, he is reluctant to jettison a central presupposition shared by sceptics, idealists, and materialists: the correspondence model of truth. This in turn affects the way he intervenes in the early nineteenth-century debate over the status of 'principles'. On one hand, Shelley rejects Hume's dichotomy of neutral fact and projected value for a view of discourse as fundamentally metaphoric and of reality as always already interpreted or value-driven. As his critique grows more confident, the foundationalist, philosophical (epistemo-logical) creed of *Queen Mab* gives way to the kind of coherentist, poetic exploration of phenomena that appears in 'On Life':

The view of life presented by the most refined deductions of the intellectual philosophy, is that of unity. Nothing exists but as it is perceived. The difference is merely nominal between those two classes of thought, which are vulgarly distin-guished by the names of ideas and external objects. . . . The words, *I, you, they*, are not signs of any actual difference subsisting between the assemblage of thoughts thus indicated, but are merely marks employed to denote the different modifica-tions of the one mind.[55]

In the new 'intellectual philosophy', then, Humean scepticism is enlisted mainly to support Shelley's nominalist treatment of 'external objects' (this line of thought dates from his claim that Hume's philosophy draws out the logic of the doctrines of Locke to an inevitable conclusion regarding 'the non-existence of external things').[56] Of course, Shelley knows from his own reading of Berkeley that there is nothing necessarily fatal to established religion in the claim that *esse* of sensible qualities is *percipi*. What he sees in Hume's work, however, is a vindication of Lloyd's marginalia to Berkeley, denying the conceivability of spirit or active substance on a model of knowledge based upon passive sensation. The mind cannot create. While Berkeley permitted the mind an intuitive consciousness of its own causal agency as a thinking being, Hume trans-lates such notions of substance, relation, and causation into the faint and languid association of ideas in the imagination, itself no iron law, but 'only . . . a gentle force, which commonly prevails'.[57] Whereas, forty years later, Monboddo is appalled that Hume should have denied the existence of everything in the universe 'besides his own perceptions', Shelley greets this conclusion with enthusiasm.[58]

How, then, are we to view the conclusions of the 'intellectual philoso-phy' presented by Shelley in 'On Life'? On one hand, Shelley's 'one mind' monism appears to push Hume's scepticism towards a conception of existence itself as phenomenal. Thus, according to Wasserman, in Shelley 'any so-called thing must be understood in the phenomenalist sense'.[59] Andrew Cooper, meanwhile, interprets Shelley's work as correcting 'Hume's neglect of the immanent aspect of experience, its becoming-ness', and rejecting epistemology for hermeneutics by shifting the terms of the question from those of causation to those of meaning.[60] This hermen-eutical turn in Shelley criticism itself instigates a view of the poet's 'mean-ing' as determined by figural substitutions rather than interpretations. According to Jerrold Hogle, for example, to 'say that "nothing exists but as it is perceived" is to argue that any distinguishable perception or memory of it has already been reflected upon, interpreted from an alien perspective'. Shelley's writing thus presents a 'centreless displacement of figural counterparts by one another' in which there is 'no "undifferentiated unity"', just a rhetoric of transference.[61]

There is undoubtedly something unorthodox, even idiosyncratic, about Shelley's scepticism and his reading of Hume. Indeed, one strength of 'phenomenological' or 'postmodern' readings is that they foreground the way in which his work glides from questions of truth and knowledge to questions of meaning. However, before accepting the claim of Hogle, Wheeler, and others, that in its wider implications Shelley's belief that 'nothing exists but as it is perceived' amounts to a challenge to the 'logocentric' tradition in Western philosophy, a further alternative should be considered. This is that Shelley's understanding of the (in)determinacy of conceptual form is itself determined not by the psychological or linguistic concerns of the late Enlightenment, but by ancient metaphysics. Hugh Roberts's argument is pertinent here. Roberts claims to identify in the influence of Lucretius an 'unrecognised "third way"' in Shelley's writing, an antirational materialism that enables the writer 'to release the kind of open-ended change that cannot be reconciled with a therapeutic-idealist politics and poetics', such as that imbibed via the organicism of A. W. Schlegel and Coleridge.[62] Lucretianism is vital, Roberts maintains, because it enables Shelley to conceive how the 'evanescent figure in the sand helps us to overcome the hermeneutic prejudice that all parts must be subsumed by and in wider wholes'.[63]

Roberts argues that Shelley uses Lucretian ideas of chaos to connect the materialism of Hume and Godwin to Coleridge's faith in the transformative powers of imagination. This in turn enables him to replace the Enlightenment narrative of progress with the idea of history as an endless cycle of decay and rebirth, driven by the pure contingency of *clinamen*. Shelley's universe then, offers no contemplative relief from humanity's fall into temporality, into history; on the contrary, it stands against the organic plenitude of a transcendental aesthetic order. Death and regeneration work hand-in-hand, like the West Wind that sweeps through Florence:

> Thou Dirge
>
> Of the dying year, to which this closing night
> Will be the dome of a vast sepulchre,
> Vaulted with all thy congregated might
> ('Ode to the West Wind', ll.23–6)

Like the mass of particles that Lucretius envisions falling through the void like 'unseen bodies of wind', the contingency behind creation is figured by Shelley as a hidden power engaged in an unceasing process of destruction and creation.[64] And yet, Shelley's West Wind, the 'Wild Spirit, which art moving everywhere', is at once figurative and literal. For Roberts, Shelley's idea of the power of the imagination is one of decay, as in the *Defence*'s depiction of 'a fading coal which some invisible influence, like an inconstant wind, awakens to transitory brightness'.[65] The radicalism behind the 'Ode to the West Wind', then, like that of 'Ozymandias', is a radicalism of death, signalling not idealistic abandonment, but the triumph of the part over the whole whereby, as Lucretius describes it, the 'earth is diminished and is increased and grows again'.[66]

There is good evidence that, before Drummond's influence weakened the link between scepticism and materialism in favour of a sceptical form of idealism, Shelley looked to Lucretius' entropic, Epicurean vision of the universe for a philosophical articulation of the relationship between atomic 'anarchy' and a non-despotic unity. *De Rerum Natura*, he affirmed in the 1817 Preface to *Laon and Cynthia*, was 'yet the basis of our metaphysical knowledge'.[67] Comments such as this notwithstanding, we must remain alert to how Shelley's reading of Lucretius is mediated by the lessons of the Enlightenment. A particular worry here is that by privileging Shelleyian ontology as Roberts does, we risk losing sight of the connection that Shelley forges between the metaphysical atomism of the Roman poet and the epistemological atomism of Hume.

What is particularly appealing for Shelley about Lucretius is the founding principle of *De Rerum Natura*, namely 'that no thing is ever by divine power produced from nothing'.[68] Perceiving that both philosophers move to supplant reification with relation, Shelley is apt to run this maxim together with Hume's attack upon the notion of a first cause effected by a divine, creative mind. Just as Hume proposes the translation of statements purporting to be about substances or entities into those regarding the associations of ideas, so Lucretius argues that the spontaneous swerve of the *clinamen* accounts for the first beginnings of the major elements through the motion of atoms. Indeed, much of Shelley's work up to 'On Life' overlays two different *kinds* of theory: one epistemological, the other ontological. 'A Future State', for instance, written in late 1818, promulgates the Lucretian lesson that death lurks everywhere in nature, and that the only immortality is atomic:

It is probable that what we call thought is not an actual being, but no more than the relation between various parts of that infinitely varied mass, of which the rest of the universe is composed, and which ceases to exist as soon as those parts change their position with regard to each other.[69]

Such ontological speculations, however, merge breathlessly with a more familiar, epistemological argument:

That is the combinations between certain elementary particles of matter undergo a change and submit to new combinations. For when we use the words *principle*, *power, cause*, &c., we mean to express no real being, but only to class under those terms a certain series of co-existing phenomena.[70]

Returning to the doctrine of immortality, Shelley concludes that 'it is enough that such assertions should be either contradictory to the known laws of nature, or exceed the limits of our experience, that their fallacy or irrelevancy to our consideration should be demonstrated'.[71] The distinction signalled by 'either ... or' is a significant one, for it marks the gap where the two philosophers upon whom Shelley is drawing refuse to meet. The abyss between 'particles' and 'terms'; between 'the known laws of nature' and 'the limits of our experience' would not easily be bridged, least of all by Lucretius, whose postulated *simulacrae* and *membranae*, the material bearers of sensation, seem, despite their poetic attraction, naïve superstitions in the face of Hume's analysis of perception.[72] Thus, Shelley's interest in relation, at this point, remains rooted in scepticism. The materiality of *clinamen*, far from depriving scepticism of its sting by privileging sheer contingency or discontinuous being over any possibility of therapeutic knowing, is fused in Shelley's thought with the epistemological problem of what constituted the limits of possible experience.

Indeed, so long as Shelley retains even a vestigial attachment to the correspondence view of truth, knowledge remains a 'problem' for epistemology – a problem, he is increasingly persuaded, materialism accentuates rather than obviates. Thus, when Lucretian tropes resurface in the *Defence*, they do so in a different light. Playfully but concertedly, Shelley challenges Peacock's post-Humean settlement in which the divorce of fact and value represents the liberation of knowledge from superstition, the advance of the historian and philosopher leaving the poet 'wallowing in the rubbish of departed ignorance'.[73] In this context, both Lucretian and Humean figures of contingency acquire a negative charge. It is poetry's therapeutic power, Shelley argues, that counteracts the mortification of sensation and 'defeats the curse which binds us to be subjected to the accident of surrounding impressions'. Reaching beyond the material phenomena of *simulacrae*, 'it strips the veil of familiarity from the world, and lays bare the naked and sleeping beauty which is the spirit of its forms'. Thus, as it 'redeems from decay the visitations of the divinity in man', poetry gives the lie to the Lucretian vision of death-in-life.[74]

Shelley's problems, of course, do not end here. Rather than removing the burden of representation, the *Defence*'s supplanting of philosophy with poetry as the power whereby we 'measure the circumference and sound the depths of human nature' transfers the problem of correspondence from the rational to the aesthetic.[75] In the *Defence*, poetry must challenge empirical 'knowledge' while at the same time asserting its own epistemic autonomy. As Shelley knew from his reading of Plato, this was a difficult line to maintain in the face of a notion of truth as correspondence. And yet, it is Plato, not Lucretius, who offers Shelley an alternative conception of truth that answers his instinct that truth should be based on relation and communication. Once again, though more surprisingly in this context, Hume is the mediator.

Hume refuses to allow his epistemological scepticism regarding the existence of other minds to overcome his conviction that the sympathetic bond between human beings is an irresistible force in human life – to such a degree, indeed, that 'the ideas of the affections of others are converted into the very impressions they represent, and that the passions arise in conformity to the images we form of them'.[76] Similarly, for Plato, the failure to arrive at a satisfactory definition of knowledge in the *Theaetetus* heightens the significance of the *Symposium*'s exploration of love, a yearning for the absolute that like unjustified true belief 'is placed between wisdom and ignorance'.[77] Both Hume and Plato suggest responses to scepticism that set aside the quest for certainty in an ideal correspondence of mind and world, form and content. Additionally, both imply that the remedy for the intellectual malady of abstract doubt about the existence of the external world can be found in our relationships with other *persons*. As Cooper argues, Shelley's Platonism encourages him to stress the importance of 'patently nonepistemological desiderata like hope and love'.[78] Thus, the bond of love in the essay 'On Love', 'which connects not only man with man, but with every thing which exists',[79] becomes in the *Defence* the property of poetry, which 'creates for us a being within our being'.[80]

As Shelley scholars know, however, there is more than one Plato. Debate has raged for decades as to whether sceptical idealism or Socratic method holds the greater sway over the poet. On one hand, according to C. E. Pulos, as Shelley sets about translating *Symposium* and *Ion*, he reacts against what he perceives to be the sophism of the dialogues – a concern which, thanks to his sceptical training in Hume, makes him receptive to Montaigne's reading of Plato as a poet who stressed the importance of intuition in the face of the unknowable. This makes Shelley, if not exactly Pulos's 'consistent Platonist in the sceptical tradition',[81] then what Tracy Ware classifies as 'a skeptical poet defending poetry' who was 'concerned to liberate the imaginative truths of Platonism from the philosophical system in which they are embedded'.[82] Ross Woodman, on the other hand, claims that Shelley's real impatience is with Godwin's gradualism, and that his conversations with John Frank Newton led him to construct his theory of poetry upon Plato's theories of (respectively) inspiration in the *Ion*, love in *Symposium*, the demiurge in *Timaeus*, and pre-existence in *Phaedrus*.[83] In this adaptation, Woodman insists, the role of Socratic *method* is vital to Shelley's purpose. Wasserman agrees, noting that Shelley encountered in Hume's *Dialogues* a dialogic approach to reasoning whose 'ironic strategy' does not refer to distrust of reason, nor 'the Pyrrhonic quietude resulting from a suspension of judgement', but is deployed 'for the purpose of an open-ended inquiry into truth'.[84] Alternatively, Hoagwood links the 'conceptual back-stitch' of Socratic dialectic to the 'epistemological circle' implied by Shelley's scepticism as 'a mentalistic or phenomenal limit to the truth content of knowledge claims'.[85] Deconstructionists like Kathleen Wheeler and Troy Urquhart, meanwhile, argue that Shelley's Socratic empiricism signals 'a transformation from dualistic thinking to thought based on relation and integration'.[86]

The complex ways in which Lucretian and Platonic influences are filtered through the empiricism of Hume and Godwin play a significant role in determining whether Shelley's mantra, 'nothing exists but as it is perceived', should be read as expressing a metaphysical doctrine, a watchword of scepticism, or, as Hogle and others suggest, the overdetermination of perception by theory. Whether or not we see Shelley's writing as 'centrifugal', then (and in what way), depends greatly upon which 'Plato' we assume guided his ideas about truth, identity, and relation. Yet here we should be aware that just as there is more than one Plato so there is more than one Shelley. There is the Shelley who seeks in the promise of the aesthetic sublime a recompense for empiricism's tragic loss of the 'world'. There is also, however, the Shelley who does not equate objectivity with correspondence *per se*, and for whom dialogue and relation *resituate*, but do not *negate* the concept of truth. Like 'holistic' Keats, this Shelley finds in Plato an account of truth as the intersubjective presupposition of dialogue.

To understand how he does this, it is important to recall Diotima's claim in the *Symposium* that love is a power that 'includes every kind of longing for happiness and for the good'.[87] On one hand, Plato appears to have little doubt that knowledge itself involves veridicality and that truth is fundamentally a matter of correspondence between belief and reality. The dialogue on knowledge in *Theaetetus*, for instance, founders not on the nature of truth, but on arriving at a non-question-begging definition for justified belief.[88] And yet, in the *Symposium*, love, plying between heaven and earth, forms the medium through which the lover, like the poet, might encounter the eternal form of the good, and experience illumination that is 'neither words, nor knowledge, nor a something that exists in something else ... but subsisting of itself and by itself in an eternal oneness'.[89] It is Plato's insistence on the connection between the evaluative and the cognitive, together with his stress on the essential role of intersubjectivity in establishing the coordinates in perception, that has attracted the attention of philosophers like Davidson. For Davidson, the *assumption* of truth in Socratic dialogue works in a very special and subtle way. As he sees it, Socrates is able to claim that he does not *know* what is true but that 'it is enough that he has a method that leads to truth', because for Plato there is no *ontological* difference between a justified belief and a 'true' justified belief.[90] In 'Plato's Philosopher', Davidson agrees with the great Plato scholar Gregory Vlastos that having experimented with a range of different methods Plato ultimately 'realises what must be assumed if the elenchus is to produce truths: the assumption is that, *in moral matters, everyone has true beliefs which he cannot abandon and which entail the negations of his false beliefs*'.[91] For this reason, truth can be said to be both objective *and* dependent upon the pragmatics of communication. Davidson unpacks this argument further in 'The Socratic Concept of Truth':

Without language, thoughts have no clear shape; but the shape language gives them emerges only in the context of active communication. What we think depends on what others can make of us and of our relations to the world we share with them. It follows that we have no clear thoughts except as these are sharpened in the process of being grasped by others.[92]

It is this constitutive role for dialogue, as we saw with Keats, which secures the relationship of interdependence between elenchus and deixis. Recapturing this antifoundationalist conception of objectivity is important in itself, but it has added urgency in the present context. For if our understanding of writers like Shelley continues to be shadowed by a conception of late-Enlightenment thought as shackled to a rigidly centred, immobile subjectivity destined to unwind into the limitlessly mobile textures and planes of postmodernity, we are almost bound to distort what is at stake not just in Shelley's theorising, but in our own. For instance, it becomes all too easy to read his claim that 'nothing exists but as it is perceived' as an early attempt to undermine the consciousness-centred model of thought by exposing the intentions of the 'subject' to the determination of incommensurable interpretations. It is my contention, however, that while Shelley frequently challenges the centrality of the subject, a centrality it elsewhere (confusingly) champions, he does so in ways that escape modern or even postmodern categories of dialectic or difference.

For this reason, Kathleen Wheeler is right to claim that Shelley's writing is revolutionary in epistemological terms, that it undermines dualistic systems of thinking. However, it is wrong to infer from this that Shelley seeks to overturn or go 'beyond' the concept of truth. Similarly, Cooper correctly indicates how Shelley becomes increasingly concerned with nonepistemological categories, in particular, the idea of love. But to assert that this represents either a retreat from reason as such, or a quasi-phenomenological open-ended inquiry into truth, as Wasserman frames it, is to miss the quite distinct sense that Shelley has of how the concept of truth relates to our methods of inquiry, indeed, to perception itself. The tendency here is to assume that the only concept of 'objective truth' at stake, the only cognitive game in town, is one based on epistemological correspondence. This plays into the hands of a critic like William Ulmer, who uses the same set of assumptions to argue that Shelley's Platonic erotics of alterity ultimately signal a 'nostalgia for identities prior to differentiation'.[93]

Instead, what Shelley finds in Plato is the possibility of a *holistic* conception of truth that overcomes the empirical division of the factual and the evaluative implicit in the correspondence model. It is this that encourages him to claim in the *Defence* that 'to be a poet is to apprehend the true and the beautiful, in a word *the good* that exists in the relation, subsisting, first between existence and perception, and secondly between perception and expression'.[94] Moreover, the Tookean–Benthamite notion that truth lies in the coherence of a linguistic community, rather than metaphysical correspondence, fits with the social dynamics of truth implicit in the Socratic elenchus. Thus, the Platonic notion of love, 'a going out of our own nature, and an identification of ourselves with the beautiful which exists in thought, action, or person, not our own' emerges in Shelley not as a *means* of attaining truth, but as a model for the kind of dialogue that *sustains* truth.[95] The celebration of this dialogue, in turn, enables poets to 'participate in the *life* of truth'.[96]

However, there is always more than one concept of truth at work in Shelley. While he flirts with holistic and relational, rather than linear or foundational models of truth, there remains even in the *Defence* the stubborn residue of the Lockean notion of correspondence as a causal relationship between entities, between mind and nature. What has often misled commentators is his Humean scepticism about our *knowledge* of that causal relationship. As Shelley writes in *A Refutation of Deism*, the 'inevitable laws' of the universe 'are the unknown causes of the known effects perceivable in the universe. Their effects are the boundaries of our knowledge, their names the expressions of our ignorance'.[97] Shelley's interest in the logocentrifugal potential of the teachings of Lucretius, Bentham, and Plato repeatedly clashes with his foundationalist instinct that truth lies in an epistemological relation of correspondence, in the relation between subject and object, rather than in the everyday praxis of human discourse. From this perspective, the 'education of error' involves rooting out the distortions wrought by language on representational knowledge, not understanding better the pragmatic presuppositions of communication. In Shelley's foundationalist pedagogy, at least, there will always be 'much work yet remaining' for philosophy.

TRUTH AND NEGATIVITY

The clash within Shelley's work between 'correspondence' and 'coherence' models of truth highlights his early engagement with one of Hume's major legacies to modern thought: the problematisation of the relation between truth and meaning. While there are signs, particularly in his later work, that Shelley was moving towards a more Socratic-Benthamite conception, his position remained ambivalent, an irresolution revealed by a comment made in a February 1821 letter to Claire Clairmont. Having complimented her on her '*Germanizing*', which 'is in the choicest style of the *criticism of pure reason*', he confesses to having only a slight acquaintance with Germans, whose 'Philosophy as far as I understand it, contemplates only the silver side of the shield of truth: better in this respect than the French, which only saw the narrow edge of it'.[98] While Shelley does not amplify his observation into a description of what the 'shield of truth' might be in the round, thick edges, dull sides and all, the *Defence of Poetry*, written in the following weeks, offers more than a few hints of a fuller conception.

Here, the incipient holism of the Benthamite-Socratic discourse of truth finds a new competitor in Shelley's thought in the shape of an idealism partly fashioned after Kant's teachings. More than just a medley of earlier prose work hurried out as a rebuttal to Peacock, the *Defence* sees Shelley turn Peacock's own beloved classical sources against him by synthesising the psychology of Humean sympathy with Plato's treatment of alterity in *Symposium* and *Phaedrus*. At the same time, Shelley deploys the *Timaeus's* mythology of how the soul, 'interfused everywhere from the center to the circumference of heaven', as Plato puts it, mediates a nonreductive relationship between particularity and unity through dialectical energies, 'herself turning into herself'.[99] These influences meld in Shelley's mind with the strain of aesthetic organicism he had found in Coleridge's *Biographia Literaria* and A. W. Schlegel's *Lectures on Dramatic Art and Literature*, whereby the reconciliation of difference or opposition, and particularly that between epistemology's damagingly divisive 'subject' and 'object', becomes the task of poetry and the creative imagination. As a result, Platonic metaphysics produces the idea of poetry as that which 'creates for us a being within our being'.[100] Thus, Shelley's myth of the 'cyclic poem written by Time upon the memories of men' becomes a decentred remedy for Peacock's linear narrative of epistemic progress.[101] Poetry is an act that partakes of that which it represents. It is an *intuition* of the secret union of fact and value, of 'truth' and 'life'.

In the *Defence* then, Shelley deploys nonlinear paradigms of metaphor, imagination, and meaning to critique Peacock's triumvirate of knowledge, reason, and truth, even though the 'truth' to be countered is not so much the oppressive and dogmatic truth of organised religion against which the poet had railed in his youth, but the tyranny of anarchic fact, the subjection to 'the accident of surrounding impressions'.[102] Poetry's figured veil redeems the ordinary by revealing philosophy's alienated truth as value-rich experience. Indeed, as Paul Fry notes, the recurring 'veil' imagery of the *Defence* is notoriously unclear on the matter of 'what covers what'.[103] Fry suggests that in the *Defence* at least 'the similarity between surface and subsurface is greater than the contrast', figuring poetry as 'a colored region behind the colors of expression'.[104] Thus, as Shelley maintains of the highest forms of poetry, like Lucretian *membranae* '[v]eil after veil may be undrawn, and the inmost naked beauty of the meaning never exposed'.[105]

This kind of language almost makes Shelley sound, once again, like Wasserman's phenomenalist, challenging linear reasoning and fact with conceptions of truth as infinite becoming. And yet, it has already been seen elsewhere in the *Defence* that what poetry 'unveils' is something other than its own ceaseless creative activity in experience. In particular, the 'naked and sleeping beauty' it discloses in the 'spirit' of the world suggests a notion of ideal essence quite in keeping with the kind of transcendentalism Shelley might have encountered in Coleridge or Plato. Indeed, the equivocation of the same passage as to whether poetry 'spreads its own figured curtain or withdraws life's dark veil from before the scene of things' perfectly reflects Shelley's double-mindedness over the question of truth.[106] Poetry, it appears, is truth-ambivalent, a 'mirror which makes beautiful that which is distorted', and yet is 'the very image of life' – but not fact – 'expressed in its eternal truth'.[107] Truth itself undergoes a transformation in the *Defence*. From the many-sided and variously textured 'shield' in Shelley's letter to Clairmont, truth is relegated, at least in its moral form, to the status of an 'empty scabbard' forever consumed by poetry's 'sword of lightning'.[108] Even here, however, Shelley's metaphor is double-edged. On one hand, far from being something that must be contemplated from all sides, truth is now overcome by poetic power; on the other, Shelley's continuing sensitivity to the claim of truth is betrayed by the underlying expectation that it is scabbards that 'consume' swords, not the other way round. Truth's enclosure, it appears, is a threat that Shelley is anxious that poetry should overcome.

Passages such as this recall young Shelley's suspicion of truth (the ultimate form) as inherently oppressive. Older Shelley is wiser, but undecided. He comes to recognise the possibility of an empirical concept of truth that is holistic rather than dogmatic, and yet he remains the captive of the notion of truth as correspondence, an assumption that informs the *Defence*'s various noncognitivist and idealist attempts to overcome reason with imagination. Certainly, his claims that 'our calculations have outrun conception' and that 'we want the poetry of life' and 'the creative faculty to imagine that which we know' challenge the epistemic centre.[109] But they do so in a way that suggests that the *only* recourse for poetry in the wake of the collapse of the Enlightenment totem of truth as correspondence is to capitalise upon the failure of representation. In this way, Shelley's ambivalence can be seen to lie between the 'shield' and the 'scabbard', between the tantalising image of truth in the letter to Clairmont and the celebration of poetry as the antidote to 'fact' in the *Defence*. This ambivalence is hidden from much modern commentary, which tends to proceed from the assumption that the only 'truth' at stake in Shelley is representational truth, or truth as correspondence. Thus, G. Kim Blank's claim that Shelley's language vacillates 'between a belief in a transcendental signified and a nihilistic materialism', overlooks the range of possibilities between these two positions scouted by contemporary thought.'[110] Similarly, while Ulmer is right to argue that Shelley's writing does not surrender itself to the power of difference in so far as it works *under the presupposition* of truth, this begs the question of whether the concept of truth at question for Shelley (or, for that matter, for us) should be identified with 'truth-as-presence'.[111]

Indeed, some commentators have come to question this very identification. Shelley's main problem, as Robert Kaufman indicates, is that the instrumental rationalism or 'calculating' reason that he sets out to overcome in the *Defence* is similar to that advocated by his philosophical mentors, particularly Paine. According to Kaufman, this launches Shelley on a quest to recover a concept of radical critique in which social 'sympathy' and 'calculation' are not estranged – in other words, a concept of reason without alienation. It is through rereading Milton, he claims, that Shelley is ultimately able to conceive of 'aesthetic experience as a formal process that produces . . . critical thinking itself as a form of truth. Such truth, for Shelley, does not inevitably translate into a progressive politics, but is nonetheless essential to it.'[112] Put this way, Kaufman's position sounds similar to the one currently being presented, though I find that the most vital source for Shelley's recasting of thought as a 'form of truth' is an emerging discourse of 'holistic', nonfoundational empiricism.

Kaufman, on the other hand, is inclined to read Shelley's strategy under the rubric of what he calls 'Negative Romanticism'. Indeed, he argues, there 'turns out to be unexpected and specific historical warrant for utilizing Adorno to defend Shelley against cultural materialist, new historicist, and post-structuralist critique'.[113] In this way, 'Shelley imagines (as Adorno will imagine) that a critical aesthetics can emerge from the confrontation with art's enactment of impasse'.[114] Yet by confining Shelley's aesthetics to an 'immanent' critique of the subject–object binary (which includes the idea of truth as correspondence and the ideal of poetry as imaginative transcendence) there is a danger of further entrenching the assumption that Shelley's intellectual reach is bounded by such binaries. My central argument, conversely, is that Shelley deals in *more* than one concept of truth. Thus, the idealistic vision in the *Defence* of what Kaufman calls 'a now-lost paradise where calculation and sympathy, word and thing, signifier and signified, are happily united in epic truth' coexists with a more pragmatic understanding of the relation between truth, communication, and the quotidian (one that does not require us to invoke Adornian notions of negative dialectic).[115] This pragmatism should by now not be surprising: while Kaufman writes in the shadow of Hegel, Nietzsche, and Benjamin, Shelley writes in the wake of Tooke, Godwin, and Bentham.

Further ramifications of this difference become apparent when dealing with a poem such as 'Mont Blanc', a work whose epistemological and linguistic bearings have generated a great deal of debate. Here, as in so much of Shelley's writing, assumptions that *we* make about the relation between truth and meaning are just as important as those that we attribute to Shelley's poem, not least because they affect how we read the poem's relation to its 'object'. Indeed, it soon becomes apparent that the poem's most conspicuous object, the 'great Mountain' (l.80), is not so much an object as *the* Object; objectivity itself: 'The secret strength of things / Which governs thought' (ll.139–40). Accordingly, the poem does not shy away from the suggestion that its gestures towards this power, 'The still and solemn power of many sights, / And many sounds, and much of life and death' (l.128–9), are, in some sense, epistemologically exemplary. The reader's attention is drawn to the very nature of reference, to the fundamental act that establishes a relation with the world as '*this*':

> Power dwells apart in its tranquillity
> Remote, serene, and inaccessible:
> And *this*, the naked countenance of earth,
> On which I gaze, even these primæval mountains
> Teach the adverting mind.   (ll.96–100)

The question that the poem attempts to answer, however, is: how and what, exactly, does the '*this*'-ness of the mountain 'teach'? The traditional reading of 'Mont Blanc' as a hymn to the chain of necessity has undergone various refinements over the years, as Shelley's materialism has been trimmed and adapted according to current theoretical preoccupations. In her celebrated essay on the poem, Frances Ferguson argues that the humanising instinct of Shelley's sublime ultimately exposes the overdetermination of reference by an incommensurable materiality. By turning, like Keats, to mute objects for conversation, Shelley betrays the impossibility of letting 'Mont Blanc be merely a blank, merely a mass of stone' as the poem 'attempts to imagine a gap between the mountain and the significances that people attach to it, and fails'.[116] For Shelley, it is love that finally compensates for the resulting void within reference, as 'emotional profligacy that continually postulates and assumes the existence of an interlocutor supplants any notion of matching one's knowledge with things as they really are'.[117] But this nonepistemological expedient merely reveals the unsustainable but inescapable 'humanizing' economy at work in the sublime, an aesthetic operation that 'imputes agency' to materiality, enabling 'the translation of the material to the human that is involved in any effort at making the scene intelligible'.[118]

Ferguson's analysis is itself based upon two key assumptions: first, that Shelley's conception of reference lives or dies by an epistemology of correspondence, and, second, that, having failed (as fail it must), his poem can provide only negative knowledge of the relation between truth and meaning. Saying nothing, but compelled to say everything, what the mountain really 'teaches' poet and reader alike is a lesson in the impossible necessity of communication, of meaning. The ineliminable role of deixis in thought turns out to be an unavoidable act of violence, as the '*this*'-ness of Mont Blanc it revealed to be purely a fiat of language. In a similar vein, Deborah Elise White reads in 'the exemplary deictic indicator "there"', the poem's enactment of a 'referential imperative'[119] that reveals 'the fundamental intransitivity of linguistic deixis'. The 'Power' of the mountain then, is just 'another name for the linguistic necessity to point or refer in the first place. It is the barren, formal, or *blank* rhetoricity that within every word says "there"...'[120]

As we have seen, however, not only are there are ways of framing the 'intransitivity of linguistic deixis' other than as 'blank rhetoricity', but, thanks to changes taking place within contemporary empiricism, similar avenues are increasingly open to writers such as Keats and Shelley. Only when we overlook these developments is it tempting to depict the breakdown of the correspondence necessary for reference as the unspeakable tragedy to which romantic writing has no answer but the repeated naming of the void and a stoic resignation to negative knowledge. And yet, appreciating the link in this period between the increasing interest in dialogue (both philosophical and literary) and nonfoundational conceptions of truth such as that advocated by Bentham enables us to understand how Keats and Shelley loosened the iron grip of correspondence upon notions of 'truth' and 'meaning'. Most importantly, it gives us insight into their gradual realisation that once a hypostasised 'meaning' is abandoned in favour of dialogue or elenchus, there is no incompatibility between indeterminacy, deixis, and objective truth. Seen from this perspective, the dynamics of 'Love' that underpin Shelley's view of relations in the natural world deflate, rather than efface epistemological paradox. 'Love' attests to the simultaneous dependence of truth upon society (the intersubjective) and of communication, in turn, upon truth (the possibility of error).

White, then, is quite right to criticise readings of 'Mont Blanc' that by rushing to establish the location of 'there' and the identity of 'thou' miss the poem's central concern with *how* these relations are established in the first place. As she puts it, such interpretations forget to ask 'how one can interpret "there," how one can speculate where it points, without first determining *that* it points'.[121] This (or to be more specific, 'this') is undoubtedly a central concern of the poem. However, 'Mont Blanc' establishes early on that the roots of reference lie not in the abyss, but in *communication*, in the 'thou' and 'this' of discourse, even in 'thou, Ravine of Arve – dark, deep Ravine – / Thou many-coloured, many-voiced vale' (12–13). Viewed in this way, the tricky grammar of the poem (whereby, as White notes, ' "There" is scarcely easier to pin down than "thou" '[122]), far from being a symptom of its irresistible rhetorical pressures, is a measure of its investment in elenchus as an activity every bit as necessary to truth as truth is, in turn, to communication. When the poet gazes upon the 'Dizzy Ravine' and seems 'as in a trance sublime and strange / To muse on my own separate phantasy', he is not drawn to meditate on the sovereignty of human consciousness. Instead, the 'human mind, which passively / Now renders and receives fast influencings, / Holding an unremitting interchange / With the clear universe of things around' is propelled into a vision of its own relationality:

> One legion of wild thoughts, whose wandering wings
> Now float above thy darkness, and now rest
> Where that or thou art no unbidden guest,
> In the still cave of the witch Poesy,
> Seeking among the shadows that pass by
> Ghosts of all things that are, some shade of thee,
> Some phantom, some faint image; till the breast
> From which they fled recalls them, thou art there!   (ll.34–48)

The Platonic paraphernalia of caves and shadows in this passage can be misleading if we forget the Socratic complexion of Shelley's Platonism, in which dialogue does not so much lead to truth as determine truth. It is only *through* its 'unremitting interchange' with others and the world, relating to a presupposed 'that or thou', that the mind is able to self-identify. Even then, as White observes, the epiphany 'thou art there!' can be an bewildering climax for a reader who, having already been led down so many referential corridors in the preceding passage, may be forgiven for wondering, not just *who* or *what* is 'there', but *where* 'there' is. Yet if we understand the interdependence of dialogue and deixis in the Socratic conception of truth that Shelley inherited, we will be less prone to view his conclusion with dissatisfaction or suspicion. In 'Mont Blanc', the indeterminacy of these coordinates ultimately reveals the nature of the relation between truth and language. Just as thought must hold 'unremitting interchange / With the clear universe of things around' – must, in other words, conceive of the contingencies of otherness – before it can obtain a sense of self, so the poem realises that these very interchanges, these 'fast influencings', are not possible without truth as a presupposition. 'Mont Blanc' confirms that the indeterminacy of 'this' and 'thou' and 'I' is a product not of the insistent contingency of grammar, but of the interdependence of communication and truth, elenchus and deixis.

The exemplary deictic indicator itself, Mont Blanc, is of course a constant presence in the poem. It is 'present' not as a something 'given' to consciousness, nor as the mark of an absence, but as the indeterminate 'this' without which all communication and interpretation would be impossible. Thus, when Shelley writes, 'Mont Blanc yet gleams on high: – the power is there', 'there' marks not the Form of Forms, nor the blank, radically inhuman power of deixis, but the importance of truth as the presupposition required for communication between Shelley and the many voiced Arve, or indeed, between text and reader. Truth cannot, indeed, be known. But the very point of the poem is that truth is not an object *for* knowledge. It is not 'Some phantom, some faint image' to be found among 'shadows that pass by / Ghosts of all things that are'. To imagine that it *might* ever be known (and that the failure to do so is an epistemological tragedy that the mind must confront, must attempt to overcome, whether through imagination or intuition) is to misconceive the nature of truth and the role it plays in dialogue. It is neither transcendent *nor* immanent. 'Negative' readings of the poem such as Ferguson's or White's miss this point.[123] Rather than betraying that the 'inmost beauty of language – the beauty of truth, the beauty of virtue, the beauty of history – lies outside any conceivable interiority', 'Mont Blanc' actually reveals how the 'beauty' of truth lies in its evading the very categories of 'interior' and 'exterior', 'inside' and 'outside'.[124] Truth is not an incommensurable something because it is not a *thing*. Silent, 'voiceless', it cannot be captured by thought *for the very reason* that it helps to form 'The secret strength of things / Which governs thought' (ll.139–40), and thus that without which, between humans and the world (between 'thou' and 'there' and 'me') there would indeed be 'vacancy'.

The linguistic mill of deconstruction is apt to grind up the varieties of objectivity at play in Shelley's work. As Hamilton argues, this results in a failure properly to discriminate the resources of Shelley's materialism from those of empiricism. 'The mistake,' he argues, 'is to think that [Shelley's] mental passiveness leaves the mind supine before an external world (empiricism) rather than empowered to participate in the natural excitation and productivity of that world of which it is a part (materialism)'.[125] My point, however, is that Shelley's writing registers the possibility of an 'empiricism' not chained to a notion of correspondence whereby the mind is 'supine before an external world'; an empiricism which is quite at ease, moreover, with both indeterminacy and objectivity. By securing reference holistically, it conforms to a discourse of reason that escapes both the synchronic and spatial mappings of the postmodern attitude and what Linda Brigham labels the '*indexical* way of referring to things' presupposed by historicism.[126]

None the less, if much modern commentary has distorted Shelley's writing because of its eagerness to dance in the ruins of reason, it must be acknowledged that Shelley himself does much to encourage this oversight. In a self-defeating strategy, he repeatedly and unsuccessfully attempts to lever the nonfoundationalist counterdiscourse of reason into an eighteenth-century view of knowledge as a representational relationship between *things*, between a 'subject' and an 'object'. This brings us back to the *Defence*. Even in this work, celebrated as one of Shelley's most logocentrifugal compositions, there is evidence of his persistent attachment to an epistemological rather than a discursive model of objectivity. As with Keats and Coleridge, the lure of the subject–object model of knowledge draws Shelley towards idealism. Ultimately, the centrifugal force of the *Defence*'s attack on knowledge is arrested by Shelley's continuing investment in a dualism, which, at its most fundamental, seeks to describe a division between conceptual scheme and empirical data, between form and content.

This problem appears at the very beginning of the essay, in which Shelley's opening gambit is a radical distinction: between reason (or 'mind contemplating the relations borne by one thought to another'; the 'principle of analysis'; the 'enumeration of qualities already known') and imagination (or 'mind acting upon those thoughts so as to colour them with its own light'; the 'principle of synthesis'; the 'perception of the value of those qualities, both separately and as a whole').[127] Yet the more elaborately Shelley unfolds the division between imagination and reason, synthesis and analysis, evaluation and enumeration, the more he alienates two kinds of mental activity, between which, since all knowing is a coming-into-being, an infinite 'unveiling', there is no fundamental distinction to be made. Fundamentally, to think of truth as an 'unveiling' means to play 'Old Harry', as J. L. Austin once put it, with 'the true/false fetish' and 'the value/fact fetish'.[128] More immediately, it means pursuing to their conclusion the *Defence's* own suggestions that the relation between 'truth' and 'meaning' is a lot tighter than the clunking apparatus of reason and imagination deployed in its introduction would permit – that truth itself, indeed, might be a pragmatic and communicative, rather than an epistemological matter.

However, by defending his account of the poetic 'origins' of human intellect against Peacock's neo-Humean narrative of the progress of knowledge, Shelley misses his target. Concentrating on overturning a culture of knowledge dominated by facticity, in which calculating reason is increasingly valued at the expense of imagination, he loses sight of his real antagonist: the correspondence model of truth itself. This is why the hierarchy of cognition in the *Defence's* exordium is so jarring, for it immediately buys into the terms of a foundationalist epistemology according to which the 'given' or raw material of perception, synthesised by imagination, must be realised in a conceptual scheme (or language) to count as knowledge. That Shelley installs poetic synthesis as the *ground* of this process – the 'principle within the human being' that surpasses the lyre by producing 'not melody alone, but harmony, by an internal adjustment of the sounds or motions thus excited to the impressions which excite them' – does not remove the dualism, it merely idealises it.[129] Kant himself had already advanced the proposition that analysis presupposes synthesis, and that the understanding '*does not draw its* (a priori) *laws from nature, but prescribes them to it*'.[130] However, Kant's argument depends not upon an empirical argument about the poetic 'origins' of thought and speech, but a transcendental argument concerning the conditions for experience to be possible. By postulating an original lyrical-synthetic act of mind as foundational in human knowledge, Shelley breathes life into the very thing that he is trying to deflate: Hume's divided universe, and the metaphysical–epistemological 'problem' of how the mind represents the world. In his eagerness to make poetry 'at once the centre and circumference of knowledge', Shelley misses an opportunity to break down the barrier between conceptual centre and experiential circumference by making the intercourse between the two reciprocal, and the difference between them one of degree rather than kind.[131]

This returns us to the problem of Shelley's ambiguous treatment of reason, itself a perennial question in Shelley studies, from Wasserman's narrative of a 'skeptical empiricism that will evolve ultimately into … idealism', to Lockridge's branding of Shelley as a 'cognitivist non-definist', to Kaufman's diagnosis of the poet's ' "Negative Romanticism" '.[132] Lockridge rightly points out that, even in his later writings, Shelley 'does not share Blake's hostility to discursive reason'.[133] Instead, reason for Shelley has the 'clearing function' of removing error.[134] As I have argued, however, the concept of 'error' performs the task of the 'object-ive' in Shelley's work. If we assume that writers such as Shelley and Keats are limited to a fundamental view of truth as ideal presence, the significance of this role will continue to be elusive.[135] And yet, one of the main reasons for this elusiveness is the difficulty Shelley encounters when he attempts to harmonise his romantic holism with the ideas of Monboddo on the relationship between thought, language, and truth.

FORM AND CONTENT

When, early in the *Defence*, Shelley suddenly swerves away from 'an enquiry into the principles of society itself', he does so in order to turn his attention 'to the manner in which the imagination is expressed upon its forms'.[136] This turn is crucial, for it marks the point at which Shelley dismisses, or at least delays, the project for a socialised conception of language in favour of a metaphysical, psychological one. The difference between these two approaches is implied by Shelley's choice of words: whereas one conceives the nature of reference to be best understood in terms of the laws that 'begin to develop themselves from the moment that two human beings coexist', the other visualises meaning as fundamentally reducible to the relationship between content and 'form'. As is the case with Shelley's theory of truth, then, the tension between these two models of meaning can be understood in terms of the difference between a paradigm based upon coherence and one founded on correspondence; while the first is linguistic and pragmatic, the second is psychological and ideal. Within this broader picture, Shelley's switch of allegiance from reason to imagination should be seen as a tactical adjustment within the correspondence model rather than a flight from it, a romantic-idealist transfer of epistemological and semantic priority from 'content' to 'form' that leaves the 'content/form' binary intact.

Indeed, Shelley had already encountered Coleridge's painstaking but broken-backed execution of the same philosophical manoeuvre in *Biographia Literaria*, a work he read in late 1817. Shelley's decision to foreground the distinction between the functions of 'analytic' reason and 'synthetic' imagination in the *Defence* reveals a renewed investment in an idealistic model of truth and language that perpetuates and intensifies the problem of how language connects to the world. Among Shelley's modern commentators, Fry is one of a handful who has accurately detected and analysed this problem. On one hand, Fry argues that Shelley not only accepts the basic premises of Tooke's theory of language when writing his *Treatise on Morals*, but also that he refuses to install thought as in any way 'prior' to language in the *Defence*. On the other hand, he notes that Shelley's uncertainty over the relationship between reason and imagination remained an obstacle to accepting the full implications of Tooke's arguments. For Fry, the ambivalence in Shelley's position is evident in the fact that while the *Defence* suggests on one level that reason at its finest 'simply *is* the imagination' the deployment of the analytic/synthetic distinction between the two faculties harks back to Shelley's earlier, Painite concern to separate figurative and literal language.[137] This means that while his work often implies that thought and language might fold into each other, 'Shelley is most frequently inclined not to accept this implication', appealing instead to the Lockean notion that 'words are arbitrary signs that obscure the pure essence of thoughts'.[138]

Certainly, up to this point at least, Shelley is quite consistent in maintaining that thought and logic are presupposed *by* language. As he puts it in a letter to Elizabeth Hitchener of January 1812: 'words are only signs of ideas, and their arrangement only valuable as it is adapted adequately to express them'.[139] This echoes Locke's claim that words '*signify* only Men's peculiar *Ideas*, and that *by a perfectly arbitrary Imposition*'.[140] The notion that the relationship between idea and word is fundamentally artificial and arbitrary enables Shelley to safeguard the mental from the linguistic, reinforcing his claim that belief is passive and incorrigible, or, as he affirms in the same letter to Hitchener, 'not a voluntary operation of the mind'.[141] As Fry points out, everywhere in Shelley there recurs the idea 'that essences are liberating while forms are oppressive,' and for the young Shelley language is the oppressive form *ne plus ultra*, the vessel of dogmatic truth.[142] An instrument of the mind, it retains the power to engender an alienated, unhappy consciousness. This concern is vividly expressed in a letter to Godwin a few months later, in which Shelley argues that 'the learning of *words* before the mind is capable of attaching correspondent ideas to them, is like possessing machinery with the use of which we are so unacquainted as to be in danger of misusing it'.[143]

This instrumentalist view of language persists even where Hume's influence encourages Shelley to dismantle epistemological barriers, such as that between the phenomenal and the ontological, or between perception and being. In the 1817 fragment 'Speculation on Metaphysics', he attempts to recover value for a jaded and sceptical philosophical culture by refashioning metaphysics as 'the science of all that we know, feel, remember, and believe'[144] and by refiguring man as 'pre-eminently, an imaginative being'.[145] However, with metaphysics itself installed as 'the science of facts', fulfilling the central epistemic imperative with 'the certainty of the conclusions which it affords', words remain marginalised. They are 'the instruments of mind whose capacities it becomes the Metaphysicians accurately to know, but they are not mind, nor are they portions of mind'.[146] The identification of the psychological and metaphysical spheres is not answered by a similar convergence of the epistemological and linguistic domains. Tellingly, Shelley does not proceed from his Humean conviction that the distinction between the '*external* and *internal*' is 'merely an affair of words' to the conclusion that the science of facts is itself determined by language.[147] His embryonic monism of mind and world always threatens to become damagingly sceptical when married to a dualism of idea and word, of bare mental content and linguistic conception, or 'form'.

As Fry's observations suggest, however, the broader picture of Shelley's thought is complex. In the years leading up to his death, Shelley struggled to adjudicate between two competing eighteenth-century models of language. On one hand, Tooke and Bentham moved to confine meaning to social, linguistic systems without any overt reference to mental 'contents'; on the other, theorists like Monboddo, inspired by Rousseau, traced reference back to its origins, to the 'primitive' but more complete expressions, utterances, and creations of earlier societies. Initially, Shelley was attracted to Tooke's linguistic deflation of abstract ideas, his rendering of truth as 'That which is TROWED', and his assertion that there is 'no such thing as eternal, immutable, everlasting TRUTH'.[148] On the other hand, Tooke's conviction that prepositions and conjunctions signalled the decline and corruption of modern language was less apt to please the young Godwinian.[149] Later, Shelley was drawn to Monboddo's Neo-Platonic narrative of the improvement of human understanding through increments of linguistic articulation, from its onomatopoeic and musical origins in the gestures of rude societies to the increasingly formal and abstract schemes developed in modern civilisations through 'rules of art'. Derived from Rousseau, this account squared with Godwin's brief discussion in the *Inquiry*.[150] Thus, as Stuart Peterfreund argues, with Monboddo's assistance Shelley is able to substantiate Asia's claim in *Prometheus Unbound* that Prometheus 'gave man speech, and speech created thought / Which is the measure of the Universe' (II.iv.ll.72–3). For both Shelley and Monboddo, he claims, the growth of a language from inarticulate cries into rule-governed signification was regulated by the unfolding '*logos*, or an informing principle that exists in both world and word alike ... an immanent "form of language," prior to logic'.[151] Consequently, like Vico before him, Shelley comes to believe 'that the problem of knowledge is in fact the problem of language'.[152]

However, critics differ on the nature of this 'problem of language' in Shelley, dividing roughly according to which of the two traditions they see as playing a more significant role in his thought. Peterfreund argues that Shelley sides with Monboddo against Tooke, cultivating the idea of logos or 'a formal principle that exists in pre-logical language and all the other "facts" of which metaphysics is the "science"'.[153] This, he claims, is reflected in Shelley's increasing use of pun and metaphor, as meaning shifts 'from the referential to the formal'.[154] Against this, Cronin identifies Bentham's claim that meaning is propositional rather than referential as a critical part of the background to Shelley's thought. A source of 'dismay' for Bentham himself, the consequent realisation that 'the limits of thought are defined by the limits of language', Cronin claims, enabled Shelley to turn the emotive, overtly fictional language of poetry into a dialectic critique of society whereby the 'poet, in struggling against one prejudice, helps to create another'.[155] Cronin links this dialectical turn to the interests that Shelley and Coleridge shared in dialogue, reader response, and wider formations of 'meaning': theories, societies, intelligible worlds.

In fact, both perspectives capture part of the truth, while missing what is really at issue in Shelley's ambivalence. Peterfreund and Cronin rightly identify a major contemporary shift in the understanding of the relationship between truth and language, and both accurately diagnose Shelley's ambivalence as a response to that change. Shelley is without doubt influenced by the theory, suggested by Tooke and Bentham, that truth and meaning are not 'given', but at the same time he is unable to relinquish the Lockean picture of reference, defended by Monboddo, according to which the linguistic domain is determined by the psychological. Indeed, as I have outlined above, Shelley would have found both traditions in Godwin's *Inquiry*.

However, neither Cronin nor Peterfreund sufficiently registers the power of the Tooke–Bentham model to transform the concept of 'truth' in ways that enable a writer such as Shelley to bypass epistemological paradox. Cronin claims that by turning Bentham's critique of poetic 'fictions' on its head, Shelley uncovers the problem of romantic relativism, making him 'pre-eminently the poet of unrealisable aspiration'.[156] Yet this begs the question of whether truth is always conceived by Shelley and Bentham as a transcendental ideal. I have argued that it is not: indeed, as Shelley was aware, Bentham (never one to allow epistemological problems to trump ethical concerns) eventually incorporates what was at first an uncomfortable finding (that linguistic fictions inhabit the entire spectrum of human experience) into a deflationary account of the truth-value of statements through paraphrasis or contextual definition. Thus, as Quine indicates, when Bentham 'found some term convenient but ontologically embarrassing, contextual definition enabled him in some cases to enjoy the services of the term while disclaiming its denotation'.[157]

The appearance of this pragmatic, holistic discourse of truth in turn raises doubts about Peterfreund's claim that Shelley's linguistics, pressing Monboddo's 'logos' to its conclusion, edge out into an untethered, centreless formalism committed to 'the drama of fostering the reign of metaphor and forestalling the reign of metonymy' through 'dialectical play'.[158] Like Cronin, Peterfreund assumes that Shelley's theoretical man-oeuvres play out as part of a game in which the ultimate goal is to understand the relationship between form and content. Shelley himself encourages this view in the *Defence* by declaring his main priority to be that of understanding 'the manner in which the imagination is expressed upon its forms'. In this respect at least, he was never to shake off the influence of Locke, Rousseau, and Monboddo. And yet, coexisting with this eighteenth-century inheritance is a more recent strain of thought, one from which Shelley breaks away at the beginning of the *Defence*, and which raises the question of whether it makes any *sense* to talk of 'meaning' – or 'truth', for that matter – in terms of a relationship between form and content.

It is this strain that resurfaces later when Shelley issues his warning to the materialists: 'whilst the sceptic destroys gross superstitions, let him spare to deface, as some of the French writers have defaced, the eternal truths charactered upon the imaginations of men'.[159] The pun on 'charac-ter' here appears to introduce two potentially embarrassing questions: first, that of how anything – even 'truth' – can shape the imagination, when supposedly the imagination alone is formative; second, that of in the sense in which truths 'charactered' or *inscribed* upon the imagination – truths so vulnerable to defacement – can be described as 'eternal'. At first sight, the warning looks like a muddle, in which the competing demands of objectivity, consciousness, and linguistic communicability are left to fight it out. But the air of paradox arises only if one approaches Shelley's caution from a perspective whereby written language is deemed to *mediate* the relationship between mind and world; a perspective, in other words, in which the linguistic always renders determination problematic. But what much of Shelley's writing indicates is that cognitive and communicative activities are not best read in terms of 'what forms what', but as social activities in which objectivity or 'eternal truth', the 'characters' of communication, and the 'imaginations of men' each supports the other. This relationship is not a metaphysical one of 'determination', but a pragmatic one of *presupposition*. It is 'transcendental' only in the limited sense that without the relations of interdependence between objectivity, intersubjectivity, and subjectivity, none of these is possible. To the extent that Shelley's work can be described as fostering a 'dialogic' model of language, then, it remains Socratic, Benthamite, and pragmatic, rather than relativistic, dialectical, or formalist.

In the end, two conclusions can be drawn regarding Shelley's evershifting attitudes towards the relationship between truth and meaning. The first is that his metaphysics block the more logocentrifugal energies at work in his theory of language. Recasting Monboddo's narrative of the origins of language as a story of the growth of synthetic imagination rather than of embryonic reason presents Shelley with an opportunity to *identify* poetic language with imaginative activity. According to critics such as Peterfreund and Wheeler, Shelley is indeed committed to such a radical paradigm shift.[160] As Fry notes, however, this manoeuvre is by no means cleanly or consistently carried through. Indeed, Shelley's construction of imagination remains, for the greater part, non-linguistic. Like Kant and Coleridge (despite their manifold differences), Shelley tends to see imagination as the synthesiser of preconscious material, connecting deep 'thought' with conscious knowledge, which is finally externalised as language. As such, imagination presumes a fundamental duality of synthesis and analysis, a distinction between 'mind acting upon ... thoughts so as to colour them with its own light, and composing from them, as from elements, other thoughts', and 'mind contemplating the relations borne by one thought to another, however produced'.[161]

At the root of this duality is Shelley's continuing adherence to a picture of a world divided between constructed 'forms' and neutral, given 'contents'. Thus, the cycle of metaphoric entropy and renewal much celebrated by some deconstructive readings of Shelley is one that supervenes upon a linear relationship of correspondence between idea and object. It is instructive to compare Shelley's position to that of Wilfred

Sellars. In *Empiricism and the Philosophy of Mind* (1956), Sellars launched an attack on the empiricist notion of factual knowledge as consisting in the mysterious alchemy of a confrontational relationship between the 'given' uninterpreted data of the world and an evaluative conceptual scheme, or 'the idea that epistemic facts can be analyzed without remainder – even "in principle" – into non-epistemic facts'.[162] According to Sellars, knowledge is always already epistemic, or evaluative. This, I would contend, is a position around which Shelley skirts throughout his career, and to which he draws closest in the *Defence*. Sellars' claim, for example, that '*being*' is logically prior to '*seeming*' completes the logic of Shelley's attack on dualistic paradigms of perception, as expressed by his mantra, 'nothing exists but as it is perceived'.[163] Moreover, it signals what is truly at stake in his constant effort to renegotiate the division wrought by Hume between a value-rich but projected 'circumference' and a factual 'centre' in human life. For grasping the 'value' horn of Hume's dilemma would have meant abandoning not just the foundational gift of intuitional immediacy, but also what is arguably the cornerstone of classical empiricism: the distinction between concept and content. As Sellars puts it, the denial of the division between fact and value 'is the denial that there is any awareness of logical space prior to, or independent of, the acquisition of a language'.[164] When the 'facts' against which Shelley rails in the *Defence* are finally overcome, what remains is what Bentham would call 'paraphrasis', truth-seeking though open-ended dialogue or communication. While he willed the end (the relegation of the factual), however, Shelley could not will the means (the removal of the epistemology of 'form' and 'content').

This brings us to the second conclusion, namely that readings of Shelley's poetry and prose based on postmodern, poststructuralist, new historicist, or constructivist models of truth and meaning are likely to be misleading when it comes to evaluating the potential in Shelley's position for summoning a critique of formalist or essentialist systems of thought. What modern criticism frequently overlooks is how the influences of Tooke, Bentham, and Godwin enable Shelley's thought to incorporate both ideas of indeterminacy and a concept of objective truth. Thus, we can admit with Hogle that Shelley's 'centreless displacement of figural counterparts by one another' is 'basic to, not a mere symptom of, his sense of thought', only if we allow that for Shelley such 'centreless displacement' itself presupposes the objectivity of truth.[165]

This is not to endorse Roberts's claim that in Shelley unpredictability becomes not merely 'a reflection of our limited ability' but 'an absolute fact about the system', a kind of Neo-Lucretian 'quantic theory of meaning, holding that meaning is not amenable to infinitely precise description'.[166] In fact, once we understand the impact of Tooke and Bentham's semantic theories upon a literary and philosophical milieu less inclined to release its hold on the concept of objective truth than modern commentary, we can see that we do not need a 'chaotic' theory of reference to explain the way in which, at its most radical, Shelley's writing manages to celebrate the destruction and renewal of 'meaning' while preserving a sense of 'the eternal truths charactered upon the imaginations of men'. It does so through the 'education of error', or Shelley's sense of the way in which discourse can only function under the presupposition that error is always a real possibility, and thus that in all human communication, as Godwin puts it, the truth cannot but be 'struck out by the collision of mind with mind'. From this perspective, Shelley's apparently paradoxical claim that truth endures even as meaning is endlessly destroyed and recreated is simply a more colourful way of arguing what Bentham's theory of fictions had already suggested: that nothing is ever constant in communication and interpretation other than the assumption that we can sometimes get things wrong.

CONCLUSION

Reading Hume's *Essays* during a bleak final winter in England in 1817, Shelley would have encountered this warning to the sceptic: 'While we are reasoning concerning life, life is gone.'[167] Hume's predicament remains paradigmatic for many writers at the beginning of the nineteenth century, and Shelley is no exception. Hume bequeaths a consciousness divided between projection and reality, confronted by the dilemma of abandoning the quest for foundations and so forsaking certainty, or pursuing facts at the price of alienating knowledge from human values. Hume's settled view, like that of Johnson, is that the demands of 'life' are inimical to those of thought. In this light, Shelley's appeals to the power of philosophy and poetry in 'On Life' and the *Defence* respectively are attempts to balance the claims of life's epistemic 'centre' and experiential 'circumference'. They form one chapter in a broader and ongoing endeavour in Western thought to regulate the competing desiderata of veridicality and life, or, in the language of Hume, fact and value. What emerges from this engagement is Shelley's double-mindedness, his ambivalence on questions of truth, knowledge, and language, reflecting *both* his critique of instrumental reason and his inability to detach this critique entirely from a moribund epistemology based on correspondence theories of truth and meaning.

In other words, even as Shelley interrogates empiricism from the perspectives of materialism or scepticism, the Platonic metaphysics of Eros or the Germano-Coleridgean aesthetics of imagination, he never completely rejects its most basic assumptions: the epistemological distinction of form and content, and the ontological distinction between word and idea. At the same time, once one strips away the metaphysical apparatus of logos and the psychological machinery of reason and imagination, it becomes clear that in the Shelleyan 'drama of fostering the reign of metaphor and forestalling the reign of metonymy', the concept of truth retains a leading role.[168] In the idea of truth as embedded in communicative action, Tooke, Bentham, and Godwin developed a pragmatic and social basis for a romantic counterdiscourse of reason. Conceived as the 'fiction' necessary for dialogue to take place, the Socratic understanding of truth as the presupposition of discourse enters Shelley's writing as an alternative form of objectivity to the consolatory, noumenal ideal left in the ruins of empiricism's quest for truth as correspondence. One of the things that makes romanticism so suggestive and yet so beguiling for modern thought is the way in which it draws together the concepts of truth and meaning *without* collapsing each into the other. Though not without misgivings, it is by conceiving of truth pragmatically, dialogically, as 'an education of error', that this is achieved in Shelley.

CHAPTER 5

The embodiment of reason: Coleridge on language, logic, and ethics

In his celebrated letter of March 1801 to Thomas Poole, Coleridge portrays himself as a man who, on the threshold of a new century, is undergoing a radical (if not quite sudden) transformation in philosophical outlook. Interleaving the language of violent revolution with the rhetoric of revelation, he writes:

The interval since my last Letter has been filled up by me in the most intense Study. If I do not greatly delude myself, I have not only completely extricated the notions of Time, and Space; but have overthrown the doctrine of Association, as taught by Hartley, and with it all the irreligious metaphysics of modern Infidels –[1]

The familiarity of this performance attests to its success: since Coleridge wrote his letter, the picture of his thought as a flight from a dogmatic materialist associationism to an equally dogmatic, 'organic' idealism has weathered well. Underpinned by the early work of Shawcross, Muirhead, Wellek, and Snyder, the scholarly consensus on Coleridge's changing views on the relationship between truth, thought, and language remained remarkably stable throughout the twentieth century. Its persistence has ensured that even today at the shoulder of the image of the Young Coleridge – Pantisocrat, Hartleian, and linguistic radical – there continues to hover the presence of Coleridge the metaphysician: Trinitarian, Kantian, and apostle of the Logos. The sense of inevitability that clings to this conversion narrative, further heightened by an air of political apostasy, is such that even those who argue that Coleridge never quite manages to disentangle himself from the unsettling implications of Hartley's thought continue to chart his career as one that slips beguilingly from uneasy materialism into disingenuous transcendentalism.[2] The political consequences of this are also widely accepted. As one critic sums it, Coleridge 'began his intellectual career as an advocate of a *civic* definition of Imagination . . . and ended it by defining the terms of an authoritarian and hierarchical culture closely linked to the *religious* sphere'.[3]

It would be foolish to deny that there is a good deal of truth in the grain of this narrative. As with many grains, however, irregularities and knots can easily be overlooked. Indeed, the image of a 'knot' in the grain is especially apt when considering Coleridge's thought and its narrativisation, both in his own work and in subsequent commentary. In this chapter, I will argue that it is precisely such an anomaly, the trace of a severed branch in his thought, whose remainder not only splits the grain of Coleridge's intellectual 'conversion' to transcendentalism, but also affects the texture of his later thinking. Pursuing this argument will involve, first, indicating the powerful but largely submerged resources in Coleridge's views on language, thought, and politics; secondly, demonstrating that the presence of the latter has been occluded by modern commentary's connivance with Coleridge's conversion narrative; and finally, revealing a Coleridgean model of truth and reason quite different from the self-defeating paradigm scouted by modern theory and historicism.

This paradigm has for a long time been a whipping-boy for critics, confirming a suspicion in some sections of modern commentary that materiality and contingency are two forces that refuse to be harmonised or finessed by Coleridge's successive appeals to association, 'polar' logic, and the metaphysics of Will. As a result, it is argued, his work remains vulnerable to the insubordination of language and history to the centripetal authority of the Logos, a susceptibility evident in the Coleridge who argues in 1795 that '[w]e should be bold in the avowal of *political* Truth among only those whose minds are susceptible of reasoning: and never to the multitude',[4] but just as apparent in the Coleridge who worries in *The Friend* over the threat that the dissemination of mere 'verbal' truth poses to the 'moral' truth underpinning a stable national consciousness.[5]

I shall argue however, that this perspective has not allowed sufficient weight to three vital aspects of Coleridge's thought. The first of these is what Heather Jackson dubs 'etymologic', the theory of language and logic that he freely adapted from John Horne Tooke's linguistic empiricism.[6] With a few notable exceptions, critics have underestimated the long-term consequences of Coleridge's interest in Tooke's attempt to construct a grammar of thought. Second, amid the considerable volume of literature on Coleridge's long and complicated involvement with Kant's philosophy, surprisingly little has been written on the holistic and *anti*-idealistic thrust of transcendentalism as a *method*. None the less, it is within the framework of transcendental argument that Coleridge discovers a model for how 'etymologic' might be extended into an understanding of the relationship between truth and communication, a model quite at odds with both materialist *and* idealist accounts. Because of this, I will maintain, Kant's role in Coleridge's thought (supplying both a method and a metaphysics) is more ambivalent than Coleridge suggests in his 'transcendental conversion' letter to Poole as well as elsewhere. Indeed, though in the end Coleridge embraces metaphysics, there is nothing *inherently* 'metaphysical' about this dimension of his thought. Finally, I will address what David Haney has identified as the 'challenge' posed to modern theory and commentary by the 'relation between hermeneutics and ethics' in Coleridge's work.[7] When read alongside his emergent ideas on etymologic and transcendental argument, Coleridge's theory of the value-ladenness of communication forms the 'knot' of his radical form of romantic critique, a counterdiscourse both to idealism and its *alter ego*, hyperscepticism, or what Coleridge calls 'hypopœsis'. Although Coleridge seems to have abandoned this counterdiscourse by 1810, I argue that it continues to influence later works such as the *Magnum Opus*.

The task of identifying the impetus for this 'counterdiscourse' has been assisted in recent years by a resurgence of interest in the links between radicalism, language theory, and the epistemology of the 'public sphere'. Thus, Richard Marggraf Turley and Paul Hamilton interpret the imagined communities of writers such as Godwin, Wordsworth, and Coleridge as attempts to 'recover a public sphere' of unfettered communication, rather than establish hegemony for a new regime of consciousness. 'In this case,' Hamilton writes, 'to imagine a language is very much to imagine a form of life ... the political consequence of a utopian moment which Augustan literary culture had contained and postponed for so long'.[8] The implications of this project are tremendous. As A. C. Goodson argues, '[u]nder terrific historical pressures, the writers concerned aspired to new kinds of holistic understanding', which in turn prove to be highly 'instructive about the formation of modern rationality in the crucible of experience'.[9] And yet, understanding what is at stake in this formation becomes a ticklish enterprise for the modern reader precisely because romanticism occupies a liminal space, a 'halfway house', as Goodson terms it, between an eighteenth-century desire for a public sphere based on free acts of communication and the 'high disciplinary' critique of language found in late twentieth-century theory.[10]

It is this ambivalence in romantic discourse that frequently wrong-foots modern criticism. As a result, alternative conceptions of truth and communication from this period have been drowned out by the clamour of the theory wars of the late twentieth century. Among the casualties is a pragmatic, communicative model, according to which truth, community, and interpretation are holistically interrelated. The 'truth' implied by this theory depends upon the social activity of communication, where communication presupposes the possibility of error, and 'error' is determined by a set of intersubjectively determined norms and values. Thus, in Goodson's 'halfway house' of romantic linguistics, language briefly emerges not as a *medium* for thought but as thought itself – not so much constitutive of thought, as *the* activity in which people engage when they communicate with each other: in other words, in the romantic 'public sphere' language and truth are exhaustively determined by the pragmatics of communicative action. I have already traced the lines of such an argument in the Socratic, 'radical empiricism' of Keats and Shelley. In this chapter, I want to go further and argue that it also forms a formidable knot in the work of the avowedly anti-empiricist Coleridge.

This knot will remain invisible unless the metatheoretical lens is adjusted. Many scholars of romantic literature, tired with the debates that raged through the 1980s and 1990s, have simply dismissed the arguments of 'high' theory and returned to the task of extending the canon or renewing the archive. So long as they remain ignored, however, the ramifications of these late-twentieth-century debates continue to have an (often unseen) effect upon the orientation of commentary, principally in the assumptions that lie behind claims that the work of romantic writing is in need of 'historicisation', 'materialisation', or 'deconstruction'. A case in point is attitudes to language: since de Man, a generation of commentators has grown used to the idea that romantic writing repeatedly *betrays* the fact that it is the nature of language to exist without essence. The template for this approach in Coleridge studies is set by Christensen's argument that Coleridge never overcomes the 'hypopœsis' that he condemns in Hartley's psychology in so far as the 'diversions, displacements, and digressions' of his own writing betray how 'truth … is morally meaningless unless communicated but is morally compromised by any vehicle of communication'.[11]

The problem with this model is that it is generally driven by a one-dimensional view of how truth and reason operate in Coleridge's work. Adjusting the lens allows us to rediscover the close relationship between truth and interpretation, and place human agency at the heart of 'meaning' without recourse to the hypostasisation or entification that de Man and Christensen find so problematic. More importantly, however, it uncovers an alternative concept of discourse in Coleridge, according to which, as William Keach describes it, '[b]eing subject to chance and to temporality, the force of language cannot indeed be entirely "reduced to necessity," but neither can it be produced or received except in relation to binding rules of meaningful, communicable thought'. It is through this counterdiscourse that romantic writing – Coleridge's included – occasionally 'imagines not an organicist or theological escape from the arbitrary but a transformation of privileged will and privileged caprice, necessity and chance, the causal and the casual, into new, less destructive, more commonly productive forms of discourse and social life'.[12] What I am arguing here, then, is that these 'more commonly productive forms of discourse and social life' are underwritten in Coleridge by a conception of truth in the public sphere, which, far from being threatened by communication, is predicated on the very notion of language as *communication without essence.*

This is not to deny the persuasiveness of the de Manian picture of Coleridge's thought; on the contrary, its plausibility and influence is part of the problem. It chimes nicely – too nicely – with Coleridge's own conversion narrative. Once one has accepted the arguments of scholars such as Mary Anne Perkins that 'the Logos is the unifying factor of Coleridge's "system" ... and the "key" to understanding every area of his thought after 1805', incorporating a 'concept of reason which includes conscience, faith and imagination', the familiar topography of the Coleridgean metaphysic quickly falls into place.[13] From this, it is no great leap to the ideology of the 'Logosophia', wherein (1) consciousness, whether of finite subject or infinite Subject, becomes the foundation of discourse; and (2) reason (encompassing 'conscience, faith and imagination') patrols a notion of eternal, ideal Truth.

Indeed, it must be allowed that Coleridge does little to discourage such readings. After 1805, his speculations regarding reason, truth, and language take an increasingly authoritarian turn. Key to this change is the 'desynonymisation' of Reason and Understanding. Hamilton has argued that the theory of desynonymy forms the leading edge of a progressive linguistics that Coleridge felt moved to camouflage with German idealism. This leads, regrettably, to 'his repression of a truly original exposition in *Biographia* in the interests of appearing in the charismatic role of the philosopher of transcendental deductions, safely isolated from the political vagaries of "common life words", and legislating for an ignorant readership'.[14] Yet, while a tradition of British linguistic radicalism underpins the technique of desynonymy, it is the centripetal tendency towards system in his thought (rather than transcendental argument as such) that guarantees that the dismantling of semantic equivalence is only ever carried out within the predetermined framework of a metaphysical hierarchy of terms. The result is that desynonymisations in Coleridge's work usually have antiprogressive bearings, most notably the discrimination of 'Reason' and 'Understanding'. As Henry Nelson Coleridge's records in *Table Talk* make clear, his uncle maintained in 1831 that the 'English Public are not yet ripe to comprehend the essential difference between the Reason and the Understanding, – between a Principle and a Maxim – an eternal Truth and a mere conclusion from a generalization from a great number of Facts'.[15]

The real problem with Coleridge's conception of Reason is not an underlying conflict between radical linguistics and philosophy *per se*, but that it is caught between two philosophical models: one constructed around relationship and communicability, the other based on ideal presence. As Hamilton indicates, the Coleridge who writes *Biographia Literaria* and *The Friend* remains convinced that intrinsic to the self-constitution of all discourses 'must be the consideration that they belong by any definition to an affective being who loves by relationship ... . Without that belonging, founded on communicability, knowledge foundered'.[16] And yet, Coleridge rarely articulates such relationships in the absence of a subtending essence whose existence is somehow presupposed. In this way, relationality is considered as intelligible only under the condition that it is conceived under a 'higher Idea' of Truth. Thus, in the margins of Edward Irving's *For Missionaries after the Apostolical School* (London, 1825), Coleridge writes of the communicative power of the Logos that 'if Christ be Truth, whatever is known as true, must be of Christ':

> But again every Thing exists in a communion of Action and reaction with other things & mediately with every other thing; and the knowledge of a Thing is imperfect without a knowledge of its Relations. But this is possible only by means of some higher Idea, which comprehends A. B. C. as *one*: and this again is rendered intelligible by some yet higher Idea, till we arrive at the UNIVERSAL IDEA ... the Identity of Truth and Being – the Form of all Forms ... the eternal self-manifestation of the Holy One ...[17]

As I will argue below, the tension between these positions – between knowledge of a thing through 'knowledge of its Relations' and through 'the Form of all Forms' – is the product of the sleight of hand whereby the presuppositions required to keep dialogue afloat in the public sphere are taken to betoken the existence of ideal entities in which ultimate epistemological authority resides. In this way, transcendental argument, itself neutral as a method, 'goes metaphysical' in Coleridge. Truth, the necessary presupposition or 'antecedent' to knowledge and communication, is accordingly reified as the absolute form of 'substantive truths, or truth-powers', since, as he insists in *On the Constitution of the Church and State*, 'an idea ... is in order of thought always and of necessity contemplated as antecedent'.[18] At the same time, in Coleridge the mediation of language ceases to be a source of anxiety when truth is seen not as foundation or telos, but as one of the more fundamental assumptions that one needs to make before one can make sense of, and be made sense of, within the communicative practices of the lifeworld. As Keats suggests, the 'beauty' of truth in this respect lies in the fact that there is very little – practically nothing – to be said about it.

An early example of this kind of thinking in Coleridge occurs in his pamphlet *The Plot Discovered: Or an Address to the People, against Ministerial Treason*, a revised and expanded version of 'Lecture on the Two Bills' delivered at the Pelican Inn in Bristol in November 1795. Coleridge's Bristol lectures frequently reflect his anxieties over the possible consequences of Godwin's proposal that truth be allowed to circulate freely among the 'multitude' through the dissemination of private learned societies. Using Hartley's associationism to rebut what he sees as his erstwhile mentor's untrammelled rationalism, Coleridge claims that Godwin's theory appears to be in 'total ignorance of that obvious Fact in human nature that in virtue and in knowledge we must be infants and be nourished with milk in order that we may be men and eat strong meat'.[19] While many readers will detect in these remarks the obscurantism of the later Coleridge, his comments on the effect of the Two Bills upon the liberty of the Press in *The Plot Discovered* reveal a quite different idea of how truth sustains public discourse:

By the almost winged communication of the Press, the whole nation becomes one grand Senate, fervent yet untumultuous. ... By the operations of Lord Grenville's Bill, the Press is made useless. Every town is insulated: the vast conductors are destroyed by the [*sic*] which the electric fluid of truth was conveyed from man to man, and nation to nation.[20]

In his essay on the political context of *The Plot Discovered*, Peter Kitson glosses this passage with the comment that '[b]y placing the political in the realms of natural philosophy, Coleridge is implying that the spread of knowledge and liberty is a natural process'.[21] While this is broadly accurate, the implication that the dissemination of truth is entirely 'natural' is a little misleading. The editors of the standard edition indicate in their notes to the same passage that Coleridge's 'electric' metaphor trades on Franklin's 'single-fluid theory – that electricity was a continuous, imponderable fluid'.[22] The key word here is 'imponderable', reflecting contemporary uncertainty surrounding the status of electricity. As Mark Kipperman notes, even before the awakening of his interest in German *Naturphilosophie*, Coleridge saw the electrochemical researches of Davy and others as replete with philosophical implications regarding human intelligence that transcended the natural.[23] Far from simply 'naturalising' truth, then, Coleridge suggests that discourse is itself dependent upon an 'electric fluid' of *indeterminable* essence that sustains communication 'from man to man'.

In this crucial sense, truth for Coleridge is as much the inexplicable precondition as it is the object of communication. It is this conception of truth that is later extended and developed by his exploration of the possibilities of transcendental argument and the relational nature of being and personhood, two of the axes that constitute what I would term Coleridge's 'truth holism'. As so often in his work, however, these axes are themselves finely poised between the holistic-pragmatic and the hypostatic-metaphysical: considered one moment as part of the background conditions of living a good and meaningful life, they all too easily inflate into the discourse of 'truth powers' and the Divine Tetractys. The same is true of the third axis, to which I now turn: the early study of the relation between truth and meaning as 'etymologic'.

ETYMOLOGIC

As Kitson argues, Coleridge's figuring of truth as the 'electric fluid' of discourse tells us a great deal about the political complexion of his thinking about truth and language in the mid-1790s. *The Plot Discovered* appears a year after the collapse of the treason trial of Thomas Hardy, John Thelwall, and John Horne Tooke in 1794. Under pressure from the very government policies Coleridge attacks in his pamphlet, however, the middle ground in the reform movement was already beginning to give way, pulled apart by Painite radicals and dissenting Christian reformers. As Kitson describes, *The Plot Discovered* was out of date even as it went to press, as the climate of the mid-nineties saw the *Plot*'s 'pseudo-historical generalisations about Anglo-Saxon democracy and Commonwealth republican ideology' edged out by 'emphatic avowals of deistic Paineite "rights of man philosophy"', which were incompatible with Coleridge's scripturally based religious radicalism'.[24] None the less, the 'commonwealth' of understanding, based on the 'electric fluid' of free communication against a background of intersubjectively determined norms, underpins Coleridge's thought around this time, a fact that went largely unrecognised until the 1970s. As Hamilton notes, Coleridge's notorious borrowings from contemporary German thought have often obscured his indebtedness to a traditionally British concern with linguistic propriety and normative features of 'ordinary' language.[25] It is the latter, which, in a brief period that left lasting marks on his work, drew him to the work of Tooke.

Tooke's impact on philosophical radicalism at the turn of the century can scarcely be overestimated. As Hans Aarsleff argues, 'Tooke's system and "discovery" came as a tonic to materialist philosophy', not least because it gave support to radical philosophy from a most unexpected quarter; since Harris and Monboddo, language theory had long been seen as a conservative redoubt.[26] To young materialists like Coleridge, Tooke's suggestion that thought is itself shaped by the words that expedite its communication offered a convincing account of how systems of belief were constituted by *discourse*, by natural languages that could in turn be changed and improved through social reform. This view of language as neither 'medium' nor 'matter' seemed to complement contemporary speculations in electrochemistry, which, as Aarsleff indicates, 'afforded a powerful analogue to the study of language and the philosophy of mind'.[27] Thus, in *The Diversions of Purley* Coleridge found a potent corroboration of his argument that a free civil society could only be maintained by the 'electric fluid of truth'. The real value of Tooke's argument for Coleridge, then, lay not in its linguistic materialism or atomism, but in its holism, or, as Olivia Smith describes it, in Tooke's belief 'that truth, freedom, and good government are interdependent', and that 'legitimate government and correct reasoning either co-exist or do not exist at all'.[28]

In order to understand the link between Tooke's arguments and Coleridge's ideal of a commonwealth of understanding based on free communication powered by a background of intersubjectively shared norms, it is important to consider how both signal a shift away from correspondence theories of truth and language, whereby meaning was held to consist in the relationship between word and idea, and truth was seen as determined by a similar correspondence between idea and object. Hume had already worried at the foundations of the correspondence model, but had not overturned it. As Quine notes, by bifurcating epistemology into a theory of meaning and a theory of doctrine, or truth, Hume attempts to explain the notion of body in sensory terms and justify knowledge of truths of nature in the same way.[29] However, by claiming that words derive their meaning from their antecedent impressions while simultaneously observing that the causal origins of those impressions remained indeterminate, Hume effectively undermines both correspondence theories. This encouraged future thinkers to speculate that meaning and truth had a closer relationship than he had allowed – or at least, that meaning and truth are determined contextually rather than causally.

In the case of Coleridge, this speculation takes the form of 'etymologic', a theory of the mutually determining relationship between grammar and logic. Following Stephen Prickett, we can roughly divide Coleridge's thinking about language into three phases: (1) an early stage, up to around 1800, when his theories are still dominated by the ahistorical, materialistic associationism of David Hartley; (2) a relatively brief period in the first decade of the nineteenth century, during which the influence of Tooke made him increasingly 'aware of the illogical complexities of language'; and (3) a final phase in which, under the sway of German idealism, he developed a metaphysics of language as constantly evolving, 'with words related not so much to things as changes in human consciousness itself'.[30] The first of these stages, which has been well documented, is evident in many of the poems from the late 1790s. For example, in 'Fears in Solitude' (1798), Coleridge describes the 'meaning' of nature in frankly causal terms:

> Oh! 'tis a quiet spirit-healing nook!
> . . .
> Here he might lie on fern or wither'd heath,
> While from the singing-lark (that sings unseen
> The minstrelsy which solitude loves best,)
> And from the Sun, and from the breezy Air,
> Sweet influences trembled o'er his frame;
> And he, with many feelings, many thoughts,
> Made up a meditative joy, and found
> Religious meanings in the forms of nature!   (ll.12, 17–24)[31]

The 'influences' that 'tremble' over the poet's 'frame' recall Hartley's account of vibrations of the 'Performance of Sensation by vibratory Motions of the medullary Particles' in the brain.[32] The poem also suggests a Hartleian link between the association of ideas – the 'meditative joy' of 'many feelings, many thoughts' – prompted by these sensory inputs and the 'Religious meanings' found 'in the forms of nature'. Here at least, the correspondence model of meaning remains intact, conforming to Hartley's argument that language is reducible to the impressions that '*excite Ideas in us by Association, and ... by no other means*'.[33] Already by 1798 however, Coleridge harboured doubts about associationism's ability to explain the *generative* power of language. Originally published in the same volume as 'Fears', 'Frost at Midnight' is often noted for its elaborate mapping of the community of 'companionable' forms linking poet, poet–child and child within a providential economy of intellect determined by the association of sensations and feelings. Even here, however, the strain placed on Hartley's causal mechanism of meaning by 'that eternal language, which thy God / Utters, who from eternity doth teach / Himself in all, and all things in himself' (ll 64–6) is evident. Ultimately, as Coleridge recounts in *Biographia Literaria*, this 'phantasmal chaos of association' proved insufficient to explain the powers binding language and intellect.[34]

This brings us to Tooke. Before his introduction to German idealism, Coleridge was impressed, like many philosophical reformers, with the far-reaching implications of Tooke's work on language, and in particular his renegotiation of the border between philosophy and philology. Here, Coleridge's thinking about language enters Prickett's 'second' stage, producing what Jackson dubs 'etymologic', a way of understanding the fundamental unity of thought and language that transcended the mechanical association of ideas. None the less, Coleridge's reception of Tooke was not free of ambivalence, even at this early stage. For Coleridge, Tooke's work had two major implications. The first – which he welcomed – is the notion that logic is rooted in grammar, and that by extension logic has an etymology. Consequently, his early etymological speculations focus on the question of how meaning and truth in the human realm are related through communicative action. In a particularly revealing notebook entry of December 1804, for instance, Coleridge attempts to improve on Tooke by demonstrating how both 'Word' and 'Truth' are etymologically related to terms of action: 'Truth is implied in Words among the first men. ... Word, wahr, wehr – truth, troweth, throweth i.e. hitteth = itteth = it is *it*. The aspirate expresses the exclamatia of action. Through, & Truth – Etymol.'[35] Lacking a firm empirical or historical basis, Coleridge's philological speculations, like Tooke's, appear whimsical today.[36] None the less, amid all the ropey etymologising, it is easy to lose sight of the principle at stake for both writers. This is conveyed by the opening phrase: 'Truth is implied in Words among the first men.' The Tookeian thought that Coleridge probes here runs something like this: if truth *does* have a close relationship with meaning, is it possible that in the human, public sphere, what binds the two together *is* communication, the reciprocal act of friendly, trusting conversation required for mutual understanding? In other words, if truth is implied in the word-act itself, perhaps truth is just what enables and sustains communication, part of what Habermas calls the 'unanalysable holistic background' of everyday discourse in the lifeworld.[37] By linking truth to communication ('truth' to 'troweth') and to physical action ('truth' to 'throweth'), Coleridge suggests that truth, word, and communicative action are linked in just such a relationship. This essentially deflated conception of truth – of truth without essence or presence – echoes the 'electric fluid' that bonds the epistemological and political commonwealth of *The Plot Discovered.* In the period between the waning of his support for Hartley and the proclamation of his conversion to the new philosophy of 'space and time', this vision acted as a placeholder for a more resolutely metaphysical solution to the problem of the relation of truth to meaning. It would be a mistake, however, to see etymologic merely as a transitional stage in Coleridge's thinking. As James McKusick argues, despite the fact that his early enthusiasm for Tooke's radicalism quickly dissipated, Tooke's philology remains 'a seminal influence throughout most of Coleridge's intellectual career'.[38]

This influence persists despite the second consequence of Tooke's work, which Coleridge deplores: linguistic atomism. While not as dogmatic as many of his followers upon this point, Tooke tends to assume that nouns are the basic units of language. As he puts it, any truly empirical 'consideration of *Ideas* . . . will lead us no farther than to *Nouns*: i.e. the signs of these impressions, or names of ideas'.[39] Against this particle-based view of language, Coleridge proposes a dynamic model based upon the *agency* of the verb, a power he links to both the act of consciousness and the Logos. This means that while for Tooke (*pace* Locke) nouns name sensations, not ideas, for Coleridge sensations only acquire meaning via a primordial verb, the 'I am', or self-inaugurating word of God.[40] By drawing the deflationary sting from Tooke's theory of language in this way, Coleridge is able to welcome the constitutive role of language in thought, and to continue to insist upon the central importance of etymology to philosophy after his 'conversion' to idealism. As he writes in literary correspondence published in 1821: 'Etymology . . . is little else than indispensable to an insight into the true force, and, as it were, freshness of the words in question, especially of those that have passed from the schools into the marketplace, from the medals and tokens . . . of the philosopher's guild or company into the current coin of the land.'[41] Some critics have identified this linkage of philology and 'Logosophia' as inherently idealising, the cunning manoeuvre whereby etymology becomes, as Jackson puts it, 'a tool won from the enemy': effectively, etymologic.[42] In this way, Coleridge is able to have his cake and eat it, accepting Tooke's etymology as a method of inquiry, while siding with Tooke's opponents like Monboddo by arguing that far from being accidental the structures of language are determined, in McKusick's words, by 'logical categories that are themselves intrinsic to thought'.[43] The roots of this revisionism are evident in the letter Coleridge wrote to Godwin in September 1800:

> I wish you to write a book on the power of words, and the processes by which human feelings form affinities with them – in short, I wish you to *philosophize* Horn Tooke's System, and to solve the great Questions ... 'Is Logic the Essence of Thinking?' in other words – Is *thinking* impossible without arbitrary signs? & – how far is the word 'arbitrary' a misnomer? Are not words &c parts & germinations of the Plant? And what is the Law of their Growth? – In something of this order I would endeavour to destroy the old antithesis of *Words & Things*, elevating, as it were, words into Things, & living Things too.[44]

Destroying 'the old antithesis of *Words & Things*' is, of course, precisely what Tooke had in mind. But while Tooke sets about resolving psychological entities (ideas) into semantic units, in Coleridge the direction of travel is reversed: words are *elevated* into Things, & living Things too'. Thus, it appears, Coleridge rejects Lockean semiotics (whereby words are deemed to be merely the 'arbitrary signs' of ideas) only to reinscribe the empiricist's problem of correspondence on a new level. For Locke, the problem of truth is a problem of how ideas correspond to the world; for Coleridge, it becomes a problem (so to speak) of how word-things correspond to the mind-world.

This is partly because, at least until he publishes *Biographia*, Coleridge continues to adhere to the idea of *correspondence* as the basic principle governing how both truth and meaning operate in human life. Indeed, it is his acceptance of a particular formulation of this model in the early work of F. W. J. Schelling (whereby knowledge is deemed to consist in 'the coincidence of an object with a subject', and truth itself is 'universally placed in the coincidence of the thought with the thing, of the representation with the object represented'), that causes the epistemological and metaphysical programme of the *Biographia* to come unstuck.[45] Against this background, the 'elevation' of words into things installs language as the privileged medium for the mind's relationship with the world, the merely *human* fulcrum of a correspondence that can only be realised *absolutely* in the divine realm. Thus, in marginalia to Moses Mendelssohn written between 1812 and 1816, Coleridge claims that while the question 'What is Truth? ... Relatively to God ... has no Meaning or admits of one reply – viz. God himself . . . i.e. the Identity of Thing and Thought, of *Knowing and Being*', relatively to the human mind, the answer can only be that 'the coincidence of the Word, the Thought, and the Thing would constitute Truth, in its twofold sense of Insight, and the adequate Expression of the same'.[46]

This in turn allows Coleridge to finesse the empirical theory of correspondence, and to distinguish between two kinds of truth. On one hand, factual or empirical truth, what Coleridge calls 'verbal' truth, consists in the correspondence of facts – or states of affairs in the spatio-temporal realm – to words. 'Moral' truth, on the other hand, consists in an ideal relationship of correspondence between words and thoughts. As he complains in an 1826 letter to James Gillman, 'the fundamental Mistake of Grammarians and Writers on the philosophy of Grammar and Language' is to assume 'that words and their syntaxis are the immediate representatives of *Things*, or that they correspond to *Things*. Words correspond to Thoughts; and the legitimate Order & Connection of words to the *Laws* of Thinking and to the acts and affectations of the Thinker's mind'.[47] By positing a fundamental correspondence of word-things to mind-world, Coleridge is able to argue in *The Friend* that the claim that truth can be as dangerous as deceit trades on an equivocation between '*verbal* truth', by which 'we mean no more than the correspondence of a given fact to given words', and '*moral* truth', that is, the expectation of a speaker 'that his words should correspond to his thoughts in the sense in which he expects them to be understood by others'. Only 'in this latter import we are always supposed to use the word, whenever we speak of truth absolutely, or as a possible subject of moral merit or demerit'.[48]

Such arguments appear to confirm the readings of those commentators who claim that Coleridge's adaptation of Tookeian linguistics reverses rather than capitalises upon the truth-deflating possibilities of etymologic. Thus, following the familiar pattern of 'high' romantic argument, Coleridge merely inflates the ontology of empirical psychology into that of an absolute metaphysics of consciousness. Striving, like Tooke, to ground the relation between language and thought in something beyond Locke's arbitrary imposition, Coleridge's etymologic becomes what Keach describes as 'an algorithm for idealist epistemological play', whereby '[w]ords-as-things thus get swept up in the grand theoretical project of the Coleridgean Logos'.[49] Rather than pursuing further Tooke's suggestion that the relationship between truth and meaning is holistic, determined ultimately by the pragmatics of communication, Coleridge posits a metaphysical essence in which sign and referent are united. Thus, reflecting on the 'education of the human race at large' in *Opus Maximum*, he rejects conventionalist theories of language in favour of one based upon a universal grammar of intellect: since '[c]onvention itself, nay, even the very condition and materials of all convention, a society of communicants, presuppose a language ... we may without hazard assume, that all the grounds and causes of language may exist in the human mind'.[50] Language's relation to truth is underwritten by the presence of Logos, Christ, or the communicative word of God. Not for the last time the potential of 'etymologic', is sacrificed to Coleridge's quest for ideal *etymologoi*. Ultimately (so this story goes), as Coleridge's philosophy becomes more 'Germanic' and his politics more conservative, his metaphysics become more hierarchical, ultimately producing the idea of an cultural elite or clerisy in *Constitution of the Church and State*, 'whose legislative grasp of noumenal reality', as Hamilton puts it, 'informs with absolute necessity the hierarchies constraining sociability'.[51]

And yet, Coleridge's plan 'to destroy the old antithesis of Words & Things' could be read as marking the beginning of his eventual abandonment of the correspondence model of truth and meaning in favour of a theory of language that rejects both the Lockean theory of arbitrary semiotic conventions and (at the other extreme) a mythology of hypostasised, 'organic' semantic origins. This strand of 'etymologic', prompted by Tooke's suggestion that truth is created by interpretative communities, stresses the constitutive power of the *activity* of communication in the establishment of epistemic norms and values. For example, one of the striking things about Coleridge's 1801 series of letters to Josiah Wedgwood on Locke and Descartes, is that in defending his claim that the 'Doctrine of innate Ideas' is not 'so utterly absurd & ridiculous, as Aristotle, Des Cartes, & Mr Locke have concurred in representing it', Coleridge instinctively turns Tookeian, posing the question: 'What is the *etymology* of the Word *Mind*?' As 'the verb "To mind"' suggests, he claims, the roots of intellect lie in action.[52] At this point, one might expect Coleridge to pursue the familiar path from philology to philosophy, or from linguistics to Logos – an anticipation which is initially confirmed by his further linkage of 'mind' to the German word *mähen*, the origin of which 'is to move forward & backward, yet still progressively – thence applied to the motion of the Scythe in mowing'.[53] However, Coleridge's desire to force his abstruse etymological speculations into conformity with his teleological imperatives is at this stage balanced by his interest in how normative and cognitive frameworks are established within the domain of *human* linguistic intercourse. Thus, in the following letter to Wedgwood, he admits to being impressed by Descartes's account of how 'Words ... become a sort of Nature to us, & Nature is a sort of Words. Both Words & Idea derive their whole significancy from their coherence'.[54] This idea that *coherence*, rather than correspondence, defines semantic and cognitive norms reveals a holistic, counterdiscourse of reason in Coleridge's thinking.

Even Coleridge's insistence on the priority of the Logos, presenting the underlying spiritual unity of truth, language, and being, is not quite the spoiler of this socialised, intersubjective, or 'deflated' idea of truth and meaning that it is often taken to be. Some commentators have pointed out that Coleridge considers language as prior to syllogistic logic only because the Logos is itself the spirit of higher Reason in words; language *speaks us*, but only because the spirit of God already inhabits language.[55] However, the concentration on the metaphysics of Coleridge's theory of language has tended to obscure what is arguably the most significant feature of the Logos: that it is *communicative*. Vital to this idea is the conception of human logic as itself founded in an act of communication, not a thing. This gives a rather different perspective on the indivisibility of logic and language in Coleridge. In particular, it reminds us that they are united in the human echo of divine communicative action. The ambiguity of the Logos in Coleridge's thought (as both communicative word and divine presence) reflects his uncertainty over whether the communicative act is itself sufficient to sustain the norms of dialogue without the presence of the paternal One, an ambivalence schematised in *Aids to Reflection*'s conception of the 'Prothesis' as an authorising essence 'transcendent to all production, which it caused but did not partake in', and which, '[t]aken *absolutely* ... finds its application in the Supreme Being alone, the Pythagorean TETRACTYS; the INEFFABLE NAME, to which no Image dare be attached', but which in the human sphere can be generalised through the Logos as Thesis, Mesothesis, Antithesis, and Synthesis.[56] Rather than being the solution, in Coleridge the 'Logos' is a name for the problem of how truth and meaning are related in discourse. Put simply: is grounding a condition of communication, or is communication a condition of grounding?

What is clear is that by the late 1820s Tooke's etymological legacy assumes a new significance for Coleridge, as *Biographia*'s Schellingian vision of aesthetic intuition as compensation for failure of absolute correspondence gives way to *Aids to Reflection*'s conception of mind, world, and language as coordinated through relationships of 'coherence'. Accordingly, Coleridge adjusts his earlier talk of revising Tooke by recasting words as 'living things'. Here, words are not *things* at all, but 'powers':

Horne Tooke entitled his celebrated work ... Winged Words. ... With my convictions and views, for [winged] I would substitute ... *living* Words. The *Wheels* of the intellect I admit them to be; but such as Ezekiel beheld in 'the visions of God' ... 'Wheresoever the Spirit was to go, the Wheels went, and thither was their Spirit to go: *for the Spirit of the living creature was in the wheels also.*' ... For if words are not THINGS, they are LIVING POWERS, by which the things of most importance to mankind are actuated, combined, and humanized.[57]

Nicholas Reid claims that the replacement of Tooke's 'Winged Words' with '*living* Words' in this passage reflects the two-tier conception of language that Coleridge developed after *Biographia*. According to Reid, the later Coleridge retained the correspondence model of meaning, but confined it to language considered as a system of conventions, the fallen language of reified and arbitrary logical forms, the 'shapes' of the mere understanding. At the same time, he became convinced that the conventional language of the apostate will was merely the reification of a deeper language. This language – the language of Reason – preceded the division of the discursive and the intuitive and manifested the *act* of 'outer-ance', whereby the world is 'formed' (in Coleridge's sense of the term) for intelligence. Just as in L. A. Reid's theories, where meaning is 'constructed' not as representation or likeness, but as '*transformation* in mode, from physical to mental' via '*formal* structure or logical relation' (like computer images from binary code), so in Coleridge's theosophy 'God the Father knows Himself in the form of the Son', and 'we paradigmatically know the world through perceptions which are formal in structure and sensuous in experience'. It is through this theory of language as fundamentally 'presentational form', Reid claims, that Coleridge escapes the Wittgensteinian charge of attaching meaning to images, in so far as he 'is not indexing meanings to reified images: he is indexing them to the imaging process'. Conceiving the formation of meaning as an imaging *process* in turn enables Coleridge finally to reject the correspondence model of meaning, and affirm in *Aids* that 'it is the Spirit which mediates between word and idea, which *determines* the word'.[58]

I have recounted Reid's argument at length because it presents one of the few concerted attempts in recent years to take seriously Coleridge's ideas about the relation between language and truth. It also indicates that Coleridge's transformation of words as 'things' into words as 'powers' is not an attempt to mystify reference, but is part of a serious endeavour to counter, once and for all, Hume's claim that in order for words to have meaning they must correspond in some way to discrete units of

experience. Coleridge's anticonventionalism and his rejection of corre-
spondentism (applied to both truth *and* meaning) is manifest throughout
his work after 1817, but is by no means confined to that period. And yet,
while persuasive in the abstract, Reid's narrative lacks context. The
missing jigsaw-piece in the background of Coleridge's changing views,
I would maintain, is Tooke's influence on dissenting and radical politics
at the turn of the century. Of particular significance is the way in which
Tooke energises debates over the reform of language in radical circles by
suggesting that 'truth' be disestablished as the foundational referent of
linguistic systems and installed – with subjectivity and communication –
as one corner of a triangle of interdependence that makes intelligent
human 'life' possible. Once we accept the accounts offered by
McKusick and Jackson regarding the persistence of Tooke's influence
upon Coleridge, the latter's insistence on the nonarbitrary 'power' of
words appears to have less to do with the formation of an 'imaging'
process, and more to do with an emergent idea of meaning as constituted
through holistic relationships between communicative action, thought,
and truth. Psychological processes are not eliminated by this model (nor
could they ever be in Coleridge), but are understood only within the
open-ended social frameworks that make them possible.

The reverberations of 'etymologic', then, are not entirely subdued by
Coleridge's transcendental 'conversion', but persist, actively shaping his
engagement with German idealism. Etymologic underpins the modifica-
tions Coleridge makes to his earlier theory of words as 'things', as well as his
increasing tendency to discard epistemological and philological speculations based on a paradigm of correspondence in favour of those built
around notions of relation and 'coherence'. Yet, more remains to be said
about just what 'coherence' means to Coleridge. This in turn divides into
two fields of concern. The first (which I will address in the third and final
section of this chapter) regards the way in which Coleridge sees the normative dimension of truth as determined by the circulation of values and
interests within a speech-act community. As he declares in *Aids to Reflection*:

Do I then say, that I am to be influenced by *no* interest? Far from it! There is an
interest in the Truth: or how could there be a Love of Truth? And that a love of
Truth for its own sake, and merely as Truth, is possible, my Soul bears witness to
itself in its inmost recesses. But there are other interests – those of Goodness, of
Beauty, of Utility.[59]

It is his insistence on the intimate relationship between truth and the
'interest' of Love that creates a bridge between the *meaning* holism of

etymologic discussed above and *truth* holism. Thus, by configuring communicative action in such a way that does not reduce meaning to semantics or linguistic conventions, but integrates what Habermas identifies as 'all three aspects of *a speaker* coming to an understanding with *another person* about *something*', Coleridge allows that within such interpretive relationships, the 'Love of Truth' is as vital a *presupposition* as the notion of, say, 'Goodness'.[60] This brings us to the second major issue raised by the question of coherence: what is the form or method adopted by intellect as it explores truth as coherence (described as such by Coleridge when he does *not* hypostasise truth as a neutral or noumenal 'foundation' of discourse and reason)? The answer to this question lies in a surprising quarter.

THE DIALECTIC OF TRANSCENDENTAL ARGUMENT

I have argued so far that the 'knot' formed by the holistic concerns manifest in Coleridge's thought has the potential to block the more stridently doctrinaire – not to say authoritarian – of his arguments on logic and language. The presence of this knot in his work also belies his own narrative of an intellectual career in which godless materialism, 'the irreligious metaphysics of modern Infidels', is overcome by the philosophy of consciousness powered initially by imagination, and later by a renascent concept of Reason. At the same time, it challenges the glossing of this 'conversion' by some commentators as the self-deconstructing act whereby intelligence, communication, and human flourishing are exposed as figured, performed or constructed by the 'rhetoric' or 'ideology' of the real.[61] Thus, while commentators such as Leask and Hamilton are right to point out that the early, 'civic' model of communicative imagination becomes increasingly difficult to sustain through German metaphysics, it is neither the case that this paradigm disappears from Coleridge's work entirely, nor that the influence of German idealism was bound to incline him towards evermore dogmatic or essentialist positions.

On the contrary, Kant's philosophy finally encourages Coleridge to abandon the idea that basic human awareness and communication are best thought of in terms of relations of 'correspondence' involving a neutral, punctual subjectivity or selfhood.[62] As Charles Taylor argues, Kant's new method, which stipulates that the intelligibility of human experience and discourse can only be expressed in terms of transcendental conditions (rather than determinate causes or logical relations), opens up the possibility of repositioning philosophy in the domain of 'agent's knowledge', or a knowledge of the conditions without which 'our activity would fall apart into *incoherence*'.[63] This in turn enables Coleridge to extend the holistic implications of etymologic, whereby Tooke's dictum of 'no man, no TRUTH' produced an argument about the indispensability of community to the formation of cognitive and semantic norms.[64] As Taylor puts it, linguistically mediated transcendental argument is forced upon us in a world where 'I can only learn what anger, love, anxiety, the aspiration to wholeness, etc., are through my and others' experience of these being objects for *us*, in some common space'.[65] Thus, when I have an uncommon insight, 'I have to meet the challenge: Do I know what I'm saying? Do I really grasp what I'm talking about? And this challenge I can only meet by confronting my thought and language with the thought and reactions of others. ... Bringing out the transcendental condition is a way of heading this confusion off'.[66] In a similar way, by refusing to separate truth and meaning from the qualitative distinctions that embed human life in a framework of values, Coleridge figures the embodied, social, and linguistic, transcendental conditions of life as the inescapable background of our 'agent's knowledge' – 'present' only in the form of presuppositions.

Of course, great care is required in reading Kant 'holistically'. One immediate problem confronting such an interpretation is that Kant does *not* find any reason to infer, from Hume's demonstration of how the conceptual panoply of the mind was underdetermined by the raw data of sensation, that there was anything faulty with the basic division of *form* and *content* that underpinned empiricism. As a consequence, Kant's attempt to build on the 'nominal definition of truth', or 'the agreement of cognition with its object', does not seek to break from the *duality* inherent in the correspondence model of truth (by questioning the underlying givenness of the object), but instead argues that this duality must be supported by a more fundamental epistemological and onto-logical unity rooted in the mind. In other words, far from being led (as Quine and P. F. Strawson would be almost two centuries later) to suspect that Hume's division of synthetic and analytic knowledge – or knowledge as '*Matters of Fact*' and as '*Relations of Ideas*'[67] – is based upon a misap-prehension of how truth is established within discourse, Kant regrounds correspondence in synthetic *a priori* plenitude.[68] Thus, the 'general prob-lem of transcendental philosophy' becomes, as he puts it in the *Critique of Pure Reason*, 'how are synthetic *a priori* propositions possible?'[69] That this problem is conceived as a question for *transcendental* philosophy, as distinct from any other form of inquiry, results from the fact that the possibility of synthetic *a priori* propositions can, it turns out, only be demonstrated transcendentally, or in so far as they form the necessary conditions of experience. For example, Kant defends the method of proof he deploys in demonstrating the 'Analogies of Experience' in the following way:

> About the method of proof, however, which we have employed ... one remark is to be made, which must be very important as a precept for every other attempt to prove intellectual and at the same time synthetic *a priori* propositions. If we had wanted to prove these analogies dogmatically, i.e., from concepts ... then all effort would have been entirely in vain. For one cannot get from one object and its existence to the existence of another or its way of existing through mere concepts of these things, no matter how much one analyses them. So what is left for us? The possibility of experience, as a cognition in which in the end all objects must be able to be given to us if their representation is to have objective reality for us. In this third thing, now, the essential form of which consists in the synthetic unity of the apperception of all appearances, we found ... rules of synthetic *a priori* unity by means of which we could anticipate experience.[70]

Synthetic *a priori* concepts not being discoverable either 'physiologically' or 'dogmatically', their existence can only be established by transcendental method. However, by assuming that the conditions of our mental coherence can only be explained according to 'rules of synthetic *a priori* unity' underwritten by the synthetic unity of apperception, Kant inaugurates a new doctrine, based on what P. F. Strawson dubs as 'the imaginary subject of transcendental psychology', whereby a fundamental argument about the 'principle of significance' in experience is needlessly dressed up in the metaphysics of appearance.[71] Thus, instead of appealing to ordinary consistency and coherence as exemplifying the unity embedded in experiential concepts, such that '[n]o faithful reports of ... experiences are in general possible which do not make use of the concepts of the objects which our experiences are experiences of', Kant, according to Strawson, all too quickly assumes that a transcendental method must be complemented by a transcendental doctrine of idealism.[72]

At first sight, this inference appears to be repeated in Coleridge. Indeed, Coleridge seems to compound Kant's error by inflating the metaphysical dimension of the argument, elevating transcendental idealism, like Schelling, into absolute idealism. Coleridge is even more inclined than Kant to fall into what Frege would later deplore as the conflation of formal and psychological arguments, equating 'logical necessity' with the limits on thought dictated by 'the constitution of the mind itself'. What I want to argue in this section, however, is that, having broken free of Schelling's influence, Coleridge's philosophy goes global to such an extent that it breaks out of idealism – indeed, out of what many would call 'philosophy' – into a world of relationships in which truth, communication, and consciousness are conceived as interdependent. Coleridge's understanding of these relationships is remarkably similar in many ways to Taylor's account of how we articulate the background of involvements that make up our 'agent's knowledge' and to what Habermas identifies as the decentred, pluralistic counterdiscourse of romanticism. Governing the form of this discourse is the method of transcendental argument first outlined by Kant.

One reason why this has not been appreciated before is the fact that Coleridge originally envisioned an entirely different, and much more localised role for transcendental argument. Once out of its bottle, however, transcendental argument refuses to be confined to a subordinate position in the hierarchy of his system. Indeed, it proves to be far more important in practice than Coleridge would have it. Before examining at this 'hidden life' of transcendental argument in Coleridge, it is important to understand how he tried and failed to lever it into a metaphysical system.

Nowadays transcendental argument is, following Kant, widely classed as an argument that purports to show that the truth of a statement in dispute is necessarily implied by the same conditions that constitute the possibility of an indubitable statement. In this way, as Taylor puts it, transcendental arguments can establish strong claims about the nature of experience through 'a regressive argument, to the effect that the stronger conclusion must be so if the indubitable fact about experience is to be possible (and being so, it must be possible)'.[73] Coleridge often identifies this kind of argument with a purely logical form of reasoning. In *Logic*, he sees transcendental argument not (as Kant did) as the foundation of scientific knowledge, but as an intermediary, connecting empirical perception and spiritual truths accessed through intuition. Noting that the ancient Greeks considered 'the mind in the threefold relation', that is, relative to the evidence of reason, understanding, and the senses, he ranks the metaphysical disciplines accordingly:

A – Noetics = the evidence of reason
B – Logic = the evidence of the understanding
C – Mathematics = the evidence of sense

Under the heading 'physics,' he lists: 'D – Empiric = evidence of the senses *Scholium*. The senses = sense + sensation + impressions'.[74] In this Kantian division of labour, 'Logic' is clearly defined as the province of the understanding, mediating between 'Mathematics' and 'Noetics':

Thus by the mathematic we have the immediate truth in all things numerable and mensurable; or the permanent relations of space and time. In the noetic, we have the immediate truth in all objects or subjects that are above space and time; and, by the logic, we determine the mediate truths by conception and conclusion, and by the application of all the world to the senses, we form facts and maxims of experience which is one of the two provinces in and on which the formal sciences are to be employed and realised.[75]

Thus, while truth may be defined verbally as ""the coincidence of the word with the thought and the thought with the thing"", and metaphysically as 'God himself', that is, 'the identity of thing and thought', epistemologically the question 'what is truth', demands a subjective criterion based in the mediation of 'conception and conclusion'. Here, 'truth may be defined [as] the coincidence between the thought and the thinker, the forms, I mean, of the intellect'.[76] On this picture, 'Logic' is limited to one facet of human knowledge because it expresses only one side of the power of self-consciousness: it is the science of understanding. As he expresses it in marginal comments to Kant, 'in Logic the mind itself being the Agent throughout does not take itself into question in any one part. It is a Teller which does not count itself; but considers all alike as Objective, because all alike is in fact subjective'.[77]

Transcendental argument, then, is the proper method for establishing the *criterion* of truth. This explains its role in *Logic*, in which Coleridge subdivides general logic into the canon or *logice simplex et syllogistica*; the 'criterion or *logice dialectica*'; and the 'organon or *logice organica, heuristica*'.[78] In other words, logic links to mathematics on one side through the purely formal logic of the syllogism, and at its other extreme, to noetics through the heuristic, metaphysical logic of discovery. Mediating between these two forms of reason is the transcendental logic of psychology. By developing 'the science of connected reasoning' in the understanding as the propaedeutic to the 'Dynamic or Constructive Philosophy', Coleridge originally planned to dovetail the relatively modest, conceptual aims of transcendental argument with the higher dialectic of knowing and being planned for the 'Logosophia', the latter involving questions of will and faith that supersede the logical categories and conceptual clarity associated with the mere understanding. In this way, the 'mediate truths' of logic would be linked to the 'immediate truth' of noetics. Tellingly, however, the section on the organon was never completed, and most of what remains of *Logic* is occupied with the dialectic.

The story of this failure (which echoes the collapse of the deductive programme of *Biographia*) can be narrated as the refusal of transcendental method to be confined to its allocated and subordinate role within Coleridge's architecture of spirit. According to his original plan, the organon was to be a form of logic that enabled the mind to make the transition from understanding to reason, from 'natural' to 'verbal' logic, and from predication and contradiction to the more fundamental act of the divine consciousness. This act in turn subtended the division between analysis and synthesis, thereby providing a metaphysical basis for Kant's location of synthetic *a priori* knowledge in the synthetic unity of apperception. It is not difficult to see why Coleridge runs into trouble. The most obvious way, one might think, of progressing from 'dialectic' or transcendental argument to a metaphysical logic worthy of theosophy and the ideas of reason would be to show how argument by way of presupposition (dialectic, in Coleridge's terms) cannot account for the totality of *its own* presuppositions. Thus, by effectively presupposing its own supersedence, it would pave the way for a higher 'polar logic' of alterity. Indeed, it is for just this proto-Hegelian move, as he saw it, that Muirhead applauded Coleridge, claiming that the latter succeeds in turning 'criticism against the critic'.[79]

However, while this may be fine in theory, in Coleridge things are not so straightforward. First, there is nothing in Coleridge to compare with Hegel's argument in the *Phenomenology of Spirit* that any 'dialectic' based on transcendental method inevitably gives way to 'dialectic' based upon negativity.[80] As I have shown elsewhere, this is because the conception of alterity that Coleridge locates at the heart of his higher logic of reason is not driven by the power of negation, but by the altogether obscurer agency of the Pythagorean Tetractys, which (among other things) involves a metaphysics of Will.[81] As he indicates in *Magnum Opus*, the 'source' of ideas is 'neither in the reason without the Will nor in the Will without the reason'.[82] What this means is that unlike Hegel Coleridge cannot *demonstrate* how the Kantian dialectic presupposes its own death through negativity. Instead, he relies upon para-philosophical means such as illustrations, flashes of insight, aids to reflection and above all the willingness of his reader to be *guided*, in order to lead his audience towards an illumination that cannot be attained without an element of volition, or faith. In this respect, as Catherine Miles Wallace points out, Coleridge envisages his relation to the reader more as a guide, albeit a 'Chamois-hunter', than as a preceptor.[83] As he argues in his appendix to the 1831 edition of *Aids to Reflection*, within 'Noetics', practical and theoretic reason must work together:

The Practical Reason alone is Reason in the full and substantive sense. It is reason in its own Sphere of perfect freedom; as the source of ideas, which Ideas, in their conversion to the responsible Will, become Ultimate Ends. On the other hand,

Theoretic Reason, as the ground of the Universal and Absolute *in all Logical Conclusion*, is rather the Light of Reason in the Understanding.[84]

Secondly, while in theory he schematically limits 'Logic' to the province of understanding, in practice Coleridge does *not* confine transcendental argument to questions regarding the way in which concepts are applied to experience. Instead, he frequently deploys the method in the realm of 'Noetics', or intuitive reason. Indeed, Coleridge routinely uses transcendental argument in support of ideas of Reason (such as infinity and immortality), not concepts (what Coleridge calls 'conceptions', such as water and table). Thus, in the *Magnum Opus*, the existence of ideas of reason, which are 'contradistinguished alike from the forms of the sense, the conceptions of the understanding, and the principles of the speculative reason by containing its reality as well as the peculiar form of the truth expressed therein', is established by transcendental argument, since that 'without which we cannot reason *must be presumed* . . . as the ground of the reasoning'.[85] Similarly, in *Aids to Reflection* he laments the decline in the appreciation of 'forethought', writing that:

[it] is at once the disgrace and the misery of men, that they live without fore-thought. Suppose yourself fronting a mirror. Now what the objects behind you are to their images at the same apparent distance before you, such is Reflection to Fore-thought. As a man without fore-thought scarcely deserves the name of a man, so Fore-thought without Reflection is but a metaphorical phrase for the *instinct* of a beast.[86]

Crucially, 'Fore-thought' for Coleridge represents not just the conceptual or even psychological conditions that make thought or experience possible, but the presupposed presence of an Idea that bears life, encompassing the very dimensions of language, love, and 'instinct' that Kant had taken such care – at least in the first *Critique* – to segregate from transcendental inquiry. This idea of 'Fore-thought' as the indeterminate precondition of coherent thought is typical of how in his later discursive writings, while outwardly concerned with system building, Coleridge thinks transcendentally. Thus, in the 'Essays on the Principles of Method', written for the 1818 edition of *The Friend* (first published in 1809), Coleridge notes that, just as 'without continuous transition, there can be no Method, so without a *pre-conception* there can be no transition with continuity'.[87] Like Fore-thought, the presupposition or 'pre-conception' underlying Method proper cannot simply be a truth of formal logic, much less an empirical fact. It must be an Idea embedded in 'life', capable of growing and seeding further thought. Coleridge calls this '*leading Thought*' in Method the 'Initiative'.[88] Towards the end of his life, in conversation with Henry Nelson Coleridge, he refers to this embodied transcendental method as 'structive' or 'Synthetic':

There are three ways of treating any subject. 1. Analytically. 2. Historically. 3. structively or Synthetically. Of these the only one complete and unerring is the last. ... You must begin with the philosophic Idea of the Thing, the true nature of which you wish to find out and manifest. You must carry your rule ready made if you wish to measure aright. If you ask me how I can know that this idea – my own invention – is the Truth, by which the phenomena of History are to be explained, I answer, in the same way exactly that you know that your eyes are made to see with – and that is – because you *do* see with them.[89]

Coleridge's deployment of the analogy of visual perception to illustrate the logic of transcendental argument (arguing from conditions of possibility rather than causes) indicates his continuing belief in the link between Kant's transcendental argument and the seminative and self-authorising power of the Ideal, 'the philosophic Idea of the Thing'. However, the 'Idea' is more than just a logical construct, it is a postulate with an existential component. Every 'initiative' of reasoning involves the input of the volitional, emotional, and ethical life of an individual. Thus, in *Magnum Opus* he argues that since in every science 'something is assumed, the proof of which is prior to the science itself',[90] an Idea is 'contradistinguished alike from the forms of the sense, the conceptions of the understanding, and the principles of the speculative reason by containing its reality as well as the peculiar form of the truth expressed therein', its 'source' being 'neither in the reason without the Will nor in the Will without the reason'.[91] Thanks to the constitutive status of the Will, the presuppositions uncovered by reflecting transcendentally on human life are, for Coleridge, as much ethical as logical:

[W]e proceed, like the Geometricians, with stating our postulates; the difference being, that the Postulates of Geometry *no* man *can* deny, those of Moral Science are such as no *good* man *will* deny. ... This then is the distinction of Moral Philosophy – *not* that I begin with one or more *Assumptions:* for this is common to *all* science; but – that I assume a something, the proof of which no man can *give* to another, yet every man may *find* for himself. If any man assert, that he *can* not find it, I am *bound* to disbelieve him! I cannot do otherwise without unsettling the very foundations of my own moral Nature.[92]

What Coleridge articulates in this passage in *Aids to Reflection* is what S. V. Pradhan usefully describes as his 'methodological holism', a method that 'does not look upon any realm of human activity as autonomous'.[93]

This holism presents an identifiably romantic shift from the quantitative to the qualitative in the ethics of human articulacy, from 'thin' to 'thick' descriptions, and from what Taylor calls the 'procedural' ethics of both Kant and the utilitarians to those whereby 'we judge the rationality of agents or their thoughts and feelings in substantive terms'.[94] By extending transcendental argument to the ethical assumptions that he cannot shake 'without unsettling the very foundations of my own moral Nature', Coleridge's argument prefigures Taylor's claim that 'being a self is inseparable from existing in a space of moral issues, to do with identity and how one ought to be. It is being able to find one's standpoint in this space, being able to occupy, to *be* a perspective in it'.[95] Indeed, perhaps more than any other writer of this period, Coleridge affirms the notion that '[w]e have a sense of who we are through our sense of where we stand to the good'.[96]

In the absence of a logical organon, then, Coleridge is forced in practice to abandon his theoretical assumption that dialectical logic or transcendental argument is merely a preparatory exercise for metaphysical illumination, as if Kant's method is just a stepladder required to reach the metaphysical springboard of 'polar logic'. The result, as transcendental argument quietly but persuasively creeps into Coleridgean method, branching out into the domains of the ethical, the linguistic, and the affective, is that 'thought' loses its centre. There is, moreover, another reason why transcendental argument secretly thrives in Coleridge's work. Etymologic helped to convince him – *contra* Kant – that the fundamental presuppositions for coherent thought were linguistic in nature. This melding of transcendental argument and radical language theory is the most significant reason behind the 'linguistic turn', as McKusick terms it, that Coleridge's *Logic* gives to Kant's critique of reason.[97] For McKusick, this turn is itself grounded in Coleridge's theosophy of the Logos. While this argument has great merit, we should not be misled into inferring that Coleridge only ever conceived this grounding in metaphysical terms. As we have seen, the Logos is defined not only by presence but also by *communication*. Communication formed the essential precondition for the 'electric fluid' of truth in society. Tookeian etymologic helped Coleridge to explain this 'fluid', but it also encouraged him to see truth, like electrochemistry, as the *condition* of life rather than its goal. Kant's transcendental argument, in turn, provided him with a logical method for understanding how such life-conditions might be articulated within reflective thought.

Once again, however, Coleridge's determination to limit the validity of transcendental argument to the psychological dimension of cognition effectively suppresses the connection between etymologic and logic as 'dialectic', and thus the idea of communication as itself a 'precondition' of knowledge. All too often, the holistic implications of Coleridge's attempt to place knowledge within an open-textured plane of interdependent human concerns is sacrificed to the perceived need for system: like Kant, Coleridge is liable to find the false security of schematism irresistible. Consequently, in *Logic* he remains convinced that transcendental argument or dialectical logic has nothing to do with either the 'evidence of reason' above it, the evidence of the senses below it, or indeed the communication of truth in everyday discourse. Thus, when in the passage from *Logic* noted earlier (in which he discriminates between verbal, epistemological, and metaphysical notions of 'truth') Coleridge identifies a *fourth*, subsidiary sense in the common currency of validation required for ordinary language, he dismisses its significance, arguing that while '[f]or rude and ponderous masses, our corn, hay, coals, and timber, the weighbridge will suffice ... medicine must have its appropriate weights ... and the experimental philosopher seeks from the artist an accuracy yet more nice'.[98]

Coleridge's insistence on determinate weights and measures for truth in language is reminiscent of the Quaker intolerance to 'laic-truth' sent up by Charles Lamb's essay 'Imperfect Sympathies'. As 'Elia' notes, Quakers refuse to take oaths because they imply:

the notion of two kinds of truth – the one applicable to the solemn affairs of justice, and the other to the common proceedings of daily intercourse. As truth bound upon the conscience by an oath can be but truth, in the common affirmations to the shop and the market-place a latitude is expected, and conceded upon questions wanting this solemn covenant. Something less than truth satisfies. ... Hence a great deal of incorrectness and inadvertency, short of falsehood, creeps into ordinary conversation; and a kind of secondary or laic-truth is tolerated, where clergy-truth – oath-truth, by the nature of the circumstances, is not required. A Quaker knows none of this distinction.[99]

This 'market-place', 'secondary or laic-truth' embedded in human conversation resembles the '*moral*' sense of truth identified in *The Friend*, that which is based on our expectation that when a speaker uses words, they 'should correspond to his thoughts in the sense in which he expects them to be understood by others'.[100] But while Lamb, keenly aware of the vital interdependence of expectations implied by this everyday 'communication' of truth, parodies the attempt to do without such a holistic framework, Coleridge subordinates pragmatic coherence to the unity conferred by an originative, ideal act of intellect. In this way, his great insight – that communication and truth are the conditions of intelligent life – is sacrificed to a metaphysical system in which *thinking* those conditions transcendentally is exclusively concerned with the 'formal' or psychological origins of the synthetic *a priori*, intellectual intuition, or whatever foundational trope Coleridge is defending at the time. In doing so, Coleridge fails to theorise the link between language, truth, and method that actually enables much of his philosophical practice. This is the real 'missing deduction' in his thought.

In this way, while transcendental argument increasingly determines the form of Coleridge's thinking about truth and language, within the schematism of his metaphysical theory it is merely the sub-discipline of 'dialectic'. Logic becomes the art of supposition, preliminary to philosophy. Significantly, this means that it is, strictly speaking, 'not philosophical; for logic . . . consists in the abstraction from all objects. It is wholly and purely subjective', and 'has no respect to any reality independent of the mind'.[101] None the less, dialectical logic remains necessary as the propaedeutic for philosophical inquiry, guarding against attempts to determine the 'thing-in-itself' by first establishing the grounds of knowledge in the subjective capacities of the mind. Kant's 'Transcendental Aesthetic' and deduction of the categories of understanding accordingly become exercises in a preparatory discipline of logical hypothesis whereby the mind sheds the naïve objectivism of materialist philosophers such as Hartley and Godwin. The failure of these thinkers lies in the fact that in neglecting the 'Hypothesis' of logical dialectic, they are led to conflate conditions with causes.[102] The result is an entirely imaginary order of speculation that Coleridge calls philosophical 'Hypopœsis'. As he argues in an 1809 notebook entry, while 'Hypothesis' consists in 'the placing of one known fact under others as their ground or foundation', whereby '[n]ot the fact itself but only its position in a . . . certain relation is imagined', where *both* the position and the fact are imagined, the status of the reasoning is mere Hypopœsis, not Hypothesis: 'subfiction not supposition'. He continues:

Atheism is the necessary Consequence or Corollary of the Hartleian Theory of the Will conjoined with his Theory of Thought & Action in genere – Words as distinguished from mere pulses of Air in the auditory nerve must correspond to Thoughts, and Thoughts is but the verb-substantive Participle Preterite of *Thing* . . . Thought is the participle past of Thing – a thing acts upon me but not on me as purely passive, which is the case in all *affection* . . . in the first, I am *thinged*, in the latter I thing or think . . . . If therefore we have no will, what is the meaning of the word? It is a word without a Thought – or else a Thought without a Thing, which is a blank contradiction.[103]

In her editorial notes to this passage, Kathleen Coburn links Coleridge's developing interest in 'hypothesis' to his reading of Kant's *Logic*, an encounter, she argues, that encourages him to distance himself further from Tooke's theories.[104] And yet, while Kant's influence on Coleridge is undoubtedly on the rise around this time, what the notebook entry confirms is the extent to which Tookeian etymologic *dovetails* with Kantian transcendental argument. Coleridge's transcendental argument is that the Will is the most fundamental 'supposition' of coherent 'Thought and Action in genere'. Without it, thought and language fall to pieces. Careless of 'supposition', however, the materialists blunder into the 'subfiction' whereby words are identified with 'mere pulses of Air', when in fact it is a *condition* of their intelligibility that they 'correspond to Thoughts'. At this point in Coleridge's argument, etymologic intersects with transcendental argument, for the embeddedness of thought in language in turn (through the etymologising of 'thought' as 'the verb-substantive Participle Preterite of *Thing*') indicates the *activity* of mind – and thus the essential agency of will – in thought. Etymology and transcendental inquiry lead to the same conclusion: Will is the most basic 'supposition' of agency, therefore of language, therefore of coherent thought. Rather than turning away from Tooke in this passage then, Coleridge is reading Tooke *through Kant*, a strategy that enables him to 'hypothesise' the interconnectedness of thought, language, and volition.

This casts transcendental argument ('dialectical logic', 'Hypothesis', or 'supposition') in a very different role to that attributed to it by Christensen's influential reading. According to Christensen, Hypopœsis in Coleridge is the cancelled figure of contingency and groundlessness that returns, like the ghost of Hartley, to haunt 'philosophy's rhetoric of the essential', undermining even the conditional certainties of Hypothetical reasoning and exposing 'the necessary artifice which installs an equivocation in necessity itself'.[105] To an extent, Christensen has a point. As we have seen, while Coleridge certainly learns from Kant the power of transcendental argument, or thinking by way of presuppositions, he generally (in theory, if not in practice) has a very different conception of the status and *nature* of those presuppositions. Thus, like Kant, he is apt to hypostasise the preconditions of thought by assuming the thing presupposed must itself have foundational status. But while for Kant this foundation is the 'I think' or transcendental unity of apperception, for Coleridge it is the 'I AM', the self-inaugurating word, or Logos. It could be argued, then, that by assuming a *holistic* transcendental argument (regarding the quotidian and pragmatic interdependence of communication, truth, and subjectivity) cannot be sustained without reference to a metaphysics of origins and being, Coleridge himself falls into a kind of Hypopœsis by hypostasisation.

What I have argued throughout this chapter, however, is that though he himself was often loath to embrace them the fundamental implications of Coleridge's arguments are more holistic than hypostasising. Indeed, the broader ramifications of what one might call his 'transcendental etymologic' are that the web of relationships sustaining truth, communication, and mental awareness do *not* require the kind of ideal architecture whose ruins deface *Biographia Literaria* and *Logic*. Once again, in order to grasp this point it is necessary to see beyond *both* Coleridge's philosophical autobiography of wayward materialism redeemed by idealism *and* the late twentieth-century critique of romanticism whose negativity trades so heavily upon it. Simply put, once we become attuned to the subtle rapport between etymologic and transcendental argument in his writing, Coleridge appears less fixated on the retrenchment of 'the essential' and more interested in the exploration of coherence through relationships that are inherently linguistic and (as we shall see in the next section) inter-subjective and value-embodied.

PRESUPPOSING OTHERS: REASONS, PERSONS, VALUES

So far in this chapter, I have argued that Coleridge's holism lurks behind more familiar and foregrounded features of his thought – idealism, formalism, logocentrism – but that this counterdiscourse remains under-represented largely through the self-fashioning of his own philosophical life narrative. For the linguistically transcendental Coleridge, basic concepts of self, language, and the 'electric fluid' of truth are interdependent. Together, they form the basic preconditions for communicative interaction between an embodied, social intelligence and the world. What remains in this section is to show how this 'embodiment' of reason is foregrounded by Coleridge, not as a constraint upon the heaven-sent Logos in the temporal sphere, but as determining the relational constitution of reason in all its forms. For Coleridge, thought only emerges through intersubjectivity, through interaction and involvement. In this way, it has an ineliminable value component: it is *ethical.*

At the heart of this idea are the relationships between language, logic, and faith. As Coleridge struggles with his lifelong goal to reconcile the claims of philosophy and religion, the balance of his later thinking shifts towards the relational, provoking the return to notions of intersubjectivity and communicability that had, for a time, been eclipsed by Schelling's metaphysics of correspondence. Theologically, this return was, for Coleridge, part of an ongoing contest between Christianity and pantheism: 'For a very long time indeed I could not reconcile personality with infinity', he recounts in *Biographia*, 'and my head was with Spinoza, though my whole heart remained with Paul and John'.[106] Above all, it is the idea of *personality* that finally triumphs in this contest, as the teachings of Paul and John overcome the limitless plains of Spinoza, and Coleridge endeavours to vindicate his belief that '[t]he Ground of Man's nature is the Will in a form of Reason'.[107]

As is well established in Coleridge scholarship, the agency of Will is pivotal in this area of his thinking. Indeed, for Coleridge, the alterity that forms Noetics, or the science of reason, is itself the product of Absolute Will. In an unpublished fragment dating from around 1818–1819, he maintains of the Will that, 'being causative of alterity it is a fortiori causative of itself[,] and conversely the being causative of itself it must be causative of alterity ... Consequently the Will is neither abstracted from intelligence nor can Intelligence be conceived of as not grounded and involved in the Will'.[108] Thus, as the following passage from the *Magnum Opus* manuscripts makes clear, the 'trichotomic' logic upon which all thought depends ultimately rests upon an alterity grounded in the Will:

> If, then, there can be no '*He*' nor '*It*' without an '*I*', and no '*I*' without a '*Thou*', the solution of the problem must be sought for in the genesis or origination of the '*Thou*'. . . . [T]he consciousness expressed in the term '*Thou*' is only possible by an equation in which '*I*' is taken as equal but yet not the same as '*Thou*', [. . . in order to do which] a something must be affirmed in the one, which is negatived in the other . . . . Now this something can only be the Will. . . . Now this equation of *Thou* with *I*, by means of a free act < by > which < we > negative the sameness in order to establish the equality – this, I say, is the true definition of a Conscience.[109]

The agency of the Will becomes a precondition of the negotiation of an alterity ('in which "*I*" is taken as equal but yet not the same as "*Thou*"') without which, in turn, basic human awareness would be unthinkable. As a consequence, Coleridge conceives of the most fundamental relations governing reality as personal *relationships* rather than logical relations: the moral awareness of *others* itself becomes 'the pre-condition of all experience'. This is most powerfully expressed in the familial model deployed to explain the emergence of consciousness (both human and Absolute) in *Magnum Opus*. Here, Coleridge distinguishes three relationships – mother/child, father/son, I/thou – whose interdependence forms the condition of possibility for the communicative Logos. Without these relationships, indeed, it is impossible to explain how difference emerges from identity. 'The whole problem of existence', he argues, 'is present as a sum total in the mother: the mother exists as a One and indivisible something.' Alterity, and with it language, is only made possible by the intervention of the father, introducing the difference-in-unity expressed in the Logos: 'The father and the heavenly father, the form in the shape and the form affirmed for itself are blended in one, and yet convey the earliest lesson of distinction and alterity. There was another beside the mother, and the child beholds it and repeats.' Finally, having left the maternal knee, 'the child now learns its own alterity'.[110] Viewed this way, personality is the key to the relation between identity and difference. Only when one thinks of the most fundamental relations as *personal* relationships, Coleridge argues, can one understand how alterity itself is possible. Only through the metaphysics of personality is it possible, by acknowledging that the claims of otherness touch us at the deepest level of our being, to resist the lure of hypopœsis, hyperrationalism, Spinozism.

Personality, then, lies at the core of Coleridge's later thought: it is the counterweight to reification and hypostasis. This is not to say that our personal relationship with God is *identical* to our relationships with other people. Being perfect, God's personhood is prothetical, it is 'personeity, differing from personality only as rejecting all commixture of imperfection associated with the latter'. This installation of God as 'at once the absolute person and the ground of all personality', represents the metaphysical edge of Coleridge's attempt to bridge religion and philosophy by reconciling 'personality with infinity'.[111] But by making the alterity outlined in his 'higher' noetic dependent upon the *willing* relationships that sustain the relations between persons, Coleridge avoids collapsing these relations into an undifferentiated foundation that could once again be made the exclusive property of philosophy. For Coleridge, personhood is prior to being, just as faith is prior to knowing.

Perhaps it is going too far to suggest that personality is such a centrifugal force in Coleridge's work. Steven Cole observes that while the 'fundamental idea of reason (its ultimate end) for Coleridge is the idea of the person as distinguished from the thing', he occasionally writes 'as though the ends of reason were indeed privately produced'.[112] His assumption that persons are not things, in other words, raises the question of how personhood is constituted in the first place. What appears to be missing from Coleridge's account is 'the question of *context*, the question, that is of where it makes sense to locate the intersubjective constitution of personhood', framed in such a way as to allow that while the claims of reason are universal 'such universality must be understood not ontologically but contextually'.[113] Cole argues that it is precisely this question that Coleridge addresses in the unpublished 'Essay on Faith', written in 1820. Here, Coleridge defines 'Faith' as '*Fidelity* to our own Being as far as such Being is not and cannot become an object of the sense',[114] arguing that 'even the very first step ... the becoming conscious of a Conscience, partakes of the nature of an *Act* ... by which we take upon ourselves ... the obligation of *Fealty*'.[115] In this essay, 'Coleridge's example of "fidelity to our own being" establishes a *relation* our being has to the being of others, and the burden of his essay is thus to show how that relation can constitute a self to which we can be claimed to have an obligation.' The 'Essay on Faith' thus offers Coleridge's 'fullest, and most compelling, explanation of how the idea of personhood is *contextually* enacted'.[116] Indeed, I would argue that Coleridge goes even further than this by suggesting that the obligation of *acknowledgement* is the most fundamental precondition of *all* recognition. Thus, whether perceiving the 'objective' world or other persons, we are bound to enter into a moral relationship that presupposes an element of will, and thus faith. As Coleridge argues, 'Conscience is the root of all Consciousness, and a fortiori the precondition of all Experience'.[117]

It is important to see that Coleridge reaches such fundamentally un-Kantian conclusions only by pursuing a method that is itself thoroughly Kantian. This is despite the fact that at least on the face of it his main endeavour in the 'Essay on Faith' and the *Magnum Opus* is to reverse Kant's proof of the existence of free will from the moral law by showing that the moral law is based on the existence of free will. This enterprise can in turn be seen as a late intervention in the controversy over Spinozism that had gripped German intellectuals decades earlier. Coleridge welcomes Jacobi's claim in the 1785 *Concerning the Doctrine of Spinoza* that the only way to neutralise the crypto-Spinozism of Kantian critique is to accept that '[f]aith is the element of all human cognition and activity'.[118] Jacobi's insistence on the priority of personhood and faith in human knowledge encourages Coleridge to develop a metaphysics of personality designed to prevent the higher logic of Noetics from folding into pantheism. Against Kant's stricture that there can never be a theology of reason, Coleridge envisages religion and philosophy in perfect equipoise, the logic of understanding blending with a logic of reason that is itself part logic, part revelation. None the less, he was not prepared to swallow Jacobi's antidote to Spinozism whole. Instead of embracing the epistemological ambiguity of what Jacobi terms in his 1815 Preface to *David Hume on Faith* as a 'knowing not-knowing',[119] as Anthony John Harding indicates, Coleridge looks to conscience as the means by which 'the self becomes aware of its own existence'. He thereby attempts to do 'what Kant did not do for himself, that is, establish *a priori* the possibility of recognising other human beings as themselves possessed of conscience and selfhood'.[120] And yet, while Jacobi's work encourages Coleridge to reject transcendental *idealism*, transcendental *argument* enables him to claim that '[t]he conscience ... is not a mere mode of our consciousness, but *presupposed* therein'.[121]

I argued at the beginning of this chapter that Coleridge's concept of rationality is pulled in different directions by two philosophical models: one constructed around relationships and communicability, the other based on ideal presence. What we can now see is that the 'Germanic' turn in Coleridge's thought that in 1801 leads him to announce the overthrow of 'the irreligious metaphysics of modern Infidels' settles nothing with regard to this dilemma. Accordingly, while it proclaims the comprehensive triumph of an immobile idealism of the Absolute, Coleridge's later thought simultaneously extends his earlier, republican-commonwealth aspirations for a culture in which (to borrow a formula from Habermas) the unity of reason lies in the diversity of its voices. Indeed, Habermas's differentiation between the later Hegel (for whom the Absolute is a 'presumption under which alone philosophy can resume its business') and the pre-Jena Hegel (who looked instead to 'the unifying power of an intersubjectivity that appears under the titles of "love" and "life"' in order to counter 'the authoritarian embodiments of a subject-centered reason')[122] can loosely be applied to the case of Coleridge. Like the later Hegel, the 'nineteenth-century' Coleridge ostensibly rejects an 'eighteenth-century', socialised conception of truth, insisting in the *Magnum Opus* that 'Reason and its objects are not things of reflection, association, or *discourse*',[123] and later defending the 'doctrine of the Trinity [as] an Absolute Truth transcending my human means of understanding it or demonstrating it'.[124] In both thinkers, however, the kernel of the earlier pluralism survives the more aggressive absolutism of the work that follows. Thus, as Coleridge's thinking after 1801 draws him onto the high plateau of German metaphysics, it also leads him back into the vale of human life. Having replaced the 'hypopœsis' of eliminative materialism with the 'hypothesis' of Kant's transcendental method, his inquiry into the 'preconditions' of coherent human life compel him to re-examine the linguistic and interpersonal relations in which human reason is embedded. This ultimately leads him to the conclusion that reason is embodied not just in communication, the 'electric fluid' of truth, but also in the ethics of personality.

This then, is what David Haney rightly calls Coleridge's 'challenge' to modern criticism: to conceive of a indeterminate critical space that is also beyond suspicion, in which the dialogue between reader and writer is shaped by the same holistic network of concerns, presuppositions, and commitments that constitutes the background to communication in general. Reflection cannot transcend, disinter, or subject such a background to radical critique because reason is embodied *by* it. It can, however, help to *change* the condition of its own embodiment by reflecting upon the presuppositions that enable it to function in the first place, presuppositions that encode not just epistemic norms, but the wider range of values that make up everyday life. In the same way, transcendental arguments are ethical for Coleridge. Coleridge's work, as Haney claims, is 'illuminated by a conversation between present and past that is not *simply* dialectical', according to which 'both partners in a conversation put their subjectivities at risk'.[125] Haney's reading, which is heavily influenced by Gadamer's hermeneutics, sets out from the claim that Coleridge's thought 'poses an interrogative challenge to modern thought precisely because he writes/speaks from within a historical, theological, and metaphysical horizon that most of us cannot share'. Utilising Gadamer's distinction between the 'aim' and the 'object' of a poem, Haney goes on to argue that:

> the aim retains a direct specificity even as the object shifts: the relationship between the poem's 'I' and 'you' can be specified (the poem's 'aim') while the 'you' or even the 'I' (the poem's 'object') may change. This helps to show how the poem can speak to us across temporal and cultural boundaries in a way that entails neither transcendental claims for a poem's existence outside of historical temporality nor the artificial narrowing of the poem's 'you' to an 'original' or 'intended' audience.[126]

If the argument of the present study has any merit, however, we must go still further and argue that Gadamer's distinction between the 'aim' and the 'object' of a poem is itself a reflection of the all-or-nothing holism presented by the interdependence of truth, subjectivity, and communication. Thus, if it appears paradoxical that 'in a Romantic conversation poem, we know that the poem is written "to" someone inaccessible to our horizon, as we both listen in on that foreign conversation and allow the poem as a whole to speak to us', it is because the poem incorporates the understanding, first, that truth is the most basic and stubborn presupposition in thought and discourse, and, second (modifying Tooke), that 'without communication, no truth'.[127] Truth depends upon deixis, but deixis is only made possible by the interaction between at least two subjects and the world. In other words, it simply makes no sense to conceive other people, other texts, other times, and so on, as operating according to discourses that are 'incommensurable' with our own. This is the watchword of holism: we either have *all* the elements for understanding otherness from the outset, or we have nothing (the latter being tantamount to saying that intelligent awareness as such is impossible). It is this 'eighteenth-century' idea of truth as the *presupposition* of communication that allows Coleridge to deal briskly with the spectre of relativism, and which underpins the Unitarian 'One Mind' metaphysics of his claim in the 1801 philosophical letter to Josiah Wedgwood that 'there is more than a metaphor in the affirmation, that the whole human Species from Adam to Bonaparte, from China to Peru, may be considered as one Individual Mind'.[128]

In this light, Haney is right to maintain that Coleridge's 'theological emphasis on the divine person universalises the notion of the person without reducing it to an abstract category'. However, while Haney sees this as the product of 'a phenomenological empiricism that places empirical understanding within the dialogic interchange that constitutes human ethical life', I believe that it is more accurate – conceptually and historically – to describe such 'dialogic interchange' in terms of transcendental argument.[129] More specifically, it is the way in which Kant's method rounds out the holism of linguistic empiricism or 'etymologic' that enables Coleridge to think about intelligent life in terms of a shared background that is as much interpersonal and ethical as it is linguistic and epistemological. As Hilary Putnam observes, it is through transcendental argument that we 'are committed by our fundamental conceptions to treating not just our present time-slices, but also our past selves, our ancestors, and members of other cultures past and present, as *persons*; and that means ... attributing to them shared references and shared concepts'.[130]

This brings us, finally, to the Good. Since our attempts to understand the world more clearly are bound to the articulation of conditions of possibility embedded in the background of our relations with *other* persons, it follows that our basic awareness of the world can only be articulated *within* a structure in which cognitive and semantic norms are imbricated with evaluative distinctions. Truth and meaning, in other words, only take shape in the context of our sense of the 'Good'. Thus, for Coleridge in *Magnum Opus*, Truth and the Good 'are coinherent but nevertheless distinct', for 'while both are self-subsistent, yet the good alone is self-originated. Truth is indeed a necessary attribute of goodness, but while we must receive the truth for the truth's sake, we love it only because it is good'.[131] This means, as he states in his 1818–19 lectures on philosophy, that any 'philosophy which strikes the words, "should" and "ought" out of the dictionary, and intellect [out] of philosophy, is only anti-philosophy'.[132] More importantly, however, it means that Coleridge explicitly collapses Hume's dichotomy of factual and evaluative judgements. He thereby removes a cornerstone of the correspondence theory of truth and finally brings down its fantasy of a purely neutral language of description. For Coleridge, as for many modern philosophers, 'theory of truth', as Putnam frames it, 'presupposes theory of rationality which in turn presupposes our theory of the good'.[133]

Many commentators have noted this move in Coleridge, but relatively few have pursued its further implications. Haney observes that the form taken by Coleridge's attack on the fact/value distinction means that 'the relation between hermeneutics and ethics in Coleridge will not allow an exclusionary relationship between prereflective direct responsiveness and reflexive "ethical" responsibility'.[134] Thus, he believes, Coleridge argues that interpretive judgement, like ethical judgement, is impossible without a fore-knowing, without 'bringing presuppositions to bear'.[135] What this demonstrates more broadly, as Charles Taylor argues, is the way in which even 'Romantic views of the self' that appear to attempt to fly the web of coherence, 'do nothing to lift the *transcendental* conditions'.[136] As Coleridge's work testifies, while *qualitative* distinctions are indispensable for defining the frameworks that help to articulate the coherence of our lives, 'this sense of the good has to be woven into my understanding of my life as an unfolding story'. But Taylor adds that this 'is to state another basic condition of making sense of ourselves, that we grasp our lives as a *narrative*'.[137] I have maintained that it is this very narrative that Coleridge's writing continually struggles to evolve, from the conversation poems to *Biographia Literaria*, and from his private letters to the manuscripts of the *Magnum Opus*.

A CHARITY-SCHOOL BACKGROUND: 'THIS LIME-TREE BOWER MY PRISON'

Haney's depiction of the ways in which Coleridge's conversation poems incorporate and enact the deictic gesture at the root of dialogue highlights the way in which the poet's commitment to holism was not erased by his proclaimed 'conversion' to idealism. Accordingly, since most of this chapter has concentrated on the prose philosophy and theology of Coleridge's later work, I will now turn to one of Coleridge's earlier poems, 'This Lime-Tree Bower My Prison', in order to retrace some of the major themes and questions raised above. The poem, in which Coleridge imagines a country walk taken by the Wordsworths and Charles Lamb (from which he is excluded through 'dear Sara [having] accidently emptied a skillet of boiling milk on my foot')[138] was first composed in an 1797 letter to Robert Southey and later revised and published in the latter's *Annual Anthology* (1800). As J. C. C. Mays's varorium text reveals, both versions have features of significance for the present discussion, revealing relationships of triangulation between truth, communication, and intersubjectivity.[139]

Like 'Fears in Solitude', which was written a little under a year later, 'This Lime-Tree Bower My Prison' can be read as a Unitarian ode to an imagined community. This community is unified and harmonised by the 'One Life' philosophy projected by a poetic voice, which, like the figures in the landscape it describes, almost vanishes into an immaterial universe 'Silent with swimming sense' (l.40).[140] And yet, the same Unitarian idea of sociability that is so crucial to the poem's imaginative trajectory from enforced isolation to shared vision can provoke an altogether less sympathetic form of commentary. Tilottama Rajan, for example, approaches Coleridge's idea of friendship with suspicion, noting that '[f]riendship as a social structure is, as Derrida intimates, homofraternal, often xenophobic and constituted around the exclusion of singularity'. Such 'limits of friendship are seen in the conversation poems, which construct a circle of friends in which Coleridge participates only voyeuristically, or into which he is admitted ... only by submitting to censorship'.[141] In the case of 'Lime-Tree Bower', it is not difficult to locate the kind of rhetoric that concerns Rajan. Thus, the image of the 'glorious Sun' (l.34) or 'orb' (l.35), which later dilates to consume in light the rook that mediates between the poet and his friends cuts a Unitarian figure of 'Life' which appears to foreclose any notion of difference that might extend to the 'dissonant' (l.77).

Its aversion to 'singularity' notwithstanding, however, the poem ranges over a wide spectrum of discursive possibilities. As so often with Coleridge, the poem is constructed around an *act* of consciousness, and, as in many of the great romantic odes, it enacts the synthetic power of the mind through the dialectical structure of strophe (meditation), antistrophe (projection), and epode (epiphany) that articulates its three stanzas. However, in 'Lime-Tree Bower', the principal action is hypothetical.

This can be seen in the very opening lines of the poem, in which the homomorphic drive noted above is unsettled at the outset by the conditional status of the poet's own vision: 'I have lost / Beauties and Feelings, such as would have been / Most sweet to my remembrance' (ll.2–4). The finely-wrought grammar of line 3, in which the modal auxiliary 'would' simultaneously carries and deflates the reader's expectations of a future perfect state, sets the base note of conditionality upon which the rest of the poem performs its task of linking the narrator with his 'friends', and, by extension, the author with the reader. Crucially, this connection occurs within a *social* space rather than any theological realm. Indeed, the entire fabric of the poet's vision is woven through *supposition*, through the conditional 'as if', so that the conjectural pastness of 'as would have been' in the opening of the first stanza is answered by the equally conjectural presentness of 'As I myself were there!' at the beginning of the third (l.46): 'A delight / Comes sudden on my heart, and I am glad / As I myself were there! (ll.44–6). This provisionality in Coleridge's epiphany is the reverse of what Paul Hamilton describes as the suspension of the aesthetic in a projected 'future-perfect state, that "will have been"' characteristic of much romantic writing, whereby the recuperation of self, knowledge, and other lost Enlightenment topoi is effected through the figurative construction 'of an otherwise irretrievably dislocated essence'.[142] Instead of the hypostasised projection of a privileged subjectivity, Coleridge's poem offers a meditation on friendship as a *precondition* of intelligent awareness. Insight is possible, the poem implies, but only on credit and charity, through trusting communication with other persons. Of course, the 'Friends' on whom the poem pins so much of its hope remain mute, and by the 1800 version have been reduced to the single figure of Lamb. And yet, however ambiguously, the poem acknowledges that the poet's experiences, whether imagined, recollected, or felt immediately 'in this bower' (l.46), can have no meaning beyond that which he can communicate to his addressees: in other words, they carry no meaning beyond that which he can assume they can understand and appreciate.

This interpretive interdependence requires from the outset not merely the poet's assumption that communication is possible, but also the realisation that this assumption in turn is part of a socially *shared* network of presuppositions that collectively form the background conditions for his own expression. In 'Lime-Tree Bower' this background is figured as nature, though here, as so often, the poem pulls in two directions at once: on one hand, largely thanks to Coleridge's flirtation with Berkeley's philosophy, nature acquires a metaphysical luminescence, bathed in blazing sunshine 'till all doth seem / Less gross than bodily' (ll.41–2). At the same time, nature becomes the stand-in or placeholder for an (unpresentable) ideal knowledge of the background conditions in 'Life' that render intelligent communication possible. Deprived of such immediacy, the poet is compelled to reflect upon what he can *reasonably expect* to be shared experience:

> And sometimes
> 'Tis well to be bereaved of promised good,
> That we may lift the soul, and contemplate
> With lively joy the joys we cannot share. (ll.64–7)

Significantly, while the 'lively joy' anticipated by the poet in contemplating 'the joys we cannot share' is not described as a singular experience, nor is it associated with any conformity to an ideal aesthetic ideology based upon a notion of reconstructed, 'dislocated essence'. In this respect, 'Lime-Tree Bower' is neither a retreat into a private world of imagination nor a celebration of an aesthetic order that derives its normative power from the negation of reason. Instead, it questioningly probes the conditions of rational communication, and in doing so uncovers what modern thinkers such as Quine and Davidson call the 'principle of charity'. Davidson explains this idea in his 1984 essay 'Expressing Evaluations':

This [principle of charity] necessarily requires us to see others as much like ourselves in point of overall coherence and correctness – that we see them as more or less rational creatures mentally inhabiting a world much like our own. Rationality is a matter of degree; but insofar as people think, reason, and act at all, there must be enough rationality in the complete pattern for us to judge particular beliefs as foolish or false, or particular acts as confused or misguided. For only in a largely coherent scheme can propositional contents find a lodging.[143]

This principle of rational accommodation to other persons is not, Davidson continues, a policy that one can choose, but is indispensable to coherent thought, 'a way of expressing the fact that creatures with thoughts, values, and speech must be rational creatures, are necessarily inhabitants of the same objective world as ourselves, and necessarily share the leading values with us'.[144] It is this very principle that, in 'Lime-Tree Bower', forms what might be called the 'charity school' that enables the poet's aesthetic education. For this reason, Coleridge's 'projected' feeling is as much an act of self-preservation as it is a gesture of generosity. By exploring the sociability that underpins his own awareness, Coleridge is not just endowing his friends with commensurate centres of self or

independent mental lives; he is investigating the background conditions
of his very ability to have an intellectual 'Life' of his own. In the principle
of charity, he discovers the 'hypothesis' – the 'as if' – that underwrites *all*
communication, and by doing so he saves the coherence of his *own* mental
life. It is *this* epiphany that drives the epodal stanza, culminating in the
closing lines of the poem (here taken from the 1797 version):

> My Sister & my Friends! when the last Rook
> Beat it's straight path along the dusky air
> Homewards, I bless'd it; deeming, it's black wing
> Cross'd, like a speck, the blaze of setting day,
> While ye stood gazing; or when all was still,
> Flew creaking o'er your heads, & had a charm
> For you, my Sister & my Friends! to whom
> No sound is dissonant, which tells of Life!   (ll.48–55)

It is tempting to interpret the 'Rook' as an aesthetic trope for the aesthetic
itself, a sympathetic form mediating the poet's feelings and those of his
friends. According to such a reading, the mobility and polymorphic
attributes of the rook (in the 1800 version it is 'Now a dim speck, now
vanishing in light' (l.72)) might explain why Coleridge was from the very
beginning concerned to contain its fleeting and indeterminate presence
within the circumference of the 'mighty Orb'.[145] And yet, the poem also
sustains a reading that identifies the indeterminacy figured by the rook as
that which results from the entirely *pragmatic* problem of putting oneself
in the place of another, and knowing that *only by so doing* – only by
appealing to *at least some* presuppositions that are shared – can one
ultimately say anything meaningful. Davidson notes in his essay 'The
Socratic Conception of Truth' that '[w]hat we think depends on what
others can make of us and of our relations to the world we share with
them. It follows that we have no clear thoughts except as these are
sharpened in the process of being grasped by others'.[146] In a similar
way, what the rook reveals to the poet is that while not all presuppositions
can be shared some at least, like the concept of truth, retain a special
'charm'. This charm is not a matter of semantics, conventions, or even
epistemology, but the realisation that communication presupposes a
shared form of Life, in which incommensurability, while occasionally an
awkward fact in human communication, can never be the rule. Linked to
his friends only by the indeterminate form of the rook, the poet realises
the constitutive role of friendship for his own thought. In Davidson's
words, '[w]ithout language, thoughts have no clear shape; but the
shape language gives them emerges only in the context of active

communication'.[147] Like the 'creaking' wings of the distant crow, 'Lime-Tree Bower' reminds us of the practical reasons why in communication, as in reason, 'No sound is dissonant'.

CONCLUSION

It could be argued, with some justification, that in this chapter I have tried (somewhat presumptuously) to save Coleridge from himself – at least, from his own narrative of intellectual growth. Accepting Coleridge's account of his life as the symbol of degenerate materialism redeemed through a spiritual philosophy of dynamic Will, I suggest, inevitably draws the suspicion of commentators rightly wary of both the 'symbol' and the philosophy behind it. What I have attempted instead is to draw attention to the *holism* in Coleridge's 'logocentrism'. In other words, without discounting his commitment to establishing apodeictic truths through a systematic discipline of thought, I have endeavoured to foreground Coleridge's interest in, and exploration of, more pragmatic paradigms of self, truth, and communication. Constructed around eighteenth-century notions of relationship and sociability, these models stress relationality rather than form in questions of truth; communicative action rather than essence in language theory; and the ethics of personality over the metaphysics of identity when treating subjectivity. Together, they make up the holism that forms the knot in the smooth grain of Coleridge's journey from materialism to idealism, and belie the notion, still common today, that this metaphysical transition is somehow an index of his political conversion from civic humanist and commonwealthsman to authoritarian defender of the clerisy. Reading Coleridge's work with an eye to its holistic phases, moreover, has an added advantage, in so far as it encourages *us* to reflect upon the holism of our own interpretive and critical judgements.

While these phases take many forms, I have argued that they can be grouped under three broad headings. Beneath the first, 'etymologic', we can identify Coleridge's first sustained attempt to break decisively with correspondence theories of truth and meaning by maintaining, against Hume, that the underdetermination of reference by sensation reveals the entanglement of truth and meaning. Adapting Tooke's arguments concerning the 'grammar' of human thought enables the early Coleridge to adumbrate the ideal of a commonwealth of understanding based on free communication, in which truth, 'implied in Words among the first men', becomes the 'electric fluid' of *indeterminable* essence that sustains communication against a background of intersubjectively shared norms.

In turn, Kant's transcendental argument provides Coleridge with a method for reflecting on the inescapability of this sociolinguistic background in a way that does not connote scepticism or relativism. Thus, by rendering Tooke's 'no man, no TRUTH' claim as an embodied transcendental argument, Coleridge 'hypothesises' the interdependence of thought, language, and volition. As I argued above, care needs to be taken in identifying this second, holistic direction in Coleridge's thought. In particular, it involves allowing greater weight to what Coleridge *does* with transcendental argument (and correspondingly, what he doesn't do with other forms of argument) than to his attempt to *theorise* this method within the master-disciplinary project of the 'Logosophia'. Only by doing this, I argued, can we understand the reasons behind, first, his failure to develop an 'organon' or preparatory method for noetics in *Logic*, and, second, the dominant role assumed in that work by the 'criterion' or 'dialectic'. Indeed, the *absence* of an organon in *Logic* underscores the fact that the principle central to Coleridgean praxis is the relation between reflection and 'fore-thought'.

And yet, as Coleridge realises in his later work, the presuppositions that 'fore-thought' contains cannot be *abstracted* by reflection, but are embedded in all human activity, in 'Life'. Accordingly, his speculations in the 'Essay on Faith' and *Magnum Opus* on the constitutive role played by the ethics of personality in thought is informed by a distinctly holistic conception of the transcendental framework within which rational beings reflect on the relations between truth, communication, and awareness. In this third strand of Coleridge's holism, the nascent intuitions regarding sociability that inform the conversation poems are made more explicit by redescribing the 'logical' relations underlying human life as personal *relationships*. By defining personhood contextually, Coleridge acknowledges that the claims of otherness touch us at the deepest level of our being. Moreover, by collapsing the dichotomy of fact and value, he is able to maintain (transcendentally) that consciousness presupposes conscience, and thus that *moral* awareness of others is itself 'the pre-condition of all experience'. Consequently, truth and meaning can only take shape in the context of a communicative act in which one brings one's moral, affective entanglements to bear, and in which subjectivity, intersubjectivity, and objectivity (the self, communication, and truth) are each necessary for the others' existence. In this way, it is what discourse presupposes that keeps it alive: truth, and the embodiment of reason within a framework of values.

Conclusion

Framing the background to this book is a question that has dogged modern thought since the Enlightenment: can the critique of reason be carried out within reason? Hume's answer to this question is no, but the cost of this refusal is the severance of his reasoning, reflective self from his everyday self whenever the former proves troublesome. More ambitiously, Kant and Hegel attempt systematically to redefine the basis of thought in light of Hume's 'no'. Though broadly in line with this project, the romantic endeavour to consecrate the other of reason in the domain of an aesthetic and imaginative conception of 'truth' is overruled by the Hegelian radicalisation of otherness as negativity. As a consequence, Hegel's damning verdict upon idealised, subject-centred reason, handed down, via Marx and Nietzsche, to modern theory, criticism, and historicism, is revisited today upon the romantic topos of self and community.

The present study is, in part, an attempt to redraw the image of reason upon which this judgement is made. At its heart is the claim that the subject-centred model gives an incomplete picture of the full range of Enlightenment rationality and romantic expressiveness. As Habermas argues, early nineteenth-century culture develops a language of decentred, communicative rationality that forms a counterdiscourse to the hypostasised conceptions of idealism. In Britain, this counterdiscourse emerges from within the linguistic and anthropological currents in late eighteenth-century empiricism. In Reid's hermeneutics of perception, in Stewart's interest in the transcendental 'stamina' of reason, and above all in Tooke's linguistic deflation of truth and Bentham's pragmatic understanding of 'logical fictions', one finds a shift away from mentalism and representationalism, towards a concern with how beliefs are justified within a community of norms embedded in the communicative practices of a lifeworld.

The romantics extend this movement by seeking to understand the *absoluteness* of these norms, sometimes as hypostasised, transcendent ideals, but just as often in terms of the nonideal, pragmatic relations of interdependence that are seen to exist between truth, communication, and the self: respectively, between objectivity, intersubjectivity, and subjectivity. The articulation and exploration of these relationships in early nineteenth-century writing constitutes what I characterise as romantic holism. The indeterminate and yet absolute 'truth' of romanticism, then, is not exhausted by the image of a transcendent, noumenal goal of inquiry; it also invokes the notion of unconditional presupposition of discourse whose indefinability is the product of pragmatic relationships between the self, others, and the world. As such, it is inseparable from other transcendental preconditions of living a life: of community, sociability, evaluation, and interpretive charity.

Accordingly, Keats's 'Cockney' critique of the nullifying gaze of representational empiricism and objectifying rationality relies on more than just the power of negativity. In elevating epistolary over epistemological 'correspondence', Keats places his faith in involvement and friendly conversation, in a sense that truth and meaning only emerge through charitable, trusting interaction (which, symbolised by the 'warm scribe' hand of acknowledgement, is denied, with devastating consequences, to the participants of Lamia's wedding feast). Like Keats, Shelley finds himself caught between pragmatic and idealistic or representational currents of empiricism – between, in his own terms, the metacritical paradigms of 'circumference' and 'centre'. As a result, his writing manoeuvres between two basic models of truth. The first is based on relation, on coherence and dialogue, incorporating 'Mont Blanc''s Socratic interplay of elenchus and deixis, dialogue and truth, in an 'education of error' that involves 'love', a sacrificial 'going out' of oneself in order to know and recreate oneself. The second is governed by the idea of correspondence between mind and nonhuman reality, according to which language is merely the instrument of a super-inflated consciousness, an idea of imagination that Shelley borrows, famously, from Coleridge. And yet, despite his attempt in *Biographia Literaria* to assemble a life narrative of materialism redeemed by idealism, Coleridge's engagement with the Tookeian linguistics of 'etymologic' is not displaced by transcendental method. Instead, the two merge, in a linguistic critique of Kant, to produce a decentred understanding of the self in terms of its 'embodied' conditions of possibility. Such preconditions encompass the ethical dynamics of interpersonality adumbrated in 'This Lime-Tree Bower My Prison' (in which language is depicted not as a 'prison', but as resting fundamentally upon an act of interpretive charity that sustains both communication and subjectivity) and systematised in Coleridge's later works, which stress the priority of faith to knowledge, of conscience to consciousness, and of personhood to being.

The implications of romantic holism for modern criticism are twofold. Commentary on romanticism will remain not only critically 'cramped' (in Rorty's terms) but also blind to the diversity of late Enlightenment and romantic conceptions of rationality as long as it bases its procedures upon a notion of radical 'otherness' that repeats by inversion the hypostasising strategy of the very discourse it aims to interrogate. In romantic studies, this problem is mainly evident (but by no means confined to) the methodologies of postmodern historicism, whose 'leap-frogging logic' of 'complex repetitive temporality' (in Levinson's terms) produces a constricted criticism, watchful, suspicious, constantly doubling back on itself, fearful of ideological contamination and unhappily obsessed with the hygiene of its own methodologies.

In reading the romantics pragmatically, and the pragmatists romantically, then, I have endeavoured to substitute dialogue-as-communication for dialectic-as-negativity. This has involved dispensing with some of the less helpful categories of metacommentary, such as 'transcendence', 'immanence', 'exteriority', 'untruth', 'aporia', and 'incommensurability'. In placing the idea of conversation at the heart of this study's metacritical framework, I have drawn upon the romantic antidualism of Quine's critique of Hume's analytic/synthetic distinction, Putnam's attack on Hume's fact/value dichotomies, Davidson's understanding of the interdependence of truth, interpretation, and subjectivity, Taylor's adaptation of transcendental arguments into holistic, 'embodied narratives' (part of his broader project to revive a 'romantic' language of expressionism), and, finally, the efforts of Habermas and Rorty to restore a romantic conception of reason as pragmatic, communicative action. Rorty himself is the self-conscious inheritor of an American 'romantic' tradition of natural supernaturalism that includes Emerson, James, and Dewey. Running through this tradition, and evident in poems such as 'Ode on a Grecian Urn', 'Mont Blanc', and 'This Lime-Tree Bower My Prison', is the romantic idea that literary interpretation is no different in kind from everyday communication, and that in criticism, as in life, even the most rigid methodologies are 'passing' in the midst of the dialogue that constitutes the self, the world, and other persons.

Notes

INTRODUCTION

1 Samuel Taylor Coleridge, *The Notebooks of Samuel Taylor Coleridge*, ed. Kathleen Coburn *et al.*, vol. 2 (London: Routledge, 1957–2002), 2368.

2 Samuel Taylor Coleridge, *Lay Sermons*, ed. R. J. White (Princeton University Press, 1972), 60.

3 Samuel Taylor Coleridge, *Biographia Literaria or Biographical Sketches of My Literary Life and Opinions*, ed. James Engell and Walter Jackson Bate, vol. 2 (Princeton University Press, 1983), 142.

4 Thomas Pfau, 'Introduction. Reading beyond Redemption: Historicism, Irony, and the Lessons of Romanticism', *Lessons of Romanticism: A Critical Companion*, ed. Thomas Pfau and Robert F. Gleckner (Durham, NC: Duke University Press, 1998), 21.

5 See Nikolas Kompridis, 'The Idea of a New Beginning: A Romantic Source of Normativity and Freedom', *Philosophical Romanticism*, ed. Nikolas Kompridis (London: Routledge, 2006). Kompridis argues that rethinking modernity's relationship with the new means at once resisting normativity and 'regarding it as a process that we should *also* embrace, something we should want to embrace for the sake of thinking and acting differently, for the sake of making the new possible' (54).

6 Richard Rorty, 'Habermas, Derrida, and the Functions of Philosophy', *Truth and Progress: Philosophical Papers*, vol. 3 (Cambridge University Press, 1998), 310.

7 This approach contrasts with Orrin Wang's dialectical reading of romanticism and postmodernism as constituting an 'infinite chain of substitutions trying to name the phantasm of our modernity'. Despite the energy and subtlety of Wang's readings, the discredited notions of immanence and transcendence are presupposed by the very aporia or 'phantasm' that drives his dialectic. Orrin Wang, *Fantastic Modernity: Dialectical Readings in Romanticism and Theory* (Baltimore, MD: Johns Hopkins University Press, 1996), 23. Instead, the present study aspires to the goal outlined by Rajan and Clark, namely, understanding 'how the present might be reread through a past that remains its condition of possibility', but in a way that obviates rather than tolerates the paradoxes that beset postmodernism's negative knowledge of its own

idealistic 'remainders'. Tilottama Rajan and David L. Clark, Introduction, *Intersections: Nineteenth-Century Philosophy and Contemporary Theory* (Albany, NY: State University of New York Press, 1995), 3.

8 This often means pushing noncognitive readings to cognitive conclusions. In her study of romantic theories of interpretation, for example, Tilottama Rajan argues that since 'outside and inside are not so much opposite as diacritical terms' discourse itself cannot be separated from the relationships between speaker, audience, and situation. Tilottama Rajan, *The Supplement of Reading: Figures of Understanding in Romantic Theory and Practice* (Ithaca, NY: Cornell University Press, 1990), 1. Responding to the 'surplus of meaning' (10) in all discourse through its own metanarratives of reading and communication, she claims, romantic literature testifies to the possibility of a kind of 'deconstruction that is postorganicist rather than poststructuralist' (1). Further questions are raised, however, if we pursue this line of thinking. The first is this: once the relationships between speaker, audience, and world are seen as *constitutive* of discourse, is there any *sense* that can be attached to the idea of a 'diacritical' relationship between the 'outside and inside' of language, or, indeed, to the idea of a 'surplus' of meaning? When we erase 'meaning', in other words, do we not also erase the 'surplus'? By folding interpretation entirely into the pragmatics of everyday communication it might be possible to abandon not only the totems of foundationalism, but also the watchwords of the counter-Enlightenment.

9 See Kathleen Wheeler, *Romanticism, Pragmatism and Deconstruction* (Oxford: Blackwell, 1993); Angela Esterhammer, *The Romantic Performative: Language and Action in British and German Romanticism* (Palo Alto, CA: Stanford University Press, 2000); Richard Eldridge, *Leading a Human Life: Wittgenstein, Intentionality, and Romanticism* (University of Chicago Press, 1997), and *The Persistence of Romanticism: Essays in Philosophy and Literature* (Cambridge University Press, 2001); Paul Hamilton, *Metaromanticism: Aesthetics, Literature, Theory* (University of Chicago Press, 2003); Russell B. Goodman, *American Philosophy and the Romantic Tradition* (Cambridge University Press, 1990); Jerome Christensen, *Romanticism at the End of History* (Baltimore, MD: Johns Hopkins University Press, 2000).

10 Richard Rorty, *Philosophy and the Mirror of Nature* (Princeton University Press, 1980), 142.

11 See James Engell, *The Creative Imagination: Enlightenment to Romanticism* (Cambridge, MA: Harvard University Press, 1981).

12 See Thomas Reid, *An Inquiry into the Human Mind, on the Principles of Common Sense* (Edinburgh, 1764): 'What we commonly call natural *causes* might, with more propriety, be called natural *signs*, and what we call *effects*, the things signified' (124–5).

13 W. V. Quine, 'Five Milestones of Empiricism', *Theories and Things* (Cambridge, MA: Harvard University Press, 1981), 67.

14 Edmund Burke, *A Philosophical Enquiry into the Origin of our Ideas of the Sublime and Beautiful* (London, 1759), 1.

15 Donald Davidson, 'Plato's Philosopher', *Truth, Language, and History* (Oxford: Clarendon Press, 2005), 224.

16 Donald Davidson, 'The Problem of Objectivity', *Problems of Rationality* (Oxford: Clarendon Press, 2004), 16.

17 It is important to distinguish (Socratic, empirical) romantic *holism* from (German, idealistic) romantic *organicism*. Holism posits the interdependence of truth, communication, and subjectivity: none of these is possible without the others. Using a plant analogy, however, organicism postulates the existence of a *higher* (transcendent) unity that exceeds the sum of its parts.

18 Wheeler, *Romanticism*, 147.

19 This is a big 'aside,' admittedly, but even here, as I argue in Chapter 5, the 'German' complexion of Coleridge's later thought has been misunderstood.

20 Esterhammer, *The Romantic Performative*, 21. Both Goodman and Richard Poirier see Ralph Waldo Emerson as a bridge between romanticism and pragmatism. Thus, for Goodman, 'Emerson is a direct link between American philosophy and European Romanticism' (*American Philosophy*, 34), while one of Poirier's main theses in *Poetry and Pragmatism* (Cambridge, MA: Harvard University Press, 1992) is that William James's pragmatism can be traced back to an 'Emersonian linguistic scepticism' (5).

21 Jürgen Habermas, *The Philosophical Discourse of Modernity: Twelve Lectures*, trans. Frederick Lawrence (Cambridge, MA: MIT Press, 1987), 5, 7.

22 Habermas, *Philosophical Discourse*, 30.

23 Ibid., 22.

24 Jürgen Habermas, *Knowledge and Human Interests*, trans. Jeremy J. Shapiro (London: Heinemann, 1972), 9.

25 Habermas, *Philosophical Discourse*, 22.

26 See Marjorie Levinson, Introduction, in Levinson, *et al.*, *Rethinking Historicism: Critical Readings in Romantic History* (Oxford: Blackwell, 1989). Levinson claims that the only way to avoid 'historicism's Hobson's choice of contemplation or empathy: in the Romantic idiom, knowledge or power' (2) is, as she puts it in her essay, 'The New Historicism: Back to the Future', to 'propose that in a real and practical way, *we are the effects* of particular pasts, to which we are related by distance and difference' (50–1).

27 See Jean-Pierre Mileur, 'The Return of the Romantic', in *Intersections: Nineteenth-Century Philosophy and Contemporary Theory*, ed. Tilottama Rajan and David L. Clark (Albany, NY: State University of New York Press, 1995), 325–48 (346).

28 Michael Scrivener, 'Inside and Outside Romanticism', *Criticism* 46.1 (2004): 151–65. Scrivener continues: 'Not to leave anyone in suspense, I will answer my own questions: yes, no, impossible to say, no, no. We are still within Romanticism . . .' (151–2).

29 Fredric Jameson, 'Metacommentary', *PMLA* 86.1 (1971): 9–18 (10).

30 Michel Foucault, *The Order of Things: An Archeology of the Human Sciences* (1966, London: Routledge, 2002), 355–6.

31 See James Chandler, *England in 1819: The Politics of Literary Culture and the Case of Romantic Historicism* (University of Chicago Press, 1998), Chapter 1. Accordingly, Chandler 'dates' his own work against that of Jameson, and Jameson's against that of Sartre and Lévi-Strauss.

32 Alan Liu, in particular, has made a series of pointed interventions in his sympathetic critique of the presuppositions of historicist scholarship, from 'The Power of Formalism: The New Historicism', *English Literary History* 56 (1989): 721–71, to 'Remembering the Spruce Goose: Historicism, Postmodernism, Romanticism', *South Atlantic Quarterly* 102.1 (2003): 263–78.

33 The idea that there is something inherently paradoxical about belief, that it is at once necessary and impossible, remains influential even among critics sceptical of historicism. Pfau applauds romantic writing for its suggestion that 'knowledge implies something holistic, not cumulative' ('Introduction. Reading beyond Redemption', 25), and uses this as a basis to argue that modern criticism should refashion itself on ethical rather than methodo-logical or technical grounds. However, when Pfau writes of 'the irreducible tension between knowledge as a formal pursuit (criticism) and as a dynamic intuition (life)' (26), he accepts the aporia that postmodern historicism inserts into thought. The otherwise welcome attempts by Rajan and Plotnitsky to redefine romantic 'idealism' as material and creative suffer from a similar drawback, evident in Plotnitsky's account of contingency as the 'unnamable even as unnamable, unknowable even as unknowable' element 'in all our theoretical or cognitive processes'. See Tilottama Rajan and Arkady Plotnitsky, eds., *Idealism without Absolutes: Philosophy and Romantic Culture* (Albany, NY: State University of New York Press, 2004), 243.

34 Hamilton, *Metaromanticism*, 233.

35 Rorty, *Mirror*, 157.

36 See Richard Rorty, 'Solidarity or Objectivity?', in *Objectivity, Relativism and Truth: Philosophical Papers*, vol.1 (Cambridge University Press, 1991): '[W]e need to say, despite Putnam, that "there is only the dialogue," only *us . . .*' (32).

37 Rorty, 'Pragmatism, Davidson and Truth', in *Objectivity*, 139.

38 Charles Altieri, 'Practical Sense – Impractical Objects: Why Neo-Pragmatism Cannot Sustain an Aesthetics', *Pragmatism and Literary Studies*, vol. 15, *REAL: The Yearbook of Research in English and American Literature*, ed. Winfried Fluck (Tübingen: Gunter Narr Verlag, 1999), 113–35 (116).

39 Altieri 'Practical Sense', 117.

40 Ibid., 126.

41 Poirier *Pragmatism*, 110.

42 Ibid., 123.

43 Habermas, *Philosophical Discourse*, 295–6.

44 For this reason, romantic autobiography need not be seen as Paul de Man's figure of reading whereby the revolving door of specular subjectivity always betrays the 'tropological structure that underlies all cognitions, including knowledge of self'. Paul de Man, *Blindness and Insight: Essays in the Rhetoric*

of Contemporary Criticism, 2nd edn. (Minneapolis, MN: University of Minnesota Press, 1983), 71. Rather, it becomes an exploration of the conditions of leading a human life; one in which not always knowing what we mean, not being able to give basic reasons for our beliefs, is seen as *enabling*, rather than undermining, our interactions with others and with the world.

45 See Richard Rorty, Introduction, *Contingency, Irony, and Solidarity* (Cambridge University Press, 1989).

46 Richard Rorty, 'Is Truth a Goal of Inquiry? Donald Davidson Versus Crispin Wright,' *Truth and Progress: Philosophical Papers*, vol. 3 (Cambridge University Press, 1998), 41.

1 ROMANTICISING PRAGMATISM

1 Wheeler claims that, like the romantics, the pragmatists rejected the 'dualisms' of 'empiricism, rationalism, or idealism': *Romanticism*, 92.

2 Rorty, *Mirror*, 358.

3 See Donald Davidson, 'On the Very Idea of a Conceptual Scheme', in *Post-Analytic Philosophy*, ed. John Rajchman and Cornel West (New York, Columbia University Press, 1985), 129–44. To Davidson, it makes no sense to conceive of 'a single space within which each scheme has a position and provides a point of view' (140).

4 Richard Rorty, Interview with E. P. Ragg, *Philosophy and Literature* 26 (2002): 369–96 (381).

5 Winfried Fluck, Introduction, *Pragmatism and Literary Studies*, vol. 15, *REAL: The Yearbook of Research in English and American Literature* (Tübingen: Gunter Narr Verlag, 1999), x.

6 Rorty, Interview, 389.

7 Ibid., 383.

8 See Marjorie Levinson, Introduction, in Levinson, *et al.*, *Rethinking Historicism*. Levinson advocates a criticism that discovers itself 'as both cause and effect of [a] constructed past', by incorporating what she describes, following Dominick LaCapra, as 'a complex repetitive temporality' (7–8).

9 Christensen, *Romanticism*, 11.

10 Fredric Jameson, *The Political Unconscious: Narrative as a Socially Symbolic Act* (London: Routledge, 2002), ix.

11 Jerome J. McGann, *The Beauty of Inflections: Literary Investigations in Historical Method and Theory* (Oxford University Press, 1985), 5.

12 Jean-Paul Sartre, *Search for a Method*, trans. Hazel E. Barnes (New York: Alfred A. Knopf, 1963), 32.

13 Levinson, Introduction, in *Rethinking Historicism*, 8.

14 Marjorie Levinson, 'The New Historicism: Back to the Future', in *Rethinking Historicism*, 51.

15 See Alan Lui, 'Local Transcendence: Cultural Criticism, Postmodernism, and the Romanticism of Detail', *Representations* 32 (1990): 75–113. Liu critiques 'high postmodernist forms' of cultural criticism which share, despite their

attempts to subdivide, 'an increasingly generic discourse of contextualism' or '*detached immanence*' (77).

16 Marjorie Levinson, 'Romantic Criticism: The State of the Art', in *At the Limits of Romanticism: Essays in Cultural, Feminist, and Materialist Criticism*, ed. Mary A. Favret and Nicola J. Watson (Bloomington, IN: Indiana University Press, 1994), 270.

17 Levinson, 'Romantic Criticism', 274.

18 Ibid., 272.

19 Ibid., 280.

20 Bernard Williams, *Truth and Truthfulness: An Essay in Genealogy* (Princeton University Press, 2002), 1.

21 Chandler, *England in 1819*, 6.

22 Ibid., xv.

23 Liu, 'The Power of Formalism', 757.

24 Frank Lentricchia, *Criticism and Social Change* (University of Chicago Press, 1983), 12, 5.

25 Richard Rorty, 'Cosmopolitanism without Emancipation: A Response to Jean-François Lyotard', in *Objectivity*, 211–22 (218). Rorty has made a career of bringing thinkers together, motivated by idea that tracing commonalities is more useful and 'edifying' than locating differences.

26 Lentricchia, *Criticism*, 5.

27 Ibid., 16.

28 Ibid., 17.

29 Ibid., 16.

30 Ibid., 13.

31 Rorty, *Contingency*, 8.

32 Rorty, Introduction, *Truth and Progress*, 4. For Rorty, the idea that there is nothing but dialogue is not threatening to the concept of truth because truth is a causal, not an epistemic concept. In discussing the nature of belief, however, 'causation is not under a description, but explanation is'. 'Texts and Lumps', in *Objectivity*, 78–92 (81). Accordingly, the pragmatist rejects both the scientist's 'positive' and the historicist's 'negative' attempts to explain the causality of thought. The point about 'truth' is not that it is unreal, but that it is not especially interesting; it does not tell us much about what human nature is or what it can become. Here, once again, Rorty follows Davidson, who sees human minds as webs of beliefs and desires, and beliefs in turn as habits of action for which the concept of truth is a precondition.

33 Rorty, *Mirror*, 358.

34 Rorty, *Contingency*, 52–3.

35 Ibid., 8.

36 Rorty, 'Texts and Lumps', in *Objectivity*, 80.

37 Rorty, *Contingency*, 19.

38 Rorty, 'Is Truth a Goal of Inquiry?', in *Truth and Progress*, 41.

39 Rorty, 'Habermas, Derrida', in *Truth and Progress*, 310.

40 Rorty, *Contingency*, 7.

41 Ibid., 19.

42 Rorty, 'Texts and Lumps', in *Objectivity*, 81.

43 Jürgen Habermas, 'Richard Rorty's Pragmatic Turn', *Rorty and His Critics*, ed. Robert B. Brandom (Oxford: Blackwell, 2000), 31–55 (32, 40).

44 Ibid., 41.

45 Ibid., 48.

46 See Rorty, 'Habermas, Derrida', in *Truth and Progress*: Rorty writes of the 'contrast between an intellectual world dominated by the "German" longing for some destiny higher than that of Nietzsche's "last men" and one dominated merely by the "Anglo-Saxon" desire to avoid the infliction of unnecessary pain and humiliation. . . . Radicals want sublimity, but liberals want beauty' (324).

47 Ibid., 311.

48 Richard Rorty, 'Response to Jürgen Habermas,' in *Rorty*, ed. Brandom, 56–64 (58).

49 Richard Rorty, 'Rationality and Cultural Difference', in *Truth and Progress*, 200.

50 Habermas, 'Richard Rorty's Pragmatic Turn', 43–4.

51 Ibid., 51.

52 Rorty, 'Pragmatism, Davidson, and Truth', in *Objectivity*, 135.

53 See 'Charles Taylor on Truth' in *Truth and Progress* for Rorty's definition of nonreductive naturalism: 'I define naturalism as the claim that (a) there is no occupant of space–time that is not linked in a single web of causal relations to all other occupants and (b) that any explanation of the behavior of any such spatiotemporal object must consist in placing that object within that single web. I define reductionism as the insistence that there is not only a single web but a single privileged description of all entities caught in that web' (94).

54 Richard Rorty, 'Inquiry as Recontextualization: An Anti-Dualist Account of Interpretation', in *Objectivity*, 109.

55 Rorty, Interview, 369.

56 Philosophers' favourite example of propositions that are putatively true by virtue of their meanings are statements of the type: 'all bachelors are unmarried men'.

57 W. V. Quine, *Word and Object* (Cambridge, MA: MIT Press, 1960), 66.

58 Ibid., ix.

59 Ibid., 1.

60 W. V. Quine, 'Two Dogmas of Empiricism', *From a Logical Point of View: Nine Logico-Philosophical Essays*, 2nd edn (Cambridge, MA: Harvard University Press, 1961), 42.

61 Ibid., 43.

62 Jerry Fodor and Ernest Lepore, *Holism: A Shopper's Guide* (Oxford: Blackwell, 1992), 6–7.

63 Ibid., 17.

64 W. V. Quine, 'Epistemology Naturalised', *Ontological Relativity and Other Essays* (New York: Columbia University Press, 1969), 82.

65 Fodor and Lepore, *Holism*, 12.

66 Quine, *Word and Object*, 20.

67 W. V. Quine, *Pursuit of Truth* (Cambridge, MA: Harvard University Press, 1990), 15.

68 Thomas S. Kuhn, *The Structure of Scientific Revolutions*, 3rd edn (University of Chicago Press, 1996), 121. As Hilary Putnam notes, Kuhn later watered down the notion of incommensurability into 'intertheoretic meaning change, as opposed to uninterpretability': *Realism with a Human Face*, ed. James Conant (Cambridge MA: Harvard University Press, 1990), 127.

69 Foucault, *Order*, 236.

70 Jean-François Lyotard, *The Differend: Phrases in Dispute*, trans. Georges Van Den Abbeele (Minneapolis, MN: University of Minnesota Press, 1988), xii.

71 Following a similar argument to Putnam, Christopher Norris argues that the incommensurability thesis is just 'a postmodern variant on the drastic dichotomy between fact and value'. See *The Truth About Postmodernism* (Blackwell, 1993) 16.

72 Putnam, *Realism with a Human Face*, 210.

73 Hilary Putnam, *Reason, Truth and History* (Cambridge University Press, 1981) 55.

74 Ibid., xi.

75 Ibid., 120.

76 Ibid., 119.

77 Putnam, *Realism with a Human Face*, 120.

78 Foucault, *Order*, xxiv.

79 See Donald Davidson, 'Mental Events', *Essays on Actions and Events*, 2nd edn (Oxford: Clarendon Press, 2001): 'Anomalous monism resembles materialism in its claim that all events are physical, but rejects the thesis … that mental phenomena can be given purely physical explanation' (214).

80 Donald Davidson, *Subjective, Intersubjective, Objective* (Oxford: Clarendon Press, 2001), 177–8.

81 Davidson, 'Conceptual Scheme,' in *Post-Analytic Philosophy*, ed. Rajchman and West, 143.

82 Ibid.

83 See Quine, *Pursuit of Truth*. Quine argues that the closest we can come to defining truth is simply to say that in calling a sentence 'true' we affirm it. Semantically, this affirmation takes the form of disquotation, as in the following formulation offered by Quine: ' "Snow is white" is true if and only if snow is white.' In this way, Quine concludes, 'the truth predicate is superfluous when ascribed to a given sentence; you could just utter the sentence' (80).

84 Davidson, *Subjective*, 217.

85 Davidson, *Problems*, 35.

86 Davidson, *Truth*, 107.

87 Davidson, *Problems*, 35.

88 Davidson, *Subjective*, 44.

89 Davidson, *Truth*, 161.

90 Ibid., 157.

91 Reed Way Dasenbrock, *Truth and Consequences: Intentions, Conventions and the New Thematics* (University Park, PA: Pennsylvania State University Press, 2001), 70.

92 Davidson, *Truth*, 162.

93 Ibid., 240.

94 Davidson, *Problems*, 16.

95 Ibid., 19.

96 Ibid., 51.

97 Ibid., 36.

98 Ibid., 74.

99 W. V. Quine, *Theories and Things* (Cambridge, MA: Harvard University Press, 1981), 20.

100 Charles Taylor, *Sources of the Self: The Making of Modern Identity* (Cambridge University Press, 1989), 49–50.

101 Donald Davidson, 'Dialectic and Dialogue', in *Language Mind and Epistemology: On Donald Davidson's Philosophy*, ed. Gerhard Preyer, Frank Siebelt and Alexander Ulfig (Dordrecht: Kluwer Academic Publishers, 1994), 429–37 (433).

102 Charles Taylor, *Philosophical Arguments* (Cambridge, MA: Harvard University Press, 1995), ix.

103 *Ibid.*, viii.

104 C. Taylor, *Sources*, 58.

105 Ibid., 32.

106 Putnam, *Reason*, 113.

107 C. Taylor, *Philosophical Arguments*, 31. Peter Lamarque and Stein Haugom Olsen come to a similar conclusion about literature in *Truth, Fiction and Literature: A Philosophical Perspective* (Oxford: Clarendon Press, 1994), arguing that like philosophy it enhances the 'coherence' (455) of the quotidian by developing 'themes that are only vaguely felt or formulated in daily life' (452).

108 C. Taylor, *Philosophical Arguments*, 32.

109 C. Taylor, *Sources*, 72.

110 C. Taylor, *Philosophical Arguments*, 32.

111 John Keats, 'To John Hamilton Reynolds', 3 May 1818, letter 80, *The Letters of John Keats 1814–1821*, ed. Hyder Edward Rollins, vol. 1 (Cambridge, MA: Harvard University Press, 1958), 279.

112 C. Taylor, *Sources*, 73.

113 Ibid., 8.

114 Putnam, *Reason*, 148. See also Davidson, *Problems*: 'disputes over values … can be genuine only if there are shared criteria in the light of which there is an answer to the question who is right' (50).

115 Eldridge, *Persistence of Romanticism*, 11.

116 C. Taylor, *Philosophical Arguments*, 10–11.

117 Jürgen Habermas, *The Theory of Communicative Action*, trans. Thomas McCarthy, vol. 1 (1981, Boston, Mass.: Beacon Press, 1984), 82.

118 Habermas, *Philosophical Discourse*, 306. Paul Hamilton has translated Habermas's picture of philosophy as a 'placeholder' for ideal communication into an account of what he calls 'metaromanticism'. For Hamilton, postmodern historicism misses the possibilities of critique offered by romantic writing, before the idea of reason became absolute in Hegel, and absolutely antinomian in Nietzsche. Metaromanticism, he argues, avoids the recuperative habits of objectivism on one hand and, on the other, the ideology of immanent critique, or the 'knowing refusal of any critical position outside a self-confirming belief-system': *Metaromanticism*, 15. Disappointed with rationalism and disgusted by the coercive power of aesthetic plenitude, metaromanticism forgoes 'mastery to occupy the more ancillary role of facilitating better communication between different discourses': *Metaromanticism*, 3.

119 Habermas, *Knowledge*, 314.

120 Habermas, *Theory of Communicative Action*, vol. 1, 42.

121 Putnam, *Reason*, 55.

122 Habermas, *Theory of Communicative Action*, vol. 1, 84.

123 Ibid., 10.

124 Hilary Putnam, *The Collapse of the Fact/Value Dichotomy and Other Essays* (Cambridge, MA: Harvard University Press, 2002), 4.

125 Jürgen Habermas, 'Philosophy and Science as Literature?', in *Postmetaphysical Thinking: Philosophical Essays*, trans. William Mark Hohengarten (Cambridge: Polity Press, 1992), 223–5.

2 PRAGMATISING ROMANTICISM

1 Wheeler, *Romanticism*, 147.

2 Ibid., 40, 44.

3 Esterhammer, *The Romantic Performative*, 20; Olivia Smith, *The Politics of Language 1791–1819* (Oxford: Clarendon Press, 1984), 23.

4 See Tim Milnes, *Knowledge and Indifference in English Romantic Prose* (Cambridge University Press, 2003).

5 David Hume, *A Treatise of Human Nature*, ed. Peter H. Nidditch, 2nd edn (Oxford University Press, 1978), 469.

6 David Hume, *Enquiries Concerning Human Understanding and Concerning the Principles of Morals*, ed. L. A. Selby-Bigge, 3rd edn, rev. P. H. Nidditch (Oxford: Clarendon Press, 1975), 25.

7 There have been recent attempts to depict Hume's work as overcoming or challenging the division between the natural and the normative. See, for example, Rupert Read's likening of Hume's '*deflationary* naturalism' to Wittgenstein and Nelson Goodman in 'In Closing: the Antagonists of "The New Hume". On the Relevance of Goodman and Wittgenstein to the New Hume Debate', in *The New Hume Debate*, ed. Rupert Read and Kenneth A. Richman (London: Routledge, 2000), 167–97 (191). See also Jacqueline Taylor's argument in 'Hume and the Reality of Value', in *Feminist Interpretations of David Hume*, ed. Anne Jaap Jacobsen (University Park, PA: Pennsylvania

State University Press, 2000), 107–36, that a dialectical relationship between understanding and the sentiments in Hume underpins his notion of 'the *emergent* normativity of moral and aesthetic judgement' (124).

8 For Jerome Christensen in *Practicing Enlightenment: Hume and the Formation of a Literary Career* (Madison, WI: University of Wisconsin Press, 1987), Hume's general project is one of exercising social power through style, whereby epistemological paradox is raised only to be exploited 'as just another articulation, a productive inconsistency' (14). Since the refinement of breakdown into recuperation is itself what sustains Hume's career, indifference to argument 'is possible because of an indifference to one's own particular opinions' (176). Thus, in 1751, Hume chides Gilbert Elliot for not debating theology with him because the latter has not yet 'reach'd an absolute philosophical Indifference on these Points. What Danger can ever come from ingenious Reasoning & Enquiry?': David Hume, 'To Gilbert Elliot of Minto', 10 March 1751, letter 72, *The Letters of David Hume*, ed. J. Y. T. Greig, vol. 1 (Oxford: Clarendon Press, 1932), 154.

9 Putnam, *Reason, Truth and History*, 127.

10 Thomas Reid, *An Inquiry into the Human Mind*, 488.

11 Ibid., 469.

12 Ibid., 123.

13 Ibid., 489.

14 Ibid., 469.

15 Ibid., 474.

16 Ibid., 477.

17 Dugald Stewart, *Elements of the Philosophy of the Human Mind*, vol. 2 (Edinburgh, 1792–1827), 56, in *The Collected Works of Dugald Stewart*, ed. William Hamilton, vol. 3 (Edinburgh, 1854–60; Bristol: Thoemmes Press, 1994).

18 Ibid., vol. 2, 66.

19 Ibid., vol. 2, 56.

20 In Daniel Rosenberg's ' "A New Sort of Logick and Critick": Etymological Interpretation in Horne Tooke's *The Diversions of Purley*', in *Language, Self, and Society: A Social History of Language*, ed. Peter Burke and Roy Porter (Cambridge: Polity Press, 1991), 300–29, notes that Paine, Godwin, and Coleridge all attended Tooke's weekly dinners between 1800 and his death in 1812 (305).

21 O. Smith, *Politics of Language*, 139.

22 John Horne Tooke, *Epea Pteroenta, or the Diversions of Purley*, ed. Richard Taylor, vol. 1 (London, 1829), 374.

23 Ibid., 10.

24 Ibid., 12.

25 Ibid., 23.

26 Ibid., 26.

27 Ibid., 49.

28 Quine, *Theories and Things*, 67–8.

29 Tooke, *Diversions*, vol. 2, 402–3.

30 O. Smith, *Politics of Language*, 134.

31 See Percy Bysshe Shelley, 'To Thomas Jefferson Hogg', 16 March [1814], letter 253, *The Letters of Percy Bysshe Shelley*, ed. Frederick L. Jones, vol. 1 (Oxford University Press, 1964): 'I have forced myself to read Beccaria and Dumont's *Bentham*' (384). Shelley could be referring to the *Traités de législation civile et pénale*, 3 vols. (Paris, 1802), *Théorie des peines et des récompenses*, 2 vols. (London, 1811), or to both. I discuss Shelley's debt to Bentham in Chapter 3, below. For the dating of Bentham's works, see Ross Harrison, *Bentham* (Routledge & Kegan Paul, 1983), xvi–xxiv.

32 Jeremy Bentham, *An Introduction to the Principles of Morals and Legislation*, ed. J. H. Burns and H. L. A. Hart (London: Athlone Press, 1970), 97.

33 Ibid., 102.

34 Jeremy Bentham, 'Essay on Logic', *The Works of Jeremy Bentham*, ed. John Bowring, vol. 8 (Edinburgh, 1838–43), 246.

35 Bentham, 'Essay on Language', *Works*, vol. 8 331. Emphasis added.

36 O. Smith, *Politics of Language*, 139.

37 Angela Esterhammer, 'Of Promises, Contacts and Constitutions: Thomas Reid and Jeremy Bentham on Language as Social Action', *Romanticism* 6.1 (2000), 67. Dugald Stewart, 'On the Tendency of Some Late Philological Speculations', in *The Collected Works of Dugald Stewart*, ed. William Hamilton, vol. 5 (Edinburgh, 1854–60; Thoemmes Press, 1994), 154–5.

38 Stewart, 'Philological Speculations', in *Works*, vol. 5, 156.

39 Ibid., 164.

40 Ibid., 162.

41 See Simon Swift, *Romanticism, Literature and Philosophy: Expressive Rationality in Rousseau, Kant, Wollstonecraft and Contemporary Theory* (London: Continuum, 2006), 17. In making this claim, Swift draws upon the work of Kant scholars such as Howard Caygill, Onora O'Neill, and Susan Meld Shell.

42 Swift, *Romanticism*, 9.

43 Ibid., 18, 11.

44 Ibid., 146.

45 Lorraine Daston and Peter Galison, *Objectivity* (New York: Zone Books, 2007), 60.

46 Ibid., 18. According to this narrative, the decline of mechanical objectivity in the early twentieth century leads to the emergence of a third code of epistemic virtue: 'trained judgement' (33).

47 Ibid., 38–9.

48 Peter Galison, 'Objectivity is Romantic', *American Council of Learned Societies Occasional Paper* 47 (1999), 17 June 2009, archives.acls.org/op/op47-3.htm#galison.

49 Foucault, *Order*, 347.

50 See C. Taylor, *Sources*, 58.

51 Percy Bysshe Shelley, 'On Life', in *The Complete Works of Percy Bysshe Shelley*, ed. Roger Ingpen and Walter E. Peck, vol. 6 (London: Ernest Benn Ltd., 1929), 194.

52 Ibid., 196.

53 Jerrold E. Hogle, *Shelley's Process: Radical Transference and the Development of His Major Works* (Oxford University Press, 1988), 10.
54 William A. Ulmer, *Shelleyan Eros: The Rhetoric of Romantic Love* (Princeton University Press, 1990), 23.
55 Shelley, 'On Life', in *Complete Works*, vol. 6, 193.
56 Ibid., 194.
57 Ibid., 195.
58 Satya P. Mohanty, 'Can Our Values be Objective? On Ethics, Aesthetics, and Progressive Politics', *New Literary History* 32 (2001): 803–33 (815).
59 Shelley, 'On Life', in *Complete Works*, vol. 6, 196.
60 Hamilton, *Metaromanticism*, 154.
61 Stanley Cavell, *Must We Mean What We Say? A Book of Essays* (Cambridge University Press, 1976), 84.
62 Ibid., 86.
63 Ibid., 258.
64 Ibid., 323.
65 Ibid., 264.
66 Ibid., 324.
67 Stanley Cavell, *In Quest of the Ordinary: Lines of Skepticism and Romanticism* (University of Chicago Press, 1988), 9.
68 Ibid., 52.
69 Ibid., 32.
70 Ibid., 61. Like Cavell, Richard Eldridge draws parallels between Wittgenstein's work on ordinary language and the romantic struggle to understand 'what our spontaneity enables and demands of us'. Eldridge, *Leading a Human Life*, 86.
71 Cavell, *In Quest of the Ordinary*, 145.
72 Ibid., 6.
73 Goodman, *American Philosophy*, x.
74 Ibid., 93.
75 Ibid., 35.
76 Ibid., 56.
77 Ibid., 109.
78 Laurence S. Lockridge, *The Ethics of Romanticism* (Cambridge University Press, 1989), 43.
79 Charles Lamb, 'Imperfect Sympathies', in *The Works of Charles and Mary Lamb*, ed. E. V. Lucas, vol. 2 (London: Methuen & Co., 1903), 60–1.
80 John Dewey, *Theory of Valuation*, in *John Dewey: The Later Works, 1925–1953*, ed. Jo Ann Boydston and Barbara Levine, vol. 13 (Carbondale, Ill.: Southern Illinois University Press, 1988), 189–251 (227).
81 Charles Lamb, 'A Dissertation Upon Roast Pig', in *Works*, vol. 2, 123.
82 Dewey, 'Theory of Valuation', 227.
83 Ibid., 245.
84 Ibid., 248–9.
85 Goodman, *American Philosophy*, 46, 81.

86 See Goodman, *American Philosophy*, 91: 'Dewey's philosophy is a culmination of the Romantic movement toward the imaginative transformation of the world, a movement including Coleridge's and Emerson's actively transformative will, as well as James's pragmatic "making of truth".'

87 John Dewey, *Experience and Nature* (New York: Dover Publications, 1958), xv.

88 Goodman, *American Philosophy*, 57.

89 For the disagreement between Cavell and the pragmatists over Emerson's place within the American philosophical tradition, see Naoko Saito, 'Reconstructing Deweyan Pragmatism in Dialogue with Emerson and Cavell', *Transactions of the Charles S. Peirce Society* 37.3 (2001): 389–406. Saito notes Cavell's argument that Emerson's dedication to a broader vision of 'life' than Dewey's 'problem-solving' conception means that 'Dewey is not Emersonian and that Emerson is not a pragmatist' (389). See also: Thomas Claviez, 'Pragmatism, Critical Theory, and the Search for Ecological Genealogies in American Culture', in Fluck, ed., *Pragmatism and Literary Studies*, 343–80; Vincent Colapietro, 'The Question of Voice and the Limits of Pragmatism: Emerson, Dewey, and Cavell', *The Range of Pragmatism and the Limits of Philosophy*, ed. Richard Shusterman (Oxford: Blackwell, 2004), 174–96, and Cornel West, *The American Evasion of Philosophy: A Genealogy of Pragmatism* (Madison, WI: University of Wisconsin Press, 1989).

90 Goodman, *American Philosophy*, 92.

91 Wheeler, *Romanticism*, 158.

92 Putnam, *Reason*, xi; Goodman, *American Philosophy*, 129.

93 William James, *The Will to Believe and Other Essays in Popular Philosophy* (New York: Longmans, Green and Co., 1904), 16.

94 William James, *Pragmatism: A New Name for Some Old Ways of Thinking* (New York: Longmans, Green & Co., Inc., 1907), 76; John Dewey, *Reconstruction in Philosophy* (Boston, MA: Beacon Press, 1948), 156.

95 Wheeler in particular exaggerates the degree of alignment between Coleridge and Shelley on the one hand, and James and Dewey on the other. See *Romanticism*, Chapters 4 and 5, in which she claims that Dewey's *Art as Experience* 'is as nearly a systematization of romantic insights into art and æsthetics as we have available' (147).

96 James, *The Will to Believe*, 72.

97 Dewey, *Reconstruction*, 100.

98 Dewey, *Experience*, 377.

99 Rorty, 'Response to Jürgen Habermas', in *Rorty*, 57.

100 Rorty, 'Inquiry as Recontextualization', in *Objectivity*, 98, 109.

101 Fluck, Introduction, *Pragmatism and Literary Studies*, ix.

3 THIS LIVING KEATS

1 Paul de Man, Introduction, *The Selected Poetry of Keats* (New York: Signet, 1966), xxxvi. David Luke, for instance, claims in 'Keats's Letters: Fragments of an Aesthetics of Fragments', *Genre* 11 (1978): 209–26, that the letters 'both generate and dramatize his ideas of poetry' (223). For Greg Kucich in

'The Poetry of Mind in Keats's Letters', *Style* 21.1 (1987): 76–94, Keats's 'epistolary acts of mind' (77) in the letters overcome 'creative torpor' and prefigure the 'doubling' strategies of his poems (89). However, in ' "Cutting Figures": Rhetorical Strategies in Keats's Letters', in *Keats: Bicentenary Readings*, ed. Michael O'Neill (Edinburgh University Press, 1997), 144–69, Timothy Webb calls for 'a poetics of the letter' to highlight the aesthetic 'autonomy' of Keats's correspondence (146).

2 John Keats, 'To George and Tom Keats,' 21, 27 (?) December 1817, letter 45, *The Letters of John Keats 1814–1821*, vol. 1, 193. Hereafter cited in notes as '*KL*'.

3 Douka E. Kabitoglou, in 'Adapting Philosophy to Literature: The Case of John Keats', *Studies in Philology* 89.1 (1992): 115–36, adumbrates an essentially Platonic reading of the poet, suggesting that Keats was introduced to Platonism while visiting Bailey at Oxford in 1817. In *John Keats* (Cambridge, MA: Harvard University Press, 1963), 255–9, Walter Jackson Bate notes that during this visit Keats also read Hazlitt's *An Essay on the Principles of Human Action* and *The Round Table*. Nicholas Roe, in *John Keats and the Culture of Dissent* (Oxford: Clarendon Press, 1997), argues that Hazlitt's influence should be seen in the context of an eighteenth-century tradition that used Shakespearean 'genius' as a model for sympathetic imagination (247).

4 The ascendancy of the negative in Keats criticism goes back to Christopher Ricks's account, in *Keats and Embarrassment* (Oxford University Press, 1974), of how, by doubling its negativity, embarrassment in Keats becomes his unmisgiving strength, a truly negative capability. In turn, Geoffrey Hartman's phenomenological rendering (in 'Poem and Ideology: A Study of Keats's "To Autumn" ', *The Fate of Reading and Other Essays* [University of Chicago Press, 1975]) of the dialectic of 'Keats's poetry of process' (139) in poems such as 'To Autumn', was challenged by de Man's argument that rather than clarifying existence poems such as 'Ode to a Nightingale' locate 'the full power of negativity' only in a contingency of the most opaque kind: Introduction, *Selected Poetry*, xxii. The negative turn in Keats criticism reaches full strength, however, in McGann's claim, *pace* Hartman and de Man, that history determines the dialectical life of poems such as 'Ode on a Grecian Urn', and thereby 'the reflexive world of Romantic art, the very negation of the negation itself': *Beauty*, 61. Marjorie Levinson extends this dialectic to the 'negative knowledge of Keats's actual life' as a performance of cultivated inauthenticity, the 'truly *negative* capability' of the *parvenu* poet: *Keats's Life of Allegory: The Origins of a Style* (Oxford: Blackwell, 1988), 6, whereby through a finely wrought 'badness', Keats effects the 'demystification of a prestigious idea of literary production' (23). Levinson's book makes two further important and related claims: first, that Keats could not enjoy a 'total understanding' (31) of his own work, because, secondly, such knowledge can only be yielded by a post-structuralist version of Sartre's progressive–regressive method whereby we deliberately 'make ourselves anomalous subjects – "bad" critics – in order to read Keats properly' (37). Levinson's first claim had, to an extent, already been countered by David Bromwich, Alan Bewell, and Paul Fry in the 1986 *Studies*

in Romanticism (25.2) forum on 'Keats and Politics', each of whom, in different ways, summon historicised readings of Keats that attempt to recover the voice of the poet from totalising critique – a project continued by Nicholas Roe in *Culture of Dissent* and by the contributors to his collection of essays *Keats and History* (Cambridge University Press, 1995). Indeed, by tracing historicism's celebration of the 'marginal' Keats to the Tory reviewers' similarly 'prejudiced understanding of his education and its effect on his poetry' (7), Roe's monograph removes much of the heat from the debate over Keatsian 'badness'. Levinson's second assertion, meanwhile, is answered by James Chandler in *England in 1819*. Chandler argues that, in the trope of 'smoking', Keats posits a reflexive, 'relative transcendence' (402), which, by historicising the situational intelligibility of his writing, prefigures and thereby obviates Levinson's own use of the progressive–regressive method. Despite this, negativity continues to haunt Keats criticism. Robert Kaufman, for example, claims to locate in Keats the emergence of an 'underlying negative romanticism' ('Negatively Capable Dialectics: Keats, Vendler, Adorno, and the Theory of the Avante-Garde', *Critical Inquiry* 27.2 (2001): 354–85 (384)), whose 'temporary negation/suspension of the ethico-conceptual' comes to fruition in 'Adorno's resistance-to-conceptual-synthesis negative dialectic' (372) and thus the idea of aesthetic modes of apprehension that 'tease us toward the critical' (384).

5 John Keats, 'To John Hamilton Reynolds', 3 February 1818, letter 59, *KL*, vol. 1, 223. In 'Keats, Fictionality, and Finance: *The Fall of Hyperion*', Terence Allan Hoagwood claims that Keats drew upon contemporary debates in the *Examiner* over the loss of the gold currency standard in order to question 'the use of signifiers detached (like paper money) from absent realities'. Roe, *Keats and History*, 127. The relationship between currency values, reference, and empiricism also forms the cornerstone of Levinson's readings of 'Lamia' and 'The Fall of Hyperion' in *Allegory*.

6 John Keats, 'To Reynolds', 21 September 1817, letter 36, *KL*, vol. 1, 163.

7 John Keats, 'To Benjamin Bailey', 13 March 1818, letter 67, *KL*, vol. 1, 242.

8 Ibid., 243.

9 See Roe, *Culture of Dissent*, Chapter 1.

10 Of course, this schematic picture is rarely clear-cut in practice. Priestley remained, like his mentor Hartley, an associationist; Bentham's theory of fictions itself owes much to Hume's distinction between 'impressions' and 'ideas', and Godwin's philosophy (crucial for considering the intellectual and cultural atmosphere in which Keats was working) incorporates – uneasily at times – elements of idealism and materialism, implying on certain occasions that truth lies in correspondence; at others, that it consists in coherence.

11 John Keats, 'To George and Georgiana Keats', 17–27 September 1819, letter 199, *KL*, vol. 2, 213.

12 John Keats, 'To Reynolds', 19 February 1818, letter 62, *KL*, vol. 1, 231–2.

13 Eldridge, *Persistence*, 12.

14 John Keats, 'To Reynolds', 3 May 1818, letter 80, *KL*, vol. 1, 279.

15 Keats, 'To Bailey', 13 March 1818, 243. Erik Gray argues that the curiously indifferent tone in some of Keats's poetry has its roots in the prosaic and tactical evasive strategies developed in his letters in the face of intractable problems or imaginative failure. See: 'Indifference and Epistolarity in "The Eve of St Agnes"', *Romanticism* 5.2 (1999): 127–46.

16 Many of these dissenting voices have clustered around the question of form. Following Alan Liu, Susan Wolfson sets out from the observation that the crypto-formalism of New Historicism has replaced aesthetic formalism 'as the universal, always subsuming all other formalisms to itself': *Formal Charges: The Shaping of Poetry in British Romanticism* (Stanford, CA: Stanford University Press, 1997), 230, a tendency that has occluded the ways in which romantic texts are themselves 'alert to form as construction' (23). The formal anomalies in Keats's final lyrics, for example, reveal an awareness of the agency as well as the historicity of poetic forms that itself becomes 'a framework of critique' (165). Others, however, draw inferences from Keats's sensitivity to form that are less supportive of historicist arguments. Thomas Pfau, one of the most trenchant critics of romantic New Historicism, argues that the 'narratives of early Romanticism and the postmodern critique of its ideological efficacy are grounded in the same epistemological paradigm, that of forms conspiring against their belated discernment, and they perpetrate the same moral utopia, that of an absolute evaluation of the other performed from a putatively value-free and clairvoyant position': 'Introduction. Reading beyond Redemption', 4. None the less, by refusing to collapse the homology of form and sensation into an indifference or identity, Keats preserves the delicate balance between the ethical and the epistemological necessary for the 'voice of critique': 'The Voice of Critique: Aesthetic Cognition after Kant', *Modern Language Quarterly* 60.3 (1999): 321–52 (349). David Ferris traces historicism's failure to detect this balance to its methodological 'classicism': 'Keats and the Aesthetics of Critical Knowledge: or, the Ideology of Studying Romanticism at the Present Time', in Pfau and Gleckner, eds., 122 and its unwillingness to embrace in full the ramifications of the Hegelian dialectic, namely, that if 'negative determination ... is never simply negation' (105), then the historical is never *simply* historical, any more than the aesthetic is purely the aesthetic. What Keats's 'Ode on a Grecian Urn' reveals, then, is how the 'aesthetic is, in fact, the rhetoric of the political rather than an ideology to be opposed to history' (123). In other words, if 'beauty is truth, then the phrase "Beauty is truth" means that beauty is beauty (just as aesthetics is politics means every politics is aesthetic)' (122). Similarly, for Hamilton, Keats's 'self-wounding critique' (*Metaromanticism*, 113), by questioning *all* habits of recuperation, undermines historicism's ruthlessly self-confirming model of *immanent* critique, offering 'a redefinition of immanence, not as the imprisonment of criticism within discourse in general, but as the transfer of authority from one discourse to another, a series of "stand-ins"' (195). While broadly in line with Pfau, Ferris, and Hamilton in their attacks on the negative dialectics of immanent critique, the present study does not join them in decrying

the blurring of the evaluative and the factual, the 'formal' and the empirical, for the reason (as detailed in the previous chapter) that the collapse of such dichotomies actually directs us to a simple, everyday conception of truth.

17 Thus, for Foucault, history betrays the alterity on which our thought depends, such 'that everything that has been thought will be thought again by a thought that does not yet exist': *Order*, 406. From this perspective, those who refuse the challenge 'to think without immediately thinking that it is man who is thinking' cannot be argued with, but can only be answered with 'a philosophical laugh' (373). For Derrida, indeed, indeterminate otherness or *différance* outstrips the resources of any truth-governed dialectic. The '*graphics of supplementarity*' are '*at once* the condition of possibility *and* the condition of impossibility of truth': *Dissemination*, trans. Barbara Johnson (London: Athlone Press, 1981), 168. Consequently, if 'truth is the presence of the *eidos*, it must always … come to terms with relation, nonpresence, and thus nontruth' (166). Postmodern historicism attempts to shape its historical 'knowledge' and dialectical 'method' in light of these claims.

18 Chandler in particular insists that 'the dialectic of historicism depends on this redoubling of the historical situation' (*England in 1819*, 38). Without this redoubling, for example, Levinson's invocation of the progressive–regressive in her study of Keats fails to register the extent to which the Sartre and Lévi-Strauss debate was itself a repetition of a romantic debate.

19 In *Hazlitt and the Reach of Sense Criticism, Morals, and the Metaphysics of Power* (Oxford: Clarendon Press, 1998), Uttara Natarajan points out that at the root of Hazlitt's moral philosophy and theory of personal identity is a principle of mental power quite at odds with Keats's selfless model of poetic genius. In doing so, she also surveys the long tradition of scholarship on the relation between Keats and Hazlitt (109).

20 In this way, Levinson argues, the 'inside-out, thoroughly textualized and autotelic accomplishment' of Keats's style achieves, by the 'triumph of the double-negative' the 'negative knowledge of Keats's actual life: the production of his freedom by the figured negation of his given being': *Allegory*, 6.

21 Keats, 'To George and Tom Keats', 21, 27 (?) December 1817, 193–4.

22 Stuart M. Sperry, *Keats the Poet* (Princeton University Press, 1973), 67.

23 Ibid., 63.

24 Keats, 'To Reynolds', 3 February 1818, 224.

25 John Keats, 'To John Taylor', 24 April 1818, letter 78, *KL*, vol. 1, 271.

26 John Keats, 'To John Hamilton Reynolds', 27 April 1818, letter 79, *KL*, vol. 1, 274.

27 John Keats, 'To Richard Woodhouse', 27 October 1818, letter 118, *KL*, vol. 1, 387.

28 John Keats, 'To George and Georgiana Keats', 14 February–3 May 1819, letter 159, *KL*, vol. 2, 103–4.

29 Chandler, *England in 1819*, 31.

30 John Keats, 'To George and Tom Keats', 21, 27(?) December 1817, 194.

31 Habermas, *Philosophical Discourse*, 297.

32 Ibid., 96.

33 See Thomas A. Reed, 'Keats and the Gregarious March of Intellect in *Hyperion*,' *ELH* 55.1 (1988): 195–232. Reed cites the effect of the disintegration of the Rockingham Whig consensus on Regency radicalism as a decisive influence on Keats's attempts to reconcile 'the necessity of suffering to personal redemption' on one hand and, on the other, 'a belief in historical progress in all aspects of culture and society' (206).

34 William Robertson, *The History of America*, 6th edn, vol. 2 (1777; London, 1792), 50.

35 Roe, *Culture of Dissent*, 39.

36 Bate writes of disinterestedness that 'within the next year the word and all it represented [to Keats] were to become something of a polar star'. *Keats*, 202.

37 John Keats, 'To Benjamin Bailey', 14 August 1819, letter 181, *KL*, vol. 2, 139.

38 As Hazlitt was later to argue, 'the height of nature surpasses the utmost stretch of the imagination' ('The Ideal', *The Complete Works of William Hazlitt*, ed. P. P. Howe, vol. 20 (London: J. M. Dent & Sons, 1930–4), 303).

39 John Keats, 'To George and Georgiana Keats', 14–31 October 1818, letter 120, *KL*, vol. 2, 397.

40 John Keats, 'To Benjamin Bailey', 22 November 1817, letter 43, *KL*, vol. 2, 185.

41 Roe, *Culture of Dissent*, 245. As Roe adds, in this respect Keats was not alone. Hazlitt, Coleridge, and Lamb all complained of the 'intellectual fussiness' of the Godwinians (247).

42 Bailey alienated himself from the Reynolds family by proposing to Miss Hamilton Gleig in Carlisle in August 1818, having been declined by Mariane Reynolds earlier that year. See Bate, *Keats*, 202–4.

43 Keats, 'To George and Georgiana Keats,' 14 February–3 May 1819, 67.

44 Thomas Paine, *Rights of Man*, 5th edn, vol. 2 (London, 1792), 1.

45 William Godwin, *An Inquiry Concerning Political Justice, and its Influence on General Virtue and Happiness*, vol. 1 (London, 1793), 21.

46 Tooke, *Diversions*, vol. 2, 18.

47 William Hazlitt, 'On Tooke's "Diversions of Purley"', *Works*, vol. 2, 280.

48 William Hazlitt, *An Essay on the Principles of Human Action*, *Works*, vol. 2, 35.

49 William Hazlitt, *Letter to William Gifford, Esq.*, *Works*, vol. 9, 58.

50 William Hazlitt, 'Coriolanus', *Works*, vol. 5, 347.

51 Hazlitt, *Letter to Gifford*, 50.

52 Ibid., 58.

53 Hazlitt, *Essay*, 21.

54 Ibid., 4.

55 Paine, *Rights of Man*, vol. 1, 35.

56 Ibid., vol. 1, 4.

57 O. Smith, *Politics of Language*, 53–4.

58 Godwin, *Inquiry*, vol. 2, 497–8.

59 O. Smith, *Politics of Language*, 21.

60 Ibid., 3.

61 William Hazlitt, 'The Spirit of Controversy', *Works*, vol. 30, 306.

62 Tooke, *Diversions*, vol. 1, 10.

63 Tom Paulin, *The Day-Star of Liberty: William Hazlitt's Radical Style* (Faber and Faber, 1998), 248.

64 In 'The Late Mr. Horne Tooke,' Hunt declares himself to be 'one of the very many who, at first sight of it [Tooke's *Diversions*] bade adieu to the leaden *Hermes* of Mr. Harris': *Leigh Hunt's Political and Occasional Essays*, ed. Lawrence Huston Houtchens and Carolyn Washburn Houtchens (New York: Columbia University Press, 1962), 140.

65 See, for example, Rajan's claim in *The Supplement of Reading* that romantic hermeneutics 'simultaneously initiates and masks the deconstruction of representation and ultimately unweaves its own recuperative strategies' (5).

66 Ricks, *Embarrassment*, 42.

67 Levinson, *Allegory*, 2.

68 Hamilton, *Metaromanticism*, 112, 133.

69 Andrew Bennett, *Keats, Narrative and Audience: The Posthumous Life of Writing* (Cambridge University Press, 1994), 1.

70 Ibid., 10.

71 Bentham, 'Essay on Logic', *Works*, vol. 8, 219.

72 Putnam, *Reason, Truth and History*, 216.

73 Robert Brinkley and Michael Deneen, 'Towards an Indexical Criticism: on Coleridge, de Man and the Materiality of the Sign', *Revolution and English Romanticism*, ed. Keith Hanley and Raman Selden (Hemel Hempstead: Harvester Wheatsheaf, 1990), 290, 283.

74 As Davidson puts it in 'Locating Literary Language': 'Writing has its ways, however, of establishing ties between writer's intentions, reader, and the world. A personal letter can take advantage of a world of established mutual connections . . . . Almost all connected writing that involves more than a few sentences depends on deictic references to its own text': *Truth*, 177–8.

75 Bennett, *Keats, Narrative and Audience*, 38–9.

76 C. Taylor, *Philosophical Arguments*, 62.

77 Habermas, *Postmetaphysical Thinking*, 117.

78 Ibid., 139–40.

79 Bate, *Keats*, 186.

80 Levinson, *Allegory*, 23.

81 Kevin Gilmartin, ' "This is Very Material": William Cobbett and the Rhetoric of Radical Oppression', *Studies in Romanticism* 34.1 (1995): 81–101 (89).

82 Ibid., 90.

83 Ibid., 95.

84 Davidson, 'James Joyce and Humpty Dumpty', in *Truth*, 156.

85 See Davidson, 'A Nice Derangement of Epitaphs': 'Here is what I mean by "getting away with it": the interpreter comes to the occasion of utterance armed with a theory that tells him (or so he believes) what an arbitrary utterance of the speaker means. The speaker then says something with the intention that it will be interpreted in a certain way, and the expectation that it will be so interpreted. In fact this way is not provided for by the

interpreter's theory. But the speaker is nevertheless understood; the interpreted adjusts his theory so that it yields the speaker's intended interpretation. The speaker has "gotten away with it" ': *Truth*, 98–9.

86 Gilmartin, ' "This is Very Material" ', 89.
87 See Keats, 'To Bailey,' 22 November 1817: 'what the imagination seizes as Beauty must be truth' (184); 'The Imagination may be compared to Adam's dream – he awoke and found it truth' (185).
88 Hazlitt, *Essay*, 21.
89 Keats, 'To George and Georgiana Keats', 14 February–3 May 1819, letter 159, *KL*, vol. 2, 81.
90 Ibid., 78.
91 Ibid., 79.
92 Ibid., 78.
93 Ibid., 81.
94 Ibid., 79.
95 Ibid., 81.
96 Ibid., 80.
97 Kabitoglou, 'Adapting Philosophy', 119.
98 Wheeler, *Romanticism*, xi.
99 Ibid., 147.
100 Donald Davidson, 'Plato's Philosopher', in *Truth*, 239.
101 Ibid., 240.
102 Kabitoglou points out that the closing lines of the ode 'not only allows for an identification of beauty and truth, but establishes a statement where the positions of subject/predicate are interchangeable': 'Adapting Philosophy', 135.
103 Keats, 'To George and Georgiana Keats', 14 February–3 May 1819, *KL*, vol. 2, 79.
104 Donald Davidson, 'The Folly of Trying to Define Truth', in *Truth*, 21.
105 Levinson, *Allegory*, 270.
106 Ibid., 271.
107 Paul Endo, 'Seeing Romantically in *Lamia*', *ELH* 66.1 (1999): 111–28 (113).
108 Ibid., 121.
109 Ibid., 124.
110 Bennett, *Keats, Narrative and Audience*, 178.
111 William Robertson, *The History of the Reign of the Emperor Charles V*, 7th edn, vol. 1 (1769, London, 1792), 25–6.
112 Robertson, *History of America*, vol 1, xvi.
113 Keats, 'To Reynolds,' 3 May 1818, letter 80, *KL*, vol. 1, 282.
114 Christopher Bode, 'Hyperion, *The Fall of Hyperion*, and Keats's Poetics', *Wordsworth Circle* 31.1 (2000): 31–7 (34).
115 Ibid., 37.
116 Ibid., 36.
117 Bate, for example, identifies this distinction as 'central' to the poem, 'though not for that reason conclusive': *Keats*, 595, while Michael O'Neill notes how the poem quickly gets enmeshed by the 'topsyturvy' arguments concerning

the relation of poet, dreamer, and fanatic ('"When this warm scribe my hand": Writing and History in *Hyperion* and *The Fall of Hyperion*', in Roe, ed., *Keats and History*, 151). Bode expresses similar doubts as to 'whether Moneta's differentiations between "visionaries," poets and dreamers make sense': 'Hyperion', 35.

118 Keats, 'To George and Georgiana Keats,' 14 February–3 May 1819, letter 159, *KL*, vol. 2, 82.

119 John Keats, 'To Richard Woodhouse', 22 September 1819, letter 194, *KL*, vol. 2, 172.

120 Ibid., 174.

121 Chandler, *England in 1819*, 31.

122 *The Poems of John Keats*, ed. Jack Stillinger, London: Heinemann, 1978.

123 See Putnam, 'Why Reason Can't be Naturalized', *Realism and Reason*: 'The elimination of the normative is attempted mental suicide'(246).

124 Denise Gigante, 'Keats's Nausea', *Studies in Romanticism* 40.4 (2001): 481–510 (510).

4 AN UNREMITTING INTERCHANGE

1 Shelley, 'On Life', in *Complete Works*, vol. 6, 194–5.

2 Percy Bysshe Shelley, 'A Defence of Poetry,' *Shelley's Poetry and Prose*, ed. Donald H. Reiman and Sharon B. Powers (New York: W. W. Norton, 1977), 505.

3 Percy Bysshe Shelley, 'To Thomas Jefferson Hogg', 26 November 1813, letter 250, *Letters*, vol. 1, 380. Translation: 'So much for this'.

4 Quine, *Ontological Relativity*, 69.

5 Shelley, *Alastor*, in *Poetry and Prose*, ed. Ryman and Powers, 69.

6 Ibid.

7 Shelley, 'On Life', in *Complete Works*, vol. 6, 193–4.

8 Hugh Roberts, *Shelley and the Chaos of History: A New Politics of Poetry* (University Park, Pa: Pennsylvania State University Press, 1997), 129. Jerrold Hogle charts the twentieth-century debate over Shelley's 'Platonism' versus his 'sceptical idealism' in his essay on Shelley in *Literature of the Romantic Period: A Bibliographical Guide*, ed. Michael O'Neill (Oxford University Press, 1998), 118–42. There is no room to rehearse here the arguments between 'Platonists' such as James A. Notopolous, *The Platonism of Shelley: A Study of Platonism and the Poetic Mind* (Durham, NC: Duke University Press, 1949); Ross Woodman, 'Shelley's Changing Attitude to Plato', *Journal of the History of Ideas* 21 (1960): 497–510; Neville Rogers, *Shelley at Work: A Critical Inquiry*, 2nd edn (Oxford: Clarendon Press, 1967); and Troy Urquhart, 'Metaphor, Transfer, and Translation in Plato's Ion: The Postmodern Platonism of Percy Bysshe Shelley's *A Defence of Poetry*', *Romanticism on the Net*, ed. Michael Laplace-Sinatra, Aug. 2003, 20 Oct. 2005 erudit.org/revue/ron/2003/v/n31/008700ar.html, on one hand, and, on the other, 'sceptical idealists' such as C. E. Pulos, *The Deep Truth: A Study of Shelley's Scepticism* (Lincoln, NE: University of Nebraska Press,

1954), Tracy Ware, 'Shelley's Platonism in *A Defence of Poetry*', *Studies in English Literature 1500–1900* 23.4 (1983): 549–66), Earl R. Wasserman, *Shelley: A Critical Reading* (Baltimore, MD: Johns Hopkins Press, 1971), and Merle R. Rubin, 'Shelley's Skepticism: A Detachment Beyond Despair', *Philological Quarterly* 59 (1980): 353–73.

9 Stuart Peterfreund's 'Shelley, Monboddo, Vico, and the Language of Poetry', *Style* 15.4 (1981): 382–400, Richard Cronin's *Shelley's Poetic Thoughts* (Basingstoke: Macmillan, 1981) and Paul Fry's essay 'Shelley's "Defence of Poetry" in Our Time,' in *The Reach of Criticism: Method and Perception in Literary Theory* (New Haven, CT: Yale University Press, 1983) each discuss the impact of the Tooke/Monboddo debate on Shelley.

10 Again, these fields are too extensive to catalogue here. Paul de Man's 'Shelley Disfigured', first published in *Deconstruction and Criticism*, ed. Harold Bloom, *et al.* (New York: Continuum, 1979), 39–73, and Frances Ferguson's 'Shelley's *Mont Blanc*: What the Mountain Said', *Romanticism and Language*, ed. Arden Reed (Ithaca, NY: Cornell University Press, 1984), 202–14, share, despite their differences, an interest in those features of Shelley's writing that exceed the terms of the conflict between scepticism and idealism, both of which retain a view of truth as 'ideal presence'. Tilottama Rajan's *Dark Interpreter: The Discourse of Romanticism* (Ithaca, NY: Cornell University Press, 1980) and *The Supplement of Reading*, together with William Ulmer's *Shelleyan Eros* portray Shelley as engaged in varying degrees of struggle with the deconstructive forces of his own writing, as does (albeit to a lesser degree) John A. Hodgson in *Coleridge, Shelley, and Transcendental Inquiry* (Lincoln, NE: University of Nebraska Press, 1989). Jerrold Hogle's *Shelley's Process* depicts a more hermeneutically liberated Shelley, a view reinforced by his essay 'Shelley and the Conditions of Meaning', in *Evaluating Shelley*, ed. Timothy Clark and Jerrold Hogle (Edinburgh University Press, 1996) and echoed by Kathleen Wheeler in *Romanticism, Pragmatism and Deconstruction*. Such appropriations of Shelley have in turn been challenged by Timothy Clark in 'Shelley after Deconstruction: The Poet of Anachronism', in *Evaluating Shelley*, eds., Clark and Hogle, 91–107. More positivist appraisals of Shelley's thought range from John Robert Leo's phenomenologically informed study of how Shelley's *Defence* intuitively moderates the claims of consciousness and world, so that 'each shift [of the imagination] creates another imaginative center which continuously decenters to a circumference, there to become a new center', 'Criticism of Consciousness in Shelley's "A Defence of Poetry"', *Philosophy and Literature* 2 (1978): 46–59(56), to Terence Allan Hoagwood's *Scepticism and Ideology: Shelley's Political Prose and its Philosophical Context from Bacon to Marx* (Iowa City, IA: University of Iowa Press, 1988), which seeks to establish the coherence of Shelley's philosophical scepticism and his political outlook. Landmark studies such as Kenneth Neill Cameron's *The Young Shelley: Genesis of a Radical* (London: Macmillan, 1950), Gerald McNiece's *Shelley and the Revolutionary Idea* (Cambridge, MA: Harvard University Press, 1969) and P. M. S. Dawson's *The Unacknowledged Legislator: Shelley and Politics* (Oxford University Press, 1980) ensured that Shelley was never going to present as

vulnerable a target as Keats for the increasingly politicised readings of the 1980s and 1990s, although Chandler's *England in 1819* is now the standard work for considerations of Shelley's relation to history and historicism. More recently, the concept of reflexivity underlying the dominant historicist mode in Shelley studies has been challenged by David Ferris's *Silent Urns: Romanticism, Hellenism, Modernity* (Stanford, CA: Stanford University Press, 2000) and Deborah Elise White's *Romantic Returns: Superstition, Imagination, History* (Stanford, CA: Stanford University Press, 2000). Meanwhile, in his elaborate study *Shelley and the Chaos of History*, Hugh Roberts has endeavoured to put many of the above perspectives in their place with an ambitious attempt to link Shelley's Lucretianism with modern chaos theory, the success of which is questioned by Timothy Morton's review in *Studies in Romanticism* 39.1 (2000): 173–7.

11 As Shelley observes in the preface to *Prometheus Unbound*: 'The cloud of mind is discharging its collected lightning, and the equilibrium between institutions and opinions is now restoring, or is about to be restored': *Poetry and Prose*, 134.

12 Shelley, *Philosophical View of Reform*, in *Complete Works*, vol. 7, 9.

13 Hume, *Treatise*, 91.

14 Percy Bysshe Shelley, *The Poems of Shelley*, eds. Kelvin Everest and Geoffrey Matthews, vol. 1 (Harlow: Longman, 1989), 382–3.

15 John Locke, *An Essay Concerning Human Understanding*, ed. Peter H. Nidditch (Oxford University Press, 1975), 140–1.

16 Locke, *Essay*, 236.

17 See Reid, *Inquiry*. Reid analyses the perception of the smell of a rose into 'A sensation' and 'some power, quality, or virtue, in the rose … which hath a permanent existence, independent of mind' (75).

18 Sir William Drummond, *Academical Questions* (London, 1805), 25–6.

19 Ibid., 28–9.

20 Ibid., 21.

21 Percy Bysshe Shelley, *The Prose Works of Percy Bysshe Shelley*, ed. E. B. Murray, vol. 1 (Oxford University Press, 1993), 5.

22 Percy Bysshe Shelley, 'To Leigh Hunt', 27 September 1819, letter 517, *Letters*, vol. 2, 122–3.

23 Shelley, *Refutation of Deism*, in *Prose Works*, vol. 1, 122.

24 Shelley, 'On Life', *Complete Works*, vol. 6, 197.

25 Godwin, *Inquiry*, vol. 2, 495.

26 Percy Bysshe Shelley, 'To Elizabeth Hitchener,' [16] October 1811, letter 118, *Letters*, vol. 1, 151.

27 Shelley, 'A Defence', in *Poetry and Prose*, 501.

28 John Stuart Mill, 'Coleridge', *Mill on Bentham and Coleridge*, ed. F. R. Leavis (London: Chatto & Windus, 1959), 103.

29 Godwin, *Inquiry*, vol. 1, 18.

30 Ibid., 14.

31 Ibid., 320–1.

32 Godwin divides perceptions into those that 'act indirectly upon the mind, by rendering the animal frame gay, vigorous [. . . or] sluggish, morbid' and those

that 'are rendered directly a subject of reasoning', ibid., 52. Compare Hume's distinction of 'IMPRESSIONS' of sensation and the 'IDEAS' of thinking and reasoning: *Treatise*, 1.

33 Hume, *Treatise*, 4.

34 Jeremy Bentham, *Deontology, A Table of the Springs of Action, and Article on Utilitarianism*, ed. Amnon Goldworth (Oxford University Press, 1983), 350.

35 Thus, while Jerrold Hogle is broadly correct when drawing a distinction between Tooke, Godwin, Coleridge, and Bentham (for whom '"thought" becomes an order able to measure ... the known world only after a visible thought-unit (or sign) is made to relate with others in a precise syntax') and Locke, Berkeley, Rousseau, and Monboddo (for whom 'Thoughts, ideas, feelings, or desires ... drive the mind to create words to be their visible embodiments' (*Shelley's Process*, 12)) this misses the crucial difference between Coleridge's organic, and Bentham's pragmatic conception of how meaning is formed.

36 Bentham, *Introduction*, 1.

37 None of these essays was published until the appearance of Bowring's edition of Bentham's works.

38 Frances Ferguson, 'Canons, Poetics, and Social Value: Jeremy Bentham and How to Do Things with People', *Modern Language Notes* 110 (1995): 1148–64 (1164). Ferguson extends this reading of Bentham in 'Beliefs and Emotions: from Stanley Fish to Jeremy Bentham and John Stuart Mill', in *Politics and the Passions 1500–1850*, eds. Victoria Kahn, Neil Saccamano, and Daniela Coli (Princeton University Press, 2006), 231–50, arguing that, contrary to standard readings, Bentham's account of human motivation 'provides a capacious view of the complex of emotion and belief' (232).

39 The only Dumont translations available at the time were the *Traités de législation civile et pénale*, 3 vols. (Paris, 1802) and *Théorie des peines et des récompenses*, 2 vols. (London, 1811), both of which were eventually translated back into English: the first in 1864 as *Theory of Legislation*, the two volumes of the second as the 1830 *The Rationale of Punishment* and the 1825 *The Rationale of Reward*, respectively.

40 See Percy Bysshe Shelley, 'To the Editor of *The Examiner*', 3 November 1819, letter 527, *Letters*, vol. 2, 142: 'Is not Mr. Bentham a Deist? What men of any rank of society from their talents are *not* Deists whose understandings have been unbiassed [*sic*] by the allurements of worldly interest?'

41 Percy Bysshe Shelley, 'To Leigh Hunt', 26 May 1820, letter 568, *Letters*, vol. 2, 201.

42 Chandler, *England in 1819*, 234.

43 Ibid., 239.

44 Ibid., 259.

45 Jeremy Bentham, *Theory of Legislation*, trans. R. Hildreth (1802, London, 1876), 11.

46 Ibid., 87.

47 Godwin, *Inquiry*, vol. 1, 181.

48 Ibid., 232.
49 Ibid., 495.
50 Ibid., 44–5.
51 Ibid., 45. See also James Burnett (Lord Monboddo), *On the Origin and Progress of Language*, vol. 2 (Edinburgh, 1773–92), 8.
52 Shelley, 'A Defence', in *Poetry and Prose*, 503.
53 Godwin, *Inquiry*, vol. 1, 23.
54 Shelley was reading Coleridge and Schlegel in late 1817 and early 1818.
55 Shelley, 'On Life' in *Collected Works*, vol. 6, 196.
56 Shelley, 'To Thomas Jefferson Hogg', letter 250, *Letters*, vol. 1, 380.
57 Hume, *Treatise*, 11. For Berkeley's arguments, see George Berkeley, *A Treatise Concerning the Principles of Human Knowledge*, ed. Jonathan Dancy (Oxford University Press, 1998), §§135–40, 154–5.
58 James Burnett (Lord Monboddo), *Antient Metaphysics: or, The Science of Universals*, vol. 1 (Edinburgh, 1779–99), 419. Hume himself, however, is not a nominalist. Despite his argument that in order to be meaningful all talk of external objects should be translated into talk of sense-impressions, when it comes to the existence of external objects he is sceptical, not dismissive. Indeed, the sceptical attitude *assumes* a distinction between the way the world is (objectively) and the way we perceive it (subjectively); it questions our ability to tell the difference, not the grounds of distinction between the two. Without the correspondence view of truth, Hume's scepticism loses its bite.
59 Wasserman, *Shelley*, 144. Wasserman claims that Shelley's scepticism tended towards an 'ontological monism' that 'defies all distinction between external and internal' (140–1).
60 Andrew M. Cooper, *Doubt and Identity in Romantic Poetry* (New Haven, CT: Yale University Press, 1988), 15.
61 Hogle, *Shelley's Process*, 10.
62 Roberts, *Shelley and the Chaos of History*, 4, 127.
63 Ibid., 235. In a similar way, Arkady Plotnisky identifies singularity in Shelley as a kind of 'radical formalization', 'A Dancing Arch: Formalization and Singularity in Kleist, Shelley, and de Man', *European Romantic Review* 9.2 (1998) 161–76 (166), which differs from both classical formalisation and formal*ism* in allowing for singularity, lawlessness, incommensurable difference '*within the same theoretical economy*' (161), and according to which Death, indeed, 'becomes a model, perhaps the model, for the structure of *every* event in life'. Plotnisky goes further, claiming that '[w]e may even define Romanticism as this magnification or/as radicalization of the individual into the radically singular' (168).
64 Lucretius, *De Rerum Natura*, trans. W. H. D. Rouse, rev. edn, Martin Ferguson Smith, 2nd edn (Cambridge, MA: Harvard University Press, 1982), 27.
65 Shelley, 'A Defence', in *Poetry and Prose*, 504.
66 Lucretius, *De Rerum Natura*, 399.
67 Shelley, *Laon and Cynthia*, *Poems*, vol. 2, 44.

68 Lucretius, *De Rerum Natura*, 15.
69 Shelley, 'A Future State', in *Collected Works*, vol. 6, 207.
70 Ibid., 208.
71 Ibid., 209.
72 For his discussion of *simulacrae* and *membranae*, see Lucretius, *De Rerum Natura*, 279.
73 Thomas Love Peacock, 'The Four Ages of Poetry', *The Works of Thomas Love Peacock*, eds. H. F. B. Brett-Smith and C. E. Jones, vol. 8 (London, 1924–34), 19.
74 Shelley, 'A Defence', in *Poetry and Prose*, 505.
75 Ibid., 508.
76 Hume, *Treatise*, 319.
77 Plato, *The Collected Dialogues of Plato*, ed. Edith Hamilton and Huntington Cairns (Princeton University Press, 1961), 556.
78 Cooper, *Doubt and Identity*, 187.
79 Shelley, 'On Love', in *Collected Works*, vol. 6, 201.
80 Shelley, 'A Defence', in *Poetry and Prose*, 505.
81 C. E. Pulos, 'The Importance of Shelley's Scepticism,' *Shelley: Modern Judgements*, ed. R. B. Woodings (London: Aurora Publishers, 1970), 55.
82 Ware, 'Shelley's Platonism', 565.
83 Woodman, 'Shelley's Changing Attitude', 497.
84 Wasserman, *Shelley*, 12.
85 Hoagwood, *Skepticism*, 31, 33.
86 Wheeler, *Romanticism*, 5. Urquhart suggests that 'Plato's Ion and Shelley's *Defence* argue the same thing – that the process of metaphor and transference makes poetry an essential part of society. 'Metaphor, Transfer, and Translation', 2.
87 Plato, *Collected Dialogues*, 557.
88 In *Theaetetus*, Socrates concludes that 'neither perception, nor true belief, nor the addition of an 'account' to true belief can be knowledge'. Ibid., 918.
89 Ibid., 562.
90 Davidson, 'Plato's Philosopher', in *Truth*, 239.
91 Ibid., 229.
92 Ibid., 249.
93 Ulmer, *Shelleyan Eros*, 10.
94 Shelley, 'A Defence', in *Poetry and Prose*, 482. Emphasis added.
95 Ibid., 487.
96 Ibid., 485.
97 Shelley, *A Refutation or Deism*, in *Prose Works*, vol. 1, 115.
98 Percy Bysshe Shelley, 'To Claire Clairmont' [18 February 1821], letter 609, *Letters*, vol. 2, 266.
99 Plato, *Collected Dialogues*, 1166.
100 Shelley, 'A Defence', in *Poetry and Prose*, 505.
101 Ibid., 494.
102 Ibid., 505.
103 Fry, *Reach*, 139.

104 Ibid., 140, 143.

105 Shelley, 'A Defence', in *Poetry and Prose*, 500.

106 Ibid., 505.

107 Ibid., 485.

108 Ibid., 491.

109 Ibid., 502.

110 G. Kim Blank, Introduction, *The New Shelley: Later Twentieth-Century Views*, ed. G. Kim Blank (Basingstoke: Macmillan, 1991), 12.

111 Ulmer, *Shelleyan Eros*, 13.

112 Robert Kaufman, 'Legislators of the Post-Everything World: Shelley's *Defence* of Adorno,' *ELH* 63.3 (1996): 707–33 (709).

113 Ibid., 707.

114 Ibid., 710.

115 Ibid., 719. Kaufman extends his argument in 'Intervention & Commitment Forever! Shelley in 1819, Shelley in Brecht, Shelley in Adorno, Shelley in Benjamin', *Reading Shelley's Interventionist Poetry, 1819–1820*, ed. Orrin Wang and John Morillo, Romantic Circles Praxis Series, 1 May 2001, 20 Oct. 2005, rc.umd.edu/praxis/interventionist/kaufman/kaufman.html. In the same collection, Mark Kipperman also links Shelley and Adorno in his 'Shelley, Adorno, and the Scandal of Committed Art.'

116 Ferguson, 'Shelley's *Mont Blanc*', 203.

117 Ibid., 207.

118 Ibid., 212.

119 White, *Romantic Returns*, 108.

120 Ibid., 111.

121 Ibid., 110.

122 Ibid., 109.

123 I would apply the same criticism to John A. Hodgson's *Coleridge, Shelley, and Transcendental Inquiry*, which moves with suspicious ease from the observation that, in 'Mont Blanc', '[s]ilence itself' is the 'ultimate trope' (81) to the conclusion that 'the only ultimate truth is the principle of metaphoricity itself. All is, and is only, metaphor' (102).

124 White, *Romantic Returns*, 125.

125 Paul Hamilton, 'A French Connection: From Empiricism to Materialism in Writings by the Shelleys', *Colloquium Helveticum: Cahiers Suisses de Littérature Générale et Comparee* 25 (1997): 171–93 (190).

126 Linda Brigham, '*Prometheus Unbound* and the Postmodern Political Dilemma', in *Shelley: Poet and Legislator of the World*, ed. Stuart Curran and Betty T. Bennet (Baltimore, MD: Johns Hopkins University Press, 1996), 254.

127 Shelley, 'A Defence', in *Poetry and Prose*, 480.

128 J. L. Austin, *How to Do Things With Words*, 2nd edn, ed. J. O. Urmson and Marina Sbisà (Oxford University Press, 1975), 151.

129 Shelley, 'A Defence', in *Poetry and Prose*, 480.

130 Immanuel Kant, *Prolegomena to Any Future Metaphysics*, trans. and ed. Gary Hatfield (Cambridge University Press, 1997), §36, 74.

131 Shelley, 'A Defence', in *Poetry and Prose*, 503.
132 Wasserman, *Shelley*, 7; Lockridge, *Ethics*, 286; Kaufman, 'Legislators', 709.
133 Lockridge, *Ethics*, 287.
134 Ibid., 289.
135 See Rogers, *Shelley at Work:* 'By "truth", like Keats and others, he [Shelley] meant "reality", "real truth"' (18).
136 Shelley, 'A Defence', in *Poetry and Prose*, 481.
137 Fry, *Reach*, 165.
138 Ibid., 172–3.
139 Percy Bysshe Shelley, 'To Elizabeth Hitchener', 2 January [1812], letter 156, *Letters*, vol. I, 215.
140 Locke, *Essay*, 408.
141 Shelley, 'To Elizabeth Hitchener', 2 January [1812], letter 156, 216.
142 Fry, *Reach*, 126.
143 Percy Bysshe Shelley, 'To William Godwin', 29 July 1812, letter 198 *Letters*, vol. I, 317.
144 Shelley, 'Speculation on Metaphysics', in *Complete Works*, vol. 7, 63.
145 Ibid., 65.
146 Ibid., 63.
147 Ibid., 65.
148 Tooke, *Diversions*, vol. 2, 402–3.
149 See ibid., Chapter 9.
150 Monboddo argues that '[i]f therefore language was invented, there must have been a first and a second language; the one altogether rude and artless, the other formed by rules of art': *On the Origin and Progress of Language*, 6 vols. (Edinburgh, 1773–92), vol. II, 6. Compare Godwin's *Inquiry*, vol. I, Chapter 6.
151 Peterfreund, 'Shelley, Monboddo, Vico', 389.
152 Ibid., 388.
153 Ibid., 389.
154 Ibid., 390.
155 Cronin, *Shelley's Poetic Thoughts*, 4, 13.
156 Ibid., 83.
157 Quine, *Theories and Things*, 68.
158 Stuart Peterfreund, *Shelley among Others: The Play of the Intertext and the Idea of Language* (Baltimore, MD: Johns Hopkins University Press, 2002), 24.
159 Shelley, 'A Defence', in *Poetry and Prose*, 501.
160 Wheeler claims to find in Shelley 'a radical interpretation of empiricism synthesized with Socratic–Platonic elements, [which] broke into new formulations of language as essentially and pre-eminently rhetorical, of imagination as constitutive of all experience ... and of metaphor, not the univocal, literal statement, as the vehicle of truth': *Romanticism*, 4.
161 Shelley, 'A Defence', in *Poetry and Prose*, 480.
162 Wilfrid Sellars, *Empiricism and the Philosophy of Mind* (Cambridge, MA: Harvard University Press, 1997), 19.

163 Sellars maintains that 'I have, in effect, been claiming that being red is logically prior, is a logically simpler notion, than looking red; the function "x is red" to "x looks red to y"': *Empiricism*, 36.
164 Ibid., 66.
165 Hogle, *Shelley's Process*, 10.
166 Roberts, *Shelley and the Chaos of History*, 253, 273.
167 Hume, *Essays*, 180.
168 Peterfreund, *Shelley among Others*, 24.

5 THE EMBODIMENT OF REASON

1 Samuel Taylor Coleridge, 'To Thomas Poole,' [16 March 1801], letter 387, *Collected Letters of Samuel Taylor Coleridge*, ed. Earl Leslie Griggs, vol. 2 (Oxford: Clarendon Press, 1956–71), 706.
2 See especially Jerome Christensen, *Coleridge's Blessed Machine of Language* (Ithaca, NY: Cornell University Press, 1981).
3 Nigel Leask, *The Politics of Imagination in Coleridge's Critical Thought* (Basingstoke: Macmillan, 1988), 2.
4 Samuel Taylor Coleridge, *Lectures 1795 on Politics and Religion*, ed. Lewis Patton and Peter Mann (Princeton University Press, 1971), 51.
5 Samuel Taylor Coleridge, *The Friend*, ed. Barbara E. Rooke, vol. 1 (Princeton University Press, 1969), 42.
6 See Heather J. Jackson, 'Coleridge, Etymology and Etymologic', *Journal of the History of Ideas* 44.1 (1983): 75–88.
7 David P. Haney, *The Challenge of Coleridge: Ethics and Interpretation in Romanticism and Modern Philosophy* (University Park, PA: Pennsylvania State University Press, 2001), 4.
8 Paul Hamilton, 'Coleridge and Godwin in the 1790s', *The Coleridge Connection: Essays for Thomas McFarland*, ed. Richard Gravil and Molly Lefebure (Basingstoke: Macmillan, 1990), 41–59 (46). See also Richard Marggraf Turley, *The Politics of Language in Romantic Literature* (Basingstoke: Palgrave, 2002). Marggraf Turley identifies a number of writers, including Wordsworth, Hunt, Keats, Shelley, and Tennyson, who, as 'part of a self-consciously political "project" that sought to modify literary taste by debating the nature of language' (xv), formed a '"community" of theorized linguistic resistance' (xxi).
9 A. C. Goodson, 'Romantic Theory and the Critique of Language', in *Questioning Romanticism*, ed. John Beer (Baltimore, MD: Johns Hopkins University Press, 1995), 4.
10 Ibid., 9.
11 Christensen, *Coleridge's Blessed Machine*, 20–1.
12 William Keach, *Arbitrary Power: Romanticism, Language, Politics* (Princeton University Press, 2004), 22.
13 Mary Anne Perkins, *Coleridge's Philosophy: The Logos as Unifying Principle* (Oxford: Clarendon Press, 1994), 3.
14 Paul Hamilton, *Coleridge's Poetics* (Oxford: Blackwell, 1983), 91.

15 Samuel Taylor Coleridge, *Table Talk*, ed. Carl Woodring, vol. 1 (Princeton University Press, 1990), 244.

16 Paul Hamilton, 'Coleridge and the "Rifacciamento" of Philosophy: Communicating an Idealist Position in Philosophy', *European Romantic Review* 14 (2003): 417–29 (418). For Coleridge, 'Unless the sympathetic chord is struck, the philosophising will remain internally incoherent … knowledge which is not communicable is nonsense, and that communicability depends not on the impersonal transmission of ciphers but on the affective resolution of information for a naturally relational being' (419).

17 Samuel Taylor Coleridge, *Marginalia*, ed. H. J. Jackson, George Whalley, *et al.*, vol. 3 (Princeton University Press, 1980–2001), 23–4.

18 Samuel Taylor Coleridge, *On the Constitution of the Church and State*, ed. John Colmer (Princeton University Press, 1976), 20.

19 Coleridge, *Lectures 1795*, 164.

20 Ibid., 313.

21 Peter J. Kitson, ' "The Electric Fluid of Truth": The Ideology of the Commonwealthsman in Coleridge's *The Plot Discovered*', in *Coleridge and the Armoury of the Human Mind: Essays on His Prose Writings*, eds. Peter J. Kitson and Thomas N. Corns (London: Frank Cass, 1991) 36–62 (52).

22 Coleridge, *Lectures 1795*, 313–14.

23 See Mark Kipperman, 'Coleridge, Shelley, Davy, and Science's Millenium,' *Criticism* 40.3 (1998): 409–36: Just as 'Davy … began to suspect that light itself was fundamental to chemistry, magnetism, electricity, and even might be a transcendent origin of human intellect as well' (419–20), so in Coleridge's Bristol circle advances in electrochemistry were taken as suggesting that 'a universe of dynamic transformation reconciling polar conflict was endorsed by empirical research into the way things *really are*' (422).

24 Kitson, ' "The Electric Fluid of Truth" ', 38.

25 See Hamilton, *Coleridge's Poetics*, 3.

26 Hans Aarsleff, *The Study of Language in England, 1780–1860* (Princeton University Press, 1967), 88.

27 Ibid., 89.

28 O. Smith, *Politics of Language*, 39.

29 See Quine, *Ontological Relativity*, 71.

30 Stephen Prickett, *Words and The Word* (Cambridge University Press, 1986), 147.

31 The text is from Samuel Taylor Coleridge, *Poetical Works*, ed. J. C. C. Mays, vol. 1, part I (Princeton University Press, 2001), 171–91.

32 David Hartley, *Observations on Man, His Frame, His Duty, and His Expectations* (London, 1791), 12.

33 Ibid., 268.

34 Coleridge, *Biographia Literaria*, ed. Engell and Bate, vol. 1, 116.

35 Coleridge, *Notebooks*, ed. Coburn, vol. 2, text 2354.

36 In her note to this passage (*Notebooks*, vol. 2, notes 2354), Kathleen Coburn argues that Coleridge was misled by J. C. Adelung's *Grammatisch – Kritisches*

Wörterbuch der Hochdeutschen Mundart (1774–86), which 'suggests, wrongly, that wahr is identical with the past tense, war, of the verb "to be" '. As for 'truth, troweth, throweth': 'The first two words are obviously connected, but neither of them with the third.' Coleridge's speculations on the origins of 'hitteth', meanwhile, 'seem devoid of any philological basis, nor is there any etymological connexion between "through" and "truth" '.

37 Habermas, *Philosophical Discourse*, 298.
38 James C. McKusick, *Coleridge's Philosophy of Language* (New Haven, CT: Yale University Press, 1986), 39.
39 Tooke, *Diversions*, vol. 1, 49.
40 See Coleridge, *Biographia*, vol. 1, 273.
41 Samuel Taylor Coleridge, 'Selection from Mr Coleridge's Literary Correspondence', *Shorter Works and Fragments*, eds. H. J. Jackson and J. R. de J. Jackson, vol. 2 (Princeton University Press, 1995), 927–8.
42 H. J. Jackson, 'Etymologic', 81.
43 McKusick, *Coleridge's Philosophy*, 42.
44 Samuel Taylor Coleridge, 'To William Godwin,' 22 September 1800, letter 352, *Letters*, vol. 1, 625–6.
45 Coleridge, *Biographia*, vol. 1, 252–4. For Schelling's influence on Coleridge, see Thomas McFarland, *Coleridge and the Pantheist Tradition* (Oxford University Press, 1969) and G. N. G. Orsini, *Coleridge and German Idealism* (Carbondale, IL: Southern Illinois University Press, 1969).
46 Coleridge, *Marginalia*, vol. 3, 849.
47 Samuel Taylor Coleridge, 'To James Gillman, Jr.', [22 October 1826], letter 1558, *Letters*, vol. 6, 630.
48 Coleridge, *Friend*, vol. 1, 42–3.
49 Keach, *Arbitrary Power*, 31–2.
50 Samuel Taylor Coleridge, *Opus Maximum*, ed. Thomas McFarland and Nicholas Halmi (Princeton University Press, 2002), 13.
51 Hamilton, 'Coleridge and Godwin', 47.
52 Samuel Taylor Coleridge, 'To Josiah Wedgwood', [February 1801], letter 383, *Letters*, vol. 2, 696.
53 Ibid., 697.
54 Ibid., letter 384 *Letters*, vol. 2, 698. Emphasis added.
55 See, for example, McKusick, *Coleridge's Philosophy*, 50.
56 Samuel Taylor Coleridge, *Aids to Reflection*, ed. John Beer (Princeton University Press, 1995), 181.
57 Coleridge, *Aids*, 7–10.
58 Nicholas Reid, 'Coleridge, Language, and the Imagination', *Romanticism on the Net*, 22 May 2001, 31 March 2006, erudit.org/revue/ron/2001/v/n22/005977ar.html.
59 Coleridge, *Aids*, 193.
60 Habermas, *Postmetaphysical Thinking*, 73.
61 I refer here to the counter-Enlightenment tendency in romantic criticism, led by critics such as Paul de Man, Jerome Christensen, James Chandler,

Marjorie Levinson, and Jerome McGann, which largely dominated romantic criticism and commentary in the 1980s and 1990s. These critics share the idea, as expressed by Tilottama Rajan in *Dark Interpreter*, that '[a]t certain critical points the Romantics deconstruct their own affirmative postulates', and that 'it is such recognitions, rather than a post-Enlightenment faith in human perfectibility through a secular conversion of the patterns of provi-dence into those of aesthetic theodicy, which prove to be the truly subversive element in Romanticism' (16).

62 On the question of the nature of Kant's influence over Coleridge's thinking about logic and language, scholarship traditionally divides into two broad camps. Ranged on one side are those who argue that Coleridge's reading of Kant contains little new of significance. René Wellek claims that Coleridge simply failed to see 'that nothing of the Kantian epistemology can be preserved in a new system': *Immanuel Kant in England 1793–1838* (Princeton University Press, 1931), 80. However, J. R. de J. Jackson counters that Coleridge's apparent inability to build on Kant's philosophy in *Logic* is due to the fact that that work was never intended to 'offer any new arguments' but is 'essentially a popularisation of the *Critique of Pure Reason*': 'Introduction', *Logic*, ed. J. R. de J. Jackson (Princeton University Press, 1981), lxii. G. N. G. Orsini combines both of these positions in *Coleridge and German Idealism* (Carbondale, IL: Southern Illinois University Press, 1969), arguing that while *Logic* 'is professedly an exposition of Kant' (115), Coleridge was hampered by the fact that he 'did not fully grasp, or perhaps did not fully accept' (256) Kant's argument for the transcendental unity of apperception in the second edition of the *Critique of Pure Reason*. On the other side of the Kant/Coleridge debate, meanwhile, are those who defend Coleridge as an innovator in logic and language who improves on Kant's theories. Thus, John H. Muirhead in *Coleridge as Philosopher* (London: Allen & Unwin, 1930) applauds Coleridge for the proto-Hegelianism of his triadic conception of reason and for turning 'criticism against the critic' (89). Similarly, Kathleen Wheeler in 'Coleridge's Theory of Imagination: a Hegelian Solution to Kant?', in *The Interpretation of Belief: Coleridge, Schleiermacher and Romanticism*, ed. David Jasper (Basingstoke: Macmillan, 1986), 16–40, maintains that 'Coleridge's conclusion is one with Hegel's: "The Subjectivity of Reason is the great error of the Kantean system"' (22). Others have argued that by playing 'Tooke', as it were, to Kant's 'Locke', Coleridge successfully introduces a 'linguistic turn' into transcendental idealism. See, for example, Tim Fulford, *Coleridge's Figurative Language* (Basingstoke: MacMillan, 1991), 106; Gerald McNiece, *The Knowledge that Endures: Coleridge, German Philosophy and the Logic of Romantic Thought* (Basingstoke: MacMillan, 1992), 21, and Thomas McFarland in his editorial 'Prolegomena' to *Opus Maximum*. In McFarland's words, '[m]uch more clearly than Kant, Coleridge sees that epistemological questions cannot be resolved without recourse to a prior analysis of the linguistic structures that constitute the means of intellectual inquiry' ('Prolegomena', *Opus Maximum*, ccxxix). My own position cuts across

these lines of debate, arguing that without Kant's method Coleridge would never have been able to develop his holistic challenge to a tradition of philosophy (Kant's included) that conceived of cognitive and linguistic relationships in terms of correspondence.

63 C. Taylor, *Philosophical Arguments*, 10–11. Emphasis added.
64 Tooke, *Diversions*, vol. 2, 402–3.
65 C. Taylor, *Sources*, 35.
66 Ibid., 37–9.
67 Immanuel Kant, *Critique of Pure Reason*, trans. Paul Guyer and Allen W. Wood (Cambridge University Press, 1997), 197.
68 Hume, *Enquiries*, 25.
69 Kant, *Critique of Pure Reason*, 192.
70 Ibid., 320–1.
71 P. F. Strawson, *The Bounds of Sense: An Essay on Kant's* Critique of Pure Reason (London: Methuen & Co., 1966), 32, 16.
72 Ibid., 32.
73 C. Taylor, *Philosophical Arguments*, 20.
74 Coleridge, *Logic*, 43–4.
75 Ibid., 36.
76 Ibid., 111.
77 Coleridge, *Marginalia*, vol. 3, 275.
78 Coleridge, *Logic*, 52.
79 Muirhead, *Coleridge*, 89.
80 See G. W. F. Hegel, *Phenomenology of Spirit*, trans. A. V. Millar (Oxford University Press, 1977), 29.
81 Tim Milnes, 'Through the Looking-Glass: Coleridge and Post-Kantian Philosophy', *Comparative Literature* 51.4 (1999): 309–23.
82 Coleridge, *Opus Maximum*, 271.
83 Catherine Miles Wallace, *The Design of the* Biographia Literaria (London: Allen & Unwin, 1983), Chapter 1: 'The Chamois Hunter'. Coleridge uses the metaphor in *Friend*, vol. 1 55: 'Alas! legitimate reasoning is impossible without severe thinking, and thinking is neither an easy nor an amusing employment. The reader, who would follow a close reasoner to the summit and absolute principle of any one important subject, has chosen a Chamois-hunter for his guide.'
84 Coleridge, *Aids*, 413. Emphasis added.
85 Coleridge, *Opus Maximum*, 270–1. Emphasis added.
86 Coleridge, *Aids*, 12–13.
87 Coleridge, *Friend*, vol. 1, 457. Emphasis added.
88 Ibid., 455.
89 Coleridge, *Table Talk*, vol. 1, 364–6.
90 Coleridge, *Opus Maximum*, 5.
91 Ibid., 271.
92 Coleridge, *Aids*, 136.
93 S. V. Pradhan, 'The Historiographer of Reason: Coleridge's Philosophy of History', *Studies in Romanticism* 25.1 (1986): 39–62 (46–8).

94 C. Taylor, *Sources*, 85.
95 Ibid., 112.
96 Ibid., 105.
97 See McKusick, *Coleridge's Philosophy*: 'Kant's critical idealism becomes in Coleridge's hands a doctrine of linguistic relativity' (51).
98 Coleridge, *Logic*, 112–13.
99 Charles and Mary Lamb, *Elia and the Last Essays of Elia*, in *Works*, vol. 2, 63.
100 Coleridge, *Friend*, vol. 1, 42–3.
101 Coleridge, *Logic*, 127.
102 This is an accusation often made by Coleridge against associationism. In *Biographia Literaria*, for example, he argues that the 'paralogisms' of associationism 'may be all reduced to one sophism as their common genus; the mistaking of the *conditions* of a thing for its *causes* and *essence*; and the process by which we arrive at the knowledge of a faculty, for the faculty itself. The air I breathe, is the *condition* of my life, not its cause': *Biographia*, vol. 1, 123.
103 Coleridge, *Notebooks*, vol. 3, text 3587.
104 Ibid., notes 3587.
105 Christensen, *Coleridge's Blessed Machine*, 19.
106 Coleridge, *Biographia*, vol. 1, 201.
107 Coleridge, 'Schema of the Total Man' (1828), *Shorter Works*, vol. 2, 1368.
108 Coleridge, 'On One Will' (1818–19), *Shorter Works*, vol. 1, 779.
109 Coleridge, *Opus Maximum*, 75–6.
110 Coleridge, *Opus Maximum*, 131–2. As McFarland notes, this account of the Logos or 'I am' was crucial in freeing Coleridge from Schelling's dyadic, 'either/or' conception of Absolute Identity (cxxxi).
111 Coleridge, *Opus Maximum*, 176–7.
112 Steven E. Cole, 'The Logic of Personhood: Coleridge and the Social Production of Agency', *Studies in Romanticism* 30 (1991): 85–111 (98, 101).
113 Ibid., 102–3.
114 Coleridge, 'Essay on Faith' (1820), *Shorter Works*, vol. 2, 834.
115 Ibid., vol. 2, 836.
116 Cole, 'Logic of Personhood', 105, 103.
117 Coleridge, 'Essay on Faith', *Shorter Works*, vol. 2, 837–8.
118 Friedrich Heinrich Jacobi, *The Main Philosophical Writings and the Novel Allwill*, trans. George di Giovanni (Montreal: McGill-Queen's University Press, 1994), 234.
119 Jacobi, *Main Philosophical Writings*, 545.
120 Anthony John Harding, *Coleridge and the Idea of Love: Aspects of Relationship in Coleridge's Thought and Writing* (Cambridge University Press, 1974), 189–91.
121 Coleridge, *Opus Maximum*, 73. Emphasis added.
122 Habermas, *Knowledge*, 21, 30.
123 Coleridge, *Opus Maximum*, 86.
124 Coleridge, *Table Talk*, vol. 1, 100.
125 Haney, *Challenge of Coleridge*, 21.

126 Ibid., 25.
127 Ibid.
128 Coleridge, 'To Josiah Wedgwood', [February 1801], letter 384, *Letters*, vol. 2, 701.
129 Haney, *Challenge of Coleridge*, xiv.
130 Putnam, *Reason*, 119.
131 Coleridge, *Opus Maximum*, 150–1.
132 Samuel Taylor Coleridge, *Lectures 1818–1819 On the History of Philosophy*, ed. J. R. de J. Jackson, vol. 1 (Princeton University Press, 2000), 265.
133 Putnam, *Reason*, 215.
134 Haney, *Challenge of Coleridge*, 5.
135 Ibid., 7.
136 C. Taylor, *Sources*, 39. Emphasis added.
137 Ibid., 47.
138 Samuel Taylor Coleridge, 'To Robert Southey', [17 July 1797], letter 197, *Letters*, vol. 1, 334.
139 See Coleridge, *Poetical Works*, ed. Mays, vol. 2, part I, 480–7.
140 Coleridge adds a note to this line in the letter to Southey: 'You remember, I am a *Berkleian*. –': 'To Robert Southey', [17 July 1797], letter 197, *Letters*, vol. 1, 335.
141 Tilottama Rajan, 'The Unavowable Community of Idealism: Coleridge and the Life Sciences', *European Romantic Review* 14 (2003): 395–416 (395).
142 Hamilton, *Metaromanticism*, 29, 32.
143 Davidson, *Problems*, 35–6.
144 Ibid., 36.
145 Indeed, it might also explain why – as the varorium version of this poem reveals – Coleridge had such trouble with these lines. Thus, in the letter, line 51 ('Cross'd, like a speck, the blaze of setting day'), which is already a substitution for the cancelled line 'H̶a̶d̶ c̶r̶o̶s̶s̶'d̶ t̶h̶e̶ o̶r̶b̶ f̶l̶o̶o̶d̶ &̶ b̶l̶a̶z̶e̶ o̶f̶ s̶e̶t̶t̶i̶n̶g̶ d̶a̶y̶', is replaced in the transcript of the poem Coleridge made for Charles Lloyd with '[?]Had cross'd the mighty Orb's dilated blaze.' This in turn is modified to 'Had cross'd the mighty Orb's dilated glory' for the *Annual Anthology*. See Coleridge, *Poetical Works*, vol. 2, part I, 484–5.
146 Davidson, 'The Socratic Conception of Truth', *Truth*, 249.
147 Ibid.

Bibliography

Aarsleff, Hans, *The Study of Language in England, 1780–1860*, Princeton University Press, 1967

Aarsleff, Hans, Louis G. Kelly, and Hans-Joseph Niederehe, eds., *Papers in the History of Linguistics: Proceedings of the Third International Conference on the History of the Language Sciences*, vol. 38, Studies in the History of the Language Sciences, series 3 Amsterdam Studies in the Theory and History of Linguistic Science, gen. ed. E. F. Konrad Koerner, Amsterdam: John Benjamins, 1987

Abrams, M. H., *Natural Supernaturalism: Tradition and Revolution in Romantic Literature*, New York: W. W. Norton, 1971

Adorno, Theodor W., *Aesthetic Theory*, trans. Robert Hullot-Kentor, ed. Gretel Adorno, Rolf Tiedemann, and Robert Hullot-Kentor, London: Continuum, 2004

  The Jargon of Authenticity, trans. Knut Tarnowski and Frederic Will, London: Routledge, 2003

  Negative Dialectics, trans. E. B. Ashton, New York: The Seabury Press, 1973

Alcoff, Linda Martín, 'Objectivity and Its Politics'. *New Literary History* 32 (2001): 835–48

Altieri, Charles, 'Practical Sense – Impractical Objects: Why Neo-Pragmatism Cannot Sustain an Aesthetics', in Fluck, ed., 113–35

Amjad, Fazel A, 'Natural and Ethical Necessity in Shelley's Epistemology', *Keats–Shelley Review* 17 (2003): 98–113

Ashton, Rosemary, *The German Idea: Four English Writers and the Reception of German Thought 1800–1860*, Cambridge University Press, 1980

Austin, J. L., *How to Do Things With Words*, 2nd edn, eds. J. O. Urmson and Marina Sbisà, Oxford University Press, 1975

Barfield, Owen, *What Coleridge Thought*, Middletown, CT: Wesleyan University Press, 1971

Barrell, Joseph, *Shelley and the Thought of His Time: A Study in the History of Ideas*, Archeon Books, 1967

Bate, Walter Jackson, *John Keats*, Cambridge, MA: Harvard University Press, 1963

Battersby, James, 'Authors and Books: The Return of the Dead from the Graveyard of Theory', in Harris, ed., 177–201

Bennett, Andrew, *Keats, Narrative and Audience: The Posthumous Life of Writing*, Cambridge University Press, 1994

Bentham, Jeremy, *Chrestomathia*, eds. M. J. Smith and W. H. Burston, Oxford University Press, 1983

The Collected Works of Jeremy Bentham, gen. editors J. H. Burns, J. R. Dinwiddy, and F. Rosen, Oxford University Press, 1968–

A Comment on the Commentaries and A Fragment on Government, eds. J. H. Burns and H. L. A. Hart, London: The Athlone Press, 1977

Deontology. A Table of the Springs of Action, and Article on Utilitarianism, ed. Amnon Goldworth, Oxford University Press, 1983

An Introduction to the Principles of Morals and Legislation, ed. J. H. Burns and H. L. A. Hart, London: Athlone Press, 1970

Theory of Legislation, trans. from the French of Etienne Dumont by R. Hildreth, 1802, London, 1876

The Works of Jeremy Bentham, ed. John Bowring, 11 vols., Edinburgh, 1838–43

Bergheaud, Patrice, 'Language, Ethics and Ideology: Dugald Stewart's "Common Sense" Critique of Empiricist Historical and Genetic Linguistics', in Aarsleff, *et al.*, eds., 399–413

Berkeley, George, *A Treatise Concerning the Principles of Human Knowledge*, ed. Jonathan Dancy (Oxford University Press, 1998)

Bewell, Alan, 'The Political Implication of Keats's Classicist Aesthetics', *Studies in Romanticism* 25.2 (1986): 220–9

Blackburn, Simon, *Truth: A Guide for the Perplexed*, London: Allen Lane-Penguin, 2005

Blank, G. Kim, ed., *The New Shelley: Later Twentieth-Century Views*, Basingstoke: Macmillan, 1991

Bloom, Harold, *The Anxiety of Influence: A Theory of Poetry*, 2nd, edn, Oxford University Press, 1997

Bode, Christopher, 'Hyperion, *The Fall of Hyperion*, and Keats's Poetics', *Wordsworth Circle* 31.1 (2000): 31–7

Bowie, Andrew, *Aesthetics and Subjectivity: from Kant to Nietzsche*, Manchester University Press, 1990

Bradley, J. L. *A Shelley Chronology*, Basingstoke: Macmillan, 1993

Brandom, Robert B., ed., *Rorty and His Critics*, Oxford: Blackwell, 2000

Brigham, Linda, '*Prometheus Unbound* and the Postmodern Political Dilemma', in Curran and Bennet, eds., 253–62

Brinkley, Robert and Michael Deneen, 'Towards an Indexical Criticism: on Coleridge, de Man and the Materiality of the Sign', *Revolution and English Romanticism*, ed. Keith Hanley and Raman Selden, Hemel Hempstead: Harvester Wheatsheaf, 1990, 277–302

Bromwich, David, 'Keats's Radicalism', *Studies in Romanticism* 25.2 (1986): 197–210

'Literature and Theory', in Harris, ed., 203–33

Buell, Lawrence, 'Ethics as Objectivity: A Necessary Oxymoron?', *New Literary History* 32 (2001): 855–7

Bulwer-Lytton, Edward, *England and the English*, 2nd edn 2 vols., London: Richard Bentley, 1833

Burke, Edmund, *A Philosophical Enquiry into the Origin of our Ideas of the Sublime and Beautiful*, London, 1759

Burnett, James (Lord Monboddo), *Antient Metaphysics: or, the Science of Universals*, 6 vols., Edinburgh, 1779–99

  On the Origin and Progress of Language, vol. 1, 2nd edn, Edinburgh, 1774

  On the Origin and Progress of Language, 6 vols., Edinburgh, 1773–92

Burton, Robert, *The Anatomy of Melancholy*, 6 vols, ed. Thomas C. Faulkner, et al., Oxford: Clarendon Press, 1989–2000

Burwick, Frederick, 'Mendelssohn and Coleridge on Words, Thoughts and Things', in *The Jews and British Romanticism: Politics, Religion, Culture*, ed. Sheila A. Spector, Basingstoke: Palgrave Macmillan, 2005, 245–73

Cameron, Kenneth Neill, 'Shelley as a Philosophical and Social Thinker: Some Modern Evaluations', *Studies in Romanticism* 21.3 (1982): 357–66

  The Young Shelley: Genesis of a Radical, London: Macmillan, 1950

Cavell, Stanley, *The Claim of Reason: Wittgenstein, Skepticism, Morality, and Tragedy*, Oxford University Press, 1979

  In *Quest of the Ordinary: Lines of Skepticism and Romanticism*, University of Chicago Press, 1988

  Must We Mean What We Say? A Book of Essays, Cambridge University Press, 1976

Chandler, James, *England in 1819: The Politics of Literary Culture and the Case of Romantic Historicism*, University of Chicago Press, 1998

Christensen, Jerome, *Coleridge's Blessed Machine of Language*, Ithaca, NY: Cornell University Press, 1981

  Practicing Enlightenment: Hume and the Formation of a Literary Career, Madison, WI.: University of Wisconsin Press, 1987

  Romanticism at the End of History, Baltimore, MD: Johns Hopkins University Press, 2000

Clark, Timothy, 'Shelley after Deconstruction: The Poet of Anachronism', in Clark and Hogle, eds., 91–107

Clark, Timothy and Jerrold E. Hogle, eds. *Evaluating Shelley*, Edinburgh University Press, 1996

Claviez, Thomas, 'Pragmatism, Critical Theory, and the Search for Ecological Genealogies in American Culture', in Fluck, ed., 343–80

Colapietro, Vincent, 'The Question of Voice and the Limits of Pragmatism: Emerson, Dewey, and Cavell', *The Range of Pragmatism and the Limits of Philosophy*, ed. Richard Shusterman, Metaphilosophy Ser. in Philosophy, Oxford: Blackwell, 2004, 174–96

Cole, Steven E., 'Evading Politics: The Poverty of Historicizing Romanticism', *Studies in Romanticism* 34.1 (1994): 29–49

  'The Logic of Personhood: Coleridge and the Social Production of Agency', *Studies in Romanticism* 30 (1991): 85–111

Coleridge, Samuel Taylor, *Aids to Reflection*, ed. John Beer, Princeton University Press, 1995

Biographia Literaria or Biographical Sketches of My Literary Life and Opinions, ed. James Engell and Walter Jackson Bate, 2 vols., Princeton University Press, 1983

Collected Letters of Samuel Taylor Coleridge, ed. Earl Leslie Griggs, 5 vols., Oxford: Clarendon Press, 1956–71

The Friend, ed. Barbara E. Rooke, 2 vols., Princeton University Press, 1969

Lay Sermons, ed. R. J. White, Princeton University Press, 1972

Lectures 1795 on Politics and Religion, ed. Lewis Patton and Peter Mann, Princeton University Press, 1971

Lectures 1808–1819 On Literature, ed. R. A. Foakes, 2 vols, Princeton University Press, 1987

Lectures 1818–1819 On the History of Philosophy, ed. J. R. de J. Jackson, 2 vols., Princeton University Press, 2000

Logic, ed. J. R. de J. Jackson, Princeton University Press, 1981

Marginalia, ed. H. J. Jackson, George Whalley, *et al.*, 6 vols., Princeton University Press, 1980–2001

The Notebooks of Samuel Taylor Coleridge, ed. Kathleen Coburn, *et al.*, 5 vols., London: Routledge, 1957–2002

On the Constitution of the Church and State, ed. John Colmer, Princeton University Press, 1976

Opus Maximum, ed. Thomas McFarland and Nicholas Halmi, Princeton University Press, 2002

Poetical Works, ed. J. C. C. Mays, 3 vols., Princeton University Press, 2001

Shorter Works and Fragments, ed. H. J. Jackson and J. R. de J. Jackson, 2 vols., Princeton University Press, 1995

Table Talk, ed. Carl Woodring, 2 vols., Princeton University Press, 1990

Cooper, Andrew M., *Doubt and Identity in Romantic Poetry*, New Haven, CT: Yale University Press, 1988

Courtney, Winifred F., *Young Charles Lamb 1775–1802*, Basingstoke: Macmillan, 1982

Crisman, William, " 'Thus Far Had the Work Been Transcribed': Coleridge's Use of Kant's Pre-Critical Writings and the Rhetoric of 'On the Imagination' ", *Modern Language Quarterly* 52 (1991): 404–22

Cronin, Richard, *Shelley's Poetic Thoughts*, Basingstoke: Macmillan, 1981

Curran, Stuart and Betty T. Bennet, eds., *Shelley: Poet and Legislator of the World*, Baltimore, MD: Johns Hopkins University Press, 1996

Dasenbrock, Reed Way, *Truth and Consequences: Intentions, Conventions and the New Thematics*, University Park, PA: Pennsylvania State University Press, 2001

Daston, Lorraine and Galison, Peter, *Objectivity*, New York: Zone Books, 2007

Davidson Donald, 'Dialectic and Dialogue', in *Language Mind and Epistemology: On Donald Davidson's Philosophy*, ed. Gerhard Preyer, Frank Siebelt, and Alexander Ulfig, Dordrecht: Kluwer Academic Publishers, 1994, 429–37

Essays on Actions and Events, 2nd edn, Oxford: Clarendon Press, 2001

'On the Very Idea of a Conceptual Scheme', in Rajchman and West, eds., 129–44

Problems of Rationality, Oxford: Clarendon Press, 2004

Subjective, Intersubjective, Objective, Oxford: Clarendon Press, 2001

Truth, Language, and History, Oxford: Clarendon Press, 2005

'Truth Rehabilitated', in Brandom, ed., 65–74

Dawson, P. M. S., *The Unacknowledged Legislator: Shelley and Politics*, Oxford University Press, 1980

Deleuze, Gilles, *Difference and Repetition*, trans. Paul Patton, London: Athlone Press, 1994

Expressionism in Philosophy: Spinoza, New York: Zone Books, 1992

Pure Immanence: Essays on A Life, trans. Anne Boyman, New York: Zone Books, 2001

de Man, Paul, *Blindness and Insight: Essays in the Rhetoric of Contemporary Criticism*, 2nd edn, Minneapolis, Minn.: University of Minnesota Press, 1983

Introduction, *The Selected Poetry of Keats*, New York: Signet, 1966

The Rhetoric of Romanticism, New York: Columbia University Press, 1984

'Shelley Disfigured', *Deconstruction and Criticism*, ed. Harold Bloom, New York: Continuum, 1999, 39–73

De Paolo, Charles, *Coleridge: Historian of Ideas*, English Literary Studies Monograph Ser. 54, BC: University of Victoria, 1992

De Quincey, Thomas, *The Collected Writings of Thomas de Quincey*, ed. David Masson, vol. v, Edinburgh, 1890

Derrida, Jacques, *Dissemination*, trans. Barbara Johnson, London: Athlone Press, 1981

Of Grammatology, trans. Gayatri Chakravorty Spivak, Baltimore, MD: Johns Hopkins University Press, 1974

Dewey, John, *Experience and Nature*, New York: Dover Publications, 1958

The Quest for Certainty: A Study of the Relation of Knowledge and Action, New York: G. P. Putnam's Sons, 1960

Reconstruction in Philosophy, rev. edn, Boston, MA: Beacon Press, 1948

Theory of Valuation, John Dewey: The Later Works. 1925–1953, ed. Jo Ann Boydston and Barbara Levine, vol. 13, Carbondale, IL: Southern Illinois University Press, 1988, 189–251

Dickie, George, 'Art and Value', *British Journal of Aesthetics* 40.2 (2000): 228–41

Drummond, Sir William, *Academical Questions*, London, 1805

Edmunson, Mark, *Literature against Philosophy, Plato to Derrida: A Defence of Poetry*, Cambridge University Press, 1995

Eldridge, Richard, *Leading a Human Life: Wittgenstein, Intentionality, and Romanticism*, University of Chicago Press, 1997

The Persistence of Romanticism: Essays in Philosophy and Literature, Cambridge University Press, 2001

ed., *Beyond Representation: Philosophy and the Poetic Imagination*, Cambridge University Press, 1996

Endo, Paul, 'Seeing Romantically in *Lamia*', *ELH* 66.1 (1999): 111–28

Engell, James, *The Creative Imagination: Enlightenment to Romanticism*, Cambridge, MA: Harvard University Press, 1981

Esterhammer, Angela, 'Of Promises, Contracts and Constitutions: Thomas Reid and Jeremy Bentham on Language as Social Action', *Romanticism* 6.1 (2000), 55–77

The Romantic Performative: Language and Action in British and German Romanticism, Stanford, CA: Stanford University Press, 2000

Farnell, Gary, 'Rereading Shelley', *ELH* 60.3 (1993): 625–50

Ferguson, Frances, 'Beliefs and Emotions: From Stanley Fish to Jeremy Bentham and John Stuart Mill', *Politics and the Passions 1500–1850*, ed. Victoria Kahn, Neil Saccamano, and Daniela Coli, Princeton University Press, 2006, 231–50

'Canons, Poetics, and Social Value: Jeremy Bentham and How to Do Things with People', *Modern Language Notes* 110 (1995): 1148–64

'Shelley's *Mont Blanc*: What the Mountain Said', *Romanticism and Language*, ed. Arden Reed, Ithaca, NY: Cornell University Press, 1984, 202–14

Ferris, David S., 'Keats and the Aesthetics of Critical Knowledge: or, the Ideology of Studying Romanticism at the Present Time', in Pfau and Gleckner, eds., 102–25

Silent Urns: Romanticism, Hellenism, Modernity, Stanford, CA: Stanford University Press, 2000

Fischer, Michael, 'Accepting the Romantics as Philosophers', *Philosophy and Literature* 12 (1988): 179–89

Fleischacker, Samuel, 'Poetry and Truth-Conditions', in Eldridge, ed., 107–32

Fleming, Bruce E., 'What is the Value of Literary Studies?', *New Literary History* 31 (2000): 459–76

Fluck, Winfried, ed., *Pragmatism and Literary Studies*, vol. 15, *REAL: The Yearbook of Research in English and American Literature*, Tübingen: Gunter Narr Verlag, 1999

Fodor, Jerry and Ernest Lepore, *Holism: A Shopper's Guide*, Oxford: Blackwell, 1992

Foucault, Michel, *The Order of Things: An Archeology of the Human Sciences*, London: Routledge, 2002

Power/Knowledge: Selected Interviews and Other Writings 1972–1977, ed. Colin Gordon, trans. Colin Gordon, *et al.*, Hemel Hempstead: Harvester Wheatsheaf, 1980

Frow, John, *Cultural Studies and Cultural Value*, Oxford: Clarendon Press, 1995

Fry, Paul, 'History, Existence, and "To Autumn"', *Studies in Romanticism* 25.2 (1986): 211–19

The Reach of Criticism: Method and Perception in Literary Theory, New Haven, CT: Yale University Press, 1983

Fulford, Tim, *Coleridge's Figurative Language*, Basingstoke: Macmillan, 1991

Fulford, Tim and Morton D. Paley, eds., *Coleridge's Visionary Languages: Essays in Honour of J. B. Beer*, Cambridge: D. S. Brewer, 1993

Galison, Peter, 'Objectivity is Romantic', *American Council of Learned Societies Occasional Paper* 47 (1999), 17 June 2009, archives.acls.org/op/op47–3.htm#galison

Gallet, René, 'Coleridge, Scholasticism, and German Idealism', in *The Middle Ages after the Middle Ages in the English-Speaking World*, ed. Marie-Françoise Alamichel and Derek Brewer, Cambridge: D. S. Brewer, 1997, 137–44

Geller, Geoffrey L., 'The Stalemate of Reason: Barbara Herrnstein Smith on the Problems of Circularity and Self-Contradiction', *Philosophy and Rhetoric* 30.4 (1997): 376–94

Geertz, Clifford, *The Interpretation of Cultures: Selected Essays*. Harper Collins/Fontana Press, 1973
  Local Knowledge: Further Essays in Interpretive Anthropology, New York: Basic Books, 2000

Gigante, Denise, 'Keats's Nausea', *Studies in Romanticism* 40.4 (2001): 481–510
  'The Monster in the Rainbow: Keats and the Sciences of Life', *PMLA* 117.3 (2002): 433–48

Gilmartin, Kevin, ' "This is Very Material": William Cobbett and the Rhetoric of Radical Oppression', *Studies in Romanticism* 34.1 (1995): 81–101

Godwin, William, *An Inquiry Concerning Political Justice, and its Influence on General Virtue and Happiness*, 2 vols, London, 1793

Gold, Elise M., 'Touring the Inventions: Shelley's Prefatory Writing', *Keats–Shelley Journal* 36 (1987): 63–87

Goodman, Russell B., *American Philosophy and the Romantic Tradition*, Cambridge University Press, 1990

Goodson, A. C., 'Romantic Theory and the Critique of Language', in *Questioning Romanticism*, ed. John Beer, Baltimore, MD: Johns Hopkins University Press, 1995, 3–28

Graff, Gerald, *Clueless in Academe: How Schooling Obscures the Life of the Mind*, New Haven, CT: Yale University Press, 2003

Gray, Erik, 'Indifference and Epistolarity in "The Eve of St Agnes" ', *Romanticism* 5.2 (1999): 127–46

Habermas, Jürgen, *Knowledge and Human Interests*, trans. Jeremy J. Shapiro, London: Heinemann, 1972
  Moral Consciousness and Communicative Action, trans. Christian Lenhardt and Shierry Weber Nicholson, Cambridge: Polity Press, 1990
  The Philosophical Discourse of Modernity: Twelve Lectures, trans. Frederick Lawrence, Cambridge, MA: MIT Press, 1987
  Postmetaphysical Thinking: Philosophical Essays, trans. William Mark Hohengarten, Cambridge: Polity Press, 1992
  'Richard Rorty's Pragmatic Turn', in Brandom, ed., 31–55
  The Theory of Communicative Action, trans. Thomas McCarthy, 2 vols., Boston, MA: Beacon Press, 1984

Hadley Karen, ' "Back to the Future?": The Narrative of Allegory in Recent Critical Accounts of Romanticism', *ELH* 69.4 2002: 1029–45

Haefner, Joel, ' "Incondite Things" Experimentation and the Romantic Essay', *Prose Studies* 10.2 (1987): 196–206

Hagberg, Garry, 'Davidson. Self-Knowledge and Autobiographical Writing', *Philosophy and Literature* 26 (2002): 354–68

Halsey, Katherine, 'Percy Bysshe Shelley and Theories of Language: A Discussion', *Keats–Shelley Review* 16 (2000): 22–30

Hamilton, Paul, 'Coleridge and the "Rifacciamento" of Philosophy: Communicating an Idealist Position in Philosophy', *European Romantic Review* 14 (2003): 417–29

Coleridge and German Philosophy: The Poet in the Land of Logic, London: Continuum, 2007

'Coleridge and Godwin in the 1790s', *The Coleridge Connection: Essays for Thomas McFarland*, ed. Richard Gravil and Molly Lefebure, Basingstoke: Macmillan, 1990, 41–59

Coleridge's Poetics, Oxford: Blackwell, 1983

'A French Connection: From Empiricism to Materialism in Writings by the Shelleys', *Colloquium Helveticum: Cahiers Suisses de Littérature Générale et Comparee* 25 (1997): 171–93

'Keats and Critique', *Rethinking Historicism: Critical Readings in Romantic History*, ed. Marjorie Levinson, *et al.*, Oxford: Basil Blackwell, 1989

Metaromanticism: Aesthetics, Literature, Theory, University of Chicago Press, 2003

' "Old Anatomies": Some Recent Shelley Criticism', *The Durham University Journal* 85.2 (1993): 303–9

Percy Bysshe Shelley, Plymouth: Northcote House, 2000

Haney, David P., *The Challenge of Coleridge: Ethics and Interpretation in Romanticism and Modern Philosophy*, University Park, PA: Pennsylvania State University Press, 2001

'Viewing "the Viewless Wings of Poesy": Gadamer, Keats, and Historicity', *CLIO* 18.2 (1989): 103–22

Harding, Anthony John, *Coleridge and the Idea of Love: Aspects of Relationship in Coleridge's Thought and Writing*, Cambridge University Press, 1974

Harris, Kenneth Marc, 'Reason and Understanding Reconsidered: Coleridge, Carlyle and Emerson', *Essays in Literature* 13.2 (1986): 263–82

Harris, Wendell V., ed., *Beyond Poststructuralism: The Speculations of Theory and the Experience of Reading*, University Park, PA: Pennsylvania State University Press, 1996

Harrison, Ross, *Bentham*, Routledge & Kegan Paul, 1983

Hartley, David, *Observations on Man, His Frame, His Duty, and His Expectations*, 1749; 2 vols., London: 1791

Hartman, Geoffrey, *The Fate of Reading and Other Essays*, University of Chicago Press, 1975

'Spectral Symbolism and the Authorial Self: An Approach to Keats's Hyperion', *Essays in Criticism* 24.1 (1974): 1–19

Havens, Michael Kent, 'Coleridge on the Evolution of Language', *Studies in Romanticism* 20 (1981): 163–83

Hazlitt, William, *The Complete Works of William Hazlitt*, ed. P. P. Howe, 21 vols., London: J. M. Dent & Sons, 1930–4

Hegel, G. W. F., *Phenomenology of Spirit*, trans. A. V. Millar, Oxford University Press, 1977

Hensley, David C., 'Richardson, Rousseau, Kant: "Mystics of Taste and Sentiment" and the Critical Philosophy', in *Cultural Interactions in the Romantic Age: Critical Essays in Comparative Literature*, ed. Gregory Maertz, State University of New York Press, 1998, 177–207

Hipolito, Jeffrey, 'Coleridge, Hermeneutics, and the Ends of Metaphysic', *European Romantic Review* 15.4 (2003): 547–65

Hoagwood, Terence Allan, 'Keats, Fictionality, and Finance: *The Fall of Hyperion*', in Roe, ed., 127–42

   Politics, Philosophy, and the Production of Romantic Texts, Corbondale, IL: Northern Illinois University Press, 1996

   Skepticism and Ideology: Shelley's Political Prose and its Philosophical Context from Bacon to Marx, Iowa City, IA: University of Iowa Press, 1988

Hodgson John A., *Coleridge, Shelley, and Transcendental Inquiry*, Lincoln, NE: University of Nebraska Press, 1989

Hogle, Jerrold E., 'Percy Bysshe Shelley', in *Literature of the Romantic Period: A Bibliographical Guide*, ed. Michael O'Neill, Oxford University Press, 1998, 118–42

   'Shelley and the Conditions of Meaning', Clark and Hogle, eds., 48–74

   Shelley's Process: Radical Transference and the Development of His Major Works, Oxford University Press, 1988

Hughes, A. M. D., *The Nascent Mind of Shelley*, Oxford: Clarendon Press, 1947

Hume, David, *Enquiries Concerning Human Understanding and Concerning the Principles of Morals*, ed. L. A. Selby-Bigge, 3rd edn rev. P. H. Nidditch, Oxford: Clarendon Press, 1975

   Essays Moral, Political, and Literary, ed. Eugene F. Miller, rev. edn, Indianapolis, IN: Liberty Fund, 1985

   The History of England: From the Invasion of Julius Caesar to the Revolution in 1688, rev. edn, 8 vols., London, 1786

   The Letters of David Hume, ed. J. Y. T. Greig, 2 vols., Oxford: Clarendon Press, 1932

   New Letters of David Hume, ed. Raymond Klibansky and Ernest C. Mossner, Oxford: Clarendon Press, 1954

   A Treatise of Human Nature, ed. Peter H. Nidditch, 2nd edn, Oxford University Press, 1978

Hunt, Leigh, *Leigh Hunt's Political and Occasional Essays*, ed. Lawrence Huston Houtchens and Carolyn Washburn Houtchens, New York: Columbia University Press, 1962

Hunter, Lynette, *Literary Value/Cultural Power: Verbal Arts in the Twenty-First Century*, ed. Sarah Poulton, Manchester University Press, 2001

Jackson, Heather J., 'Coleridge, Etymology and Etymologic', *Journal of the History of Ideas* 44.1 (1983): 75–88

   'Coleridge's Lessons in Transition: The "Logic" of the "Wildest Odes"', in Pfau and Gleckner, eds., 213–24

Jackson, J. R. de J., *Method and Imagination in Coleridge's Criticism*, London: Routledge & Kegan Paul, 1969

Jacobi, Friedrich Heinrich, *The Main Philosophical Writings and One Novel Allwill*, trans. George di Giovanni, Montreal: McGill-Queens University Press, 1994

Jacobus, Mary, 'The Art of Managing Books: Romantic Prose and the Writing of the Past', in *Romanticism and Language*, ed. Arden Reed, London: Methuen, 1984, 215–46

James, William, *Pragmatism: A New Name for Some Old Ways of Thinking*, New York: Longmans, Green & Co., 1907
  The Will to Believe and Other Essays in Popular Philosophy, New York: Longmans, Green and Co., 1904

Jameson, Fredric, 'Metacommentary', *PMLA* 86.1 (1971): 9–18
  The Political Unconscious: Narrative as a Socially Symbolic Act, London: Routledge, 2002

Jessup, Bertram, 'The Mind of Elia', *Journal of the History of Ideas* 15 (1954): 246–59

Jones, John, *John Keats's Dream of Truth*, London: Chatto & Windus, 1969

Kabitoglou, Douka E., 'Adapting Philosophy to Literature: The Case of John Keats', *Studies in Philology* 89.1 (1992): 115–36

Kant, Immanuel, *Critique of Pure Reason*, trans. Paul Guyer and Allen W. Wood, Cambridge University Press, 1997
  Prolegomena to Any Future Metaphysics, trans. and ed. Gary Hatfield, Cambridge University Press, 1997

Kaufman, Robert, 'Intervention & Commitment Forever! Shelley in 1819, Shelley in Brecht, Shelley in Adorno, Shelley in Benjamin', in *Reading Shelley's Interventionist Poetry, 1819–1820*, ed. Orrin Wang and John Morillo, Romantic Circles Praxis Series, 20 Oct. 2005, rc.umd.edu/praxis/interventionist/kaufman/kaufman.html
  'Legislators of the Post-Everything World: Shelley's *Defence* of Adorno', *ELH* 63.3 (1996): 707–33
  'Negatively Capable Dialectics: Keats, Vendler, Adorno, and the Theory of the Avante-Garde', *Critical Inquiry* 27.2 (2001): 354–84

Keach, William, *Arbitrary Power: Romanticism, Language, Politics*, Princeton University Press, 2004
  Shelley's Style, London: Methuen, 1984

Keats, John, *The Letters of John Keats 1814–1821*, ed. Hyder Edward Rollins, 2 vols., Cambridge, MA: Harvard University Press, 1958
  The Poems of John Keats, ed. Jack Stillinger, London: Heinemann, 1978

Kelley, Theresa M., 'Keats, Ekphrasis, and History', in Roe, ed., 212–37

Kipperman, Mark, 'Coleridge, Shelley, Davy, and Science's Millenium', *Criticism* 40.3 (1998): 409–36
  'Shelley, Adorno, and the Scandal of Committed Art', in *Reading Shelley's Interventionist Poetry, 1819–1820*, ed. Orrin Wang and John Morillo, Romantic Circles Praxis Series, 20 Oct. 2005 rc.umd.edu/praxis/interventionist/kipperman/kipperman.html

Kitson, Peter J., ' "The Electric Fluid of Truth": The Ideology of the Commonwealthsman in Coleridge's *The Plot Discovered*', in *Coleridge and*

the Armoury of the Human Mind: Essays on His Prose Writings, ed. Peter
  J. Kitson and Thomas N. Corns, London: Frank Cass, 1991, 36–62
Knights, Ben, *The Idea of the Clerisy in the Nineteenth Century*, Cambridge
  University Press, 1978
Kolb, David, 'Authenticity with Teeth: Positing Process', in Kompridis, ed.,
  60–77
Kompridis, Nikolas, 'The Idea of a New Beginning: A Romantic Source of
  Normativity and Freedom', in Kompridis, ed., 32–59
  ed., *Philosophical Romanticism*, London: Routledge, 2006
Kucich, Greg, 'Keats's Literary Tradition and the Politics of Historiographical
  Invention', in Roe, ed., 238–61
  'The Poetry of Mind in Keats's Letters', *Style* 21.1 (1987): 76–94
Kuhn, Thomas S., *The Structure of Scientific Revolutions*, 3rd edn, University of
  Chicago Press, 1996
Lachman, Lilach, 'Keats's *Hyperion*: Time, Space, and the Long Poem', *Poetics
  Today* 22.1 (2001): 89–127
Lacoue-Labarthe, Philippe and Jean-Luc Nancy, *The Literary Absolute*, trans.
  Philip Barnard and Cheryl Lester, State University of New York Press, 1988
Lamarque, Peter and Stein Haugom Olsen, *Truth, Fiction and Literature:
  A Philosophical Perspective*, Oxford: Clarendon Press, 1994
Lamb, Charles and Mary Lamb, *The Works of Charles and Mary Lamb*, ed. E. V.
  Lucas, 7 vols., London: Methuen, 1903
Lamennais, Hugues Felicite Robert de, *Essay on Indifference in Matters of
  Religion*, vol. 1, 1817; trans. Henry Stanley, London: John MacQueen, 1895
Lawrence, Christopher, 'The Power and the Glory: Humphry Davy and
  Romanticism', in *Romanticism and the Sciences*, ed. Andrew Cunningham
  and Nicholas Jardine, Cambridge University Press, 1990, 213–27
Leask, Nigel, *The Politics of Imagination in Coleridge's Critical Thought*,
  Basingstoke: Macmillan, 1988
Lentricchia, Frank, *Criticism and Social Change*, University of Chicago Press,
  1983
Leo, John Robert, 'Criticism of Consciousness in Shelley's "Defence of Poetry"',
  Philosophy and Literature 2 (1978): 46–59
Levinson, Marjorie, *Keats's Life of Allegory: The Origins of a Style*, Oxford:
  Blackwell, 1988
  Marilyn Butler, Jerome McGann, and Paul Hamilton, *Rethinking Historicism:
  Critical Readings in Romantic History*, Oxford: Blackwell, 1989
  'Romantic Criticism: The State of the Art', in *At the Limits of Romanticism:
  Essays in Cultural, Feminist, and Materialist Criticism*, ed. Mary A. Favret
  and Nicola J. Watson, Bloomington, IN: Indiana University Press, 1994,
  269–81
Lévi-Strauss, Claude, *The Savage Mind*, London: Weidenfeld and Nicolson, 1966
Lindop, Grevel, 'Lamb, Hazlitt and De Quincey', *The Coleridge Connection:
  Essays for Thomas McFarland*, eds. Richard Gravil and Molly Lefebure,
  Basingstoke: Macmillan, 1990

Liu, Alan, 'Local Transcendence: Cultural Criticism, Postmodernism, and the Romanticism of Detail', *Representations* 32 (1990): 75–113

'Remembering the Spruce Goose: Historicism, Postmodernism, Romanticism', *South Atlantic Quarterly* 102.1 (2003): 263–78

'The Power of Formalism: The New Historicism', *ELH* 56 (1989): 721–71

Locke, John, *An Essay Concerning Human Understanding*, ed. Peter H. Nidditch, Oxford University Press, 1975

Lockridge, Laurence S., *The Ethics of Romanticism*, Cambridge University Press, 1989

Lovell, Ernest J., 'Shelley's Prose: The Growth of a Moral Vision', *Prose Studies* 3.2 (1980): 152–64

Lucretius, *De Rerum Natura*, trans. W. H. D. Rouse, rev. edn, Martin Ferguson Smith, 2nd, edn Cambridge, MA: Harvard University Press, 1982

Ludwig, Kirk, ed., *Donald Davidson*, Cambridge University Press, 2003

Luke, David, 'Keats's Letters: Fragments of an Aesthetics of Fragments', *Genre* 11 (1978): 209–26

Lyotard, Jean-François, *The Differend: Phrases in Dispute*, trans. Georges Van Den Abbeele, Minneapolis, MN: University of Minesota Press, 1988

The Postmodern Condition: A Report on Knowledge, trans. Geoff Bennington and Brian Massumi, Theory and History of Literature 10, Manchester University Press, 1984

MacKenzie, Iain, *The Idea of Pure Critique*, London: Continuum, 2004

MacKinnon, D. M., 'Coleridge and Kant', in *Coleridge's Variety: Bicentenary Studies*, ed. John Beer, Basingstoke: Macmillan, 1974, 184–203

Marggraf Turley, Richard, *The Politics of Language in Romantic Literature*, Basingstoke: Palgrave, 2002

McFarland, Thomas, 'Aspects of Coleridge's Distinction Between Reason and Understanding', in Fulford and Paley, eds., 165–80

Coleridge and the Pantheist Tradition, Oxford University Press, 1969

Romantic Cruxes: The English Essayists and the Spirit of the Age, Oxford: Clarendon Press, 1987

McGann, Jerome J., *The Beauty of Inflections: Literary Investigations in Historical Method and Theory*, Oxford University Press, 1985

McKusick, James C., 'Coleridge's "Logic": A Systematic Theory of Language', in Aarsleff, *et al.*, eds., 479–89

Coleridge's Philosophy of Language, New Haven, CT: Yale University Press, 1986

McNiece, Gerald, *The Knowledge that Endures: Coleridge, German Philosophy and the Logic of Romantic Thought*, Basingstoke: MacMillan, 1992

Shelley and the Revolutionary Idea, Cambridge, MA: Harvard University Press, 1969

Mettrie, Julien Offray de la, *Machine Man and Other Writings*, trans. Ann Thomson, Cambridge University Press, 1996

Michael, Jennifer D., 'Pectoriloquy: The Narrative of Consumption in the Letters of Keats', *European Romantic Review* 6.1 (1995): 38–56

Mileur, Jean-Pierre, 'The Return of the Romantic', *Intersections: Nineteenth-Century Philosophy and Contemporary Theory*, ed. Tilottama Rajan and David L. Clark, Albany, NY: State University of New York Press, 1995, 325–48

Mill, John Stuart. *Mill on Bentham and Coleridge*, ed. F. R. Leavis, London: Chatto & Windus, 1959

Milnes, Tim, *Knowledge and Indifference in English Romantic Prose*, Cambridge University Press, 2003

  'Through the Looking-Glass: Coleridge and Post-Kantian Philosophy', *Comparative Literature* 51.4 (1999): 309–23

Modiano, Raimonda, *Coleridge and the Concept of Nature*, Basingstoke: Macmillan, 1985

Mohanty, Satya P., 'Can Our Values be Objective? On Ethics, Aesthetics, and Progressive Politics', *New Literary History* 32 (2001): 803–33

Morton, Timothy, Review of *Shelley and the Chaos of History* by Hugh Roberts, *Studies in Romanticism* 39.1 (2000): 173–7

Muirhead, John H., *Coleridge as Philosopher*, London: Allen & Unwin, 1930

Müller, Johannes von. *An Universal History, in Twenty-Four Books* [trans. J. C. Prichard], 3 vols., London, 1818

Natarajan, Uttara, *Hazlitt and the Reach of Sense Criticism, Morals and the Metaphysics of Power*, Oxford: Clarendon Press, 1998

  'The Veil of Familiarity: Romantic Philosophy and the Familiar Essay', *Studies in Romanticism* 42. 1 (2003): 27–44

Newey, Vincent, 'Keats, History, and the Poets', in Roe, ed., 165–93

Nietzsche, Friedrich, *Untimely Meditations*, trans. R. J. Hollingdale, Cambridge University Press, 1983

Norris, Christopher, *Against Relativism: Philosophy of Science, Deconstruction and Critical Theory*, Oxford: Blackwell, 1997

  Reclaiming Truth: Contribution to a Critique of Cultural Relativism, London: Lawrence & Wishart, 1996

  Spinoza and the Origins of Modern Critical Theory, Oxford: Blackwell, 1991

  The Truth about Postmodernism, Oxford: Blackwell, 1993

  Truth and the Ethics of Criticism, Manchester University Press, 1994

Notopolous, James A., *The Platonism of Shelley: A Study of Platonism and the Poetic Mind*, Durham, NC: Duke University Press, 1949

O'Neill, Michael, ed., *Keats: Bicentenary Readings*, Edinburgh University Press, 1997

  'Keats and the "Poetical Character"', in *Placing and Displacing Romanticism*, ed. Peter J. Kitson, Aldershot: Ashgate, 2001, 157–65

  'Keats's Poetry: "The Reading of an Ever-Changing Tale"', in O'Neill, ed., 102–28

  '"When this Warm Scribe my Hand": Writing and History in *Hyperion* and *The Fall of Hyperion*', in Roe, ed., 143–64

Orsini, G. N. G., *Coleridge and German Idealism*, Carbondale, IL: Southern Illinois University Press, 1969

Paine, Thomas, *The Age of Reason*, 2nd edn, 2 vols., London, 1795
   Common Sense, Philadelphia and Charlestown, South Carolina, 1776
   Rights of Man: Being an Answer to Mr. Burke's Attack on the French Revolution,
     5th edn, 2 vols., London, 1791–2
Paley, William, *The Principles of Moral and Political Philosophy*, London, 1785
Park, Roy, 'Coleridge and Kant: Poetic Imagination and Practical Reason',
   British Journal of Aesthetics 8 (1968): 335–46
Pater, Walter, *Appreciations*, London, 1895
Paulin, Tom, *The Day-Star of Liberty: William Hazlitt's Radical Style*, London:
   Faber and Faber, 1998
Payne, Michael and John Schad, eds., *Life, After, Theory*, London: Continuum, 2003
Peacock, Thomas Love, 'The Four Ages of Poetry', 1820, *The Works of Thomas
   Love Peacock*, 10 vols., ed. H. F. B. Brett-Smith and C. E. Jones, vol. 8,
   London: Constable, 1924–34
Perkins, Mary Anne, *Coleridge's Philosophy: The Logos as Unifying Principle*,
   Oxford: Clarendon Press, 1994
Perry, Seamus, *Coleridge and the Uses of Division*, Oxford: Clarendon Press, 1999
Peterfreund, Stuart, 'The Color Violaceous, or, Chemistry and the Romance of
   Dematerialization: The Subliming of Iodine and Shelley's *Adonais*', *Studies
   in Romanticism* 42.1 (2003): 45–54
   Shelley among Others: The Play of the Intertext and the Idea of Language,
     Baltimore, MD: Johns Hopkins University Press, 2002
   'Shelley, Monboddo, Vico, and the Language of Poetry', *Style* 15.4 (1981): 382–400
Pfau, Thomas, 'The Voice of Critique: Aesthetic Cognition after Kant', *Modern
   Language Quarterly* 60.3 (1999): 321–52
   'Introduction. Reading beyond Redemption: Historicism, Irony, and the
     Lessons of Romanticism', in Pfau and Gleckner, eds., 1–37
Pfau, Thomas and Robert F. Gleckner, eds., *Lessons of Romanticism: A Critical
   Companion*, Durham, NC: Duke University Press, 1998
Plato, *The Collected Dialogues of Plato*, ed. Edith Hamilton and Huntington
   Cairns, Bollingen Ser. 71, Princeton University Press, 1961
Plotnisky, Arkady, 'A Dancing Arch: Formalization and Singularity
   in Kleist, Shelley, and de Man', *European Romantic Review* 9.2 (1998):
   161–76
Poirier, Richard, *Poetry and Pragmatism*, Cambridge, MA: Harvard University
   Press, 1992
Pollock, John, 'Epistemic Norms', in *Epistemology: An Anthology*, ed. Ernest Sosa
   and Jaegwon Kim, Oxford: Blackwell, 2000, 192–225
Pradhan, S. V. 'The Historiographer of Reason: Coleridge's Philosophy of
   History', *Studies in Romanticism* 25.1 (1986): 39–62
Prickett, Stephen, 'The Ache in the Missing Limb: Coleridge and the
   Amputation of Meaning', in Fulford and Paley, eds., 123–35
   Coleridge and Wordsworth: The Poetry of Growth, Cambridge University
   Press, 1970
   Words and The Word, Cambridge University Press, 1986

Priestley, Joseph, *Disquisitions Relating to Matter and Spirit*, London, 1777
  Doctrine of Philosophical Necessity Illustrated, London, 1777
  An Examination of Dr Reid's Inquiry into the Human Mind on the Principles of Common Sense, Dr. Beattie's Essay on the Nature and Immutability of Truth, and Dr. Oswald's Appeal to Common Sense on Behalf of Religion, London, 1774
Pulos, C. E., *The Deep Truth: A Study of Shelley's Scepticism*, Lincoln, NE: University of Nebraska Press, 1954
  'The Importance of Shelley's Scepticism', *Shelley: Modern Judgements*, ed. R. B. Woodings, London: Aurora Publishers, 1970
Putnam Hilary, 'After Empiricism', in Rajchman and West, eds., 20–30
  The Collapse of the Fact/Value Dichotomy and Other Essays, Cambridge, MA: Harvard University Press, 2002
  Realism and Reason: Philosophical Papers, vol. 3, Cambridge University Press, 1983
  Realism with a Human Face, ed. James Conant, Cambridge, MA: Harvard University Press, 1990
  Reason, Truth and History, Cambridge University Press, 1981
  Renewing Philosophy, Cambridge, MA: Harvard University Press, 1992
Pyle, Forest, 'Kindling and Ash: Radical Aestheticism in Keats and Shelley', *Studies in Romanticism* 42.4 (2003): 427–59
Quine, W. V., *Elementary Logic*, rev. edn, Cambridge, MA: Harvard University Press, 1980
  From a Logical Point of View: Nine Logico-Philosophical Essays, 2nd edn, Cambridge, MA: Harvard University Press, 1961
  Ontological Relativity and Other Essays, New York: Columbia University Press, 1969
  Pursuit of Truth, Cambridge, MA: Harvard University Press, 1990
  Theories and Things, Cambridge, MA: Harvard University Press, 1981
  Word and Object, Cambridge, MA: MIT Press, 1960
Quinney, Laura, 'Weiskel's Sublime and the Impasse of Knowledge', *Philosophy and Literature* 18 (1994): 309–19
Rajan, Tilottama, *Dark Interpreter: The Discourse of Romanticism*, Ithaca, NY: Cornell University Press, 1980
  The Supplement of Reading: Figures of Understanding in Romantic Theory and Practice, Ithaca, NY: Cornell University Press, 1990
  'The Unavowable Community of Idealism: Coleridge and the Life Sciences', *European Romantic Review* 14 (2003): 395–416
Rajan, Tilottama and David L. Clark, eds., *Intersections: Nineteenth-Century Philosophy and Contemporary Theory State*, Albany, NY: University of New York Press, 1995
Rajan, Tilottama and Arkady Plotnitsky, eds., *Idealism without Absolutes: Philosophy and Romantic Culture*, Albany, NY: State University of New York Press, 2004
Rajan, Tilottama and Wright, Julia M., eds., *Romanticism, History and the Possibilities of Genre: Re-forming Literature 1789–1837*, Cambridge University Press, 1998

Rajchman, John and Cornel West, eds., *Post-Analytic Philosophy*, New York, Columbia University Press, 1985

Read, Rupert, 'In Closing: The Antagonists of "The New Hume". On the Relevance of Goodman and Wittgenstein to the New Hume Debate', in Read and Richman, eds., 167–97

Read, Rupert and Kenneth A. Richman, eds., *The New Hume Debate*, Routledge, 2000

Redfield, Marc, 'Response: Reading the Aesthetic, Reading Romanticism', *Romanticism and the Insistence of the Aesthetic*, ed. Orrin Wang, Feb. 2005, Romantic Circles Praxis Series, 20 Oct. 2005, rc.umd.edu/praxis/aesthetic/abstracts.html#redfield

Reed, Thomas A., 'Keats and the Gregarious March of Intellect in *Hyperion*', *ELH* 55.1 (1988): 195–232

Reid, Nicholas, 'Coleridge, Language, and the Imagination', *Romanticism on the Net* 22, May 2001, 31 March 2006, erudit.org/revue/ron/2001/v/n22/005977ar.html

'Form in Coleridge, and in Perception and Art More Generally', *Romanticism on the Net* 26, May 2002, 31 March 2006, erudit.org/revue/ron/2002/v/n26/005699ar.html

' "That Eternal Language," or Why Coleridge was Right about Imaging and Meaning', *Romanticism on the Net* 28, November 2002, 31 March 2006 erudit.org/revue/ron/2002/v/n28/007208ar.html

Reid, Thomas, *Essays on the Intellectual Powers of Man*, Edinburgh, 1785

An Inquiry into the Human Mind, on the Principles of Common Sense, Edinburgh, 1764

Ricks, Christopher, *Keats and Embarrassment*, Oxford University Press, 1974

Roberts, Hugh, *Shelley and the Chaos of History: A New Politics of Poetry*, University Park, PA: Pennsylvania State University Press, 1997

Robertson, William, *The History of America*, 6th edn 3 vols., London, 1792

The History of the Reign of the Emperor Charles V, 1769, 7th edn, 4 vols., London, 1792

Roe, Nicholas, 'A Cockney Schoolroom: John Keats at Enfield', in O'Neill, ed., 11–26

John Keats and the Culture of Dissent, Oxford: Clarendon Press, 1997

'Keat's Commonwealth', in Roe, ed., 194–211

ed., *Keats and History*, Cambridge University Press, 1995

Rogers, Neville, *Shelley at Work: A Critical Inquiry*, 2nd edn, Oxford: Clarendon Press, 1967

Rollins, Hyder Edward, ed., *The Keats Circle: Letters and Papers and More Letters and Poems of the Keats Circle*, 2nd edn, 2 vols., Cambridge, MA: Harvard University Press, 1965

Rorty, Richard, *Contingency, Irony, and Solidarity*, Cambridge University Press, 1989

Interview with E. P. Ragg, *Philosophy and Literature* 26 (2002): 369–96

Objectivity, Relativism and Truth: Philosophical Papers, vol. 1, Cambridge University Press, 1991

Philosophy and the Mirror of Nature, Princeton University Press, 1980

'Response to Jürgen Habermas', in Brandom, ed., 56–64

Truth and Progress: Philosophical Papers, vol. 3, Cambridge University Press, 1998

Rosenberg, Daniel, '"A New Sort of Logick and Critick": Etymological Interpretation in Horne Tooke's *The Diversions of Purley*', in *Language, Self, and Society: A Social History of Language*, ed. Peter Burke and Roy Porter, Cambridge: Polity, 1991, 300–29

Rubin, Merle R., 'Shelley's Skepticism: A Detachment Beyond Despair', *Philological Quarterly* 59 (1980): 353–73

Rule, Philip C., 'Coleridge and Newman: The Centrality of Conscience', in *The Fountain Light: Studies in Romanticism and Religion in Honor of John L. Mahoney*, ed. Robert J. Barth, Gainsville, FL: Florida University Press, 2002, 231–55

Saito, Naoko, 'Reconstructing Deweyan Pragmatism in Dialogue with Emerson and Cavell', *Transactions of the Charles S. Peirce Society* 37.3 (2001): 389–406

Sandback, Shimon, 'Keats. Altered by the Present', *Comparative Literature* 35.1 (1983): 43–54

Sartre, Jean-Paul, *Critique of Dialectical Reason*, vol. 1, trans. Alan Sheridan-Smith, ed. Jonathan Rée, London: NLB, 1976

Search for a Method, trans. Hazel E. Barnes, New York: Alfred A. Knopf, 1963

Schlegel, A. W., *A Course of Lectures on Dramatic Art and Literature*, trans. J. Black, 2 vols. London, 1815

Scrivener, Michael, 'Inside and Outside Romanticism', *Criticism* 46.1 (2004): 151–65

Searle, John, 'Literary Theory and its Discontents', in Harris, ed., 101–35

Sellars, Wilfrid, *Empiricism and the Philosophy of Mind*, Cambridge, MA: Harvard University Press, 1997

Shaffer, Elinor S., 'Metaphysics of Culture: Kant and Coleridge's *Aids to Reflection*', *Journal of the History of Ideas* 31 (1970): 199–218

Shawcross, J., Introduction, *Biographia Literaria*, by Samuel Taylor Coleridge, ed. J. Shawcross, 2 vols., Oxford University Press, 1907, xi–lxxxix

Shelley, Bryan Keith, 'The Synthetic Imagination: Shelley and Associationism', *The Wordsworth Circle* 14.1 (1983): 68–73

Shelley, Mary, *The Journals of Mary Shelley 1814–1844*, ed. Paula R. Feldman and Diana Scott-Kilvert, 2 vols., Oxford: Clarendon Press, 1987

Shelley, Percy Bysshe, *The Complete Poetical Works of Percy Bysshe Shelley*, ed. Thomas Hutchinson, London: Oxford University Press, 1934

The Complete Poetical Works of Percy Bysshe Shelley, ed. Neville Rogers, 2 vols., Oxford University Press, 1972

The Complete Works of Percy Bysshe Shelley, ed. Roger Ingpen and Walter E. Peck, 10 vols., London: Ernest Benn, 1926–30

The Letters of Percy Bysshe Shelley, ed. Frederick L. Jones, 2 vols., Oxford University Press, 1964

The Poems of Shelley, ed. Kelvin Everest, *et al.*, 3 vols. to date, Harlow: Longman, 1989–

The Prose Works of Percy Bysshe Shelley, ed. E. B. Murray, 1 vol. to date, Oxford University Press, 1993–

Shelley's Poetry and Prose, ed. Donald H. Reiman and Sharon B. Powers, New York: W. W. Norton, 1977

Simpson, David, 'What Bothered Charles Lamb About Poor Susan?', *Studies in English Literature* 26.4 (1986): 589–612

Sitter, John, *Literary Loneliness in Mid-Eighteenth-Century England*, Ithaca, NY: Cornell University Press, 1982

Smith, Barbara Herrnstein, *Contingencies of Value: Alternative Perspectives for Critical Theory*, Cambridge, MA: Harvard University Press, 1988

'Value/Evaluation', in *Critical Terms for Literary Study*, ed. Frank Lentricchia and Thomas McLaughlin, University of Chicago Press, 1990, 177–85

Smith, Olivia, *The Politics of Language 1791–1819*, Oxford: Clarendon Press, 1984

Snyder, Alice D., *Coleridge on Logic and Learning*, New Haven, CT: Yale University Press, 1929

Sperry, Stuart M., *Keats the Poet*, Princeton University Press, 1973

Spinoza, Benedict de, *The Collected Works of Spinoza*, trans and ed. Edwin Curley, 2 vols., Princeton University Press, 1985

Stevenson, Warren, *Divine Analogy: A Study of the Creation Motif in Blake and Coleridge*, Salzburg Studies in English Literature: Romantic Reassessment, ed. James Hogg, Institute für Englische Sprache und Literatur. Universität Salzburg, 1972

Stewart, Dugald, *The Collected Works of Dugald Stewart*, ed. William Hamilton, 11 vols., Edinburgh, 1854–60; Bristol: Thoemmes Press, 1994

Strawson, P. F., *The Bounds of Sense: An Essay on Kant's* Critique of Pure Reason, Methuen, 1966

Swift, Simon, *Romanticism, Literature and Philosophy: Expressive Rationality in Rousseau, Kant, Wollstonecraft and Contemporary Theory*, London: Continuum, 2006

Taylor, Charles, *The Ethics of Authenticity*, Cambridge, MA: Harvard University Press, 1991

'Leading a Life', in *Incommensurability, Incomparability, and Practical Reason*, ed. Ruth Chang, Cambridge, MA: Harvard University Press, 1997, 170–83

Philosophical Arguments, Cambridge, MA: Harvard University Press, 1995

Sources of the Self: The Making of the Modern Identity, Cambridge University Press, 1989

Taylor, Jacqueline, 'Hume and the Reality of Value', in *Feminist Interpretations of David Hume*, ed. Anne Jaap Jacobsen, University Park, PA: Pennsylvania State University Press, 2000, 107–36

Thorslev Jr, Peter L., 'Dialectic and Its Legacy', in *Coleridge's Theory of Imagination Today*, ed. Christine Gallant, New York: AMS Press, 1989, 103–12

Tooke, John Horne, *Epea Pteroenta, or the Diversions of Purley*, ed. Richard Taylor, 2 vols., London, 1829

Towsey, David, 'Platonic Eros and Deconstructive Love', *Studies in Romanticism* 40.4 (2001): 511–30

Trilling, Lionel, *Sincerity and Authenticity: The Charles Eliot Norton Lectures, 1969–1970*, Oxford University Press, 1974

Trott, Nicola, 'Keats and the Prison House of History', in Roe, ed., 262–79

[Tucker, Abraham], *The Light of Nature Pursued*, 3 vols., London, 1768

Ulmer, William A., *Shelleyan Eros: The Rhetoric of Romantic Love*, Princeton University Press, 1990

Urquhart, Troy, 'Metaphor, Transfer, and Translation in Plato's Ion: The Postmodern Platonism of Percy Bysshe Shelley's A Defence Poetry', in *Romanticism on the Net*, ed. Michael Laplace-Sinatra, Aug. 2003–20 Oct. 2005 erudit.org/revue/ron/2003/v/n31/008700ar.html

Vendler, Helen, *The Odes of John Keats*, Cambridge, MA: Harvard University Press, 1983

Voltaire, François-Marie Arouet de, *The Age of Louis XIV*, trans. Martyn P. Pollack, London: Dent, 1926
  Philosophical Dictionary, trans. and ed. Theodore Besterman, London: Penguin, 1971

Wallace, Catherine Miles, The Design of the 'Biographia Literaria', London: Allen & Unwin, 1983

Wallace, Jennifer, 'Tyranny and Translation: Shelley's Unbinding of Prometheus', *Romanticism* 1.1 (1995): 15–33

Wang, Orrin, *Fantastic Modernity: Dialectical Readings in Romanticism and Theory*, Baltimore, MD: Johns Hopkins University Press, 1996

Ware, Tracy, 'Shelley's Platonism in *A Defence of Poetry*', SEL 1500–1900 23.4 (1983): 549–66

Wasserman, Earl R., *Shelley: A Critical Reading*, Baltimore, MD: Johns Hopkins Press, 1971

Webb, Timothy, ' "Cutting Figures": Rhetorical Strategies in Keats's *Letters*', in O'Neill, ed., 144–69

Weisman, Karen, 'The Bounds of Lyric: Romantic Grasps upon the Actual', *European Romantic Review* 15.2 (2004): 343–49
  'Shelley's Ineffable Quotidian', in Curran and Bennet, eds., 224–31

Wellek, René, *Immanuel Kant in England 1793–1838*, Princeton University Press, 1931

West, Cornel, *The American Evasion of Philosophy: A Genealogy of Pragmatism*, Madison, WI: University of Wisconsin Press, 1989

Whalley, George, 'Coleridge's Debt to Charles Lamb', *Essays and Studies* 11 (1958): 68–85

Wheeler, Kathleen, 'Coleridge's Theory of Imagination: a Hegelian Solution to Kant?', *The Interpretation of Belief: Coleridge, Schleiermacher and Romanticism*, ed. David Jasper, Basingstoke: Macmillan, 1986, 16–40
  'Kant and Romanticism', *Philosophy and Literature* 13 (1989): 42–56
  Romanticism, Pragmatism and Deconstruction, Oxford: Blackwell, 1993
  Sources, Processes and Methods in Coleridge's Biographia Literaria, Cambridge University Press, 1980

Wheeler, Samuel C., III, 'Language and Literature', in Ludwig, ed., 183–206

White, Deborah Elise, *Romantic Returns: Superstition, Imagination, History*, Stanford, CA: Stanford University Press, 2000

Willey, Basil, 'I. A. Richards and Coleridge', in *I. A. Richards: Essays in his Honor*, ed. Rueben Brower, *et al.*, Oxford University Press, 1973, 227–36

Williams, Bernard, *Truth and Truthfulness: An Essay in Genealogy*, Princeton University Press, 2002

Wittgenstein, Ludwig, *On Certainty*, trans. Denis Paul and G. E. M. Anscombe, ed. G. E. M. Anscombe and G. H. von Wright, Oxford: Blackwell, 1969

Philosophical Investigations, 2nd, edn, trans. G. E. M. Anscombe, Oxford: Blackwell, 1958

Wolfson, Susan, *Formal Charges: The Shaping of Poetry in British Romanticism*, Stanford, CA: Stanford University Press, 1997

'Introduction. Keats and Politics: A Forum', *Studies in Romanticism* 25.2 (1986): 171–4

Womersley, David, *The Transformation of* The Decline and Fall of the Roman Empire, Cambridge University Press, 1988

Woodman, Ross, 'Figuring Disfiguration: Reading Shelley after de Man', *Studies in Romanticism* 40.2 (2001): 253–88

'Shelley's Changing Attitude to Plato', *Journal of the History of Ideas* 21 (1960): 497–510

Youngquist, Paul, 'Rehabilitating Coleridge: Poetry, Philosophy, Excess', *English Literary History* 66.4 (1999): 885–909

Index

CAMBRIDGE STUDIES IN ROMANTICISM

General Editor
JAMES CHANDLER, *University of Chicago*